ing both the traditions we come from and the challenges we face.

At once a stark portrait of the American economic machine and a celebration of its cast-offs, *Not Working* ultimately gives testimony to the strength of the human spirit in adversity. For what it reveals of both the flaws of our society and the nobility of the individuals within it, it will be read and cited for many years to come.

Jim Kiernen

Investigative journalist **Harry Maurer** was born in Pennsylvania in 1948 and raised in Yellow Springs, Ohio. Since graduating from Columbia in 1970, he has traveled extensively throughout Europe, Latin America, and the United States, writing full-time. His articles on labor, economics, and international affairs have appeared in such magazines as *The New York Review of Books, The Nation, The Progressive*, and *Ms*. Formerly an editor at *The Nation*, he is currently living in New York City and writing his second book, on international cartels.

NOT WORKING

NOT WORKING

An Oral History of the Unemployed

Harry Maurer

HOLT, RINEHART AND WINSTON
NEW YORK

Published by Holt, Rinehart and Winston, 383 Madison
Avenue, New York, New York 10017.
Published simultaneously in Canada by Holt, Rinehart and
Winston of Canada, Limited.
Library of Congress Cataloging in Publication Data

Maurer, Harry.
  Not working.
  1. Unemployed—United States—Interviews.
I. Title.
HD5724.M335   331.1'37973   79-1296
ISBN: 0-03-044131-5

First Edition

Designer: Cathy Marinaccio
Printed in the United States of America
10 9 8 7 6 5 4 3 2 1

**To
J. Leo Chapman,
with love**

Contents

A Note on Organization

Documentary filmmakers often shoot twenty times as much film as they use in their final version. The resulting problem of organization is similar to the one I faced after gathering a mass of interviews—which, when transcribed, filled a huge number of pages—on a subject so multifarious as unemployment. Briefly I toyed with the two most extreme methods of organizing them: to offer no thematic grouping at all, but simply to present each interview as a self-contained chapter, so that the table of contents would be no more than a list of names; or, on the contrary, to suppress individuals in favor of themes by breaking up the interviews into their relevant parts, so that each chapter on a specific subject—losing a job, financial pressures, racism, and so on—would contain small pieces of many interviews. Finally, I chose an approach that preserves individual voices intact, but also arranges them in chapters reflecting what seems to me the most important themes.

Still, the task of selection and placement was not simple. I did my best to let the interviews speak for themselves, grouping people according to which part of their talk was the most vibrant, intimate, and original—that is, which aspect of the experience touched them the most. Some people, for example, spoke with greatest heat about being fired; others, about looking for work; others, about schemes for making a buck. Each of those subjects seemed to form a natural chapter. Two groups of people—minority youth and older professionals—seemed so cohesive and faced such egregious obstacles that I felt they required their own chapters. Chapter 2, the longest in the book, also has the broadest focus; in it, people tell how the general experience of unemployment—rather than any one feature of it—has affected them. But there was always something of an arbitrary quality about my choices. Most people in this book could have fitted into at least two different chapters, and in fact, in a very few cases I did divide interviews in two.

One final note: All names in this book have been changed, as much to protect the guilty as the innocent. Naturally, anonymity was requested by most people who talked to me about breaking the law—whether their crime was to traffic in stolen goods, to sell marijuana, or simply to work off the books a few hours a week. But many people whose claim to unemployment compensation was lawful, and who had no unreported income, also asked that their identities be disguised, usually so that their troubles would not be laid bare to neighbors, colleagues, or relatives. I often changed the names of companies that people used to work for and placed the speakers in another town or city.

Acknowledgments

My first and deepest thanks go to the unemployed men and women who gave of their time to make this book possible; such life as its pages contain springs from their vitality and candor. Thanks, too, to Rob Fasano, the finest travel companion an itinerant interviewer could have. Whether we were driving interstates that seemed endless, combing city outskirts for a cheap motel, pitching a tent in the rain, or spending long, often discouraging days at unemployment centers in search of people to interview, Rob's generosity, flexibility, and funny stories made the experience a pleasure. He made first contact with several people who appear here and sat in on a number of interviews.

Other friends who housed me on the road, or who offered suggestions and leads, include Phyllis Applebaum, Laura Bernay, Jim and Kathy Driscoll, Ginger Gray, Kathy MacKenzie, Colleen McGrath, Charlo Maurer, David Porter, and Benito Romano. My parents, Robert and Charlotte Maurer, gave encouragement and support, as always—and lent an aging, indispensable Ford, which performed miraculously. The 40-Plus Clubs, the United Auto Workers, and Techno-Economic Opportunities Institute of Palo Alto, California, graciously permitted me to contact and interview their members. Barbara Durr, Robert Hatch, and my editor, Natalie Chapman, brought their keen critical talents to bear on the rough draft, helping to shape it into a book.

Special thanks go to those who inspired this effort. Francis Greenberger, my agent, had the idea in the first place. And of course, Studs Terkel, interviewer par excellence, whose work has blazed the trail for other "oral historians," deeply influenced the making of this book.

NOT WORKING

INTRODUCTION

This book is about the unemployed. But unlike most books on the subject, it is really about people, not numbers. Indeed, this book is *by* unemployed people: their words fill these pages. It is about secretaries, construction workers, stockbrokers, teachers, welders, engineers, truck drivers—their ideas, feelings, tales. It is about politics and economics as well, but of the personal variety, not the kind of numerical abstraction that is usually invoked to analyze unemployment. The people in this book talk about unemployment as an urgent reality: about pounding the pavement and drinking wine on the corner; about receiving pink slips and writing résumés; about watching soap operas and seeking interviews; about stealing watermelons and committing suicide; about cursing God and praying for the strength to get out of bed.

There are many people in this book whose living rooms have turned into prisons without bars, and others who gleefully feel they have escaped jobs that were jails. There are people who have been broken by years of idleness, and others who have discovered emotional resources that allow them to endure—even, in a way, to triumph. In short, the men and women in this book vary enormously. Yet amid the variety there is a common feeling, stated with bitter clarity at times, only half spoken at others, and occasionally not yet formed as a thought but rather as a troubled notion whispering behind the words. It is that a crime has been committed.

Unemployed people have been robbed of something, and they know it. The bewilderment they often express is like that of the homeowner who returns to find rooms ransacked, valuable and beloved objects missing. The sense of violence and invasion, the feelings of fear and loss and helplessness descend with the same stunning force when a worker is deprived of work. And the loss is much greater, because work, if the longing of the unemployed is any indication, remains a fundamental human need—even in the crushing form it has increasingly assumed in the modern world. It provides not simply a livelihood, but an essential passage into the human community. It makes us less alone.

But why bother about the unemployed? Why write this book at all? Part of my hope is that readers who are or have been jobless might find something of themselves here, as well as new ways to understand and cope with unemployment, thus making the experience less like solitary confinement. And I am convinced that the common tendency to think of unemployed people as mere numbers—as a more or less depressing

1

percentage droned by the newscaster each month—must be battled. It is much easier to shrug off percentage points with a turn of the channel than it is to shrug off the trauma in the lives of *individuals*.

And a time is upon us when ignorance of the human cost of unemployment becomes ever more dangerous. In the last decade the American economy has undergone a sea change. The high growth rates and low inflation that the country enjoyed, almost without pause, from 1948 to the early 1970s have given way to the phenomenon called stagflation, meaning the baffling mix of slumping growth and brisk inflation. Since stagflation shows no sign of disappearing, and since a slow growth rate means slow creation of jobs, unemployment in the eighties cannot be dismissed, as it often was in the preceding decades, as a negligible ache in an otherwise healthy body. The affliction has settled in. It may well grow worse. And to understand its malignancy fully, we must listen to the steadily larger group of Americans who are suffering.

Simply to *define* that group, however, is a tricky problem. Most people know that the officially determined rate of unemployment is a gross underestimate, omitting as it does all workers who are so discouraged that they have stopped looking for work; housewives, students, and others who would look if they thought work could be found; many people who are "disabled" or "retired"; and part-time workers who would like full-time jobs. True unemployment is approximately double the official rate. Thus, when I began gathering interviews for this book, I found nearly as many doubtful cases as classic ones. Should I have included as "unemployed" the aspiring rock-and-roll star who finagled his way onto unemployment in order to find time to practice? Or the nineteen-year-old high school dropout who has never landed a job? Or the unwed mother who would work if she could find a day care center for her kids?

I never devised a set of well-defined rules, but in the course of driving twelve thousand miles and talking to hundreds of people around the country, I did arrive at guidelines (some of which I violated according to my quirks or hunches). I decided that anyone collecting unemployment could fit into the book, no matter how thoroughly fraudulent his or her claim. Anyone whose life was largely centered on the search for work, or largely shaped by an inability to find it, I also considered unemployed. I usually steered away from welfare recipients and retired people, judging that those were related but separate realms. On the other hand, I did talk to some elderly workers who had been laid off years before and "retired" because they couldn't find another job. Hoboes were out, as were full-time hippies, the idle rich, and most others who preferred not to work at a job.

Such choices gave rise to a certain irony. While one thinks of the unemployed as inhabiting the dismal underside of American society,

2

those people commonly considered to be "unemployed" actually belong to a privileged group: They have worked in the relatively recent past. I met many of the people in this book at unemployment centers; that meant they had been jobless for less time than the maximum unemployment claim—generally under a year—and at least had an income less paltry than welfare offers. There are few spokespeople here for the "hard-core" unemployed—convicted criminals, for instance, or long-term mental patients—whose original problem may have been unemployment, but who are presumably so beaten by poverty and despair that work is now hardly a possibility.

Nevertheless, the anger and grief in these pages show that even a "short" stretch of unemployment can cut deep enough. Jim Hughes, the jobless welder, has a simple term for it. He dreams of filing a lawsuit against the company that fired him unjustly. His grounds? "Human damage, you might say."

Looking back two years, I see that I brought to this book a peculiar attitude toward the unemployed. I wanted to measure the human damage, but from the point of view of people's success or failure to cope with it. I wondered why some men and women plunge into depression, alcoholism, and even suicide when they lose a job, while others cheerfully rearrange their lives and emerge the stronger. Why do some families splinter under the strain while others pull together? The questions linger, but as I moved from town to town, interview to interview, my growing outrage told me the approach was faulty on two counts. First, the psychological reasons for someone's response to misfortune are buried too deeply in the caverns of personality to be unearthed in a two-hour talk. And second, by picturing unemployment as a sort of contest in which individuals succeed or fail, I had adopted the characteristic American tendency to blame the victim. No doubt people have varying reserves of courage, resilience, confidence, and ingenuity. But that misses the point, which is that no one today, weak or strong, should have to undergo trial by idleness. The failure is collective, not individual. We do not take care of our own.

The suffering, of course, is proportional to the burden borne. Art Finch, thirty-four-year-old father of three, is naturally more alarmed at being laid off from his American Motors job than is his teenage co-worker who still lives at home. And the pressure mounts not only with family responsibilities. Age, class, education, status, race, sex—all these factors help or hinder survival. Money in the bank has its influence, too. My best lesson about the context of unemployment came from Juan Camacho, the farmworker from Gonzales, California. Like other farmworkers lucky enough to be legal residents, Juan rarely stays unemployed for months at a stretch. But if he and his wife are jobless for

3

just two weeks, they can't meet bills for electricity, the trailer, the car. Two weeks more and they have to borrow money for food.

How people respond to unemployment is ruled by the interplay between their personality, the objective situation, and a third important factor: ideology. The way they *think* about being unemployed—which really means the tangle of ideas, observations, myths, and precepts they have woven into a vision of their place in the social structure— profoundly affects their ability to endure it. This ideological aspect boils down to one basic question: Who is to blame? And here the unemployed tend to be of two minds. For the record, they usually give an explanation for their joblessness that places the onus elsewhere—on a foreman who's a bastard, or discrimination of some sort, on a heartless company, on the economic downturn. But what astonished me—more than any other discovery in the course of writing this book—was the degree to which unemployed people blame themselves.

Often such feelings lie below the surface of speech, but one does not have to be an expert prospector to read the terrain. Jim Hughes, who says he was fired without cause, nevertheless hates to apply for unemployment compensation. "That kinda hurt my pride a little. More than a little. . . . I guess it was from the way I was brought up. Do things for yourself. Reward yourself. Nobody gives you anything for nothing." Which is to say, I've failed because I'm not the ideally self-reliant individual. Or take Kristen Jacobs, who feels her college degree qualifies her only for unskilled labor. She is disgusted about that, and yet: "At times I have a very low opinion of myself. . . . Partly it's because I don't feel I'm making the supreme effort to get a job. I mean, I'm not following up absolutely everything in the paper that I might have." She is echoed by Martin Penn, the unemployed anthropologist: "I think when I get an interview I have pretty good rapport with the person except that I have a tendency to put myself down too much. Maybe I'm too apologetic." Meaning, in both cases: I've failed because I'm doing something wrong.

Many older people express it by saying that at some earlier time they made a crucial mistake, usually by demanding too much out of life. Dorothy Feiberman, who left a good job when her company relocated: "My parents were fearful people and tried to impress upon me that I should carve out a secure career. . . . I knew that advertising wasn't secure, but when you're young, you don't think about those things. Now I think they were right. . . . Had I known what lay ahead of me, I would have moved to Timbuktu with that company, I'll tell you." Eddie Vargas, the skilled machinist: "Sometimes I think it's all my fault. I should have opened my mouth at such-and-such a time. I should have taken such-and-such a job when I had the chance. I shouldn't have listened to that teacher when he told me to aim high."

Grace Keaton, abruptly fired after twelve years with a publishing firm, says it most plainly: "I was persuaded that I must be not only as bad as the company must have thought I was to fire me, but much worse than that. Probably the world's worst. Probably I didn't deserve to live. . . . It's the brutality [of being fired]. It may be more like rape than death." She is right: rape victims frequently report the same sense of guilty responsibility for the violence they have suffered.

The paradox can be explained only by the always puzzling ability of people to believe two contradictory things at the same time and by the power of ideology to smother reality. Unemployed people feel they have been robbed of something, yet on a deeper level they feel it was their fault. (In some cases, of course, it was. Abraham Rosner lost his stockbroker job partly because he hated to drum up business on the phone. Jeff Weinbaum, former tape editor at a record company, admits: "I thought very narrowly about doing the job but not the strategy of keeping the job. . . . There were a lot of temperamental people involved, and I was certainly among them.") But even when workers were axed by a willful employer or when hundreds were laid off at a time, the ache of personal failure is felt. Having absorbed a value system that grotesquely glorifies professional success, unemployed Americans cannot help thinking they fall short as human beings. And the more thoroughly they accept American mythology regarding beneficent competition, equal opportunity, and the entrepreneurial spirit, the deeper their shame.

Plagued by self-doubt, many people offer an account of their unemployment that relieves the emotional stress. The notion of revenge, for example, serves well. Mary Volino, fired when she was pregnant, says, "Anyway, I got [unemployment]. And I decided to run it to tilt. Just run it, man, to the bloody end. And I did. Seventeen months of unemployment. I understand that [the company's] interest rates go up, and I just wanted to blow them right out. . . ."

Many other people soothe the personal sting by insisting that someone else—usually some distinct social or ethnic group—is taking all the jobs. Blacks and Latins feel that whites get them, women say that men do, "legal" immigrants blame their plight on "illegals," and in the wake of affirmative action programs, white men say that only minority groups or women have a chance. On occasion, the complaints may mask a halfhearted effort to find work. More important, they reflect the inevitable polarizations of a society that is permeated by prejudice—and that forces its members to compete for an insufficient number of jobs.

In fact, discrimination cannot be overestimated as a terrific obstacle to the unemployed. And for the unemployed black worker—or Native American, or Chicano, or woman—the problem is not simply the fact of discrimination but the pressure that the *fear* of it causes. The job search is disheartening enough without the constant worry that rejections are racially motivated. "You go in and you see that white employer sitting there, and you just get a feeling of 'Wow, is he going to hire me?' " says Ron Brett. "As opposed to just coming in there and sitting down and talking to him. All those other feelings come in there because you know that he is different than you, and in a sense you can't take him as a person." Perhaps the most depressing stories come from older workers, who suffer from almost universal age discrimination but whose predicament is not so widely known because they have not organized as powerfully or militantly as blacks or women. Several people in this book, laid off in their fifties from high-level positions, face the devastating prospect that they may never work again at *any* job since they are considered "overqualified" to do simpler labor.

I was surprised by the number of unemployed who said that religion—usually some form of born-again Christianity—was their source of strength. One reason is that their belief in a benign Being makes them feel less alone—and unemployment can be a very lonely ordeal. They also feel sure that passionate faith will bring good things in its wake, that God will provide. "So I have been trusting the Lord to supply me with a job," says Eddie Vargas. "As long as I put Christ first in the picture, I know He is going to supply my needs." Equally important is the sense that whatever happens, it is probably for the best. To the evangelical Christian, unemployment may be confusing and painful, but at least it is not a meaningless disaster since the Lord presumably has his reasons. And in any case, it is not this world, with its tribulations, that matters, but the next.

On the other hand, a touch of cynicism helps some people. Indeed, cynicism as a world view amounts to the mirror image of fundamentalist Christianity; it is amost a religion in itself. Rather than believe all is for the best because the Lord is in command, cynics feel that all is for the worst—and draw similar comfort from it. If everything and everyone are corrupt, if life is simply a battle to take advantage, then why feel bad about unemployment? Why work anyway? While no one in this book expresses it so nakedly, the attitude can be glimpsed, particularly among the few cases of classic unemployment fraud—those who, like Dave Yalman, get themselves fired and use unemployment to finance long vacations.

Other people raise muddier moral questions, since the varieties of lawbreaking that one encounters among the unemployed are infinite. Virtually every jobless person I met supplemented unemployment checks with some sort of odd job or part-time work, a brand of illegality that seems as broadly accepted as petty income-tax evasion. For others who have a large off-the-books income, like the neighborhood marijuana dealer Al Salvatore, it is the unemployment money that becomes a pleasant supplement. And there are the numerous artists, here represented by novelist Dick Franco and rock singer Freddie Dreyfus,

6

who see unemployment as an unofficial government subsidy to creative people. Says Dick, "We don't have the de' Medicis anymore. . . ."

Finally, there are the very few—and very lucky—people for whom unemployment turns out to be a blessing. Laura Gordon, the former New York public-school teacher, is typical of them. Laid off during the fiscal crisis, she was surprised to feel "an enormous relief. . . . It began to dawn on me that I might as well face my negative feelings about teaching." Months of unemployment gave her the time to ponder. It "forced me to face myself, in a way. All the questions of security, identity, loneliness, independence. . . . I thought my job defined me and gave me security, and it was like a door I never looked behind." While she has not settled on a new path, she feels the work she chooses will be more heartfelt, risky—and therefore satisfying.

It would seem that for anyone with equal courage and drive, unemployment might be what it was for Laura: a time to rethink, to change direction if need be. But it takes nothing away from her to say that what Laura and those like her in this book—Ruth Paster, Susan Casey, Jack Dustin—have in common is based as much on privilege as on personality. They are all relatively young; the oldest is thirty-seven. All but one are single, and none has a child. They come from comfortably middle-class families and with one exception are well educated. They have acquired the habit of introspection and have the financial resources to cultivate it. They have options and are aware of them. Most workers, especially those in the lower echelons, can only dream of such favorable circumstances. All too often their restive impulses must be stifled in the interests of putting food on the table.

A hundred times in the course of writing this book, I found myself wondering why people talked to me at all. Why did so many say yes when accosted outside an unemployment center by a stranger who wanted to ask personal questions about a painful subject? At times, of course, they just found it hard to say no, and I shamelessly took advantage. A few were intrigued by the chance to be in a book. "Hey, I'm gonna be a star!" crowed one youth. Others were flattered by my interest, which may have seemed sweet at a time of ebbing self-esteem. And the majority, I suspect, simply felt the need for release. As we talked, they looked for ways to explain, to comprehend, to justify. Spouses and friends, perhaps, had heard it all before. Or perhaps the doubts and discouragements were more easily revealed to a stranger. In any case, I was welcome.

Far more often, it must be said, I was not. Most people I approached at unemployment centers refused to meet with me. And of those who agreed, I actually managed to talk with only a minority—perhaps one in three. Having agreed, apparently against their better judgment, people used ingenious and infuriating ruses to give me the slip. The most common was simply to fail to keep our date. Time and again I arrived at someone's house to find him or her not home. Frequently, too, I was given the wrong address, or an address that didn't exist, or an address where the person had lived years before. One Friday I remember with particularly bitter amusement. I had spent Thursday at the unemployment center in Salinas, California, speaking with unemployed farmworkers. Although the people there—mostly Mexican immigrants—had obviously been suspicious of the *gringo* who spoke Spanish and claimed to be writing a book, five had agreed to talk with me the next day. Not one of them showed up. By Friday afternoon it seemed I had driven down every side street in Salinas, looking for nonexistent houses that had been described to me in convincing detail. At four I went back to the unemployment center to see if I could snare a latecomer and thus not lose the entire weekend. There I met Juan Camacho, who said he lived in a trailer park in Gonzales—twenty miles away. With the deepest skepticism and in an ugly temper, I set off one Saturday morning for Gonzales. To my surprise, there was Juan, who gently scolded me for being half an hour late. He had been worried that I wouldn't come at all. . . .

Throughout, I was troubled by what Studs Terkel calls "this thief-in-the-night feeling," the knowledge that I was taking much and giving little. The irony of the fact that I was happily employed writing a book about unemployment did not escape me or my companions. I could not afford to pay for their time. And the interview experience tends to be one-sided. By the end of a talk—especially if it had been one of those exciting encounters during which the air seemed to become supercharged—I knew some of my host's secrets, while he or she knew nothing about me. Usually, then, the tape recorder was turned off, we breathed a little more easily, and the questions came: about *my* life, *my* work, *my* hopes. Even so, the exchange was rarely equal, and I would leave amid handshakes and smiles and wishes of good luck, feeling burdened by the weight of what I had received. There was every chance I would never see my host again. And what of me had I left behind? Perhaps only the fact that I had listened well.

Or maybe, it occurred to me later, another, more subtle sort of exchange was taking place. What led me to the thought was the word *worthless*. No other term is used so often by unemployed people to describe how the experience affects them. Julie Jacobsen's lament "I feel worthless and useless and tired of trying" echoes dozens of others. Yet *worthless*, used that way, is a curious word. Unlike *stupid* or *lazy*, it does not refer merely to oneself. Rather, it implies the existence of someone else; it is an intrinsically social term. The question it raises is: worthless *to whom?* And the answer, I think, is: to the community.

Much has been made recently of the widespread cry for work that has meaning. The search for fulfillment is here, too; many of the people in this book would not take any job, just to be working. But more basically, what they want is a productive role and the sense of belonging that comes with it. That sense, like good health, often is taken for granted until it vanishes.

Thus, in some tiny way, talking to me may have restored something to my companions. After all, I was writing a book and they were helping me. In recording the talk, we were making something. We were part of the shared tasks that make up a society. "Well," they nearly always said afterward, "I hope that'll be of some use to you." Perhaps it is not too farfetched to think that when I arrived at someone's house, tape recorder in hand, among the things I offered was the chance to feel, for an hour or two, less "worthless."

What broader implications—what hints of the future—are to be found in what these women and men say about their lives? In order to answer, one must move from the realm of individuals back to that of percentage points.

Unemployment in the United States, comparatively speaking, has been extraordinarily high for many years. Since World War II, the level of unemployment that the government considers "full employment" has been double or triple that of most major capitalist nations. And even that odd notion of full employment has grown steadily less "full": In the late 1940s it was 3 percent, during the 1960s, 4 percent was the accepted figure, most economists have now boosted it to 5 percent, and the more conservative suggest it should be 6 or even 7 percent. Most laymen, however, less interested in rationalizing away the deficiencies of the system, still consider the current official rate of around 6 percent extremely high—especially since, as noted above, the real rate is closer to double.

Why do we tolerate the fact that one of every ten American workers is unemployed or underemployed? The answers are complex, rooted deeply in our history and culture. But here again, ideology plays a crucial role. The doctrine is familiar to anyone who has been schooled in America, who watches TV or reads the newspapers. It runs more or less as follows: In the "free enterprise" system, people achieve according to their merits. Bright, ambitious, and hardworking types naturally rise to the top, while the less deserving sink. Overcoming obstacles is not only possible, but part of the test. The unemployed, therefore, must be a shiftless and lazy lot who don't really want to work. Such notions have been around since the birth of capitalism and always have had the same result: to reconcile workers to drudgery at low wages by keeping alive their hopes of getting ahead and by playing on their fears of sink-ing into the despised underclass on the dole. Employers, who have the most direct interest in a cheap and docile labor force, always have been the most righteous advocates of rock-ribbed individualism. And the media echo the themes—for example, by endless reports on welfare and unemployment "cheating," which reinforce the image of the poor as a pack of thieves while masking the woeful inadequacy of benefits to provide a humane standard of living.

It need not be that way. Between 1960 and 1970, while unemployment in the United States averaged 4.8 percent, in West Germany it was 0.6 percent; in Japan, 1.3 percent; Sweden, 1.7 percent; France, 2.0 percent; and Great Britain, 3.1 percent. The same differential has prevailed in the 1970s, though stagflation has brought higher unemployment to all those economies. Furthermore, most of the other countries have unemployment benefits, provisions for retraining and relocation, and protection against layoffs that are much more generous than American counterparts. Economic and demographic factors partly account for the differences, but the most important ingredient is political. Workers in Europe (Japan, for cultural reasons, is something of a special case) are highly organized and less under the sway of individualist ideology. In several countries, social democratic parties with a working-class base hold power. Unwilling to let workers pay the price for strains in the economy, they have imposed full employment (or near to it) as the top social priority.

What would it take for Americans to make the same commitment? Only a political breakthrough similar to the one that came during the Great Depression. In 1933 one-quarter of the nation's work force was unemployed. At the time there was no unemployment insurance and hardly any other provision for relief of the poor. As Frances Fox Piven and Richard Cloward point out in *Poor People's Movements*, "The dole was anathema to the American spirit of work and self-sufficiency. Therefore, it should be dispensed to as few as possible and made as harsh as possible to discourage reliance upon it." But as the magnitude of the disaster began to sink in, attitudes "began to change among some of the unemployed. . . . [I]f so many people were in the same trouble, then maybe it wasn't they who were to blame, but 'the system'." The new outlook led to an unprecedented phenomenon: massive demonstrations and organizations of the unemployed. The Unemployed Leagues, Unemployed Councils, and finally, the Workers' Alliance of America proclaimed that society should provide jobs for its members, and if not jobs, then at least some means to avoid starvation. Washington responded with public works programs, unemployment insurance, and the welfare sysem, all now widely regarded as essential.

Yet having accepted social welfare programs, the country stopped short of the more important recognition: that to hold a job should be the right of every citizen, a right ranking with the freedoms of speech, press, religion, assembly, and so on. As the people in this book convey all too clearly, Americans still instinctively link work with merit, they still view a job as a privilege that only the worthy may enjoy, and they are resigned to unemployment's being ever with us. One hopes it will not take another Depression to bring about the next breakthrough; perhaps prolonged stagflation will prove to be catastrophe enough.

After all, the concept of the right to a job is not altogether foreign. In 1945 the Senate (but not the House) passed a Full Employment Bill which declared that "all Americans able to work and seeking work have the right to useful, remunerative, regular and full-time employment" and stated it to be the government's duty to create enough jobs to allow citizens to exercise that right.Repeated polls have shown that the public favors a government guarantee of jobs for all. Yet the sole serious reform proposal Congress has passed is the Full Employment and Balanced Growth Act of 1978, known as the Humphrey-Hawkins Bill after its two sponsors, the late Senator Hubert Humphrey and Representative Augustus Hawkins. Its basic provision commits the government to achieve nothing more ambitious than 3 percent unemployment among persons twenty years and older within four years of passage.

And even the modest and toothless Humphrey-Hawkins proposals almost did not become law, largely because the merest mention of full employment puts the business community on a war footing. Its objections are familiar, having been advanced against the New Deal programs: first, that full employment is impractical, if not impossible, and second, that it would destroy capitalism and with it our individual liberties. The former claim is based on the notion that full employment would be destructively inflationary. Numerous experts—not to mention the experience of other countries—challenge that assumption and the underlying one that inflation is caused primarily by rising wages. As for the second objection, it is hard to take seriously since hysterical warnings about the death of "free enterprise" have been used to delay every major social welfare proposal in the last 150 years, from banning child labor to allowing trade unions to organize—yet capitalism survives. The liberties actually in jeopardy are more likely to be those of employers to hire and fire at will, to break union organizing drives, and to pay meager wages, all of which would be more difficult were it not for the mass of unemployed.

American history suggests that when the demand for full employment is widespread enough to make it a priority—and a political reality—a way will be found to make it work. But such a time seems distant, even given the volatility of public moods. For the great majority of people in this book, political action could not be a less urgent concern. Their struggle is to survive with grace and dignity: to stay off the bottle; to keep from screaming at the spouse; to get up in the morning and face the classified ads. Even their anger, which in other circumstances might offer a path toward understanding and action, becomes merely an albatross. "And what's bein' mad gonna get you?" says Jimmy Green. "That don't get you nowhere, bein' mad. I mean, just 'cause you're angry at bein' unemployed, that ain't gonna make nobody jump up and give you a job. You get better treatment if you're pleasant and smilin'."

Such protest as occurs rarely goes beyond a kind of silent striking back (or fantasy thereof), reminiscent of Ralph Ellison's Invisible Man in his subterranean room, tapping electricity to power his hundreds of light bulbs. George Muravchik, the unemployed engineer who is illegally collecting welfare and unemployment at the same time, has a novel view of citizenship: "Since I have a hunch that the federal government and the state government have part responsibility for this unemployment situation, it's up to me to find out how to get money and live as best I can. To fight the system. That's a right, because I'm a citizen." Others dream of filing suits against companies that discriminate, but "How are you ever gonna prove it?" Only Giorgio Ricupero, sixty years old, has actually joined a group that fights to publicize the problems of the elderly unemployed. His conclusion: "You can write an awful lot of letters, and still nothing happens."

In fact, there are very few organizations of the unemployed—and that is astonishing, given the millions of Americans out of work. Such groups as exist almost all limit themselves to helping their members find jobs. Typical of these are the 40-Plus Clubs, established in ten cities to aid jobless executives over forty years old. As Dorothy Feiberman makes clear, the collective support and training in job-hunting techniques offered by the clubs are invaluable to the lucky few who have access to them. But these groups rarely try to speak for all the unemployed, nor do they suggest any solution to mass unemployment.

There is, in short, something missing here: a profound sense of the common predicament and how it might be changed. That sense probably has not been widespread since the Depression; no doubt the New Deal reforms helped defuse it by making the conditions of unemployment a measure less desperate. Instead, today there is diffuse anger, a suspicion of injustice, a confusion about one's place in an inhumane system. For that reason most of the people in this book leave me, at least, with a sadness that underlies my celebration of their extraordinary toughness and vitality. They persevere—magnificently, in many cases. But the price for simply persevering is paid in the coin of isolation, powerlessness, and uncertainty. Says Laura Gordon: "You can think about the politicians or the society, but it's like dropping something in a lake and watching the ripples, ripples, ripples. Nothing to get a handle on."

Is unemployment any different when there *is* something to get a handle on? Susan Ingham, Mabel Lockwood, and Julie Jacobsen, the three women who make up a chapter on "Fighting Back," would say so. Or, even more to the point, listen to the men and women caught up in the union struggle that is the subject of the last chapter of this book. Each of them suffers all the slight irritations and wrenching anguish of unemployment. Yet each understands clearly why he or she is out of work, knows that others are out for the same reason, and believes, with Rosie Engels, that "if people don't stick together, there's no way you're gonna get anyplace."

Rosie's union brother, Dirk Robinson, has been waiting for a year for a labor arbitrator to decide if he should get his job back. Blacklisted in the region, he cannot find other work. He says he has lost everything: wife, children, friends, house, savings. Even so: "I'd like to go back to [the company]. Even though I feel very, very bitter towards them, I liked the job I had there. And if I go back, I'll be going back a winner. I'll feel like I won the battle; I stuck it out. If the people there can see that I stuck it out, with the divorce and all, and came back in there a winner, maybe it'll change a couple of people's minds. Because I think they need that union in there." This is not the voice of a man who has lost everything. Dirk Robinson knows his choices mean something—his battles make a difference to other men and women. In that knowledge, he has gained at least as much in human stature as he has lost in human damage.

1

GETTING FIRED: "Sorry, Frank . . ."

For many people, the experience of unemployment is molded by its first brutal, traumatic moment: being fired. The blow frequently comes with no warning, after years of service to a company. I realized, after hearing an astonishing number of such horror stories—a few of which make up this chapter—that the key question they raise concerns power in the workplace: who has it, who doesn't. It is interesting to note that none of the people in this chapter belonged to a labor union, which might have protected them against the company's power to hire and fire at a whim.

GRACE KEATON

She is in her late thirties, a small, animated woman. She is divorced and has a daughter in college. Her apartment is in a handsome old building with large rooms, high ceilings, and a river view from every window. Books cover two walls of the living room; on the other walls hang prints, mostly of antique watercolors of European cities. She is about to leave the apartment for a new job in another city and is unhappy about it. She worked in publishing for nearly fifteen years before being "thrown to the auditors" by her last company.

As she talks, she wraps the tape recorder cord around and around her fingers.

I started in publishing in 1961. It was the beginning of the era of merging and wheeling and dealing and conglomerates that made publishing the darling of Wall Street in the late 1960s. The industry was getting faster, and it was exciting in a way. In some cases publishing was being taken out of the hands of the stuffy old clubs, the old boys, and being given to intellectuals in some instances and drummers in others. In many ways it was a liberating combination. One hoped for a breath of fresh air and fewer celluloid colors.

I did publicity and promotion in hardcover briefly and then went to a paperback house. I was there for twelve years. A long time. I worked my way up dutifully by hard work and learning my trade and so on, to a good and interesting job at a level where the corporate pressures began to be felt on the job. I felt them through my boss and his boss. Pressures for more income, control of costs, control of industry, to reduce staff periodically. The pressures for ordinary business goals became greater and greater, producing a job that was more and more tense and less and less desirable. But I couldn't walk out because of the salary. I had a child to support and me to support. It's hard to back away from it when you are in it, though it's perfectly clear now how tense I was for years. It was not so clear then.

The parent firm was a conglomerate. A holding company. They buy and sell real estate. They own TV and radio stations. They have a chain of tree-trimming companies, a loan company, gold mines, grapefruit groves in California, and God knows what else. It's very much like working for GM without a union. The pressures are very heavy. They have bought more and more and more. The corporate expansion has been headlong, to say the least. And the differences in pressure are not

17

discernible between it, even though it's a publishing company, and General Motors or ITT or anybody else. In fact, they may be greater. Because every product you make is a new product. In publishing you can't keep producing Ford whatevers.

What led up to your getting fired?

Nothing led up to it. It was almost a total shock, with the exception of a few days beforehand, when I was just feeling something funny and dreadful. I couldn't even tell you what. I would see two people together in a place that was unusual to see them together. That kind of thing. But I had an appointment with my boss at 10:30 one morning, and I came in with my pile of work, and I said, "Do you want to begin with this contract?" And he said something like: "No, I want to begin by talking about your leaving this company." This company I had been with for twelve years. I didn't die, but I can't tell you why not.

Moreover, this was a man I had been almost nauseatingly loyal to, and I *felt* loyal to. I would never speak to his superiors without his presence or without his explicit approval. And I defended him to my staff and to outside people. I would say, "He's really a good guy, he's really fair, he really does everything he can, he really, really, really." And he did not have the slightest hesitation in what he used to characterize as the corporation's "breaking my knees." They take you in a back alley, and they break your knees. Put out a contract on you. And he just did. He looked at me. . . . I worked with this man for eight or nine years in one capacity or another. A lot of my promotions came through him. And he just did it.

I speculate now that the pressures finally reached him beyond his psychological control. And that he got more and more nervous and trembly, and his main goal more and more was holding on to his job and retiring with a good pension. And so on. I still don't know what precipitated all of this. I asked him what it was, and he said, "It's a fait accompli. I've got it all signed. I got you a very good severance arrangement." Now, what's very good at that place is considered starvation at a lot of places. I mean, after twelve years, what could possibly be very good? Maybe another twelve years' pay. But not much less than that.

I said, "What do you mean? I want to know. You still have a job. I want to know what happened." At this point the personnel personage came in. I couldn't believe that the corporation apparently required a witness, but that came to be standard practice, too. So I ignored him. And Fred said, "Well, there's really nothing I can tell you. You can ask me questions if you want." It was clear that there was very little point. He'd not only gotten everything in writing, but they had covered themselves by not firing me. They had eliminated my job. And they have technically not replaced me. They moved one person into my office with what sounded at the time like about half my functions. Someone to whom I had also been enormously loyal, and who I just couldn't believe, couldn't believe was doing this.

The meeting would have been three minutes long if Fred had had his druthers. It was unpleasant and uncomfortable, and he didn't want to go on a moment longer than he had to. Certainly he didn't want any personal emotion mixed up in it, which is the kind of person he is.

In any case, it was total shock. I guess my mouth hung open for thirty seconds or so, and I said, brilliantly, "What do you mean? What do you mean?" But he had just said in no uncertain terms, "You are fired." And I said, "What do you mean? What do you mean?" And then I said, "Why? Why? Why? Why? Why?" He had all his speeches prepared, and I didn't, so his were shorter and evasive. He said it was all done. There was no going back. It was all signed, and the separation agreements were to his mind very generous. And there was no changing anything, and that was the way it was, and he was not about to give me any good reasons for this. Or any reasons for it. I was supposed to ask him questions. So I said, "Well, is it this? Is it that? Is it this? What is it?" He said, "Yes, sort of, well, no, well. . . ." He just didn't want to talk about it. He wanted me to disappear. He just wanted me to drop out of the earth. You know, I probably should have clammed up and said, "I want to call my lawyer." But I don't have a lawyer.

I finally left his office. I don't think I could have been in there more than fifteen or twenty minutes. I went down to my office and started packing things up. Fred said magnanimously that he would have a truck deliver things to my house. That's almost unheard of. Normally it's "Lady, get your ass in gear and get out in five minutes and don't come back. And where are the keys to the office?" God, I mean, immediately, in one minute, you're a pariah. You are trespassing. It's just remarkable, the violence.

It was the worst blow I ever had. I've been divorced. My father died a few months before I got fired. Both constitutionally and by event I've been through a lot of emotional upheaval in my life, and I've never been through anything like getting fired. Never. It's funny—for a long time the first thing I asked everybody was "Have you ever been fired?" Because I had the feeling that they could not possibly understand anything I was going to say unless they had been. And for a while that was true. I was persuaded that I must be not only as bad as the company must have thought I was to fire me, but much worse than that. Probably the world's worst. Probably I didn't deserve to live. It doesn't simply take away your self-confidence. It destroys you. Utterly.

The amazing thing is that I have had this same thing described to me by people who were fired where they just cut out a department or closed a plant. They say the same thing. There is something in the act. . . . I suppose there is something in our faith in and attitude towards work that says if you work well, you're going to be rewarded. That this is one of the virtues of our society and the capitalist mode. That there is something healthy, to use an old-fashioned word, about working well. So that if you're going to approach justice, that's where you're going to approach it. "Good people always get jobs." How many times have you heard that? It's a lot of horseshit. It's not true. But still, we believe it—and it's devastating, therefore, to be fired. I have still not recovered from it. I have had three job offers since then. Those offers have made no dent in that part of me that feels destroyed.

I was also furious. I was just furious. I felt completely betrayed. Which I was. There's very little doubt about that. This had apparently been going on for quite a while. There was every opportunity to say to me, "This is going to happen; get out and look for a job." In fact, I had been out looking for a job for a while because of all this dreadful corporate pressure. And I had turned down a job. And other things had come up that I hadn't investigated because I thought, "Oh, you know, what the hell. They've changed the pension law, and I'm going to be fully vested soon. And there are things about this job that are attractive, and maybe the people who are running the corporation will decide to retire to Tahiti and some good people will come in." You know, that sort of indecisive thing you do. So I was absolutely devastated.

I must say my spirits were kept up by friends in the industry who called. A lot of people called. I owe a million deep-felt thank-you notes. They helped me look for another job. Somebody directed me to the unemployment office. Everyone who'd ever lost a job called up and said something nice. I think that probably got me through. I felt I had not been completely abandoned by everybody, that not everybody would be willing to betray me in the same way. The feelings were so elemental, and so strong, just overpowering. Betrayal. Depression. Shock.

Do you have any idea now why you were fired?

I think ultimately because they didn't like me. I think it's probably that simple. There are still people in the company who are quasi alcoholics or who don't do any work. They're still there. And people who don't make waves. I had a lot of people working for me, and I was under a lot of pressure. I'm probably the kind of person who under those circumstances is not invisible. Probably what it came down to was simply that I was not liked. But I don't really know. It could be that I am taking the rap for things that went wrong. They saved some money on my salary, needless to say. I don't know how heavily any of these things weigh. But I never got any explanation.

Now I have decided to leave the city. I chose a job far away from here because I thought it might somewhat mitigate that work obsession. I'm going to a more leisurely city, a place where the industry is more leisurely, and certainly to a more leisurely job. I think I want to heal, in a way. And I think that may be very sensible, a smart thing. But I can't imagine ... you know, you remember emotional experiences, and at some point you say, "I cannot summon up that experience anymore." It's just too long ago, or it wasn't strong enough. I can't imagine that happening with being fired. I think till I die, I will be able to summon it up again like dehydrated horror. If I just sprinkle a few drops of water on it, I will be able to summon up that first numb horror, rage, and the depression afterwards. Just total wipeout.

It has to have a lot of kinship with death. I have not been through a lot of unexpected death in my life. My father died. He was almost eighty-seven, and he wasn't ill, just running down. I lost one other person. (I love that term for death. "I lost," as though you misplaced [laughs].) After the deaths I could almost feel processes of catharsis and consolation working. But with being fired I haven't had any. They just haven't occurred. Perhaps because death is more real, and this is less real. But for example, I almost lost my old sleep patterns. I wake up almost routinely at dreadful hours like four and five in the morning. And part of that half-waking nightmarish thing that goes on has to do with the event of being fired, or whose fault it was, or nightmares about my boss or about the office. Not things about going hungry or being without a job. It's the brutality. It may be more like rape than death. Being brutalized, violated, and being helpless. There is nothing more clearly the exercise of power than that. I mean, you can kill someone, and that's also the exercise of power, but it's no clearer. This is clearly power. It's frightening.

FRANK CAPEK

He lives in a middle-class housing development on the West Coast. The neighborhood, built in the late 1960s, still looks raw and incomplete; the trees are not yet as tall as the one-story houses. He is a stout man, Czech-born, but now an American citizen. He has been out of work six months, looking for a job as "an engineer, draftsman, designer, machinist, anything." Asked what he does with the rest of his time, he gestures in disgust at the living room, which he is painting. He jokes *about his heavy accent: "I am over the most difficult times that I have with the language. I used to ask for the veal cutlet and get the shrimp. And I pay the $9, $10. I was happy to get something." He lives with his wife and daughter.*

In 1958 I came to the United States. I started as a mechanical engineer with a steel mill in Chicago. I turned them down when they offered to help me get the master's degree at company expense. And I said that I appreciated it, but that I was so green, so new, and so happy with my work in Chicago that I would just like to continue. I said, "If you people like my work, please let me stay here. It would be hard to move a second time so soon after the separation from my country." Today how I look at it is I made a big mistake that time. It never comes back, that kind of opportunity.

After two and a half, three years I left and went to work for an aerospace corporation. I was working on equipment for the space program that took the men to the moon. Very, very exciting project. I'll never forget it in my life. I had all kind of work, sometimes sixty hours a week. And I made tremendously good money. I bought a house together with my wife.

At that time another aircraft company had a big, big contract. The personnel department was recruiting, and they had a big advertisement in *The New York Times* a couple of times. Good, flashy advertisement. All kind of relocation expenses for mechanical engineers, aerospace engineers, anyone with aircraft experience. So I responded. I said, "Let's find out." I went into an interview, and I met their reps there, and they liked my background. They liked my résumé. They liked my work and my capability. So they gave me a call in about two, three weeks. "Frank, if you're still interested, remember we talked so-and-so?" I told them it depends on the money. They offered me almost 40 percent more than I was making. I had a permanent good job there after five years' employment. And suddenly I get 40 percent more. A very senior manufacturing engineer position, besides relocation expenses. Very good as far as paying all kinds of costs. I just think it over, talk it over with my wife. How can I gain that much, even if I stay with where I am forever? OK. Accept the offer. I accept it. Very rapidly we get the moving truck from the warehouse and they pack up everything and we get the limousine out to the airport. That's all, good-bye.

I move across the country and report to the new company. Got into the engineering department. Working on rockets, missiles. It was an interesting, challenging job. A place to learn for any engineering person. But you have reviews every four months. You find out that you are just a number. The salary increases all go to the seniority guys. The new guy, you are just like a slave. You have to work two or three times harder than a ten or fifteen years' seniority guy. And if you are not performing, you are very soon out the door. They have no mercy with family or whatever. You have to be on the ball. Especially new guys.

In 1969 the company lost almost every government contract. The missile program was chopped down. They had a lot of opposition from the government, so we had to feel it. When a program is down, there is no work. Who came last, he goes out first. And I was one of them. After a year they gave me a nice letter: "Sorry, Frank. We have such-and-such a situation. Work load, the contract, the problems. We have to include you in the surplus list. If anything goes better, we're going to call you back. Please advise us if you're changing your address and so on." After one year. I had just bought this house.

Almost immediately Frank found an engineering job with an airline. "Fortunately at that time the depression or inflation or whatever was better than now." After three years he was laid off again and found another job with a company producing everything "from tanks to recreational vehicles."

After two years there, the aircraft company did call me back. In 1974. And what happened? I found out that the company still has not changed anything. But I accepted the recall because the benefit package and the insurance package and everything else is better than any other places. You have more benefit to the salaried employee than anywhere. This is the nation's number one defense contractor. If you have a dentist bill or anything with the doctor, a baby or whatever, you're almost not paying a penny. In other places it is not so. So I accepted. I thought maybe this time it lasts longer.

Unfortunately it was only two years. In March of 1976 I'm out again. They had a budget problem, with the cutbacks and the allocations for the missiles—you know, with the money they thought they were getting. They chopped down to half or so. They told us that we lost the project because the $400 million become only 200. That's how it goes. There is no mercy. And now I'm still out, and I don't know, I think this company has ruined my life.

What makes me mad are those people who are sitting there and getting fat with the salary increases and doing nothing because of seniority. They have less right to a job than the subcontractors who come in from outside and carry the work load. They do nothing, just sit around the coffeepot. It's just impossible. You just have to throw up when you see that system. I have a couple of friends including a Czech who survived ten or fifteen years. I visited their work stations, and they're just laughing. They have a hard time to get through eight hours sitting there and doing nothing. They walk around. They go down to the credit union, and they sit in the cafeteria. They get coffee breaks every half hour or more. Talking, talking, talking. Visiting each other. Going home and making out tax returns and everything else you can think. And this is all the highest-paid people. They're not performing. Just a joke, an insult against the working professionals.

This last layoff I contested because I learned about the open-door policy. It's only a gimmick, but I figure, what can I lose? Let me knock on the president's door and tell him, "I'm working hard. I'm performing. And you people are selecting me as the number one who gets fired from my department. But look at the other people not working. See this, see this, see this. What's wrong here? What's going on?" I went to two different offices and told them my feeling about the company. That they pulled me out of a permanent good job and moved me across the country. And now I am fifty-four years old. I have a family. I have a house. I have less and less chance to go anywhere. I said, "You people have no mercy. Give me a broom or give me some other assignment. I'm going to take it, because I have no other choice."

But the open-door policy is just a gimmick. I thought I had a right to appeal, but they just . . . it's only an option you can take, probably by state labor law. You can complain if you don't like it. You can use the open-door policy and tell your superior you feel this way or the other way. But basically nobody gets any medicine there. You just tell the story and walk out. Strip off your badges. You're still out. They tell you about the budget, about their problems. They tell you that you have no seniority, that they have seniority people who have more rights than you have. I told them the seniority guys aren't working at all. It didn't matter.

One time they almost escorted me out from the plant. I had the right to go to the manager on the last day, but they thought I was fired already. I told them I still have one interview with the manager. Tomorrow at eleven o'clock. And they grab me in the neck and want to throw me out.

So I just came home and told my wife, "That's it again." They give you a week or two severance payment and some other things, they pay you vacation, and good-bye. Now I wonder if I will find another engineering job. As a mechanical engineer it's very, very hard to find a meaningful job. I am getting old, and when one mechanical engineering job pops up here or there, they have wholesale applicants. They get forty or fifty résumés on one opening.

The company isn't even cooperating when other companies call for references. I feel they're giving me a hard time about recommending my services to some other places because I contested my case and everybody knows I was resisting. I was a bad guy. I used the last chances to survive, to give my family bread every day. I called them and one manager said that. "Frank, don't ask me. I can't recommend you." He was very strict. "Don't ask my help. They are mad." All because I contested my rights. I have no union. I have nothing. I just used those one, two, three, four steps to expose my situation and let my superiors know what's going on in this and that department. And how they're working. But it seems to me they know. I didn't tell them anything new.

DAVE YALMAN

He lives alone in a one-room apartment in Philadelphia. When he is unemployed, "The park becomes very important to me. I'm a big walker. Just give me a pair of sneakers and I'll walk across a mountain. . . . And I'm a pretty social person. I have a lot of people that are dear to me in the city, my parents and stuff like that. I go out a lot. I visit people a lot and have people visit me." Someday he would like to be a film director.

I'm twenty-six years old, white, born in the Bronx. Middle-class Jewish background. As far as this last job goes, I got it through the job-counseling center that the unemployment office sponsors. They referred me. It was a small magazine. I worked there for eighteen months. At first my position was relatively creative. Some telephone sales for advertising space, but the thing that excited me was that I wrote the entertainment section of the newspaper. Which was good, because I'm into movies and stuff like that.

But the paper got into such bad financial condition in the recession that my section was eliminated. I was reduced to doing really boring stuff. All typing. Bills. And they couldn't afford to give me a raise. At least they kept giving excuses. I couldn't even get a cost-of-living raise. They were not just into doing that. I was really up a creek. I couldn't afford to leave the job because I was broke. And I was almost in tears. I felt like a vegetable.

So I decided to get myself fired. I decided to be good to myself and take the consequences as far as getting fired goes. I didn't know if they were going to contest unemployment or not. But I just knew I had to get out of there. So I really fucked up. Fucked up everything I could possibly do. The system I adopted was—well, I had to type bills during the day. What I decided to do was just make a mistake on each bill I typed. Make major errors like getting the name wrong or getting the address wrong, so it would go all the way out and be returned again. "No such person at this address." Get the wording of the ad wrong. Get the amount wrong. Just make one big major boo-boo on each bill. Every single bill.

I decided this on a Friday, I remember, and I said to myself, "Well, look, in a couple of weeks—they're pretty thick, but they're going to have to catch on." So I would type something wrong on each bill, and I would invariably get half of them back at the end of the day. They would catch the mistakes. But the other half they missed. And my boss started to say, "Dave, you're really not doing well. What's happening?" And I would say, "I don't know, I'm certainly trying to do them right." There was a definite chance they could have fired me for cause. As far as unemployment goes, there's cause and incompetence. If I had come in late every day and shouted on the phone all the time, they could have said, "Good-bye, we're not giving you unemployment after what you pulled." So I tried to clean up my act, relatively speaking. Which wasn't easy to do since I didn't exactly have a good reputation there. So I was punctual. I was a fast worker, did everything on time. Except that I didn't do anything right.

Eventually they caught on. My boss called me in one day and said, "Look, Dave, it's obvious that you're not doing the work because it's boring. I know it is. You're bored silly. We're gonna have to let you go, and we'll give you unemployment." He obviously felt very guilty, which surprised me. I came to realize afterwards that it was because he had promised me a lot of things that never happened. He was very quick to promise things, and he had done that to me, and I had been disappointed. He definitely felt guilty about that.

So I said, "Oh, really? Well, if you think that's best."

And I lived happily ever after.

JEFF WEINBAUM

He is twenty-seven years old, single, a musician. After earning a master's degree in music from the University of Michigan, he worked for *eighteen months at a record company. Now he gives violin lessons to supplement the $42 a week he receives in unemployment benefits. He also composes and performs with a group that plays avant-garde chamber music.*

My official title at the company was tape editor. It's the equivalent to film editing, to montage. When you make a record, the original material is edited down into the performance that you decide is the best one. You take a great bulk of material and edit into one supposedly best performance. Obviously there are technical and artistic considerations involved in doing that, and in a small record company the tape editor winds up being responsible for both. But I wasn't the producer of the records, which means ultimately it wasn't my decision if the performance I had edited was the appropriate one. Finally, I lost the job because of disagreements over that.

The company has always had trouble with tape editors because . . . well, I guess it's just because of the nature of the situation. The tape editor has to really cater to the boss. The boss wants to be catered to. That's his privilege, and he makes use of it. And so the tape editor is in a very delicate position, and I didn't handle it too delicately. In big companies such as Columbia Records that situation is avoided because there's a strict division between engineering and management. The person who physically cuts the tape is an engineer, a union member. He has no responsibility for artistic content. The producer is management. But in a small company this division is very unclear. So I couldn't make up my mind whether I was an engineer or management. I was both and really neither.

In other words, I was responsible for the work, but I didn't ultimately have control of it, which is a difficult situation. Plus the fact that I was not nominally the producer kept my wages down. I started at $3 an hour and worked up to $175 a week. I felt it was nowhere near enough compared to the concentration I was putting into this tape editing.

And I got very cocky about it. I behaved as if the job were mine forever. It was a very funny situation because most of the time the boss left you completely alone. The engineers worked more or less on their own. Every once in a while he'd just come in and take over, then drop out again in the middle and let you finish the work. I felt very much in a vacuum. I mean, if I wasn't going to be responsible for the work, I wanted more direction. What I finally said to the guy was: "If you want it a different way, tell me what you want, and I'll do it for you. But I'm not going to second-guess. I can't edit according to what you want unless you tell me. You have to take my word that I have listened through all these seven hundred tapes and this is the best one there." I believed that. I believed that I made the best possible choices. But he would come in and say, "Listen, this isn't the best." And I'd say, "Yes, it is the best. This one is bad, and all these other possibilities are no good for various reasons. I've done the work. You haven't." But that wasn't the appropriate attitude.

How did you actually get fired?

Well, I was working on Beethoven's Ninth for about two months. I had just finished editing an enormous amount of material. The complete Ninth Symphony plus two overtures and several other pieces.

First the editing has to be approved by the boss and the conductor. Then you go to the next step, which is mixing. You take the edited tape and process it electronically so that it sounds the way the producer wants it to sound, which involves balancing the various tracks. Sometimes filtering it, sometimes limiting the dynamic range. There's a lot of technical things involved with transferring from the tape medium to the record medium, which have different characteristics. You have to mediate between them.

So I had a big disagreement with the boss about a specific movement in the Ninth, namely the fourth. I thought there was only one rendition of it that was even acceptable at all, and that the others were terrible. The boss thought that the one I thought was the worst was the best. So he got this idea. It was late on a Thursday evening. Everybody was tired, and we were having this disagreement. So he called in his secretary, who has some musical background, and we had a blindfold test. We played both versions and then asked her which one was the best. Now this was obviously not a great idea [*laughs*]. Anyway, she chose mine. I have a feeling that clinched it. Boy, was that dumb.

I came down with the flu that weekend. I had it for ten days. The night before I was planning to return to work I got a call about six o' clock at night from the chief engineer, who's a young guy. He's also been subsequently fired. This happens to everybody at that place. You really have to toe the line or you get booted out. Apparently they had just that minute decided to fire me. They didn't even wait until I came back to work after being sick ten days. Which I thought was kind of low.

That episode with the Ninth was the last time I saw the boss. He never talked to me personally about it. He had this flunky do it.

So at that point I went on unemployment. Now they could have been bitchy about it. They could have said that I behaved provocatively and therefore I wouldn't have been eligible. Instead they just said that I was unqualified. That enabled me to qualify for unemployment. They said I just hadn't been the right person for the job, which is theoretically not my fault.

Do you think you behaved provocatively?

I guess you could look at it that way. I hadn't toed the line in a certain sense. But I hadn't been trying to lose the job, that's for sure. I just didn't really think through what it took to keep the job. I thought very narrowly about doing the job but not the strategy of keeping the job. You know, who I had to flatter, who I had to go along with, et cetera. There were a lot of temperamental people involved, and I was certainly among them. And being the lowest-ranking temperamental person, I was the first to go.

After getting fired, I sort of wanted to end it on a "no hard feelings'" type of note. I wanted to accept some of the responsibility and have him accept some. I wanted to say, "Well, I didn't do as well as I should have," and he would've said, "Well, we know that, but you didn't do as badly as you could have." It was really a fantasy on my part. I think it was caught up with my whole attitude towards the job. While I was there I wanted to belong, to feel needed, to feel useful. To feel like I was at home there. In other words, in order to release my creative energies I had to have that feeling of being at home. That was important to me. But maybe that's just an excuse. Anyway, I didn't approach it as just a job, where my involvement was limited to what I had to do for the job.

CARMEN GONZALEZ

She is about twenty-five, a tall, shy, olive-skinned woman dressed in denims. Her accent and slang testify to her Puerto Rican background and her years in the United States. She is going to college near her home in downtown Washington, D.C. She has been unemployed for nearly a year.

Through my friend Michael I got into working with a society of antique collectors. I worked there for two or three years. After my boss retired, Michael took over the position, and he became too personal with me. You know, to me he's still a friend, but to him I was something else. If I didn't do what he wanted me to do I was going to be fired, or it was going to be down on my record.

I was a librarian. I had to keep all the records. The society gets all these gifts, and they have seminars in the summer, and people would come to make studies. So I had to keep in mind all the regular library work, plus where people were going to stay and where to send them papers and things like that. It was interesting. I liked it.

But my friend Michael, he lived across the street from me, and he wanted to know everything. Like when I got home from work, he would be calling me and wanting to know where I was going. Like what time I got out of school—OK, that's all right; it's my job, and they should know what time I leave school. But when I got home from work he would be calling me and wanting to know where I was going and what time I would be back. He would tell my boyfriend not to come and pick me up, stuff like that.

So like I said to the girl who interviewed me at the unemployment office, I can't say and put it on paper that he felt anything for me. I'm not inside him, you know. A lot of men rap to a girl but they're not really interested. They're just doing it to do it. If I were to say he loves me, then later on he could say, "No, I never said that to her." He could deny it.

It seems to me from the story that he does, but I didn't want to put it down in writing that he loves me. He asked me to go out, and he wanted to know everything about my personal life. He asked me to go camping. Then one time we got this very big and expensive gift from a gentleman who is a member of the society. He has sort of like a mansion and a library with all these original French and Italian arts and stuff like that. Paintings and books that you don't even want to touch because they're so delicate and beautiful. There were more than two thousand books. I had to take them out and catalogue them. And one day Michael was standing next to me, and he stopped and said, "Don't you feel the vibrations between you and me?" I looked at him. I said, "Look, don't make me laugh." It was just funny. I said, "You're just a comedian." He says, "I'm not, I'm not! This is not a joke, Carmen. This is serious. Don't you feel something after all this time that we've been friends and we've been working together? Don't you feel something?" And I said, "No, honestly, no. I care as a friend, and you're very intelligent, and you are a very interesting person to talk to. But as far as emotional feelings are concerned, no."

So after that he kept getting very upset. He didn't talk to me for weeks. And when he did it was mainly to put me down. This was the way he was. And I cannot work for somebody who makes me feel useless. Who has to recheck everything I say and do. You know, I'm typing and he has to be standing there looking at what I'm doing. He used to tell me that he was doing me a favor, that he didn't need someone like me. So I said, "Why don't you fire me then? I mean if you don't need me, you're just wasting your money." But he never did fire me.

I remember the first time I left. I called him from school and told him that I'd have to stay at my dance class for maybe an hour because we're practicing for a performance. So he says OK. I got to work earlier than what I told him. I said, "I'm here," and I started doing my job. The library is full of people. And he gets hysterical, screaming at me for being late, "What the fuck. . . ." Just the language, you know, upset me. I was so upset. I said, "Look, if I start fighting with you in here, we're just going to have a show." So I sat there and kept doing my job.

But the next day I called him up and said, "Look, I don't think I'll be coming there anymore." So he says OK. Then Saturday afternoon he calls me and says, "What are you doing?" I go, "I'm going out." And he says, "Look, I called you, but don't think I'm kissing your ass." I go, "Don't put thoughts in my mind. I feel I could tell you whatever I have to say." So he says, "I called to apologize. I don't do this to anybody, but I called to apologize. I've thought it over and I admit I was wrong. I didn't know you were that sensitive." I said, "It has nothing to do with being sensitive. I have taken enough put-downs. I live with it at home and I don't have to take it on the job. I'm not starving yet." So he says, "Will you come back?" And I said I would think about it. I took a week off, and then I felt, well, why not? Everybody was shocked to see me back.

He went along perfectly for a month. He said, "I promise you that we're here to work and that's it. We're here on business." But a month went by and he started it all over. When he insulted me I never answered back. I feel that you shouldn't get that low.

But finally I was in no mood to hear whatever he had to say. So I told him, "Look, you keep your personal feelings within you and it will be better that way. I'll continue working and that's it. But if you find that I can't continue working here with you because it's too impossible, then tell me and I'll leave." All of a sudden he came out and said, "You know what you are? You are a very spoiled little bitch." That hit me. Maybe because it's true I'm spoiled in some things, but it really bothered me. So I stood up and told him, "Look, I don't have to take this. You know what? You are a bastard, that's exactly what you are. And I don't have to take this. You can continue doing the work because I'm leaving and I'm not coming back."

He started screaming to me that he had fired me, and I said, "No, you didn't fire me; I'm leaving." So he said not to give his name as a reference, not even to mention that I worked for him. And when I went to collect unemployment, I had to go through this whole process of writing letters and getting photocopies, and I had to tell everything that went on.

First the girl asked me, "Well, I read in your application that the reason for your quitting is personal. Would you like to talk about it?" I said, "Sure, I'll talk, but do I have to?" So she says, "Yeah, we have to find out why." I started telling her what happened, and she started asking me if I ever went out with him, if I was ever alone with him in his apartment, how long do we know each other and how old is he and everything. I said, "I don't know, I never asked him." I said, "As a matter of fact, I don't know anything about him except that he lives alone, he's kind of weird, and he's a librarian." Then she kept asking me if I ever answered back when he rapped to me, you know, like encouraging him to keep talking to me. So I said there were days that we never talked to each other, and I never spoke with him unless it was necessary. And I was over to his house once, but it wasn't only me. It was a party for people from the office, so I wasn't there alone. I never did visit him alone because I felt I would be teasing him. That might not have been my intention, but he'd probably feel that I was teasing him by being alone in his house. He always wanted me to come and hear this record or that record, but I always told him to give the record to me and I'd listen to it in my house and bring it back.

Well, I got the unemployment. But I feel a big problem in my getting another job is that I don't have a reference from this last job where I worked five years. Interviewers question that, you know. The reference is very, very important. They really question you. They ask, "What do you mean, 'personal reasons'?" Then they look at you like—I don't know, especially a female, when you tell a male what happened to you or why it's personal, he looks at you like he was saying, "All you women, you like to tease." It makes you feel funny. I feel guilty out of nothing. I never felt and don't feel that I teased Michael or encouraged him to go that far. And I don't like to share all these things with everybody. But they always ask why you left, and you have to tell the truth.

MARY VOLINO

She is a transplanted Manhattanite living in a small rented house in a suburb of San Diego with her husband, a salesman of industrial chemicals, and her baby. She graduated from a commercial high school and married at nineteen. She is now twenty-five. For two years she worked in a small company that makes sports equipment. She started out in the accounting department, then was transferred to purchasing.

I wasn't in purchasing but a month when I realized that I was pregnant. I had a male boss, but I went immediately to my old boss, Joan. She had a lot of influence on the whole company, or so I thought. I told her I was pregnant and she said, "Wow, that's fantastic." I said I didn't know if I would have the baby because I wasn't sure what I wanted at that point. And she said, "Well, listen, don't worry about it." I told her I would like a job to come back to if I decided to have the baby. "Don't worry about anything like that," she said, "except that in your seventh month, I don't think it would be a good idea if you stuck around because you'll be too big." So at that point I figured, well, yeah, that sounds logical to me. Besides, I'd like some time for myself. It'll give me a few months before I have the baby, and then I'll go back to work. So I tripped along on my merry little way.

I didn't get along with my boss, Don. He was extremely chauvinistic, and he became unglued when I started to wear maternity clothes. He would scream and start picking on me. He was weird. Women frightened him. So here I am getting bigger and bigger and they're fighting with me because it's time for my raise. He keeps putting me off and telling me, "Well, since you're leaving, there's no reason for you to get a raise." And I'm saying, "But I've worked all this time without a raise; I'm due for a raise right now." And he says, "No, I'm working it out, I'm working out something good for you where you can get it all in one lump sum when you leave." We're going through this constant battle, back and forth, and he's saying that the woman, Joan, is the one that's holding my raise back, and she's saying it's him.

So he starts in about my seventh month when I'm just realizing that I can't give up this job so easily. I really need the money. He keeps saying to me, "Well, when are you going to leave?" I keep saying in a couple of weeks. We're going back and forth like this. God knows why. Some people said the front office didn't think it looked good to have me so big. Also, the president of the company was constantly afraid that I would fall down and hurt myself. I think it was mainly because I didn't have a good rapport with Don. But it was this constant general feeling, you know, that I was the first woman ever to get pregnant there and they didn't know how to handle it. Subsequently, a few girls after me have gotten pregnant, and they've let all of them go, too.

So I'm just assuming it's OK, you know. And my girl friends are figuring the same. There was one other girl who was all hopped up about it because she felt that now she didn't have to worry about getting pregnant. She'll have a job to return to, too. Now I understood that it would be unlikely for them to keep my particular job open for six or nine months, but I thought I'd have *something*. They'd put me *somewhere*. State law says that you cannot be let go because of pregnancy, and there has to be a job waiting for you after six weeks, if I'm not mistaken. Because six weeks is when your doctor says you are allowed to return to work. And it was like an understood fact from the very beginning. I mean, it was never brought up. I talked about it with the other girls in the office. I never went back to Joan and made sure, definitely, because she had said it in the beginning. Why should I assume otherwise? Don had told me specifically that he couldn't keep the purchasing job open, and I had said, "Yes, I understand that," but he said, "There's got to be something else. You can pitch in somewhere."

Anyway, the day that I was leaving they had this form the supervisor is supposed to fill out. One part says, "How do you rate this employee?" Me and Don were joking around, and he told me to fill it out and say if I was good, excellent, or what. I filled it out and brought it in to Joan. And where it says "Remarks," I had put down "Nine months maternity leave." She took it and scratched it out and said, "We don't have anything like maternity leave. If you want a job, you're going to have to come in and fill out an application." Just like any other fuckin' slob on the street.

Well, I was crushed. I mean I was literally crushed. She intimidated me like crazy, this woman. She had like a B.A. in psychology, and she was a CPA. All the power this fucking woman held. She just held so much power that I was totally intimidated by her. When she said that about coming in and filling an application, I just looked at her. Because I loved that job. I mean, as bad as it was, it was the first job that I ever felt capable and confident in. So I just got up and walked out of there defeated. I didn't know how to deal with it. I was trying to keep myself together. A brave front. Walking out with my head held high. If I could have I would have cried hysterically. You've gotta realize too that when you're pregnant you get docile. I don't know, you're very different. I'm sure now I would say something to her, but then I was like totally blown out. I mean totally.

They bought me off with a $200 baby gift. A check. And they took taxes out of it.

Then I had a big legal battle at unemployment. At first I waited a month before going. I bought Joan's shit hook, line, and sinker: "You quit and that's it." She sold me a bill of goods and I bought it. But my husband kept saying, "Go, go, it's legal." So finally I went. Unemployment didn't know how to handle my case because there was nothing written down except the thing about maternity leave that Joan scratched

34

out. I explained it to the guy and he couldn't believe what was happening, this whole thing I was telling him, and he said, "Wow, I don't know, I've got to talk to my supervisor." The supervisor called me and kept asking me over and over again the facts. What was said back and forth. Plus Joan, the bitch, was giving him the runaround. She wouldn't answer the phone for about a week. And they kept writing on the papers, "Quit because of pregnancy."

I finally said, "Listen, talk to Don. Maybe he'll help me." And I called him hysterically. He knew what financial position my husband and me were in. And I said, "Don, you've got to make them give it to me. You can't say that I quit. Get that last piece of paper. It's written on there that I requested a maternity leave." And he said, "All right, don't worry, I'll take care of it." I don't know what he did, but I got the unemployment. And then I found out from friends that he got put on the rack by Joan. He had his door open, and he yelled, "Well, I was going to lay her off anyway."

So everybody figured he had been stabbing me in the back. I did too for a long time. I thought maybe he had never really liked my work, and that I'm so incompetent that they never wanted me back. I carried this around for months. And then I thought about it, and to console myself, I figured he had to cover his back, too. I guess the way he decided to cover it was to say that it didn't matter whether I got unemployment or not because I was about to get laid off anyway.

Anyway, I got it. And I decided to run it to tilt. Just run it, man, to the bloody end. And I did. Seventeen months of unemployment. I understand that their interest rates go up, and I just wanted to blow them right out of the fucking world. Fuck them like they fucked me.

After you found out what the law was, did you think about suing them and making them take you back?

I didn't want to work for those fuckers anymore. I just don't want to be around them. Besides, I've been able to stay home with the baby, and if I can collect unemployment, screw them, why not? It would have been a good thing on principle to fight it, but I wouldn't have been able to walk into that place. I haven't been there since. I wouldn't go there again. Especially an insecure person like me. I'm very insecure, and when people say these things to you, whether to your face or behind your back, it kind of fucks with you. I felt that for a long time.

2

OUT OF WORK: "Human Damage, You Might Say"

People change during long months of joblessness. Their confidence waxes or wanes; their goals shift; they discover unsuspected sides of themselves. Their attitudes toward work, society, and life are shaped anew. The people in this chapter talk about those changes and reveal a tremendous variety of reactions to unemployment.

JIM HUGHES

A green house surrounded by cornfields on the outskirts of a small town in Indiana. The house is so close to the road that passing cars almost drown out conversation. It is a sweltering July day. Jim comes to the door shirtless, a paunchy man of thirty-five with longish sandy hair and mustache. Except for his years in the Marines he has lived his whole life within ten miles of this house. He is a welder. At night he takes classes in X-ray technology. "My education will be completed in August of next year. Unless I decide to go further, but I don't think I will. Then I feel I'll be able to find work without any problem."

He chain-smokes. His wife sits down to listen in between chores. His five-year-old daughter peeks out from the kitchen.

He is "a die-hard Republican. I kinda follow Reagan more than I do Ford. Though if Jerry Brown had won the Democratic nomination, I'd have crossed over. He seems to be on the ball. But that's about as far as it goes for politics with me. I don't think much of politicians. If they'd have seen this recession comin', maybe they could've done somethin' about it. But there was nothin' nobody could do about me getting fired. I don't blame it on society. . . ."

The whole thing started back when I was fired without just cause. I was working until last July in a tool and engineering shop. And the foreman for some reason—now this is my personal opinion, but a lot of the other fellows I worked with felt the same way—just picked me out and put lots of pressure on me and fired me. Right after that they came up with a big layoff. The more people they had out of the shop at that time, the better for them. So I feel it was a combination of a personal thing and the fact that he had pressure on him to get rid of people. I don't feel I was at fault.

I had some anger, really, because I had never been fired before. I felt my work performance was good. Excellent, really. But he kept putting pressure on me for more and more work. I was doing three times the work they normally wanted on the day he fired me. And he fired me for poor work performance. There was a parking violation, other little things. Like tardiness. I was buying this house at the time, and I think on three different occasions I notified him that I would have to be late. And he still used that as an excuse. So it had to be a personal thing. I liked the job. I liked the people working there. I hated to lose it.

So I went to the unemployment office. That kinda hurt my pride a little. More than a little. I didn't really want to go, but I felt that I had to in this situation. I felt that I wanted to get them for all I could. I wanted a little bit of revenge. But even though I paid that money in, I still didn't like to go. I guess it was from the way I was brought up. Do things for yourself. Reward yourself. Nobody gives you anything for nothing. This is the attitude I had at that time. Still have that attitude somewhat. But I've had to swallow that pride.

When I first applied, the unemployment office turned me down. So I had to get a lawyer, go to hearings, subpoena witnesses. It was April when I got fired, and it wasn't until the next December that the unemployment office finally decided in my favor, that I had been fired without just cause. So I didn't get any unemployment all that time. Only welfare.

It was rough. Of course, I went out almost every day at first and tried to find work, but it was in the middle of the recession. There was just no work available. There was nothing there at all. And this came as a surprise because I had never really looked for work before. The day I graduated from high school, a friend of mine said, "Hey, we need a fellow up here." I went in the next day and had work. I got home from Vietnam on Friday, and on Monday I was back to work at the same place. They always had something for me. So this time around, first thing I did was call them. They said, "No, we don't have anything. Things have dropped." It kind of made me feel bad because I never had that experience of going out and trying to find a job. When I lost this job, it was a completely different world than before.

The first week I was out looking for something every day. Then slowly it got to where the money situation only allowed me to go out looking for work maybe once a week. Then it got to once every two weeks. I couldn't put gas in my car. I had like $400 worth of monthly bills. I was used to making $600 and I was cut to zero. I had money put away, enough to live on. A few dollars, not too many. It wasn't bad the first month. Well, the first two months. But after that the money depleted.

After the first thirty days it was beginning to run out. I knew in the next few weeks I was gonna be at zero. So I went to welfare. Then I *really* had to swallow my pride. That first day at welfare was quite a day. I've tried to push it out of my mind because they really kind of step on you. I got the feeling that they have an iron hand over you, and you're nothing. I got the feeling they didn't care. They make you sit— well, it's a common thing, even in a doctor's office you hear people complaining about this. But the sitting and waiting. Waiting for nothing. And they give you as little information as they can possibly give you. I don't think—and it's a personal opinion again—I don't think they wanted to help you as much as they should have. I mean, their job is to help. I don't think they were doing their job. You get a feeling of rejection. Especially the feeling that they're better than you. No equality. No equality whatsoever. I waited all day and they told me I would have to come back the next day. I hated to go back but I knew I had to. And then they told me I couldn't draw anything for thirty days because I'd been fired. So I had to wait another month, and I didn't get my first check until July 30. From April to July, zero money.

Then there was a food stamp problem. I qualified for food stamps, but I actually had to go out on my own to find out my rights. They didn't tell me I didn't qualify for food stamps. They just didn't say anything about it. They only tell you what you ask. Which I guess is all right. They're not breaking any rules. But they're not helping you either, and this is what they're for. So I had to get kind of forceful with 'em. I don't feel that I'm better than anybody else, but I didn't feel like I was gonna be pushed around. And I finally did get someplace. I said, "Look, I either get food stamps or I'm gonna make some phone calls." I actually had to raise my voice. A few swear words. Threaten to call a few people, like my congressman. I've met the man, talked to him. And it seems if you threaten them a little bit, they bend a little more and say, "Well, OK, we'll give you something."

It wasn't long before everything was gone. I had swallowed my pride and I was upset about everything. Welfare started giving us $224 a month; but they always gave you a hard time, and you had to go there almost every month for something. The fact of being off work and just laying around with no money. No money to put in the gas tank of the car to go look for work. There was the threat of the utility companies turning the electricity off. The telephone. Furnace running out of fuel all the time. They turned the phone off during that time, but I always managed to borrow some money someplace to keep the electricity from being turned off. I average around $36-a-month electricity, and I think at one time I had an electric bill of $200 and some. It got awful tough. Sometimes we'd be completely flat zero broke. We ran out of food a couple of times. No money to buy food stamps. Wasn't nothing we could do. We just went without. We didn't eat. That's true. Sometimes for three and four days at a time.

And pretty soon you start creating your own problems. I drank a little heavy. Started drinking when there was nothing to do. When the money ran out I couldn't afford it, but any chance I got I did. And I had too much time on my hands. Too much of being home. I think it hurts your relationship, your marriage and so forth. I know in some cases of welfare the father has to leave the home to be able to survive. I wasn't gonna let that happen. I had that gnawing at me. And the wife and I had problems. We started to have little arguments. It wouldn't have happened if I'd been working. They were senseless. They were over little or

41

nothing. We'd just bitch at each other for nothing. We had nothing else to do, just bitch at each other. I constantly raised hell because I was unhappy. She left me at one time for three or four weeks. In fact, it still affects our marriage. We see a shrink regularly. Every week. And even with going and seeing a shrink it's rough.

It's hard to even remember how I passed my time. Pushed it so far back in my mind. Even that short a time ago. You just get up in the morning and wait to go to bed at night. You can't wait till it's time to go to bed. When you go to bed you can't sleep. Worrying about things. But when you get up in the morning, you just can't wait till it's time to go to bed. You sit and wait. For what I don't know. I just kept waiting on something. That's a helluva thing to get a feeling like that. That's when it's time to see a shrink.

There wasn't nothing to do but just lay around. Try to borrow some money. By that time you'd borrowed from everybody, and they wasn't gonna give you any more, because they knew they weren't gonna get any back. If your electricity was working, you watched the TV. Or listened to the radio. And just get up in the morning and wait for bedtime.

For a while we visited friends, but it got to where we didn't have the gas to go. So most of our friends didn't have too much to do with us, I guess. There was one, of course, there's always one who sticks by you. But we didn't associate too much with people. 'Cause we didn't have money to associate and do the things we used to do. I borrowed money off of them until they wouldn't give me any more. And after that I didn't go around because you felt embarrassed, you couldn't give 'em back what you borrowed. You end up having to use your friends, and that's a bad scene. And I wouldn't tell anybody when we needed help worst, when there was no food. That's one bit of pride I had left. I wouldn't tell anybody. It was about the *only* thing I had left. I could do without. There'd be enough to feed the child, and even then she'd be hungry most of the time.

We had creditors after us constantly. Constantly. It got to the point where you'd look at the mail, you'd know what it was, and you just throw it aside. They just want their money, wondering when you're gonna pay. You try to explain the situation 'cause they understand to a certain point. But they're interested in their money. They don't care about you really. I can see their point somewhat. I did keep most of my bills up, just couldn't keep them all. One month it'd be somebody, and the next it'd be somebody else. I'd revolve 'em around to where they wouldn't complain too much, but there was constantly somebody complaining. They never repossessed anything. I don't know how I did it. I really don't. Somehow I did it. There was never once a threat of repossessing.

When my wife left, that was the worst. I had a little bit of money. Less than $100. I made that last me all month, and somehow I managed to keep booze around pretty much of the time. I don't know how I did it. I guess by stretching a dollar. And I had no idea what was going to happen to me. No idea, no hopes, no nothing. Everything had went down the tubes. I knew things had to get better because they couldn't get worse. That's the attitude I had. It's the wrong attitude to have, I guess, but sometimes you get to a point of wanting to give up. You know you can't give up. But when you can't do anything, you have a feeling of total worthlessness. You're just worthless.

In September, after six months out of work, he found a job for $2.50 an hour. "That was only $5 more take-home than I would have got on unemployment. On $2.50 an hour in this area you don't make it too good. But it was a stepping-stone." He worked there three months, then found another job as a welder at higher pay. After two months he was laid off for lack of work.

All I know is I went in one morning. There was a pink slip, and I just packed up my tool box and left. Didn't ask any questions. Went to the unemployment office. No hassles this time.

When I came home, I went out looking for work that next morning. I've had a couple of possibilities since then, thinking I was going to get a job here and there. It's taking them a little longer to say no. At least this time it's not just "Well, we're not taking applications." This time they're giving a few interviews. And giving me a little better chance. Everything is better this time. The unemployment check is coming through. No waiting period. There's enough money to cover the bills. Just barely, but there's enough to get by on. We're not starving this time. We don't run out of food like we did. And we don't have the problem of utilities. Being on unemployment isn't all that bad, compared to being on welfare.

But it's starting up again. I've been off about four months now, and it's starting again. I got to find work, even if it's digging ditches, because there's no way I'm going to go through that again. I'm foreseeing these things coming. Trying to do something about 'em before they happen this time.

But I have a different attitude now. I know my pride isn't as big as it used to be. It's made me a little short-tempered, short-fused. It's changed the relationship with my family. It's changed the whole surrounding. Before, things always rolled along real smooth. Now I've seen the rough part of life. I know what it's like now. Before, I didn't know what the rough part was. I've seen combat in Vietnam, but as far as how it is out in the world, I know what it's like. Maybe not as rough as what it was during the thirties. But I'm always gonna look back on this and say, "Hey, I've been through it. I know what it's like." It's been rough. Human damage, you might say.

43

RUTH PASTER

She is thirty-seven, a native Californian. She has worked in television most of her life. Her jobs have included publicity director, story developer, consultant, features editor, and producer. Her husband is a successful lawyer. Their large house is in a canyon near Los Angeles favored by professional people who like its mildly bohemian tone.

Eight months ago she was fired from a network news program along with most of the staff.

The firing itself didn't affect me. I was angry at the way it was done. It was really my first encounter with the brutality of network politics and how it can absolutely stop looking at people as people. I had never really believed that would happen. So it didn't leave me with a feeling of worthlessness—anything but that. At first I felt kind of—I don't want to say proud, but *special*. Yeah. Like "Fuck them."

But later on, depression is a mild word for what I felt. And it wasn't so much that I was out of work; what depressed me was that I didn't know what I wanted to do, that I was not looking for a job, that working didn't mean anything to me. It was not like the depression I had during my first stretch of unemployment, which was: "Jesus Christ, I don't know if I'll ever work again." It was more a combination of "I don't want to write the letters and I don't want to go on the interviews." For two reasons. One, they might reject me, which is unpleasant. And two, they might hire me. Nothing turned me on. No job possibilities excited me. I was depressed not because I felt "I'm unemployed, and nobody loves me." It was more like "I'm unemployed and don't care."

And it wasn't the kind of thing I could talk over very much with my husband. I was feeling like I didn't want to do anything and there wasn't anything I *could* do, but whenever I said that to John, he'd say it was a lot of crap. John's very practical. His attitude is: You do by doing. Also I think that there are certain kinds of depression that you can't share. One of them is that ultimate depression, not over growing old, but over "What do I really want to do with my life?" If the answer is a big zero, that's not something you can share. You've got to go through it alone.

I guess I was reacting to getting fired and to the letdown from the usual hysteria that I get into when I'm working. For the first four months I did absolutely nothing about getting work. I slept a great deal and watched a lot of television. Really hated it. I mean, there are certain things on television that I love and wouldn't miss for the world, like "Masterpiece Theatre," but the whole soap opera scene is another thing, and I would find myself watching all day. Then I would put myself together and cook dinner for John. I'd cry a lot. After a while I sat down at my typewriter and wrote some letters. That made me feel better. But I would write the letters and then say, "Well, I certainly have to give people two weeks to receive the letter, the way the mails run. I can't call them right away." Then I'd give them a week to read the letter. So it took me three weeks even to pick up the phone. And then, if they didn't return my call, I wouldn't call them back. I remember friends calling me about jobs and saying, for example, "Ruth, there's a job open at CBS in children's programming." I would put off calling. If it was Monday, I'd say, "Well, I don't want to call on Monday because it's after the weekend and you always have a lot to do." [laughs.] So Monday would go. Then I would say, "I certainly can't call them at 11:45 because they're going out to lunch." Somehow I would miss Tuesday, and you obviously don't want to call anybody on Wednesday, and the week would go by. Finally, I realized that people would stop helping me if I didn't start making some of those phone calls. I remember I called CBS and talked to the secretary. I said, "Sarah, I hear there's a job open in children's programming." She said, "Ruth, I don't think they're going to fill it," and I said "Oh," and was relieved. I had done my little thing and didn't have to worry about it. Then I started to pace myself and say, "I'll make two phone calls a week and write two letters." Absolutely no motivation.

When I work, I work too hard. It consumes me 100 percent. Friends go out the window; my husband goes out the window; weekends go out the window. I get totally overwhelmed by the pace and the pressure. And I bring everyone into this horrendous work orbit. So being unemployed was a shock and a luxury at the same time.

But I went into therapy with this problem, this incredible work anxiety. I'm slowly discovering that it has nothing to do with work. It's really been the anxiety that has made me perform, whether it's anxiety for promotion or anxiety to please or whatever. What has depressed me is that as that anxiety goes away, I am finally faced with the choice of what I want to do. Although I can get turned on by a specific job that is offered to me, I have been chosen, I have not done the choosing. That's kind of depressing. There must be people who desperately care about what they're doing. They'd do it even if they weren't getting paid. That's a whole different definition of work, and that's really what I'd like to find.

Instead, when I lost my job, I felt like I didn't want to do anything. Well, that's not true. I read a tremendous amount. But again it was part of this whole work thing in my head. I used to read a tremendous amount of fiction. Now I hardly read any fiction at all. I find myself reading George Sand's biography or Strachey's memoirs or Freud's biography or Virginia Woolf's letters. I am fascinated by the degree of passion that motivates people. But it's sort of unfair to myself, too. You can get very disgusted if you compare your life to George Sand's [laughs]. But I have a tremendous curiosity about whatever that thing is that people have found that keeps them interested in themselves. I think when you work, you can get so much involved that you lose sight of what's right for you and just go crashing ahead. But finally, you reach a point where you wonder what it's all about. Well, that hit me when I got fired. I guess you finally realize that there isn't an answer, but you somehow keep looking for it. And you laugh about it a lot.

It put a strain on my relationship with John. When I was unemployed years ago, he would come home and be assailed for hours with the fact that I was nothing and a nobody and would never work again. I didn't want to do that this time. So he would come home, and I'd just lie. He'd come home and say, "How was your day?" I'd say it was fine. "What did you do?" I would offer some fabrication. "Who did you call?" Sometimes I would say some names 'cause I really didn't want to go into it. And I resented doing the housework. When I have a job, all the housework is shared equally. But I feel since I'm not working, it's up to me to cook the dinner and do the laundry and shopping. And yet a part of me resents it. If it were reversed, it would be totally different. When he comes home and says, "I'm absolutely exhausted," I get very angry at the fact that he's working. And thoughts rush through my mind like: "You just wait till I'm working again; this is all gonna change."

Money is another problem. I left the job with enough money to carry me. And the fact that John's working gives me that excessive luxury of evaluating where I'm going and what I want to do, and what does television mean, and I'd rather be a painter, and all that crap. But even though I won't starve, I need my own independent money. John pays the rent and all the major bills. I have enough to pay for the groceries and for all my own needs. So it hasn't come to where I have to say to him in the morning, "I need $5." But a while back I did need money for something important—for therapy—and John said, "Look, if it's that important to you, then look for a job." I think that's what got me moving. I realized I couldn't wrap myself up in this cocoon of dependency. I had to go out and do something. That, and I felt, "OK, God damn it, I'll show you. I'll get out and get a job, and I'll make twice as much money as you, and then we'll see who'll do the dishes."

Sooner or later, unless you are really out to destroy yourself, the pendulum swings back. You get so anxious and depressed by not doing anything that you realize you have carried it to the limit. I began to see what I was doing. I mean, I was reading *The Savage God* and Sylvia Plath, all these books about suicide. It was getting worse and worse and worse. So finally, I started writing those letters. I remember my first interview. It was at a publishing company. I walked in, and the woman looked at me and asked, "Well, what do you want to do with mass-market paperbacks?" I couldn't think of a thing. Not a thing I wanted to do there. I somehow lied, but after that interview I was more depressed than ever. It wasn't until I had a good interview at ABC, with a man in the local news division who was interested and bright and had some respect for women, that I felt I still cared about anything. It was very exciting. I felt, "All is not lost," even though I didn't get the job. It made me see there was still some grain of passion in me somewhere.

I think what happened to me was that by being in therapy and not having to deal with the day-to-day pressures at work, I finally had to look at myself. Being fired started a lot of things going in my head that had nothing to do with my marriage or what job I would find next, just a realization that I've been on a treadmill my whole life. I've questioned things that I never questioned before. I've gone beyond that feeling of "No one is going to want me" to "What do I want?" I've also realized, after the experience with my last job, that I'll never commit myself in that way again. I guess I was burnt more than I've been willing to admit. I've learned that particularly in the networks, it doesn't really matter how hard you work. The decisions on whether you go or stay have nothing to do with your work. I'd always heard about that, but I'd never seen it happen. People's lives destroyed like that. Mine wasn't, but there were people who needed the money and who cared and who didn't want to be fired. I can honestly say that I would never again work in the entertainment department of any network. I would rather not work for another two years than take a job that I didn't like, where I would drive myself crazy over something I don't care about. Because what is the point of working that hard when it all goes down the drain? What does it really mean? What do you have to show for it? Now I no longer fly into a frenzy after every interview, wondering if I'm going to get the job or not. If I get it, OK; if not, that's OK too. I've changed.

ROBIN LANDAU

She grew up in Stamford, Connecticut. "My mother does nothing, and my father is in real estate from his father. He owns shopping centers and apartment buildings." She lives on the East Side of Manhattan

and studies child psychology part time. She has been collecting unem-
ployment for nearly a year. Before that she worked for a company in the
garment center ("I just hated the people there—they were loud; they
were obnoxious") and a film production company. "I was a gal Friday
and assistant film editor. I couldn't take the typing and answering
phones, and I found out that editing is supertechnical. You can't be
creative because the producer and director always tell you what to do."
She left there for a job in publishing. She is twenty-four.

I had a friend at a big publishing company. I forget what she was, but
she had a pretty important position. She told me a good job was opening
up and she would help me get it. So I went there. I was happy about it
and real excited about getting a new job which I could train for and
maybe enjoy because I love books and I love reading. But I'm just not a
business person. I can't take it. It drives me nuts. The job was in the
trade sales department. And the company is like this huge publishing
house on the thirty-ninth floor of this office building. You've got to
zoom up at 8:30 every morning and zoom down at 5:30 [laughs].

And publishing . . . I thought publishing would be exciting because
you're around all these books. What a *drag* publishing is. The only
people who work in publishing are these creepy librarian women or *au
naturel* girls. Like these whole-wheat girls who would look better if they
put on some makeup. But no, they won't wear makeup. And they sit
around and sit around, very bright, but Christ, so boring. I like to be
around men, and the only men who work there are these old men who
were like . . . the editors? No, not the editors, I forget what you call
them. And it was really hot. It was last summer. And all I did—you had
to memorize like two hundred names of people. It's so big. And these
salesmen would call up from around the country and go [mocks deep
voice], "Well, Brentano's in Ohio just ordered fifty thousand copies of
such-and-such!" Then you'd have to call up some other woman, and it
was just a lot of phone work and a lot of names and a lot of bullshit. All
mass production. I quit after two weeks.

I mean, at first you're excited about a job. You think it's really something and it's going to lead someplace. But the first day you're there, to
hate it? I mean to really *hate* it? I hated it the first day; I couldn't stand
it. But my parents had said, "Robin, I don't care what you do, just get a
job. Just get something so at least you're partially supporting yourself
[laughs]. Because we're so sick of supporting you, and you're old
enough that you have to learn responsibility." I *am* responsible 'cause
every job I've ever had they've always liked me and I've always shown

up on time and I've always done what I was supposed to do. And I've always hated it [laughs].

Anyway, it was summertime, and my parents actually saw that I was going a little nuts and a little bit off the wall in publishing. I don't know what it is about me, like I'm materialistic and I'm bullshitty, but I'm also extremely, extremely sensitive. In the business world I just can't make it unless it's fun and people are nice. But people are not nice in business that much.

I didn't collect unemployment until three months after I quit. 'Cause I'm scared to ask people for favors. I was scared to go back to the place I worked before the publishing company and say, "Could you please say that you laid me off instead of I quit?" And I left there on very good terms. I still see the people. So finally one of my friends said, "You're a stupid idiot; why don't you just go and ask?" After three months I got up enough courage to go. Otherwise I wasn't going to get unemployment. Now that I look back on it, it was so stupid of me. Why not ask? So you get a rejection? It's just that I can't take rejection either [laughs].

How did you feel about taking the unemployment money?

Great! Oh, it was the best thing that ever happened to me. It was like a free $85 a week. Just to enjoy myself and fool around with, for doing nothing. For doing nothing. I mean when I was working, I was taking home maybe $40 more. Busting my ass. Well, not busting my ass, but just being very depressed and wasting a lot of time for $40 more a week. And here I was collecting $85, doing nothing. It was the best thing that ever happened to me. It was like a gift from heaven. Pennies from heaven. Dollars. It's terrific.

The fact is that I hate working. See, I would be good at volunteer work with children or something. But the thing I really hate about work is getting up so early. Such an ungodly hour. And it's just too much. You work, you come home, you eat dinner, you're so tired, and you have to wake up the next day. And your weekends are the big thing. Weekends are such a drag because they're just so crowded with all these crazy people who do the working and go out to unwind. You can't enjoy yourself on weekends. I would much rather go out on a weekday night. So I'm a lot happier when I'm not working.

And I certainly feel no guilt whatsoever about taking the $85. I think this government and the whole world is crazy and war-happy, and that I wasted a large part of my life by working for these people, doing nutty jobs. That's not what life is about, sitting in an office nine hours on your ass, typing or taking orders from somebody. So I feel they owed it to me.

So during the summer I went to the pool and I played tennis and I got skinny and I got a suntan. I was living here, but my parents belong to a club and my friends have tennis courts and pools and I have a car, so I took the car with me and my friends to the Hamptons. I'd bop around there, and I was really relaxing and getting mellow and nice again. What my parents don't understand—but I think now they do—and what people don't believe is that . . . well, a lot of people want to be famous or they want to do something constructive in their life. But I was so happy for six months. I was doing nothing, and I think I could be happy doing nothing for the rest of my life. I have friends and I like to read and I like to go to museums and I like to paint and I like to sculpt and I like to do crafts and I like to go to theater and I like to go to movies and I like to go to parties and I like to dance and I like to have a good time and I like to travel and I also like to be serious. But I think my whole life I could do that without getting a job. People just do not understand that. They go, "Oh, Robin, you can't be happy doing nothing." And I was going, "But I am happy." For a while I was denying it: "This is wrong, Robin, you should do something constructive. Society! You should have a job or something." But finally I came to the realization—well, I always had the realization, but I finally admitted to myself that, yes, Robin is very content doing absolutely nothing. I mean not nothing, but not a job, not having to be famous, not having to be well known, not having to make money.

I guess I went back to school because of what my father said. One day he said, "Well, Robin, what's going to happen if I'm not around anymore?" When he said that, I started to cry hysterically. My father's an idol to me. I think he's wonderful, a terrific human being and wonderful about everything. I just started to cry and said, "Don't you ever say that to me again," and he goes, "It's true. What's going to happen if you don't marry somebody wealthy? What's going to happen if you never get married?" See, my whole life is dependent on a man to get married and to make sure he's wealthy. But I would never marry just for money because I couldn't do that. I would get sick to my stomach if somebody touched me who I didn't love. So like I need both. I need love and money. And it's pretty hard to find. So I said to myself, "Let's get your life together." So I bopped into school, and I'll be happy being a child psychologist every now and then.

I can't live on $85 a week. I don't pay the rent. My parents pay the rent. I pay everything else and I still have to take money from them. It happens to be very difficult for me to live on $85 a week. I feel horrible about taking their money. But I've gotten past the point of feeling horrible; I feel one step worse than horrible: I feel like I don't care. Like the part about being horrible is already over because I know that I'm horrible and awful. I'll never make anything out of my life, so I like to live off of other people. So I feel like the only attitude to have is to not care and be thankful that they can do it. I do appreciate it and I don't really take advantage. It's also . . . you know, in a certain way they never taught me responsibility with money. All of a sudden I got out of school and there was this great pressure. Now be responsible! But during my whole life there wasn't even a gradual buildup. I got everything I wanted, everything. And all of a sudden I got out of college and I was so shocked. "OK, now do it yourself." But I was never taught. You don't do that to a person. I blame them for doing that. I'm not placing the guilt on them. The thing's on me. It's my fault. But they should've taught me. They should have been more responsible in that respect.

I mean, some people function best when they work. A lot of people need work, the responsibility, something to occupy their time. Because they don't have that many outside interests, and it does take up a large part of your life. But I'm very unliberated because I think men should still support women. Unless the woman finds something that interests her and she wants to work. But she shouldn't have to. That's not really my point of view on men and women, but on men and me. I don't really believe that about women. That was wrong to say. I just think that for me it's right. I don't want to be liberated in that way.

Basically I'm happy with myself. I think Robin's a good, together, nice person. But as far as ever having a goal or as far as ever having a future, I don't think I'll ever have one. It does get depressing at times and I think that maybe I should. But I'm just not made that way and it never seems to work for me. Like I probably would be happy just getting married and having a family and being rich and having a good time. I mean, not screwing around because I'm pretty straight sex-wise. I'm pretty monogamous. I just like to fall in love and get married and be very happy. I guess I sort of live in a fantasy-type world [laughs].

ANTHONY PASTORINI

He has a round, boyish face with long reddish hair swept across his forehead. He wears blue jeans, sneakers, and a flannel shirt untucked in back. He's slightly overweight and given to fantasy. "I read everything. I must have read umpteen hundred books. Can't keep much of it in my head, but I keep enough that it helps out when the need arrives. Like, you need a bomb built? I can build a bomb 'cause I read a book on how to disarm 'em. I've lived quite a big life in twenty-one years." He has recently written a 375-page detective novel and sent it to a publisher, who suggested he take creative writing lessons.

*He prefers to meet at my motel on the edge of Minneapolis. Around
us, a desolate cityscape of vacant lots and small factories.*

I was born in Minneapolis in '54. Dad's a mailman. Mother's a typical
housewife. Normal life. Grew up, went to school. Quit school when I
was fifteen and got my equivalency diploma. I bummed around for a
while, worked in my dad's tree nursery up north when he retired. Then,
when I was sixteen, I illegally joined the service. Lied about my age. I
didn't have anything else to do. I was going nowhere. I figured it would
be a good education. Maybe learn something I could use on the outside.

On the whole I had a good time in the Air Force. Did just about
everything, but mostly was an engineer on aircraft. I was in Vietnam,
Guam, the Philippines, Japan, California, Texas, Washington, and many
other places. Continually moving around. Finished up by getting
wounded in Nam. Helicopter. We were just flying a mission. We got
knocked out of the air. The next thing I knew I was waking up on a
transport coming back to the States. They temporarily sewed me up,
then put in a pin and a joint. I used to kid the guys around base, "Man,
I'm just as good as anybody else in show biz, I got a pin just like Evel
Knievel." And I did.

Then I got discharged three months early. They found out what my
age was. They had me up for falsifying enlistment papers. They said,
"Well, you can get out or stay in and face a court-martial." So I got out
with an honorable discharge and full benefits.

It's a popular belief, you know: Join the service, learn a trade. Well,
you may learn a trade in the service, but you can't apply it when you're
on the outside. Unless you're something like a personnel manager or an
accountant. Most of the people that go into the aircraft field, if they're in
anything but electronics they can't get a job on the outside. Can't qualify. Have to go for three years of college. Eight hours a day, four days a
week for a P and A license. That's power plants and aircraft. It's a
license to work on any kind of aircraft. You have to go through this
college. You gotta get it all on paper. And nowadays most of the college
kids that get diplomas, they can't get jobs.

It was a year before I found my first job. I went around to all the
airports, putting applications in. I got the same reply from all of 'em:
"Sorry, no previous experience, no license, I can't help you." They
won't let me touch a Cessna, a $100,000 airplane, when in the service I
was working on $7 million jets. Doing the same type of work. More
complicated. More hydraulics. I can't touch a plane on the outside. And
I'd say 95 percent of the people who are getting out of the service are

like that. They're out of a job. I know there's quite a bit of turnover, but the first year they're out, they reenlist. I knew quite a few while I was in. They went out and I'd run into them again at different bases, back in the service. 'Cause there's just no way to cope with the outside. If I had my choice I'd reenlist, but I can't because of me lying about my age before.

At first I lived with my uncle and aunt, rent-free. I was collecting unemployment, so I was giving them $80 a month for food, telephone expenses, and stuff like that. I took care of their kids. They felt it was enough, but I didn't. I felt that I should give them more, but they insisted on me keeping it. Save the money for a car or something. So I saved up quite a bit of money. Got a car. And then I started really going all over the place for a job. I even went down to Ohio. They're building a nuclear reactor down there. I was trying to get a job as a construction worker, laborer, you know. No luck. Kind of hard to believe I can't even swing a shovel or a pick. I've done it before. But it was, "I can't use you. No experience—no job."

After a while you get disgusted, disappointed. You really get hyped up about a job, right? You're figuring you're going to get it. Go in there with a great attitude and everything. They come up with this thing: "No previous experience? No job." Like one job was driving truck. Little delivery van. I couldn't even get a job doing that. No previous experience. I've driven just about everything the service has. No previous experience, no job. Another thing: If you're under twenty-one, forget it, you can't get a job. Any of the security places, playing guard, you can't get a job.

You get disgusted and slack off, you know. A little thing in your head starts saying, "Why the heck should I go out there if they're gonna say the same thing the last place did?" Like I went to one place yesterday. Bell Telephone. Went in there, did it. They said they'd let me know. Most of the places say that. "We'll let you know." You go to the unemployment office every morning when it opens. Eight-thirty. You go into their card files and microfilm room. You go through them. Get everything. You call the places and make appointments. You go out and fill out applications. I must have given out fifteen hundred copies of my discharge form within the first six months. But nothing, not even a call saying that we can't hire you. I think it's pretty ridiculous. A guy's got that time under his belt, he's got a fairly good head on his shoulders, so they tell me. Fairly good education and no criminal record. I haven't had a ticket in my entire time of driving. Won't hire me. No experience. You can't get experience unless somebody breaks down and hires you.

I started to get into arguments at home. The slightest little thing would set me off. I slacked off about getting a job. I'd go to one or two places a day, where before I was going to ten, fifteen places every day. And if the kids started goofing around, I'd get mad and I'd start yelling.

53

Storm out of the place. A few times I just walked away. For two or three days. Walked clear into the city, walk around for seven or eight hours, talking to people. Thoughts go through your head like you haven't thought of your entire life. "I wonder where I can get a gun?" Things like that. Everybody thinks of suicide, mostly everybody, when things get down. But I used to sit around thinking of ways to do it. Painlessly, of course. Weird thoughts go through your head when you're sitting around with no money in your pocket. Every time you walk by a bank you think of somehow ripping it off. Or some way to turn a fast buck real quick. At first I was buying lottery tickets. I gave it up.

One outlet—when I was in the service I took up karate, and when I got out I took it up till about three months ago. It was an outlet to an extent. But every once in a while the instructor would get me mad and I'd go at him full force. They had to pull me off him one day. Things get built up inside of you and you gotta let them loose. And sometimes the slightest little thing will let it all out. Not anymore. I've settled down, cooled down. Takes a lot to set me off now. Takes a lot. But during that period . . . slightest little thing, I'd go right through the roof. Pretty bad.

I was going down to my old neighborhood in Minneapolis and hanging around with what the police would call unsavory characters. It was a motorcycle gang. We'd cause malicious destruction. You know, no irreparable harm, but we'd razz the police and cause all sorts of problems. Stop our bikes right in the middle of the road. Fifteen of us, right? Just stop right then and there, right in the middle of the road, and get off. Cause traffic jams. Ride around our bikes on people's lawns. Turn over cars. Start fires in trash cans. Not the little round ones—the dumpsters. They had to call the fire department. Rode down to City Hall, downtown, where they got the big statue. Sat up on one of the hands. Police came. Got us. Took us away. Didn't arrest us or anything 'cause they figure we're off on some locoweed or something, which none of us were. The mayor's car, we filled it up with rotten eggs. Oh, it was a mess. You should see—we got write-ups from the newspapers for some of the dumb things we did.

You figure you're doing it against the last guy that says, "No thanks, we can't hire you." Taking it out on something else besides your friends and people around you. Against the last person or last company. See, everybody was down on companies. We felt a lot of the places had a policy that you have to have experience or they won't hire you. So we were just doing it to get out the meanness, just plain meanness. Most of the guys were out of work. They were down-and-out about not having a job and just plain disgusted about everything. So they'd go out on these little binges, tear up some neighborhood. Everything that could be replaced or fixed, you know, no permanent damage. We might let the air out of tires, but we weren't gonna slash 'em.

Then I decided, well, this ain't getting me nowhere. I was looking around. Looking at myself. I was getting pretty well down physically and every other way. Pretty well down the drain. I was up to 285 pounds. I had a full beard. My hair was down to my shoulders. Unclean. I had an apartment by then, and it was a mess all the time. I was putting quite a few beers away. Hanging around at the clubhouse. So I said, "Well, I ain't getting nowhere," so I started really putting in a lot of hours looking for a job. It was partly because a friend of my uncle's who's a lieutenant on the police force was telling me about some clowns getting blown away downtown. For nothing at all. Just goofing around on a corner. Well, this shook me up a little bit. And one of the gangs in our area had their clubhouse raided by a couple of guys with sawed-off shotguns. A thing like that gets you a little nervous. Three people got killed; nine ended up in the hospital. One of them is paralyzed from the waist down. Things like that. They get you thinking, "I'd better get out of here before something like that happens to me." So I shaved everything off. Got my hair cut. Cleaned up. Sold my bike. Got a small car. Started looking for a job.

Found one in a junkyard. Nasty old place. I couldn't complain. It was a job. Paid $3.75 an hour, which is outstanding for a junkyard. I had to lie to the guy to get it. He asked me if I had ever used a cutting torch. I had seen my dad do it, so I said, "Sure, sure, sure." He said, "All right, let's see you use one." So I went out back to start it up and started cutting. So I got hired.

I went back to the area where I was supposed to be working right? It was a pool of hydraulic fluid, oil, gasoline, everything. Highly volatile. And I was supposed to be out there cutting up cars, you know. See, they yank the engines out of the cars, and most of the time they'll break the transmission parts, the casings. All the fluid ended up right where I'm at. When I got off at night I had to take a scraper, a paint scraper, and scrape an inch of sludge off my combat boots. I told them they better get a water hose and better lines for the acetylene and oxygen or they're gonna blow me up and the whole place with me. They said all right, we'll see about it. I went at it, cutting away.

First I set a car on fire. I'd be cutting the part, and the heat and flame would go past it. And the sound-deadening material in the cars would ignite in flames real quick. One started burning and they couldn't put out the fire. Neither could I. They had to call the fire department. The firemen came out there and fined them $250. They still wouldn't run a hose out. Gave me a bucket. I'm supposed to run 150 feet to get a bucket of water and run back while the car's on fire.

Some of the cars they never took the gas tanks off. Just drop them over there for me to cut the parts off with the gas tanks still in. Finally one exploded. A chunk of metal flew back and the tank smoldered for about three minutes. I didn't know it; otherwise I'd have been gone like the wind. So I cut the part off, figured I'd take it up front. Started to walk back up there, and I got about thirty feet from the thing before it went off. It picked me up about ten feet and laid me against a set of tires. I weighed 250 pounds, so that's quite a bit of pressure. And I got burned by a piece of insulation that was soaked in gas. It hit my arm, and as I brushed it off the skin went right along with it. It just peeled off. So I said, "Well, I think you better put a fire extinguisher back there and a water line. Cover the area with water. Water's a little heavier than oil, and it'll keep it from igniting that much." So he said, "We'll see." I went back to work the next day. Doctor bandaged me up, and I went back. They wanted me to cut the rear end of this car. I said, "Take the gas tank out." He said, "No, no, there's no need. There's no gas in it." I turned off the torch, set it up, and said, "Give me my money. I'm quitting. Unsafe working conditions." They said, "All right." Gave me my money and I walked out the door.

This whole period has taught me not to expect too much. You hope for a job, but you don't go overboard anymore. You sort of take things as they come. You get hired, you get hired. You don't, you don't. Some people get really mean from not getting a job after that long. I was for a while. Came out of it. I'm looking for a job. It's about all I can say, looking for a job. A lot of people are rejoining the service. I even went to one of the enlistment places, right? Just to see if I could get back in. And the guy there said, "Heck, if you hadn't of gotten out of the service you would have been a great recruiter." I just said, "Thanks. Thanks a lot."

ROLAND BATALA

He is reluctant to be interviewed. Finally he agrees. But when I find his house, in a beautiful old neighborhood near a large eastern university, no one answers my knock. I call from a public phone, and he answers. "You have to come around back," he says in a strange tone. I soon see why. He is living in a tiny corner of the basement that he has divided into two "rooms" by hanging a curtain. There is hardly space in the bedroom area for a bed and chair. The ceiling is crumbling. He owns the house but has been unemployed so long that he is forced to rent it out in order to pay the mortgage.

He is a handsome African with parallel scars on each cheek. His speech is lightly accented, his grammar a bit exotic. A proud man, he is not happy to be seen occupying his own basement. But he is too polite to refuse. And he is eager to talk.

I came from Ghana about fourteen years ago. I'm thirty-four, so I have spent most of my working life in this country. I got my bachelor's degree in New Orleans. Then I went to school at Columbia for a master's in biochemistry. I got it in 1972. But I figure I haven't had much luck—not in the job market anyway. I've been out of work for more than a year now. My last job was with the city department of personnel. They were using federal funds in the program, and they said it ran out. So everybody had to get off of it. It wasn't just me. My manager had to leave, too, because he was on the same federal funds.

Since 1972 I've worked here and there. It's tough looking for a job, and I guess for me it's also tough keeping it. I found that many companies have hired me just . . . It's just a cover-up thing, because sometimes the heat is put on them. They don't have too many black people on their staff, and I'm a black man. And they know they have to hire somebody, you know, so they hire you for a while and then find some reason to get rid of you again.

I've worked in pharmaceutical houses, laboratories—different places. And I've had to take some companies to the Fair Employment Practices people. I didn't think I was getting fair treatment, and in the end I knew I wasn't wanted around those places anyway. The last one was here in the city. I reported them to the Fair Employment Practices people, and they didn't act on it. They didn't act on the case for about two years. Then someone, I don't know who, brought the case up to them again. They wanted me to report everybody and the money that's involved and all that. But I don't want to keep all those things in me for so long. I'll probably get ulcers [laughs]. So I try to forget these things because they are not so good. It's no good keeping in bad memories for too long. I try to forget them if I don't like them. So I just didn't respond because two years was such a long time to look into a case like that. No doubt I was disappointed in the government officials who really didn't do their job, because they were the ones who were supposed to look into this thing.

Anyway, many companies, from what I have seen, don't take all those things too seriously about hiring minorities or hiring women. A good example is the university here. The government is keeping after them year after year. "We will cut off your grant," and all that. I have been there many times, they have my applications. I'm qualified to do a lot of things. But they will never hire me. And the government knows they don't have enough black people, and that there are people like me looking for work. But nothing will be done.

The best job I had was at a pharmaceutical house. Heavens, my supervisor did all sorts of things to make me very unhappy on the job. Like he insulted me a lot, in every way possible. He would push me. I mean, not really touch me, but making gestures like that. And he insulted everything I did. My work, my presentations. It was a sales job, you see. I had to call on doctors. And I knew my presentations were just as good as anybody else's because we used to have meetings and I saw what everybody was doing. I didn't think mine were really bad. But he condemned everything, and I knew it just wasn't fair. One time he took some of the sales that were coming out of my territory and put it somewhere else, so it would make my own territory look like it wasn't doing too well. They used to give bonuses at the end of the year, but they didn't give me any. Many, many things were done like that, which just made me feel that they were trying to push me out. I believe because I am a black man. I believe so. Because I don't see any other reason. Why else? Why couldn't I stay in?

It's very tough for me to prove what was going on. That's very tough. You have to tape things, and then try to replay them in front of the judge. And that might not be admissible evidence because maybe I taped it falsely, you see. All these companies know the laws, and they know how to get around them. So I know some black people will make it, but actually I think it's just getting worse and worse for blacks.

After leaving that place I got another job. This was in a paint store. I would have liked this job. I was put in quality control. And I didn't last on that job for more than two months [laughs]. Because I was black and all the white people were actually making the paints. You see, I had to make recommendations. I had to say, "Add this. Add that." They would bring me the sample, and I had to test it and see if this is good enough or you ought to do some more mixing or whatever. And they just couldn't stand that. They couldn't stand that. Because I was black and a supervisor. I had to leave that place because I got so much hell from the foreman, from the manager of the plant. They were just pushing me out. Two people resigned, and they said they resigned because I was black. They absolutely resigned. Then many of the rest, they made fun of me. Laughing and poking fun. And my car—one time they took off the license plates on my car and threw them away. So many little, little things that you figure if you stay on they may harm you personally. And I just knew it wouldn't work.

I even tried real estate. They can let you work six months without a license. And I tried that. You know, I got the six-month permit, and in six months I never sold one house [laughs]. I figure that for many of the clients it was tough to buy a house from a black man. Very tough. Which is very strange. I don't know why it would be. You know, I tell them, "I have this degree," and all that stuff, but still I found out it was tough for them to accept. Maybe they feel I would get the commission, and they don't want to help. I don't know what they are thinking.

So I've been looking for research work or maybe work in a laboratory or a hospital. And I should be able to do some teaching job. Unfortunately, though, I don't have the state teacher's certificate. But parochial schools could take me without those credentials. I have visited all the hospitals and labs and have been interviewed, but generally they tell me right away that they don't have any openings, and when an opening comes they will let me know. But they never let you know anything. I have applied in New York. I went to Philadelphia. I have my applications in in Washington. I have interviewed several times at the university. They've given me tests. They've given me ratings, and they pass me on my ratings. It's just a matter of getting some professor that I could work with. They say they have to present my name to all these people when there are openings. But heavens, with all the pressure they are getting, they just don't do a thing.

Lately things have been very quiet. I have been bitten so many times that I'm cautious now. Fed up anyway. I don't think I look so vigorously now as probably I should. Because I think I'm discouraged. I have gone so many times. I've hit my head against the stone wall too many times. I feel I should even get out of this place for a while. Go somewhere else, and then maybe later on start anew. Because it's so bad to go to an employer and show so many months that you haven't worked. If I go away to a job, then I can come back and say, "I just came back from this job." And then I can have recommendations. So this is my move. I'm looking into foreign governments now. I started applying for foreign positions. In black countries. Probably I can find one that might use my talent.

It's affected my outlook on life a lot. I don't dress so hot anymore. I just put on anything I have. Shabby clothes, shabby coat. I mean, when you don't feel too good inside and there is no money in your pocket, it's no use getting into a suit. I guess it affected the way I walk, the way I dress, and where I go. Before I used to like to dance, go to parties, go to clubs, and many of these places you have to pay $3 or $5 just to get in. And I find I can't go because I don't even have the money in the first place. Probably just because I didn't have the means, I became more lonesome than ordinarily. So it's really a bad psychological state. I don't feel too good about myself.

But I try not to be bitter. That bitterness is just going to eat me up inside. It's going to be destructive to me. I'm probably going to get hypertension or ulcers. Because I can't just go out and start punching people in the nose. "You didn't give me a job." [laughs]. Didn't give me a job.

I was married before, you know. And when I lost that good job at the pharmaceutical house, the wife got a divorce. So it's destroyed my family and destroyed a lot of friendship. And I own this house, but I can't live in it. I have to rent it out so that those people can pay for it, so I don't lose it. That's why I end up in the basement. I can't look many of my classmates in the face. Who are maybe doctors or who are at least working. There are many, many people who I have lost touch with. Very good friends. Because I know if they invite me to dinner, I can't bring them here. I'm really ashamed to bring anybody here. I am ashamed that my condition is so bad, compared to theirs. And that despite how much I tried, I can't get a job to earn the money to improve my standard of living. I don't think they would understand. I wouldn't want to take the chance.

And then I go into a lot of regrets. Like I'm wasting my life. So many months. Because when you go into the American system for so many years, you develop a sense of joy from accomplishment. And when I'm not accomplishing anything, I feel very sad. All the college I've been through, all to waste. I'm not really achieving anything at all. Every day is just wasted. I feel a deep sense of emptiness.

And not only that—it makes you wonder. Why go to college? Why waste all this time? Why go to all this trouble? And if you have children, what are you going to tell them? Are you going to encourage them to go to college and get their degrees? Because they are going to grow up black, and maybe they won't even get a job or they won't be able to live a decent life. So this is why I figure I have to keep on struggling. I have to keep on struggling.

CLARK HOOVER

He is forty-one—balding, slightly overweight, dressed in a sports shirt and Bermuda shorts. He is not used to talking about himself and uses awkward, quasi-bureaucratic phrases—a habit probably picked up during years of police work. He lives south of Pittsburgh in a suburban development still being carved from rolling hills. We sit on his back porch, overlooking a half acre of churned dirt that someday will be his yard.

I started working as a policeman in 1960. I spent nine years in the Pittsburgh department and then transferred to a smaller department in one of the wealthy suburbs. I spent six years there, until in the summer of 1975 I was responding to a call at 4:00 A.M. Somebody was breaking into a house. I was the closest car to it, so I went in. And during the course of my travels to the location, even though I was traveling with the siren going and the emergency lights flashing, a car blew a stop sign and hit me broadside. I ended up with a fractured back, a brain concussion, and leg injuries. I was in the hospital for almost four months. And when I got out and went back on duty, I found out that with the injuries I had and the loss of memory that followed, I could no longer pursue my profession.

The main problem was the back injury. I couldn't protect myself any longer, in the event of a bar brawl or something like that, without a real possibility of getting badly hurt again. And there was no chance of getting a desk job. It was a small department, and the only positions available were out in the street in the squad. I worked for four months, from May of '74 through August, but it became quite obvious to me and my superiors that I was no longer competent to handle myself or protect the life and property of the citizens I was getting paid to protect. So I had to take a medical retirement. And I haven't worked since then.

This of course threw me into a dilemma. I was used to making about $1,275 a month, and I was knocked down under $500 a month. And I've got untold medical bills, which I hope will eventually be picked up by workmen's compensation or the insurance company of the other driver. But that's in litigation now. Workmen's comp feels that the insurance company is liable, which I'm sure they are, but the insurance company is holding off as long as they can. In the interim, workmen's comp isn't picking up any bills because of their stand, which is that the other company is liable. So in the meantime, I'm left hanging in between. I'm obligated for the doctor bills and hospital bills, which so far run over $10,000. This has been going on since 1975, and the best information my attorney can give me is that it may be another couple of years before the thing is ever brought to court.

Where I go from here I don't know. The doctors have me under total disability now as far as any type of physical work is involved. And I'm also limited to desk jobs that don't demand too much in the way of powers of concentration because of the blow on the head and the injury to my brain in the accident. For a while I almost completely lost my ability to concentrate. I could be sitting and talking to somebody and five minutes later I couldn't recall whether I had seen them or talked to them, let alone remember what was said. The doctors said it would level off, which it has done. But my memory is still far from what it should be. I can recall my past pretty good, but recent conversations or events fade away. So I'm really not physically able to qualify for any job with any real responsibility.

When I first got out of the hospital, I started talking to friends and acquaintances to see if they knew of anything that would fit my particular need for employment. I got some pretty good leads, but one of two things always happened. In the first place, I was looking for work just when the country was heading into the recession. So the job openings just weren't there. Companies were cutting back and phasing out jobs. I don't recall coming closer to a job than being put on the waiting list. And in any case, the jobs that approached what I need in terms of salary all required a rigid physical and mental aptitude test, and I knew I couldn't pass either one. I knew I'd get washed out. Some people said, "Well, you could always get a job at a gas station or a grocery store." Maybe that's true. But I can't really be on my feet for that many hours every day. It would cost me more in medication and doctor bills to try and keep going than I would be bringing in. It's an avenue I explored, but it just wasn't to be. I talked it over with my doctors and they strongly advised against it. The work would be too hard on my back.

So it's been a very frustrating year. All of a sudden I'm not the independent individual I had grown to be in forty-one years. Just the opposite. At times I found myself almost pleading for some form of employment. And I see nothing in the future that's going to change it. I've run out of friends and relatives. Naturally I scan the newspapers and go to the state employment office, but they haven't come up with any leads at all. Jobs just aren't available. You'd think in the times we're living in that this would be one area where there wouldn't be any difficulty. There are so many things that need to be done. But industries and private businessmen can't afford to expand their payrolls. It's bad news.

I finally came to the point where there was no place to turn but the state of Pennsylvania for unemployment benefits. It took me a long time to even attempt to go down there. I felt very defeated by it. Emotionally I was down. I felt degraded. Maybe that's just the way I am, and maybe I shouldn't feel that way. Maybe I should feel grateful that I've received some help from the state. And I am grateful that I've received some help from the state. And I am grateful for what I've gotten. But I went through—well, I guess I'd call it agony before I could bring myself to go down there. I'm sure some of it was pride. I wasn't prepared to accept the—I was going to say humiliation, but I guess I won't use that word. It's a helpless feeling. Like you're using the last resort. I would find myself thinking, "Gee, I hope I don't meet anybody I know." Of course, the people where I had been working knew about it because they had to send in a report. I felt that was degrading, too, but you can't feed your family on pride.

So I found myself down there in line with the 7 percent or 8 percent—I don't know what the exact percentage is now—of unemployed people in this state. My position is probably a lot different from the ordinary working individual who's unemployed, because of my limitations. Nevertheless, I'm standing right alongside of him in line down at the unemployment office. Why I'm there, why he's there is basically immaterial. The fact is we're there going through the same thing. And it's very distasteful. When I get down there, I almost have the feeling that the people behind the counter are saying, "Well, here's another bloodsucker." Maybe this isn't fair to the people down there. It could be that I'm too sensitive. But the way they look at you and talk to you, it's the feeling I get.

I've always worked. All my adult life. I've been very active. Even when I was in school I did a lot of part-time work and enjoyed it. So it's been quite an emotional adjustment to have it pulled out from under me all of a sudden—my power to earn, my power to go out and support my wife and kids. It's pretty easy to fall into the attitude of feeling you're useless. I have a tendency to feel guilty because my wife goes off to work every day, and my son has been working at a little dry cleaner's trying to make a couple of bucks for himself. And here sits Dad, the old man, more of a liability than an asset. That weighs on my mind quite a bit. It's depressing for an individual who does want to get out and be independent and be the breadwinner in the family. I can't fulfill those ambitions. And I find that it's easy to start feeling sorry for yourself. It happens particularly when I come home from a stay in the hospital. You can destroy in one hour what the doctors tried to do for you in two weeks, just by sitting and succumbing to the thought that you're no good anymore. And that's the worst thing a person can do.

So I try to keep busy with little things. I don't care if it's scrubbing the floors for the wife or doing the dishes; at least it keeps my mind away from the deteriorating thoughts. I have my therapy, of course. I'm trying to strengthen myself through exercises, so that takes up part of my time. I follow up on job possibilities if I run across them. In the summer, with two teenagers at home. there always seems to be something I'm involved in. The main thing is to avoid sitting and twiddling my thumbs. If I do that, I get too depressed.

I also have a lot of faith in God. It's been a real blessing because it's pulled me out of some tailspins. The worst was when I was confronted with the fact that I couldn't continue as a policeman. That was a terrific blow. I was angry at everybody, including God. When you're so sure that you can continue, and then you find out that you can't because of your own weaknesses, it's very hard to accept. I enjoyed police work. There were a lot of times when it was difficult, sure. But I honestly tried to be a public servant. It was my life. It had been for all my married years. And it was plucked away from me in a couple of seconds, and to have to be told I couldn't continue. . . . It was a terrific emotional trauma. I'm not through it yet. I sometimes wake up at night and think of the hopeless state that I'm in, and I figure, "What the hell's the use?" But somehow I've been able to continue on and not make my condition any worse.

The financial problems are another thing. Put yourself in the position of earning $700 every two weeks, and all of a sudden it's cut by more than two-thirds. Well, you have obligations that you've assumed, and those people want their money. Sure, they understand your position, and they'll go along with you for a little while; but then you start getting the phone calls and the nasty letters. My wife is working, thank the good Lord; but she's a secretary, and that isn't the highest-paying work.

My biggest problems have been with the doctors and hospitals. The medical profession has applied more pressure on me than any businesses or places that I've had loans. The doctors want their money when they want it. They don't care where you get it or what you do to pay it. I talk to them and tell them my situation as far as being unemployed. They usually say, "Don't worry about it." And then you get a letter in the mail that they're turning it over to a collection agency. It's hard for me, because if I had the money I'd certainly pay them. Some of them say, "Just send in a few bucks a month." Fine. That's what I'm trying to do. And then all of a sudden you get a call from a collection agency, and they want full payment in five days, or else. Well, you can't get blood from a turnip. I tell them, "I'm unemployed. I don't have the money." They say, "Go borrow it." Go borrow it? How are you gonna borrow it if you can't pay it back? "Well, go get something from your mother. Can't you borrow from your in-laws?" Things like that. They call the wife at work, which is embarrassing for her because she can't tell them any more than I can. It's humiliating and it's nerve-racking. They know that sooner or later they'll get the money, but boy, they don't back off. I've had them call me three days in a row. And when you get two or three of those a day, that gets to you in a big hurry. You don't want to answer the phone. Because you don't know what to do. My savings are completely depleted, so I just have to tell it like it is and hope they'll understand. I suppose they could get a judgment against me and take the house. I'm not sure they won't try it. I just hope we can hang on until the lawsuit comes through. My attorneys tell me I have a good case, but I could lose everything before it gets settled.

These last few years have changed the way I feel about almost everything in this country. For one thing, I'm much more aware of the unemployed than I was when I was working. I've met a lot of people who are in a more desperate situation than I am, and I feel for them because I've seen it from the other side of the fence now. Before, unemployment was just a figure of speech or a certain percent. I'd say, "Gee, that's a shame," and then ten minutes later I'd forget about it. But when you're in that minority on the job market, you have a different view of things.

I pay much closer attention to politics than I ever did before. I read a lot more and watch all the candidates on TV. Naturally all of them are saying that more jobs will be available when they're elected. Unemployment will go down. They're gonna make a Utopia for us. I think it's a bunch of BS myself. I don't see any way they're gonna drastically change the economy. These candidates must think the American people are ignorant imbeciles. There's no possible way they can fulfill the commitments they make, unless they go in even bigger for mass production of arms for war. And I certainly don't want to see that happen. Then everybody would lose, not just the 10 percent unemployed.

It's somewhat frightening. You don't really have the power of choice that you think you have. I hope and pray that this recession will pull out and pull out in a big hurry because the way it's going now it's damaging the real foundation of our country. It's deteriorating faster than we can build it up. I'm always reading in the paper or seeing on TV that they say unemployment is gonna drop. But every time I go down to that unemployment center there's more people there. And to see all those people and look at their faces and wonder if their position is worse than yours or whether it's better than yours, it's a hopeless feeling. It's a feeling I never thought I'd have to experience in all my working years.

LAURA GORDON

She is a striking woman—dark-haired, dark-eyed, twenty-six years old—who lives in Brooklyn's Park Slope section. Formerly a schoolteacher, she is now a sculptor. Her apartment, full of light and plants and pottery, gives a feeling of extraordinary calm, as she does herself. She lost her teaching job because of the New York fiscal crisis.

The school system kept me hanging for two or three months. I didn't know until school began whether or not I would have a job. The union didn't know what was happening. The city didn't know what was happening. My principal didn't know what was happening. But finally it came down to either starting the year in a slot in my school that didn't look at all secure or transferring to Manhattan to teach severely disturbed children—which I didn't feel capable of doing—or leaving. I decided to leave. I wanted to finish my master's degree, and I said, "What the hell, why take a job when I'll probably just get bumped in a few weeks?"

During those months of waiting I was looking to my principal for a lot of support. He kept telling me. "It's all right; we'll see what we can do." I don't think I realized how bad those months were until much later. In the long run what I felt was an enormous amount of rage. Feelings of rejection, of humiliation. And it was frustrating because there was nobody to let that rage out against. It was faceless. I couldn't beat my fist against them or fight them or scream at them. It came down to my director and my principal, but they had nothing to do with it. You can think about the politicians or the society, but it's like dropping something in a lake and watching the ripples, ripples, ripples. Nothing to get a handle on.

When the first day of school came, I thought I had licked it. I thought I had worked it through and straightened everything out. But that first day came, and I woke up and of course I wasn't going. The dream I had that night was that several of the children came running to my door and rang the bell. "Miss Gordon, Miss Gordon," they shouted. "Where are you, where are you? We're waiting for you." It was a very emotional dream. I felt this tremendous sense of loss; even though I wanted to speak to them, I couldn't reach them. The school is a block from me, and I still have trouble walking down the street. I'm afraid I'll meet one of the children.

It felt like all my independence was being ripped away from me. I had lost my job. Truly lost it. Now what was I going to do? In a sense it was easier because I went back to graduate school. And at first I thought it was just the loss of money that was taking all my independence. But then I began to feel it on a psychological level. What is my identity? OK, I'm not a teacher. Am I a student? It's difficult when you strip away all the things that supposedly hold you together in terms of an identity. Your work, your money, whatever is power to you, whatever is responsibility, whatever means freedom and choice. I had to ask myself, "Who am I now? What will I do now?"

At the same time I had a sense of partial relief. I had been teaching children with very poor self-images. They were bright, but they had difficulties, hyperactivity, things like that. And I had to work with teachers who were sometimes more disturbed than the children. So I felt an enormous relief not to have to deal with them anymore. And not to have to get up in the morning and have this whole thing structured. It began to dawn on me that I might as well face my negative feelings about teaching. I don't think I'm that kind of person. I like it much more if I can create something for myself and not have a nine-to-five job. But I don't know if I ever would have left if I hadn't lost the job. I chose it, without even thinking, because I felt that teaching was secure and structured. And now here I was for the first time having to structure my own time. Discipline myself.

At first there were a lot of times when I felt paralyzed. I was going to school part time and working on my sculpture. I got offers to substitute-teach and turned them down. I felt I'd rather do my own work. But there were times when I didn't feel like going to school. I didn't feel like working. I couldn't motivate myself. It couldn't come from inside. I felt paralyzed. It was at those moments that feelings of rejection, feelings of being cut down, feelings of loss came over me. I felt like other people were controlling my life. I say "paralyzed," but I wouldn't necessarily stay in bed all day. I would get up, but I didn't feel like being engaged at all. Some days I'd just stay home. I got more interested in reading, music, writing, sometimes just cleaning. And this is interesting: I felt like I went through many stages of my life. I felt like I was an old person who'd lost a loved one or lost whatever it was that gave meaning to their life. I felt like I had children, which I don't. I felt like I was a housewife. I stayed home and took care of the house and thought, "It's almost three o'clock; I should pick up the children. And I have to shop because I have to cook." I lived days like that, sometimes weeks like that.

It forced me to face myself, in a way. I mean, I was facing myself before, but it got me to other levels that I might not have dealt with until much later. I thought my job defined me and gave me security, and it was like a door I never looked behind. I never said, "My God, what's behind it? What would happen if I lost the job?" As a child I never thought of how I would support myself, what I really wanted for myself. Also as a woman. For a woman to do that today, to really understand that nobody's going to come riding in on a white horse to take you away, isn't easy. That feeling still comes over me pretty often. I wish that someone would come and make all this disappear. But I chose this position. I didn't marry young. I didn't have children. So I'm alone, and it forced me to think constantly: What shall I do? What do I really want to do? What's most feasible to do? Where can I do it? Will I do it alone? Will I do it with other people?

One thing that's helped is being in therapy. That means constant dealing with my feelings and thoughts. Unemployment wasn't the first thing that really blew my mind about what I'd do when I had to face myself. But it did bring up other things. And in the therapy I had an outlet to think about them and explore them. There was somebody echoing my thoughts. There was a mirror there.

What did you learn from that?

A number of things. It was very slow. But over the months I think what I learned was about my responsibility for myself. In a deep sense. I still haven't mastered it, but I got a glimpse. I saw that no job, no person, no thing, no money, no nothing is going to do it for me. I have to do it myself. Even if I lived in a society where work was nonexistent. I'd have to produce myself. It became very clear that I had to find my own meaning of things, and I had to find new outlets for myself, even the old ones that I had forgotten. And financially—ultimately that's the big issue—I had to find a way to maintain my own independence. Also, being fired forced me to spend a lot of time alone. At a fairly early time in my life, I had to deal with what it was to be alone, to walk the streets alone, to eat alone, to sleep alone and think alone. I used to fear being old and alone. But now when I think about the future, I don't have that fear so much now. That's been an enormous change for me.

Now is the time that I'm really having to come to grips with all of it. School is over. My unemployment has almost run out. The last month or so has been very difficult. I wonder constantly what to do. But I've come to realize that anything I really love, I can make my work. I can do it myself if I want; I can do it with other people if I want; I can do it through a system or on my own. I guess I knew that before on some level, but I don't think I would have chanced it. Probably would have stayed in some little niche.

I still don't know precisely what I'm going to do, but I have a much stronger sense of well-being than I did a few months back. I don't feel lost. Well, I feel lost, but I don't feel my *self* is lost. You are who you are no matter what your job is. Maybe it takes people a lifetime to learn that. I hope I've gone through a big chunk of it with this experience of unemployment.

Not too long ago I went to a concert where some of my brother's friends were playing. It was like a dream, meeting all these people that I knew when I was growing up. And of course, what they asked me was: "What do you do?" That was the question. *What do you do?* What do you do with yourself? Because that's who you are. It's synonymous. And they were all responding the same way. All of them except a man who I knew as a child, who I loved very dearly. He has gone blind. And he was the one who could reach me. He couldn't even *see* me. He wanted to know what I did, but it didn't matter to him when I said, "I lost my job, Andrew. And I'm confused, Andrew. And it's difficult, Andrew." I had tears in my eyes, I can still feel it. He had his arms around me, and he said, "It doesn't matter. Do what you love. Just keep doing what you love." I was so touched by that and the contrast with everyone else. It kind of summed up the whole experience. What do you do? Trying to get away from that and realizing that it's all right. I mean, I don't have to wait for Andrew to throw his arms around me and say, "It's all right." I can say to myself that it's all right.

SUSAN CASEY

Another schoolteacher, also a victim—or beneficiary—of the fiscal crisis. She lives with her boyfriend, an Olympic-class track champion, on East Ninth Street in Manhattan. The apartment feels half vacant even though she moved in a year ago; records are piled in a corner, the walls are blank. A gaily colored hammock hangs from the living-room ceiling.

My principal warned us when we came back to school in the fall that there were definitely going to be layoffs this year. He said it was no idle threat, the way it had been in years before. The city really had no money. All this time, of course, the principal and assistant principals had no real idea what was happening. They had to get their information from other people, who also didn't know. Nobody seemed to know, except that the ax was going to fall soon. My principal had suspicions, from what the superintendents were telling him. He said he was told that about 20 percent of the school was going to be let go. Of course, none of us believed it because you can't imagine how the school's going to function with 20 percent of its staff gone and all these monies gone. Well, about a week after school began they started telling people that they were going to be excessed or sent to other schools. Then a teacher's strike came for about a week and a half, and during that strike I was sent a letter saying that I was laid off.

I was a little shocked at that, but I wasn't really depressed because it hadn't struck me yet how difficult it was going to be to survive without the salary. I knew it was going to be hard; but I thought I'd probably be able to find some other work, and the unemployment was $95 a week. It's not a lot, but it certainly was going to pay my rent. And I had my family. I knew I wasn't going to starve. Plus I kept hoping that they would recall me, because they did say that people who were laid off were going to be put on the preferred list to be recalled. So I thought, "I'll wait. Instead of looking for another job, I'll see what happens. Maybe I'll get recalled, and then I'd just have to quit whatever job I had found." But as it turned out, from listening to the gossip, it didn't look as if they were going to be recalling people for quite a while. I finally did get recalled, just last week. After eleven months. They sent me a certified letter saying that they had positions. I'm ignoring it. My form of revolt [laughs].

But you don't sound very angry about getting laid off.

I was a little angry. But after I began hearing stories about what had happened to the teachers who were stuck in the system, I began to think that my position wasn't half bad, that I was the luckier one. The teachers who were excessed got sent to other districts, and a lot of them ended up in really rough areas. At least I was laid off and allowed to collect unemployment. If these other teachers didn't like their jobs, they could just quit. And many people don't feel that they're in a position to do that. They make $17,000 a year, with every vacation day that exists. You're just not going to find that kind of job anywhere else. Even though the conditions they work under are very, very bad. I went back and visited my old school a few months ago. It's pathetic. They're running the school on 20 percent less staff. They've got forty kids piled in a classroom. They've eliminated all the extra programs: no gym, no music, no art. They shortened the schoolday. And of course, the teaching has to be minimal. I know I had a difficult time with thirty children in a classroom, and the contract said there definitely would never be more than thirty-two children in a class. Now they have forty, and if they want to make it forty-five or fifty, they can. All the teachers are depressed. The change from the way it was before—which wasn't good—is so drastic that they're discouraged.

So as time has passed, I've begun to realize that the board of education really did me a favor. Even though teaching is a good job in many ways, it's also a very frustrating job because you're not really teaching. You're a disciplinarian. But you choose to be a teacher, you choose to be in that system, and you choose to follow its rules. I never felt I'd be able to leave that job on my own, but having been forced out, I realize that there were any number of things I could do if I really wanted.

But being laid off must have been a lot more emotional for me than I allowed myself to feel because now I'm so violently angry at the board of ed and this lousy system they've set up that frustrates everybody who's in it. I used to be disgusted at the inefficiency of the bureaucracy. But I began to see that the evil of the whole system is its impersonalness. I mean, you can't blame any one person. I'm not angry at my principal, and I'm not angry at the other teachers who kept their jobs, because they have to feed their families. I'm not angry at the people who work at the central board because they have the same excuses for keeping their jobs. But there they are, hacking away, firing people left and right who are the sole breadwinners for their families. And they don't care. There's no compensation. "You don't like it, it's tough." They send people helter-skelter all over the place to find jobs wherever they can, and their attitude is: "If you don't like the job, you can quit." And yet there's no one person you can blame. It's that impersonal board of ed up there that's making all these decisions, and it's not even *their* fault. They blame the city. You know, "The City." I just feel that it's very evil. Before, I never thought about the system as being the least bit symbolic or political. I just felt, you live in the city, you adjust to the circumstances and the institutions that are there. And you work because you have to work. Now I feel much more critical about the kinds of organizations I'll work for and the kinds of things I'll support because I feel I must take responsibility for the kinds of jobs I have. I can't just be an impersonal, idle part of it. If you work, you contribute to a system, whether you think it's good or bad. So you have to make a choice as to what kind of system you'll work for.

A lot of my friends think I'm berserk. They say, "Look, you were offered the job back, now take it! How can you turn down $17,000?" But I almost feel I'd be going back on my word by taking that job now. I realize that people's attitudes about the job you take have nothing to do with the quality of the job or whether it's socially useful or not; they have to do with the amount of money. It's just a question of "Well, can you maintain your life-style?" But my life-style is very much as it was before, and I've discovered I don't need to preserve it by supporting something I feel is negative. I would be very willing to teach, but not for the board of ed.

STEVE LACARRIERE

A Native American pueblo outside Albuquerque, New Mexico. A harsh landscape of dry reddish hills. dirt roads, scattered low houses of adobe with pickup trucks in front. I wait for Steve, who is in Albuquerque fetching a load of lumber. He arrives, wearing a cowboy hat and denims. He is twenty-four and looks older. "I was born in Murphy, Idaho. That's south of Boise. A little tiny town. We're from South Dakota originally. See, we're Sioux Indians, and around here is all Pueblo Indians." His brother is married to a woman from the pueblo; they have six children. Steve is single, living here until he can find a job.

He is helping build an addition on the house. "You don't want to feel like you're not pullin' your share. I don't want no pressure to build up like last time I was out of work. I'm pretty much at oaoo, and my brother's made it pretty easy for me. He tells me, 'Well, hang on, something will come along.' So I'm hanging on. When I turn twenty-five, I should get a trucking job. I know there's jobs out there. I'll go out and do the really long runs. I don't mind those kinds of runs. I like to drive solo. . . ."

As soon as I graduated from high school, I went to work. This was in Boise. I started doing roofing. Ever since I was twelve I've known how to do roofing work because my father's a carpenter and all my uncles are

71

carpenters and all my brothers are carpenters. I learned roofing from them. So I went on my own when I was about nineteen and worked for four years. Making good money.

But then everybody stopped buying roofing. Really, it was strange. There was a fuel shortage, and then all of a sudden everything went haywire. Nobody was buying roofs. I couldn't find work nowhere. I'd been working for this one company almost three years, and I couldn't believe it when they went into that slump. 'Cause they had kept me busy through the snow and everything. There was always work, even in the hard winter up there. And all of a sudden they hit that slump, and there was *nobody* hiring.

I called all the roofing outfits and they didn't need me because they already had men that had been working for them five or six years. So I went to the unemployment office and used their job service to look for a while. But the situation was just too bad. There wasn't that many openings. You had to have college education for most of them. And I was looking for *anything*, from car wash to anything else. I'd get out to the car wash and find thirty-year-old men washing cars. It was like everything just went crazy all of a sudden. And *I* started to go stir crazy. You get frustrated, going to job interview after interview with these little referral cards. You go out there and all they do is tell you, "Well, we can accept it but we can't give you a job because we already got somebody. We'll keep you on referral." In four months I must've put out over a hundred referral cards. That's just too many to get nothing, not even a response.

So what do you do all day? You go home and you sit. You become a real TV bug. And you begin to get frustrated sitting at home. Everybody in the household starts getting on edge. They start arguing with each other over stupid things 'cause they're all cramped in that space all the time. I was living with my brother and my sister and my mother. And we all got hit. My brother got laid off, and then my sister was out of work. My mother was retired. The whole family kind of got crushed by it. That's a lot of frustrated people, sitting there together so long.

To burn up your energy, you start getting crazy. I didn't like that. I felt like decking the people at the unemployment office, right? 'Cause when you had to go there and sign up for your checks, that's about the worst humiliation you ever have to go through. A lot of these people seem to feel like you're taking it out of their pocket. Actually it's the money you put away for this. But the way they treat you, you really get pretty mad. I've seen a lot of people get mad down at the unemployment office. I've seen it to the point where one guy actually knocked another guy down. But I try to forget about it [laughs]. That was a really bad time. It was just so hopeless.

I was out of work four months that time. Frustrated. Bad atmosphere at home. And back then I was drinking pretty heavy. Well, I was doing that ever since I was little. You get to drinking too much. I would hang out in a bar, go in there and shoot the bull with the guys, you know. Pretty soon I was drinking heavy. To the point where I was getting everybody at the house pretty well mad at me. See, I was drinking up my unemployment checks. I'd go out and fill out referral cards all day and then get drunk when I didn't find nothing. What it came down to is I was an alcoholic. That's what it came down to. You might think alcoholics are guys on skid row. Shit, no. Alcoholics can be fifteen, seventeen years old. So I found I was at the point where I was becoming an alcoholic. Where I cared more about drinking than I did about anything else. And it really got bad on unemployment. That's when I really started drinking. I mean, I'd spend $30 a night drinking beer, and that's in 30-cent glasses. When you add up $30 in 30-cent glasses . . . that's about as much as you can drink. I drank to the point where I'd have so much alcohol in my blood, a few more points and I'd have been in what they call a state of death [laughs]. I never could handle it. I don't understand why I drank it. Once I got into a fight with my brother about it.

Did it get to the point where your family said, "Hey, you better cut this out?"

It got to the point where I tried to commit suicide last June. And I almost did it.

See, I had been going to this program for Indians in Boise. I'd go down there for job referrals, but their jobs were just about the same as the unemployment office. It wasn't much good. But they wanted to send me for schooling because I did finish high school. That's a remarkable thing for a lot of Indians, you know. A lot of Indians don't finish high school. So they wanted to send me to school for a lot of things. Artwork and stuff like that. I didn't want to go. I figured if there's somebody out there with a really super talent, he should be the one to take the money and go. Then they asked me if I wanted to drive truck. That's something I always wanted to do. So they sent me to school for a month and a half on a program called CETA. When they came up with that I was really surprised 'cause they paid me $3 an hour to go to school. Plus they paid for the school and everything that goes with it. Then they paid me $100 a week until I found a job.

While I was in school, I didn't worry about drinking. I was engrossed in the truck driving. I really got into it. I didn't see no reason to drink. But when I got out, they said to put in applications at all the trucking companies. I did that, but they wouldn't hire me because I'm only twenty-three. You have to be twenty-five. Because of insurance reasons. So here I was, I had all my papers and everything, and I still couldn't get work. Only this time I was getting $100 from the government to do almost nothing. I was working with the program, doing little things like picking up old people that couldn't get to the hospital. And it kind of got to me again. I was getting paid for doing little things. I shouldn't have gotten paid that much. You start feeling you're taking too much for nothing. The program didn't care, but I didn't want it. Your conscience bothers you. And being unemployed again, the same syndrome happened. It was only one month, and it started getting me. I started drinking again, and that's when it really got bad.

So one night my brother came in just in time to stop me from killing myself. With a gun. He came home and found me doing it. I was drunk, drunk out of my mind, and I couldn't get the bullet in the chamber of the rifle. I don't remember very well what led up to it. But I can always remember that ugly point right before taking your life, when you're thinking about what you've actually accomplished. That split second when the barrel is in your mouth and you're trying to get the bullet in the chamber to blow your brains out. I can always sit back and remember that goddamn scary point.

It's just lucky for me that my sister and brother stuck by me at that point. I'm really glad they stayed by me. It was really a bad time, frustration added on frustration, and they helped me. That makes a hell of a lot of difference, people that care for you. I mean, they could have kicked me out when I was drinking so much, but they didn't. Or they could have said, "You lousy bum, why aren't you out working?" They could have thrown ridiculous questions at me. Instead they'd say. "Go down to the unemployment center." I'd go down and there wasn't nothing there. But they stuck by me.

Anyway, if my brother hadn't come in, I probably wouldn't be here now. He took away the rifle and flagged down the sheriff. There was this one good sheriff, too. I'll always remember him. His name was Pat Condon, and he's a really young sheriff. He said he don't usually get friendly with his prisoners, but he talked to me. And he took me up to the university hospital and they put me in a psychiatric ward. They sent a few shrinks in and they talked to me. They said, "You're not suicidal, you're just a frustrated alcoholic." That's what made me think: "Man, he called me an alcoholic." I never thought of it that way. That night I started thinking, "I have a problem. I have a real serious problem." And the next day I started calling around. They've got a rehabilitation center there in Boise. It's run by Indian people. So I went there. and I met the director of it, whose name is Martha Tucker. She's really good people. She talked to me when I was going through the shakes. And they helped me until I left Boise. They don't cast you aside. 'Cause alcoholics get into down periods just like anybody else, but I mean down periods when you're sitting there thinking about going out drinking. I try not to let things get me down that bad anymore. Because I know how far you can go. How far I could go if I just take like two drinks. I know I could pull the trigger. No problem. That scares the hell out of me.

I'm glad I found out early, you know. I'm only twenty-four and that's pretty early. I could have gone along kidding myself until I'm forty. I wonder where I'd be then. 'Cause the first thing you got to do when you get into Alcoholics Anonymous or something like that is admit you're an alcoholic. That's the worst thing. You say, "I don't want to admit that." A lot of people won't. They made up their minds they ain't gonna admit it. But hell, the next day I was willing to say I was an alcoholic. I knew there was something wrong. When you get to the point where you're getting a gun, there's gotta be something wrong. And when the psychiatrist tells you it's not in your head, it's in your drinking, then you know something's wrong. When you drink your money up to the point where it's all gone, even if you drop to the floor pulling it out of your pocket, you know something's wrong. And there was the scary thought of knowing I might end up on skid row. Where all the people kick you when you're sleeping in doorways and stuff.

Three weeks after I stopped drinking, things started looking up. The program told me to put in an application with this trucking outfit. Next thing I knew, they hired me because I was a minority. I filled the minority bill. That's what a lot of employers hire minorities for, to get their minority quota filled up. This outfit had one black guy in Seattle and me [laughs]. We were the minority bill. That's pretty funny 'cause everybody else was Anglo. We were the only minorities there.

I drove for them a year. Hauling mail. I drove the crappiest run. Nobody wanted it. I asked them for a sleeper run, but they wouldn't put me on it because I wasn't twenty-five. And then the government started dropping runs, and everything went all to hell. I thought I was set because the mails, you know, they've got to keep moving all the time. But they kept dropping all these runs. and finally last month I got laid off. Couldn't get no work in Portland with other companies 'cause of my age, so I decided to come down here to New Mexico.

Being out of work this year's a different thing, though. It doesn't scare me that much. People are going back to work. The only places where they ain't working is the overpopulated areas. It's not like it was a year and a half ago. My whole family's working. My sister went out and got a trade. She went into dog grooming. Now she's grooming animals—poodles, they call 'em. Poodles and all them other little furry animals. And my brother's working in a gas station. I just have to wait a few months till I turn twenty-five. Then maybe I'll get a trucking job. I'm gonna keep on hanging in there till I'm twenty-five and get back out on the road again. I like living on the road. So the pressure's not building up too bad now. I'm not too frustrated.

JUAN CAMACHO

He lives in a trailer park outside Gonzales, California, with his wife, Consuela, and family. They are both farmworkers. The trailer is cramped but well kept. An image of the Virgin dominates one wall. Four small children orchestrate a constant uproar—fighting, howling, laughing, demanding food. A young man, introduced as a relative of Juan's, comes home and sits on the couch, watching the tape recorder suspiciously. Juan speaks in Spanish with the deferential, embarrassed manner of a poor man honoring a guest. Consuela sometimes breaks in to disagree, emphasize a point, or urge more potato soup upon us.

I'm forty-nine years old, and I first came here to the Salinas Valley in 1967. I was born in Mexico. My father left the family some land in a little village about eighteen hours by car from the Texas border. But the land wasn't any good and we didn't have any machinery, so the harvest wasn't enough to keep us. Finally we had to leave the land. At the age of sixteen I crossed the Texas border for the first time, a little *mojadito*.* All my life I came to Texas to work in the season. Finally I found out that they were paying better wages here in California, so I emigrated and got my residence visa. That was in 1967. Since then I haven't suffered so much. I used to have to cross the river in order to get into Texas, and more than once I almost drowned. But I had to come. It was a necessity. I've worked in everything that has to do with the fields.

Right now I've been out of work for about a month. My wife can't find work either. Normally I work with a labor contractor. He hires me day by day and gets me work in the fields for a company or a rancher. At this time of year I should be working in the tomato harvest, which lasts two or three months. But last year the contractor I was working for hired me out to one company during the tomato season. There was a union election, and Cesar Chavez's union won. The company wouldn't negotiate with Chavez. So there was a strike. It lasted about two weeks. And now nobody who was there last year can get a job. The contractor made up a list of about eight hundred people. Since I had always worked for this company in the past, I was on the list. But I think the company looked at the list and threw out the people who were there last year. Maybe they

---

*Wetback.

don't want another strike. But it seems to me—how can I put it in other words?—it seems to me like discrimination. They should give last year's people work anyway, since they won the elections. Instead, the company is working with the same contractor but with different people.

CONSUELA: With the Teamsters there's more work than with Chavez's union. Ever since Chavez came in, there's been less work.

JUAN: Well, I think Chavez is OK. It's the companies that don't want to negotiate with him because if they do, wages go up. A lot of ranchers won't agree to higher wages, so they don't plant their fields, or at least they plant crops that don't take so much work. This whole valley used to be planted in lettuce, but lettuce takes a lot of work. So now they're planting grapes, and with grapes there are only four months of work. And when the harvest comes, all sorts of people come up from Texas. They stay for the season and then go back. So I don't think it's Chavez's fault. At a lot of the companies where he won the elections, they don't want to give his union the work.

But the real problem is that there are too many people. Especially in the Salinas Valley. People come here because of the climate and because the pay is better. In this valley the pay is higher than anywhere else. Some people are earning $3.40 and $3.50 an hour. I've worked in other places where you get $2.50 an hour. Just beyond Salinas, near Santa Cruz, they pay $2.50. So everyone comes here.

I've never seen so many people looking for work as this year. You go to see a contractor, and he's got such a pile of illegals that he tells you, "Oh, I'm sorry, there's no work." The contractor I usually work for said to me just the other day, "Hombre, where are all these people coming from?" I told him, "I don't know; I guess they're looking for work like the rest of us." [laughs.]

But you can understand it because the pay is so bad in Mexico. The field workers there earn 40 or 50 pesos* a day. And life is very expensive there, too. So they come here, and they can earn almost $4 an hour. The highest wages the contractors are paying is $3.15 an hour. The unions are paying $3.40, and some companies $3.50. The contractors always pay less. I work with contractors because I can't find a job with a company. It's hard to get in, for the same reason: too many illegals.

So that's how it is. No work. If la migra† shows up today and deports some people, there'll be work tomorrow. Or if they'd just pass the law that they were talking about and that was supposed to pass, to fine the bosses who hire illegals, then I think there would be more work for us legals. What happens now is that la migra throws them out just over the border, and they stay a week or two and then come back. Now I hear that

---

*About $2.
†The Immigration and Naturalization Service officers.

they're dumping some of them as far away as León or Guanajuanto, so they don't come back. Or at least it takes longer. But I think the solution is for the government to throw out the illegals once and for all. The way it is now, neither the illegals nor the legals get enough work. Of course, that's the way I started, too. [laughs]. I remember times in Texas when I would go for a month or two without work, just living off the grapefruits that I could steal.

As soon as one company lays me off, I go around to all the others to look for work. Normally I'd be working now for one company through the tomato season. But then I'd have to go look for other work. So that's what I do now that I'm unemployed because of the strike last year. I go out to the fields in my car. Wherever I see teams working, that's where I go. From field to field, I ask for work. I go out every day. I cover the whole area between Gonzales and Greenfield. It's about fifteen miles. Right now I'm the only one of us who's going out to look, but when I find a job, then maybe on another day there'll be work for my wife.

I go out at 5:00 A.M. When it gets to be 8:00 or 9:00, I know I don't have much of a chance to join up with a team, so I don't bother to run around anymore. Sometimes I hang around the union hall till noon to see if there's a call for people. They make a list at the hall of thirty or forty men, whoever's there. If they get a call for men, they take them off the list. Twice I missed work because I left the hall and came home just at the time that there was a call for men. You have to be there to get the work.

On Monday my contractor has promised to get me work in the chili harvest. He says it's about to begin. That's the hope I have right now. I've had bad luck for the last month. Right across the road here there was a gang, and one day la migra came and took eight. They were illegals. I went to the boss and asked for work, and he said to go to the union hall in Salinas. When I got to the office, the union had already sent eight new men. So that's why I didn't get it that time [laughs].

When la migra comes and takes people away, you've got the best chance to go to the field and get work. But only for a day or two or three. Then the illegals come back. The bosses don't tell you that they're letting you go to hire the others. They just say there's no more work. Do you know why they like illegals better? Because they'll put up with anything. For example, there are foremen who are always scolding. If you ask another worker for a cigarette or something, they're on your back, and they know that the illegals won't answer back a single word. The illegals just let them say what they like. And another thing: The illegals work cheaper. Even I would do it in their situation. They come from so far away, and they suffer so much to come.

Right now I have a plan. If I don't get work next week, I'm going to try in Fresno. I've heard on the radio that there's work there. I'll leave the trailer and the family and go up alone to see what God sends my way.

What are you living on these days?

While I'm on unemployment, I get $74 every two weeks. I think I get so little because I don't work steadily. There are some people who are getting as much as $100 a week, but they had steady jobs. We get some help from welfare for Consuela and the kids. They give us food stamps and medicaid. And sometimes they give us money if we need it. But if I get work, they subtract what I earn from the welfare check. If they're supposed to give Consuela $200 and I earn $50 this week, they take it out. All in all, it's barely enough. Barely enough. Sometimes there's not enough to pay the bills. We just limit ourselves and pay them somehow and get along as best we can. We just eat potatoes and beans. We don't buy anything we don't need. We buy whatever is nutritious and cheap. The thing that goes first is meat. Because meat's the same as milk, and it's better to get milk for the kids. The most important thing is to take care of them. A grown person won't be hurt if there's nothing to eat but a potato or two. But the kids can't do without milk.

CONSUELA: Every now and again we can get meat. Maybe once a week.

JUAN: Another thing I do is sleep late, until ten or eleven. That way I can avoid having three meals [*laughs*]. I skip lunch. Because if you get up late, you don't need it. For us just a month of unemployment is a serious thing. We fall way behind with the bills. Even a week is bad. We can't pay the electricity, the trailer, and pretty soon we get behind one bill and have to pay two together. That's the worst. Just now I fell behind one payment on the car and one on the trailer. So I got a $300 loan from a friend. Pretty soon I'll have to pay that back. As soon as I get a steady job, I'll get the money together and pay him. I've borrowed a few times from this friend. He's got a very good job, and he speaks good English. He charges high interest, but if I tell him I need the money for four months and I pay it back before that time, he doesn't charge me all the interest that we agreed to. He just charges me one or two months.

Last year I was unemployed in the winter, and I had to do something I'd never done before: buy food on credit. The children were crying because they were hungry, and I didn't know what to do. We couldn't buy milk for them or anything. So I had to humble myself and go ask the woman in the store if she would give me some credit. I was forced to embarrass myself in front of this woman. She asked me if I had anyone around who would vouch for me. I said, "OK, I'll bring someone." And she said, "Well, an awful lot of people have run off. There was one man who spoke to me about what a terrible time he was having—like you— and asked for credit. To this day he owes me $70. I never saw him again." But she gave us credit anyway. Since then, if I go a week or two without working and we haven't got money to buy food, she gives us credit. When I get work I go and pay her. We've maintained the credit because it's very important to us. When I'm not working we can get food for the kids.

If I can get work even for two days a week, that's about $50. I can budget the $50 for milk and gas for the car, and if I owe the store I can pay them something. Or if an electricity bill arrives, that's about $25, so we pay that and keep the other $25 for expenses. But there have been times when we had nothing to eat at all. That's why I had to humble myself and ask for credit. I had to do it. Like I said, when you're grown up, you can live with being hungry. But not little children.

RON BRETT

He lives in a black neighborhood in Dayton, Ohio. He refuses to be interviewed at home, so we talk sitting on the grass in a park. He is shy and rather formal: "I guess I'm a loner. I don't mind it so much. I'm Christian now 'cause I have the Lord. So I don't really feel like I'm completely alone. But generally, I think I'm a loner." He has been out of work for a year and has just been "saved."

I was born in Dayton and grew up here. I went to elementary school, junior high, and then high school here. After that I went to the University of Dayton for a little while. But I found myself really needing some money [laughs]. So I decided to check out the job market. Well, it just so happens that I fell into getting unskilled work, like factory work and janitor work. That's mainly what I've been doing, is unskilled labor. Work where you can use your hands.

The last job I had was at a machine shop. I was a machine operator. You know, pushing a couple of buttons and watching to make sure the tubes went into the machine straight. Well, after two and a half years I found myself wondering, "Wow, am I just gonna do this for the rest of my life?" And I started thinking that that might happen. So I decided I better come out of there. As it turned out, I ended up not going in to work, a couple of times, and I didn't call. I did that a couple of nights in a row, and the third night I came in. The foreman was standing there at the time clock, and he said that I was terminated. Which was what I was hoping would happen.

There wasn't any one thing that made me decide to leave. It was everything combined. I was having to force myself to go to work. That's really heavy, to get up and have to force yourself to go somewhere when you don't want to go. When that time rolled around and I had to go to work, I just hated to do it. I couldn't relate to most of the guys. I wouldn't talk to anybody. I'd eat my lunch alone. And then I think the foreman felt a lot of racial animosity towards me. It wasn't an outward thing, but whenever I came up on him, it would seem like he was afraid of me, and I was afraid of him. When I came out of there after eight hours, I'd be so numb that I'd feel like I left my mind elsewhere. And I'd have to find it. I felt like I just deposited my mind at the door.

But I can't put the total blame on that place because my personal life wasn't going very well at the time either. I happened to get that job at a time when my personal life was down-and-out. So it was a bad thing all around. It was a very searching year for me in 1976. I knew I was looking for something because my life was so empty. I said, "Hey, there must be something more than just doing what I'm doing." So I started searching, and I realized that maybe Jesus was the answer. So then I came to the conclusion that Jesus is the answer. But if it weren't for 1976, that terrible year I had in '76, I might not ever have come to Jesus.

What made that year so terrible?

[Laughs.] Well, I got myself caught up in some really strange desires, which it took a lot of money to satisfy. I drank pretty heavy, and on top of that I was seeing a woman who was a prostitute. So actually what I was doing was working to satisfy those two desires for drinking and sex. I would be with the woman maybe twice a week, and it cost a lot of money. And if she wasn't around, I'd be drinking. I felt myself thinking, "Wow, why am I doing this?" I was at rock bottom. So that's one more reason that I hated the job because I knew that I was just doing it to get the money for what I was doing. I was a slave to that job and to my desires. A lot of times I would go to work drunk because it made it a lot easier. Even though it was dangerous, it gave me some peace of mind. So when I got fired, I knew that something was starting to happen. Something good [laughs].

And around springtime I decided to turn to Jesus. I started going to Jesus People Church. People witnessed to me, and I realized I needed Jesus. I knew my soul needed to be revived and brought alive. So I went to church, and I got saved, and that was it.

Getting saved is when you turn to Jesus with a full commitment. In other words, Jesus is the center of your life, and you live for Him. When we talk about getting saved, we're talking about Jesus coming into your life. It's total commitment. A lot of people just believe in Jesus. They believe, but they don't live their lives for Him. That's the difference from what I've done. That's what changed my life.

How did it change?

Well, I must admit I don't have a job [*laughs*]. But I have peace of mind, which is something I've been looking for for a long time. Jesus helped me to enjoy life without worrying about anything. I used to always worry about money, about this, about that. . . . I'd think, "Wow, am I gonna get a job?" I still worry about it, but I know that I shouldn't because I know Jesus is right there, and He's gonna get me a job. So I don't worry that much. I go to the unemployment center, and I check out the papers. I call people up. That's what I've been doing for the last six months. Looking for work, but not real intensely. I find myself in a position where I don't want work like I had before, which is mainly what you're gonna get if you're unskilled. So I've been looking mostly for jobs outside of factory work. But I haven't had any luck.

I guess one reason why I haven't been putting that much effort into it is because I get discouraged quite a bit. I get all kinds of feelings, you know. . . . Sometimes I think it's maybe because they don't think I would fit into that job. Sometimes I think it's racial. All kinds of thoughts go through my head. A couple of times I'm sure it was a racial thing. I went into this one place, and they right away told me, "Hey, we don't have any openings." I could tell by the way the guy addressed me that there was no room for black people in the job. And I went to this other place where the man said, "Well, we're looking for a certain kind of person." What that meant, I don't know. I took it that the certain kind of person shouldn't have black skin.

That kind of thing used to make me very angry. It doesn't bother me as much now as when I was in high school. Back then I'd be walking down the street and people would be hollering, "Nigger!" That still happens. Like this guy the other day—I came out of my house, and a guy was riding by. He said, "Black boy, you come out to —" Some suburb, I don't know which one it was. "You come out there, you ain't gonna come out alive." I said, "What? This is still happening?" Those are isolated incidents, but it still enters into the picture when you go looking for a job. You go in and you see that white employer sitting there, and you just get a feeling of "Wow, is he gonna hire me?" As opposed to just coming in there and sitting down and talking to him. All those other feelings come in there because you know that he is different than you, and in a sense you can't take him as a person. You'd like to, and that's what you should do; but all this other stuff comes in.

And even that's not as discouraging as seeing how many blacks are out of work. How many black males are out of work. That's what bothers me. You wonder sometimes why this is. Why, when you go into the ghetto, you see black men just walking the streets. No jobs. It really makes you wonder. Are they going through the same things I go through? And maybe do they not have jobs because they don't want to put up with it? I see black men all over, sitting around idle, not doing anything. It bothers me. And it scares me because I'm thirty-five years old, and unemployed, and black, and I wonder when I'm going to get that chance to be able to contribute something. Where I have a good job and I can really feel important on the job. Right now I just don't feel important. I don't feel significant. Unemployed, no money, thirty-five years old.

And then I go downtown and I see all these white dudes in suits. I'll be thinking, "Wow, they're human just like me." But ... [laughs]. But they may be my enemies. I don't know. Every time I see a white man in a suit I go through changes. I guess I'm looking at the power structure there. When I look at all those men in suit and ties, I get to thinking, "Hmm. Would I be like that?" Not that I want to be, but I think of at least having the opportunity to get into business college or business school. I think all kinds of stuff. Like the fact that for every three or four of these white men that are dressed like that and have a business career under their belt, there may be one black man. Probably even less. One black man who is able to go through business college and get a good job. And sometimes, walking on the street, I feel like I have to step out of their way. Then I say, "The heck with that. They're gonna step out of my way." Or not even that. Shoot, why should either one of us have to step out of the way? We should just walk normally. But I really think about those guys.

Before I had Jesus, I was always angry about things like that. I always had this anger and animosity towards white people, towards society. I still get that, but it's not as intense. I used to walk around with a snarl on my face. And when I'd get high, I'd be thinking all kinds of thoughts about the white man. Like going out and killing a white man. Throwing a Molotov cocktail in somebody's window. I don't feel that now. Jesus keeps me cool. I don't have to be mad at the white man because I know anger isn't going to do me any good. To stay angry, stay bitter, isn't going to do me any good because it's a waste of energy. It's not gonna change anything anyway. The white man is always gonna discriminate, so why worry about it?

There's something else I think about. Here we are in 1977. The recession is supposed to be going down. They say that the rate of unemployment is going down. Yet I think about all the people I see at the unemployment service. And I usually go and give blood over at the blood plasma place. You get a lot of people down there without work. Hundreds come in there every day. It's crowded all the time. The place stays open from 7:30 in the morning until 5:30 at night, and you get people coming in there constantly. It's depressing. That's the only word I can think of. You get a lot of blacks and a lot of students because they're sort of in the bottom echelon like unemployed poor people. Now I know that those people, if they didn't really have to go in there, they wouldn't do it. I know I wouldn't. If I had a choice, I wouldn't do it. But I have to get some money. So I go. First you have to sit and wait. Then they check your blood pressure and do some tests on you. Then you gotta go wait again till a table opens up. It's pretty depressing to have to go through all that just to get $6, or $9 they give you the second time, if you go twice a week. You figure, why go through all that? Getting pricked and having these big needles stuck in you for $6. Every time I go in there I think, "Wow, is this really, *really* happening?"

Then I think of all the people who are working and never had the experience of going into a blood place and giving blood because they need the money. They've always had money. It really makes you think. I feel I'm a person who's willing to work and contribute something to the work force. But I'm not going to take just any job. I'm gonna be fussy. I think I have the right to be fussy about what kind of job I'm suited for. I'm not saying that I'm qualified, but I do have the right of choosing what area I want to go into. And I don't think the unemployment service should have the right to cut off your benefits. I think they should carry you as long as necessary. No, what do they do? They just cut off one unemployment extension. You can only have two extensions now. Because they feel that there are jobs available. But what kind of jobs are we talking about here? We're talking about dishwasher jobs, janitor jobs. Those kinds of jobs are around. But can you survive making $2.50 an hour? No way. I couldn't. And I don't think anybody else could. And I don't think that's being unreasonable.

So it really causes you to wonder when you see all this going on around you, and they say that the unemployment rate is going down. Are they talking about the hard-core areas? The inner city? Have they been to those blood plasma places? What are they looking at, when they say that? Are they just referring to the one-third or one-fourth of the working class that maybe are out of work for two or three weeks and then they've got a job again? Who are they actually talking about?

GEORGE MURAVCHIK

He is an electrical engineer living near "Silicon Valley" in California, an area known for its large number of companies that specialize in electronic circuitry based on tiny wafers of silicon. But he is hardly the stereotype of an engineer. Whether by temperament or circumstance, he has become a bohemian of sorts. He dates the change to 1970, when massive layoffs hit the valley: "This area was like a desert of dying engineers. The engineers in the Santa Monica unemployment office had their own special room. I saw what was happening, and I said, 'Hey, the only thing is to go back to school.' I discovered Berkeley. The college kids were rioting, and I was an engineer with a very narrow mind. A family man. I thought it was a great country. Vietnam, who cares? But these guys opened my mind so much that I was able not only to survive but adapt to the lack of a job and a new way of life." In 1971 he left California to work in Chicago—his hometown—for three years.

He talks intensely, hurrying from subject to subject. He wears a yarmulke and has a handsome pepper-and-salt beard. He is forty-six years old.

In 1974 I left Chicago and came back out to California. All I could find was a couple of temporary jobs. Through job shops. In California today most of the companies won't hire you direct. If they don't know you, they're not gonna spend the money on you. There are so many people coming to the area that they don't have to. They hire through job shops. They're like an employment agency for engineers, technicians, draftsmen, anything technical. The job shop hires you, screens you, and sends you out to whatever companies they get calls from. Say Memorex wants to hire ten electrical engineers, ten test engineers, twenty testers, some designers, et cetera. They send this entire list to the job shop, and the shop says, "I got 'em all for you." Or half. "Fine, send them down." So the job shop calls me up and all the other guys and says, "George, go see this man." If the man likes me, the job shop hires me, not the company. You get good money from the shop, but no fringe benefits. The jobs can be ninety days, thirty days, sixty days, a year. They may turn into something permanent if you're lucky.

So I had a few nice jobs. One with an electronics company. They ran out of money. Then I got a job with a computer products outfit. They ran out of parts, had to lay me off. The following year, 1975, I got a job with them again for two months. Ran out of parts. Had to let me go. Then I worked as a speed-reading instructor from April to August of '75. Since then it's been nothing.

I'm on unemployment insurance. I've got two extensions coming, thirty-two weeks. I'm on welfare. Sometimes I get government loans and grants for going to school. I get a little bit of disability. Not much, but every little bit helps. All told it comes to about $500 a month. If they keep doing it, I can just live tax-free [laughs]. I don't like it, but they're forcing me.

I thought you couldn't be on unemployment and welfare at the same time?

That's what you think.

How did you do that?

I'm not talking. No, I'm not gonna say. It's there. I look at it this way. Since I have a hunch that the federal government and the state government have part responsibility for this unemployment situation, it's up to me to find out how to get money and live as best I can. To fight the system. That's a right, because I'm a citizen. So I have this income, that's all. It doesn't matter how or where or when. I don't want it, but I have to have it in order to live.

What's the disability for?

Back in 1972 I was examined by a psychiatrist who said I was a manic-depressive. I didn't believe it. So I went to a medical center and stayed there for a couple of weeks. They said, "You're a manic-depressive." I believed it. Because I know those people; they're pretty straight. So I take lithium carbonate and it's under control. It's a miraculous thing they developed a few years ago. But there are some side effects from the lithium that make it difficult to do some of the things I used to do. Whether it's temporary or not, it's there, so I put a claim in for disability and I got on. It's not much, but it's enough.

Now I'm looking for a company that will hire me so I can work steadily for a minimum of five years. That's my minimum. I'd like to work longer. But the longest job I've had in engineering has been five years. I don't care if it's a big company or a small company, I want to get steady work, because the Bay Area is the place I want to live in. And I want to be a whole human being. I want to work. I don't want to be told I'm overqualified because that's bullshit. I don't even care whether it's engineering. I wouldn't mind driving a bus. The money is good, $7.60 an hour. The only problem there is that you've got to be an ethnic minority to get in. And they tell me I'm not a minority. I tell 'em I am a minority [laughs]. But according to the government I'm not. That's crazy too. They have this affirmative action bit, which is nothing more than placing minorities. Namely blacks and Chicanos. Even if they're incapable of doing the job. And they tell me, "No, you can't do it because you're not with affirmative action." So that's one thing I'm up against. Another thing is my age.

So you go to the unemployment office. They list IBM runoffs of jobs. And if you look closely, there will be a little four-letter word saying "Mand." Mandatory listing. This job may have been filled internally two months ago, but the companies have to list it by law. The job may not even exist. A lot of companies will advertise openings just to get exposure, and the jobs aren't there. All kinds of funny games are going on. You don't know what's happening till you get to see the guy. There are companies that are getting eight hundred résumés a week. Some are getting two hundred, three hundred a day. They get filed in the waste-basket at the end of the week. A friend of mine gives a seminar on how to hunt for jobs. She told me, "White résumés are a waste of time. Get parchment, get yellow, get off-white, anything that will attract their eye. You have eleven seconds' reading time for someone to decide whether he wants to see you." Well, with numbers like that we're worse than cattle. They're not interested so much in who can do the job well. Not since the Depression have you had such an employer's market of all these talented people. Not only engineers and technicians. You got teachers, plumbers, electricians. . . . This is the competition I face.

I sent out about fifty résumés a week for a while. Didn't get much of a response. Then I got to the point where I figured I'm gonna refuse résumés entirely. When a man says, "I want a résumé," I'll say, "I can see you. What time can you see me? Tomorrow?" And they do. They'll see you in person. They may say, "Don't you have a résumé?" And I'll say, "I'll bring it with me, but it's a junky one. I haven't updated it." When the guy gets to the point of having fifty résumés, he either can't make a decision or he's gonna screen everybody out. I don't want to be screened out.

But I'll never get discouraged because life is meant that you shouldn't get discouraged. Sometimes it's a fight, but it doesn't hurt. It hasn't hurt me. I dump all this shit on my psychiatrist [laughs]. Mainly I feel numb to it. I know I'm gonna get a job sooner or later. Two years, three years, six months. In the meantime I know I can survive. So what have I got? I have a bicycle. And the beautiful California sunshine. And the moun-tains, some good food, and some good female companionship. And I have two places to stay. I used to have an apartment—$125 a month. Finally I couldn't afford it. So I moved into a synagogue up in San Bruno. I store my clothes in a rabbi's garage. I can sleep outdoors on the lawn or indoors on a couch in the office. And then over in San Francisco I have a little yeshiva where I can stay for free. If I want to, I can contribute. They have good kosher food. Some of my food stamps are going to support the yeshiva. They don't have any money.

How do you pass your time on a typical day?

Well, I wake up about 6:00 or 6:30 and pray and do yoga. Then I bike down to a place for breakfast. You can sit by the pool and have fresh squeezed orange juice. It's delightful. When I finish there, if it's a day to go to the unemployment office to collect money, I'd bike over there and collect. Then I'd make some phone calls from there to some companies that may be hiring. A lot of days I pick up the paper and there are jobs listed. I say, "Hey, I'm gonna get a job. Look at all these jobs!" And I call up. They tell me to send in a résumé. That could be frustrating, but I'm used to it. I call the man up, and I say, "Hello, Joe? Hi. I'm interested in talking to you on this job. I'll bring a résumé if I have to, and I can make it between such-and-such a time." Or I say, "When is it convenient for you?" I let him have the ball, but I throw it. He either picks it up or he doesn't. If he doesn't, I say, "Well, you don't want to hire anyway, good-bye." I have to do that. I'm not gonna run out there if he's not serious.

So I look for jobs in the morning. Then I call up one of my woman friends and say, "Hey, I'll be available for lunch at such-and-such a time." I arrange to have a good lunch somewhere. Then I might go to the Berkeley campus because I get my mail there. That place is another buffer for me, besides religion. When I bike or drive or walk through the university, looking at the trees, I relax. It has a very calming effect on me. I look for my mail, and sometimes I get surprised by getting money in the mail. I know some people around there, and I talk to them about what's happening in the country. On Mondays I go to my group therapy from 2:30 to 4:30. Tuesdays I go to unemployment, and once in a while I have to go to the welfare place. Sometimes I go into San Francisco to look for work there. Or I go to the beach. It's a very easy way of life, even though it may seem to be chaotic and wasteful. I keep myself in shape by biking and mentally in shape by other things. Sooner or later things are gonna break.

If I didn't have my religion I would probably go a little kookie. I'd probably go boozing or whoring. Maybe I'd start a little riot. But the Torah is an unusual piece of work. The rabbis say if you read the Torah, study Torah, you don't need a psychiatrist. And I believe 'em. There's stability in my religion. It gives me not only a place to go on a Sabbath, but also a day of rest. From Friday night to Saturday night I have twenty-four hours of peace. No television, no telephone, no car, no bike riding, nothing but walking, praying—not in that order. Making love is legal. Lying on the grass, reading, having good kosher meals at people's homes, and just getting together with people.

I wake up very early and I pray. I go into the chapel. I put on all the prayer things and I pray. I have communion with God every day this way. Very, very enlightening. Puts me into a high, a spiritual high. That's how I'm able to go out every day and say, "Well, maybe I'll find a job."

Do you ever pray for a job?

Sure. Oh, yeah. He expects it. First I thank God for being a Jew, and then I pray. I say, "Look, I'd like to have my daughter out here to go to school, and I'd like to find a nice woman to marry, and it means money. I know you don't understand what money is. It's not part of your business. I would like a job, a good-paying job." So He understands. But being spiritual, He doesn't really know what money is all about [laughs].

I have a friend, Irv, who's a Ph.D. in chemistry out here. I met him on the unemployment line, and he says, "Those bastards. They think this is a welfare check they're giving me. I earned this money. I paid it." I can see it's getting to him. I say, "Irv, ignore these people. That's their job. Just be thankful that your children are alive and healthy and that you're getting some money to pay for everything." No, he's angry. Some people even refuse benefits. Well, I'm not proud. I want to live. I want to live like a human being, not like a beggar. And it doesn't get me down because I know it's not my doing. I didn't lose my job because I was a screw-up guy and got fired. I lost my job because of economic conditions. And the only thing I can do is do a little better than survive.

It's true that it's a weird life I lead. It's like the old Jewish tale of the Jews moving from one part of town to another. Being destitute. But as my psychiatrist explained, I found stability in the midst of chaos. To you it may seem unstable, but amidst all the chaos I have a place to live. Two places. In very spiritual headquarters with all the religious books I want. And the other place with all the kosher food I want. And with beautiful rabbis and people that come in who are beautiful. I can worship in either place. So it's stable. I go once a week to my group, and that's stability because I dump a lot of junk out on them. I have my psychiatrist, and I go to movies, and I have dates with divorced women. It's a very fine life.

JACK DUSTIN

He is a slender young man with long, frizzy red hair and a beard. He wears jeans, an Indian cotton gauze shirt, and a string of pukka shells around his neck. He lives with his girl friend, Vicky, in Chicago—an old neighborhood of weathered churches, huge maples, and dilapidated but handsome apartment buildings that are beginning to attract remodelers. We're in the park near his house. He seems boyishly excited about the balmy weather.

He waited three months after being fired before claiming unemployment. "I come from a very religious family. And we were very poor. My father worked three jobs. He was a teacher, a welder, and he had a

89

paper route with two boys. He had high standards for everything. So I worked my ass off, following in his footsteps. I had a lawn-mowing business when I was ten with about 150 customers.

"My father would never do something like take unemployment. I felt too proud to take it, too. I'd like to justify it by saying I paid into it all the years I worked, but I still feel a little uneasy. It took a lot of talking to my friends before I went. There's the insinuation of being lower-class...."

When I was twenty I was going to the University of Chicago, and I got a summer job as a bookkeeper in a grain elevator. When the summer was over they asked me if I'd like to stay on as an assistant supervisor. I was married at the time and I was thinking about a career, being a professional, all kinds of good shit like that. So I worked there for another year and they asked me if I would be a broker for the company. I said, "Yes, of course." I worked there two more years and then got fired three months ago.

The company was one of the largest grain companies in the world. My job was to buy grain from farmers and dealers all over the West and Midwest and then sell it to other dealers. I did the whole range of speculating on the market: buying futures, taking cash positions and future positions, liquidating them, stuff like that. I did a lot of export business, too, because the company owns a big grain elevator here. Sales to the Far East, delivering rail freight.

I thought I really liked it. It was kind of a little game. I was making about twenty-five grand. I bought new cars every year, you know, and just lived the way a businessman was supposed to live [*laughs*]. Especially while I was still married, I found myself falling into the role of a businessman. Going out on business trips and entertaining and socializing. It was really strange because it didn't fit in with me. I didn't completely lose my identity, though. I always had my long hair. I was chastised for that in the straight businessman's world. But it was all a joke to me.

Then at the end of two years the company started a big drive to hire college graduates. They had just named a new personnel manager for the whole country, and he started flying around and talking to people in the various divisions to see what the situation was. Basically he was exercising his newfound strength in the company. To do that, he had to do something big. So he went on a recruiting drive to get people who would raise the status of the company. He hired people from the best colleges. Harvard, Yale, Cornell—a bunch of East Coast preppies. They may not have been the best students, but they had degrees from the name colleges.

They started trying to fit these guys into the system. And I knew the company fairly well. I knew how many offices and how much space they had. Well, they hired an awful lot of people. More than they had room for. So I was kind of gearing myself up for the end, because it was mentioned several times by my friends there that it was too bad I didn't have the education. I hung on because the money was so good. But eventually my boss said, "It's coming from the head office. They want to see these preppies get a place in the company." And I said, "That's fine. I'll leave. No problem." It was kind of mutual because I had adjusted myself to it a while before. And there was no feeling that I hadn't done an adequate job. My boss even said to me, "My God, I wish you had that degree because I don't want to get rid of you."

I still resented it a lot, though. I resented the fact that somebody I didn't know, and who didn't know me or what kind of job I could do, was dictating my life. And it was uncomfortable. It changed my life a lot because all of a sudden I didn't have the income and the life I used to have. But I wasn't unhappy. In fact, I was very happy.

Why so happy?

Well, that didn't come right away. At first I was depressed. God, was I depressed! In the days right after my boss talked to me, I was really down. Really, really, really down. The first thing that went on was: "What are people gonna think?" Then: "What are my parents gonna think?" I was embarrassed about the fact that I was fired, and that it was because I didn't have the education. In fact, I told a lot of people that I quit. And then I started thinking, "What's my life gonna be like? What am I gonna do without the money? I've still got bills to pay. How am I gonna meet those bills?" It was very negative, very depressing. To have to think I would have to completely leave the style of life I had lived for those years. It hurt. It hurt a lot. I'd lay in bed at night and wonder what was gonna happen.

But there were other things that were starting to happen in my life at that time. Basically I met a certain lady, and we talked about a lot of things. It made me see myself and how materialistic I was. See, it was really strange for me to be a big businessman. When I was married, I was aiming to be a very, very rich man. A very successful man that everybody would look up to. But after I got divorced, I felt that I was just out for myself. I was making money, but the job itself wasn't all that important anymore because the responsibility of having a family and building for the future wasn't there. I got married when I was nineteen. And I felt I had missed a lot. I had lived a life that was very straight. I never played around on my wife at all. And then all of a sudden I was free. And I was twenty-two, just twenty-two. I had all this money and nothing to do with it. No support payments, nothing. So I decided I was going out to get everything I had missed. And I got it [laughs]. I got a lot of it. I went completely off the deep end.

It was funny how it started. I went to the same bar a lot, and I went out with a couple of the waitresses. Then I got a couple of phone calls from other ladies who said, "Hey, I heard about you from so-and-so." I'd say, "Who?" They'd mentioned the name, and I'd go, "Oh, OK." So we'd go out. I just fell into the role. I let myself go. I let everything go. Different women, buying sports cars, spending extravagantly. I started living in a condominium with a couple of friends. We partied and danced and got drunk and stoned all the time. It was a crowd of very physical people. Most of the women were looking for men with money, and I had the money. It was easy. One person after another would find out you had money and would want to meet you. It just went like that. It was all purely apart from any real reason to go out with someone. It was just the fact that you had money and could treat them to movies and operas and ballets and restaurants, all that shit.

I guess you'd say I was being a playboy. I figure when you're spending maybe 70 percent of your income on different women and different frivolities, you're a playboy. I wasn't thinking about personal relationships. There was no depth to anything. It was purely sexual, just the physical feelings. I even was a gigolo for a while because through the business I used to meet some of the richest people in the city. Their wives liked me because I was the oddball, the stranger, the one that made people think. I was exciting to them. I did strange things like make love in the park in the middle of the night. To them it was intriguing. And people who are looking for a little excitement do some weird stuff, let me tell you [laughs].

All that was sort of like the job—I thought I liked it at the time. Then when my boss talked to me I realized it was coming to an end. Like I say, it hurt bad for about two days. Then I resigned myself to the fact that it was over, and I was gonna go on from there. It was the end of a future. I had to start thinking about other things that would make me happy. All of a sudden the money wasn't there, so you wonder about other things. It made me go from thinking about sex all the time to more meaningful things. At least to me they're more meaningful. It completely changed my ideas of relationships. I couldn't take out women all the time and spend money on them like it was going out of style. I had to be more conservative. I had to find women who didn't expect to be taken out on the town every night. That's when I started being with Vicky a little more. We'd do things that didn't cost a lot of money. She liked it, and I liked it. It changed my whole outlook. She was the first lady I had met that I could just talk to for hours.

So when I actually quit working, I felt great. I had about two months' notice, and I had planned for it. It felt good to have all my days for me. I did a lot of thinking, a lot of working with my hands, things that made me happy when I was younger. I got back into painting and music. Vicky and I moved in together and started talking about going into real estate. She's got some money, and I have a little bit. We want to buy something, fix it up, and then sell it. Right now we're looking into some apartments in this section of the city. I used to work with my hands a lot when I was growing up. I helped build the house my family lives in. And now I've got the time to do it again. It's nice.

I had to think a lot about whether to go back to the grain business. While I was working, I had offers from other companies, and I always said, "No, I won't do it because I'm doing so well here." But afterwards I asked myself if I should go back to those companies that wanted me before, so that I wouldn't have to lose my money or my life-style. I weighed the pros and cons of it. I tried not to let the fact that I was fired affect the way I felt about the industry. I kept an open mind and said, "Maybe it's really good work. A lot of people are happy at it." So I thought about whether I really liked it. And I said, "Well, lookit, I had to make fifty to one hundred calls every day. I had to talk to the same people every day, who said the same things." Some people I enjoyed talking with, but it was maybe three calls out of the one hundred. The rest of it was business. No personal relations. There was a lot of haggling about prices. There were a lot of conversations about who was responsible for what. Why did you make this deal? Why this, why that? You had to justify everything to your superiors. As long as you could do that, it was cool. But I really felt like I was getting an ulcer. I was there for eleven or twelve hours a day, going, going, going. I just felt too mellow for that [laughs]. Some people love to be pushed all the time. I don't. That's why I never did go back or even inquire.

I've still got a little money, and I've got things I can sell. I've got thousands and thousands of dollars of personal possessions. Even if I had to sell them at a big loss, I could still make the bills. And I realize that these possessions are just worldly goods. I can get along without them. I haven't sold any yet except my car, and that was easy. I thought I loved the car, but when I sold it I felt good. I had money. I paid my bills. Everything was cool [laughs]. I think sometimes of the memories attached to my things, but I also think of why I bought them in the first place. Lots of times I'd buy things because my friends were buying them. I always wondered if I was buying friendship with my money, and I think I was.

I still feel the way I did when I stopped working, that I'm on vacation. And I hope that feeling always stays with me. Because what I'm doing now is fun. I get up around noon. Make a few phone calls about real estate. Wander down to the place we're thinking about buying. Talk to the residents or the contractors who are going to do the work. I spend a lot of time putting numbers down on paper to see if it's gonna be a money-maker or a money-loser. I have meetings with people in the city government—electrical inspectors, the department of buildings. . . . Or maybe during the day I'll do some painting or sketching or photography. Then in the evening we're usually over at some friend's house, or we have people over. Listen to some music, fix dinner, wash the dishes. Around midnight we take off and go play a little pool, or walk through the park, or just walk around the neighborhood. We've walked all over looking at buildings at night.

We usually hit the sack around three and talk till the sun comes up. Then sleep till noon. We play tennis a lot, too. Real tennis nuts. Do some hiking, some running.

Mainly for me it's just going out and seeing what I am. I had to get to know myself after those years at the company. So I go walking in the woods, or by the lake, and watch the colors and think about what makes me happy. What *really* makes me happy. And I see that living around here makes me happy. Being free to do what I want makes me happy. I've got a zillion house plants, and they make me happy. Talking makes me happy. A lot of things that don't cost money. And I don't put money down because it makes you happy, too. It's just that you have to temper all parts of your life.

In fact, I don't know when I've ever been so happy. Sitting out here, not a worry in the world. Isn't it a gorgeous day?

FREDDIE DREYFUS

He is twenty-five, a rock guitarist and singer. Other people his age might call him hyper. The interview amounts to a monologue, with a rush of ideas, memories, and stories tumbling from his lips. "I was brought up in Rye, New York. We had about ten acres, with woods and a grand old house. My father was a corporate attorney. He's very Germanic-Russian, like Dostoyevsky. He had a lot of moral conflicts. He would walk the estates. He worked and worked. And I had to cut the grass. Without a tractor. I had to cut it beautifully, formally, with sweeping curves. I did that even when I was eight years old, up until I left home, which was as soon as I could."

After a few stabs at college he dropped out to open a boardinghouse in "a big old southern mansion like Tara. It was a dilapidated crate. We *fixed it up, and for four years the tenants had the privilege of three hundred acres run by crazies. Then we had a big yard sale for three days, sold everything, and I walked out with about $70. And a tire iron under my arm, because me and my partner were trying to kill each other. . . ."*

I moved to New York and I wanted to make it in rock music. And I wanted a really firm foundation, so I figured I'd get a job for a while and eventually get on unemployment. That was my idea. It's what I've always wanted as an artist. I wanted to establish a firm home that was safe, and I was willing to work twenty or thirty weeks to get it together. And then have just enough money coming in to live on and perform my art.

The job I got was as superintendent and handyman at this disco place on the East Side. It's all mirrors and plastic vines and flowers hanging from the ceilings and colored lights on the vines. And it gets ripped up every night. Linoleum on the dance floors gets knocked out; chairs are broken; sometimes there's blood on the carpets. Kitchen clogs up. And I have good manual skills, because I was brought up with saws and drills and plumbing and stuff. I thought on that job I might find some avenues into my career because the guys who own the club also back films and music and shows. In fact, that's one of the reasons I got fired. I was starting to get close to one of the owners. I spent two solid days working on his apartment. He would just take me out of the club, because he's the owner.

The other reason was the time clock. For the first few months I was there I just refused to punch in and out. I said, "I will not. I'm the super and my hours are sometimes very long and late, sometimes early. I demand that freedom." I had the right to be that way because that's a very strange job, being the super of a place like that. But during the last two weeks my boss, the man who directly supervised me, insisted that I use the time card. Well, I still didn't punch it half the time. I would just do my hours. The first week I recorded thirty-one and a half hours, and the next week it was thirty-five hours or something. He took me in his office and used the two events, the apartment and the time clock, as an excuse to fire me.

I only lasted eighteen weeks there, so I needed four more for unemployment. In the meantime I got a job as super of two buildings. So I had to work on these buildings. I was rehearsing almost every night with my band, Reefer Madness. Late at night, from like eleven to two. Plus I was fucking like a maniac with Nicole, and I wanted to do nothing else but that. She's the only girl I really fell in love with here in New York. So it was a very full time.

Through *The New York Times* I got another superintendent job at a health center. I liked that job. But I had to be there at seven every morning and leave at three. It was hard, with rehearsals at night. I would be so tense from having to wake up in the morning that at eight I'd call up all my band members just to talk to them. They'd say, "What are you doing, we just came home from rehearsal!" I'd say, "I'm at work." [Laughs.]

Well, after nine weeks Dr. Adams, who is the head of the hiring, fired me. He said that I wasn't making my hours. I wasn't, it was true. Once I got caught asleep in one of the therapy rooms, with the door locked. One of the doctors opened it with a key, and there I was, curled up. I wasn't a dedicated super. Didn't give a flying fuck about the health center. And I knew that if I treated the job the way I felt about it, the deterioration curve would be about right to get me on unemployment. I wouldn't have to make it happen. The only way to get on unemployment is by natural process. So I did. I was hassling them for a raise, and finally Dr. Adams came to me and said, "What would you do if you were in my position? You don't always come exactly on time, and you want a raise. So why don't we just let it go?" I said, "Fine," because that way I felt completely free of obligation. He said, "What you do is good. But you don't do that much. You just waste time and hang out." I said, "I agree." I used to go for two-hour lunches at Zum Zum [laughs].

So now I get $60 a week unemployment. That's $240 a month that comes in the mail. And I'm the super for these buildings, so I don't pay any rent. The apartment I live in is $300 a month. I get $150 off and $5 an hour for any work I do. I always do thirty hours a month, so it comes out to a free apartment. It used to be off the books, but it's going on the books now. So every fourth week we report all four weeks as one week, and I lose my unemployment for that week. And people are starting to give me money for my art, which is the whole point of unemployment. I've got another six months to go, and so far in the last month I've gotten $3,800 in investments in my art. Which will all have to be paid back. I'm $3,800 in debt. But they're all loans on very good terms, from people who are interested in my music.

Lately I've been spending all my time on the phone. Hardly any socializing. Trying to make this rock thing happen. I wake up to the phone at 8:30. By myself, usually. I'm on the phone till noon. Take a walk, smoke a joint, usually come in and practice for about half an hour and get back on the phone. Rehearsal starts around one, goes to four. Come home, slowly. Visit friends. Sometimes go out at night. Usually end up playing or writing songs into the night. Don't read anymore. I used to read like a madman. Can't read. Can't harness my mind to anything else. Occasionally I put a day or two aside and just do building work or go be with a girl. But I don't even do that too much. Spend my time on the phone or at meetings. It's my only priority. The people I've met in the last two months have been incredible. Things have intensified. Some producers are interested.

So I need unemployment. It's a definite part of the social system. It's another method of survival. But it has to be tied with some other thing to be fulfilling. In itself it's not much. It's just a way to get through a certain period. It's not a great living. I grew up in a home where my father made $100,000 a year. So I know about things like that. But it's not important, having fine wines and the best cuts. Granted, you sure can't have it on unemployment. But the stakes are high for me because I'm trying to be a rock star. And I'm competing. The other day I was playing a new song for this producer who wrote a lot of big songs. And he said, "I don't like it. It's cheap." I was hurt. He said, "Look, if you want me to be your uncle Ted, I'll tell you it's a beautiful song and I'll suck you off if you want." Which he would. "But if you want me to talk to you professionally, then I'll just level with you. I think you're a talent, but when I listen to you I'm listening to you in comparison with McCartney and Stevie Wonder. If I say I don't think the song is good, I'm talking about really high standards, and you're gonna have to meet those standards to deal with me on a professional level. So don't be offended." This is the kind of thing I'm getting into. It's very exciting. And it's demanding. We're going on tour soon, I think. It's pretty sure. So I gotta go out and buy a six-foot mirror and stand in front of it hours every day, while my tapes are playing, and practice my moves.

It's hard to be an artist. They don't reward you much for it, unless you pull off this big gaudy scheme or after you're dead. There's so many breaks against you. If you imagine society as a body, the blood system of the society doesn't circulate to the arts until many of the cells have died. The supply of money is very sparse. And you have to work your way in, like any other profession. But it's hard to work your way in because there are no incremental salary increases. Artists have to go it on their own. That's why, when they rise up, they're with kings. Because they made it. But most of them don't. So unemployment is really important for my type of person. A lot of my friends who are actors and actresses are on it. But I can see a whole spirit in the nation welling up against people on unemployment. You know that story "The Lottery," where the girl gets stoned to death? Well, I think about some pretty, sexy actress type who just wants to live glamorously, and she's on unemployment. I can see how people could begin to hate her. But on the other hand, if she ever became Marlene Dietrich, then we'd thank God that she was allowed to live and not become a secretary.

My father climbed to the top of the world, more or less. He lived in the most elegant town in New York State and in one of the finest homes in the town. But now he has severe heart problems. He has had operations. And his whole life is going to be like that. Chest pains and muscle spasms from tension. So I had the good grace to be born on top of the shit box, and I've seen what it takes to make it. And I could see that it's not the only thing. To get it, at least if you're working nine to five, you really have to bust ass. I know how hard my father busted ass. And I figure if I'm gonna bust ass that hard, it's fucking well gonna be doing something I like. So I'm doing rock music. It's the only thing I can do that hard.

ART FINCH

A beefy, stolid man of thirty-four. Before going to work in the Kenosha, Wisconsin, plant of the American Motors Corporation, he ran a dry-goods store in western Wisconsin. "But we had a fire and got burned out. Lost everything we had. So that's why we moved back around here, to the area I'm familiar with. I was born just a few miles from here. And the AMC plant is probably the highest-paying in all Wisconsin. When I was laid off, I was making roughly $6.48 an hour. Plus overtime, and I was working second shift, which means a 5 percent premium added to that $6.48."

His wife, Nancy, listens as we talk. We're in the dining alcove of their apartment, in a newly built complex near Kenosha. Two towheaded children wander in and out. A baby sleeps in a crib.

I started with American Motors in 1974. It was easy to get work then. In fact, I would guess they hired at least a thousand people at that time, between June and September of 1974. But that was their peak period. That's when their sales were really coming on. Last year they had a record year. And now everything is down. They're the worst auto maker in the country for sales.

So I got laid off in March. The cars weren't selling. They had a big backup of cars, and they were laying off a lot of people. The idea was—or what they told us anyway—that we'd be off just long enough to bring down the inventory, sell off the '75s and '76s. So I wasn't too concerned about it at the time, for the simple reason that I had almost four months of sub pay credits accumulated. I don't know if you're familiar with that. It means that while you're unemployed, you draw 95 percent of your pay. Your credits are accumulated by the hours worked. If you work a long time, you build up these credits. When I was laid off, I had fifty-some credits, I think. And while you're off, with each unemployment check you get one from sub pay. With my four dependents, I drew a pretty good amount. For every check they take off X number of credits.

Well, my sub pay ran out two weeks ago. Jeez, I had no idea we'd be out this long. When I was laid off, that's just about the time Ford and Chrysler were calling back, and they had been really hurting a couple of years before. So I figured to be off for a month or two. It was the spring of the year. It was OK with me. It was just like a vacation because the money was there. In fact, I probably made more money by not driving to work and using the gas. I didn't mind a bit. It was like a nice little vacation. Or so I thought at the time [laughs].

During the first few weeks it was just lazy and boring. Nothing to do. I mean, what are you going to do? You sit here and watch television for a while, and you can only stand so much of that. You can drive around, but you can only do so much of that. You take the kids fishing; you putter around. I thought I'd be back to work within a few weeks. Nothing to be concerned about. But still, I feel better when I'm working. Hell, I put on weight like you can't believe. I sit around, get lazy. I oversleep. I figure maybe I'll get up in seven hours, but then I feel so good lying there that I don't get up. I get lazier day by day. Since I've been off I put on twenty pounds. Just sitting around, you grab some cheese or something. It's the boredom of not doing anything, and no exercise at all. Just makes you feel lazy and terrible. And now it's increasing more and more. I'm getting so restless that it's hard to sit down for more than an hour. This is getting to be true even at night. I'm restless from the time I get up till the time I go to bed again.

And after a while I began to realize that maybe they weren't gonna call me back right away. I don't know exactly when it was. Maybe a month ago, I realized that I only had a few more sub pay checks coming and the prospects really looked bad for me going back to work. At the time of layoff, according to all the reports that were around, it was just a matter of clearing out the huge flow of cars that they had. Evidently they didn't clear 'em out [laughs]. They just aren't selling. And as the quarterly reports come in, talking about bad sales at American Motors, you begin to think, "My God, here they've got 300,000 cars, and it's getting to the end of the '76 season. They're gonna have to ship those cars and sell 'em." And you realize that that's just not gonna happen to a small company like AMC. You know, to Ford 300,000 cars is nothing. But to American Motors that's a lot of automobiles. After those reports came out, that's when I felt the worst about it. Really bad depression. I got crabby and ornery.

It's not a whole lot better in any other industry. Because so much depends on auto workers, for one thing. Steel workers depend on 'em, everybody that makes the parts. So I'm certainly not alone. I would like to have more control over it. But I think the thing that this country really ought to start doing is holding all the imports down. At least until these other countries are buying what we're exporting. It's kind of ridiculous. There's probably a ratio of twenty to one against us. And it's hurting us. Of course, labor is cheap over there, which in a way I guess is our own fault. Our unions are so goddamn powerful. It's gimme, gimme, gimme. But then again you read in the papers that the major car companies are making a billion and a half dollars' profit for their shareholders. Well, Jesus, I think the worker is entitled to some of that, too. So I don't really know where the answer lies. If I did, I would be fighting right alongside Jimmy Carter or somebody. But I'd like to see the imports stopped tomorrow.

You can't really blame the company. They're trying to sell cars. They've got obligations to their stockholders. And it's not like they say, "Well, I don't like this guy, so I'm gonna slow down car sales to lay him off." I don't think it's that at all. I do think they could hold down the prices on the cars. Just about any product they could probably hold the price down. Without making the huge, huge profits that they do. That would improve things. But I see a lot of people working for American Motors—well, I'm sure any other company or industry has it—you see a lot of foreign cars pull into the parking lots. Well, that's fine. Sure, they're economical. But so are a lot of American cars. It may not be as good a quality car, but it's a little less expensive too. But these people come in their BMWs or their Audis, even Volkswagens. They're cutting their own throats and mine while they're doing it. *That* I really am against. I just don't think that's right.

Just about any foreign product can be made as well in this country. It's probably a little more expensive, but they could hold down the costs. I say we should stop the imports, more than anything, and put our own people back to work. It's just a stupid vicious circle. When I'm laid off, I can't buy a new car. So nobody can make one for me, and that's two more people off work there. How many people off work for one car? As each one gets laid off, it just goes further and further down. That's why I feel that the imports are what's killing our country. More so than the high union wages. Because the profits are definitely there.

For now there's not much point in me looking for another job around here. All the decent-paying plants are either laying off or are at capacity. The places that are hiring want very skilled labor, and I'm unskilled. My unemployment check is $122 a week. Now that's not a hell of a lot of money. But if I take a job working forty hours and bring home only $140, I don't feel I'm gaining a damn thing. So the only thing that makes sense is to wait it out and hope to get back into AMC. You have to think awfully, awfully hard about leaving it for the simple reason that the money and the benefits are so good. I got a thirty-year plan, right? Sure, thirty years is a long time. But hell, you can retire and still be reasonably young and enjoy life and have a good income. Plus the fact that even if you're on the assembly line, doing one particular job, by the time you get in two or three years' seniority—under normal conditions, that is; the way things are now, who knows?—you can keep picking better jobs. And after ten or twelve years, or maybe fifteen, there's so many jobs that are so easy that it would be impossible to leave. So I think I would spend thirty years there.

I'd like to be back in business for myself. But the money's not there to go into it. I'm not saying it won't happen if circumstances are right. If I happen to come into some money or win a lottery or something. I don't feel that I'm a puppet or a robot to American Motors. I don't feel that way at all. But to be my own boss and do something I really, really enjoy. . . . As compared to not minding the factory. If American Motors were a job where I hated to get up in the morning, and Sunday night I'd say, "Oh, Jesus, tomorrow's Monday already," I wouldn't go. I'd work for half the money rather than do that. But I don't mind American Motors, and I don't mind getting up Monday morning and going to work. It's not like I can't wait until Monday morning gets here, either [laughs]. But I think anybody who's reasonably intelligent would much rather do things for themselves than for somebody else. Make money for themselves rather than the company.

How long do you think it'll be before you have to go to work?

Soon. Very soon.
NANCY: Yesterday. [They both laugh].

KATHY DRYSDALE

She grew up in Jackson, Tennessee, one of eight children in a poor family. "I got into the twelfth grade, lacking three months from my diploma, and I got in trouble. You know how young girls do when they're in school?" She dropped out, had the baby, and worked five years as a clerk-typist, then came north looking for "something more exciting." There was no office work, so she took the next best thing: the assembly line at American Motors Corporation. She lives with her two daughters, aged ten and eight, in a predominantly black neighborhood of Milwaukee.

I got hired in at American Motors in June '74. June 12, as a matter of fact. I would have been one of the lucky ones who are still working if I had gone in in February. A lot of people got hired in in February, but I didn't make it. So, after I got hired in, it was the regular thing. I guess they try you out to see if you really want to work. They put you in this unbelievable job, just to see if you can do it. They scare the heck out of you. I was on the line, and I had to get under the front of the car where the motor goes. I'd crawl under there with two guns. I had to take one and do some wiring, and then I had about seven screws to put in there. And I mean you had to do it like this, you know [*snaps fingers rapidly*]. Because the line would never stop. You had to be out of there within a minute. So I was really running. I'd wake up during the night almost crying and saying, "I know I can do it. I've got to do it because I got hired in. It's not going to be like this forever." That first week I was so afraid that I wasn't going to get the job. I was just frantic. Because I knew I had two little daughters, and I really had to learn the job or else get kicked out.

Finally I got that together after about a month and a half. Then later they transferred me to another section, into the inspection division. I really enjoyed that. The people were lively and everybody was pretty nice. It seemed as if the nights wouldn't just drag by.

But then came the talk about layoffs. People started coming around and saying, "Hey, how much time you have?" You say, "About two years." They say, "Hey, you're gonna get laid off." Well, I don't want to hear it, you know? It's just hearsay. But the people in the plant hear it from somebody, and they pass the word around. It's a rumor. And you get so tensed up. I learned one thing: Don't ever tell anybody you only have a year or a year and a half. 'Cause they'll tell you, "Hey, you're out, that's it." They don't wait until somebody else comes around and informs you properly. So I heard that for about two, three weeks straight. It was really beginning to upset me. Because I was thinking, "What am I going to do? I can't just sit at home." I've been working just about ever since I was thirteen years old. Now I'm twenty-seven, and sitting home with nothing to do? Some people would try and cheer you up. They'd say, "Well, they'll probably be hiring again after vacation." And I'd say, "Yeah, I got laid off once before for about two or three weeks, and they hired me back in." But I think people could see that downfall look on my face. It's like being kept in the dark because you're wondering if they're going to get you next. Lots of people have already been laid off, and you're on that border line. You've been there before, and they didn't get you. But you know all the time that they're gonna get you next. But you don't know when.

I was frightened. I didn't want to be laid off. And then there were those people with ten, fifteen, twenty years who were saying, "I wish they'd lay me off. I'm tired of working." Well, they don't really want that. I know it's a lie. Why come to work every day if you really want to be laid off that bad? Because a person with that much time can afford to take off. They can use up their casual days or anything. But when somebody reports to you and says, "You're going to be laid off indefinitely," then hey, you feel like you're out in the world all by yourself. You wonder what you're going to do. You've been out working, struggling, trying to get . . . and you can't get. And you think, "How am I gonna get it? What am I gonna do?" It really is something to think about, something to frighten you. So I always say don't ever let people tell you what they think when it never happened to them. Let it happen to them, and they'll realize. They say all those things—"I don't want to work"—well, quit your job, so I can get it! Because I want to work! I'm one of those determined people. I enjoy working. I mean, you've got to sweat a little, you got to give a little in order to receive. 'Cause these people ain't givin' away nothin'.

So one day—it was a Thursday; they usually inform you on a Thursday—here come the foreman and the steward. My steward had been telling me he didn't know exactly what they were gonna do. But that Thursday he came around and said, "We're gonna try and get you to work next week, but then you'll be laid off indefinitely." Oh, God. I said. "All right." And the next week I only worked one day, and that was it. That was during the week in March when the real big layoff came. A lot of people got kicked out.

It wasn't so bad at first, especially after my sub pay came through. I was getting $122 a week unemployment, plus sub pay. It came to about $170. That was pretty good. When I was working, I was taking home about $15 more. So I felt pretty secure when I was getting sub. But I still didn't like it. It's just the idea of sitting down. I'd rather work for what I receive. It's all right receiving it, and it's my money true enough; but yet and still, why sit down when I can be putting my body to some other use?

During the first few months I did a lot of sewing. I would do it just about every day. I was used to doing something, and I had nothing else to do. Actually it started before I got laid off. I had this outfit I had cut out for my oldest child. It had been lying around for about two years. When I switched from working nights at the plant to working days, I needed something to do in the evenings besides watch TV. So I started sewing on that outfit, and I finished it after a week. Then I got enthused about it after I quit working because I knew Easter was coming up and I couldn't afford to buy anything. So I said, "Well, heck. Why should I just sit around? I've got a sewing machine. I gotta pay for it. Might as well go on and fix something for the kids, and me as well." So I made our Easter outfits. And people noticed. They'd say, "Hey, that's really nice. Where did you get that from?" I'd say I made it. They'd ask me to make them something, and I'd say, "Well, there will be a slight fee, but I'll make it for you."

I'd start sometime around nine. I'd get up and get the kids off to school, and then I'd start. Watch TV and sew until about eleven. But after a while I started pulling away from it. I made two outfits for two fellows I know, and the last one took me about two weeks to finish. Whereas I should be able to make two outfits in a week. It seems as if I couldn't concentrate. You have to read the stuff on the pattern to make the outfit, right? I would read it, and I would understand it; but yet and still, I *wouldn't* understand it. I started seeing double, I guess [*laughs*]. I'd be sitting there so long, and if you do anything for a certain period of time, it starts getting next to you. So I'd just kind of close my eyes a little and rub my forehead and try again. That didn't seem to work. And I started getting nervous. My doctor asked me about it. You can probably tell just sitting here. I am getting really fidgety, and I think it's because sitting around the house has started to get next to me. So I'd leave the house just to get some air. That would make me feel better after a while, but when I came back in I wouldn't feel like going back to my sewing. Gradually I started pulling away from it. And it seems like now when I go in and try to start sewing, I don't have the patience to do it. I want to do it, but I don't have the patience.

It's like something is pulling me down. I can't understand it. I don't have any energy. Something just seems like it's taking over. As if my body was useless, and I can't do anything. Sometimes I don't even get up till about twelve. And I don't want to clean up, even though I can't stand to see things out of order. I have to make myself get up and do it. Sometimes I just sit around and look at the walls until they're caving in on me.

And I've been full of worries about money. I knew the sub pay was gonna run out sooner or later, so I was trying to pay everything up. It would have been all right if the sub pay lasted as long as unemployment, but it ran out last week. And when you know it's gonna run out, you still have to worry about how much you spend. Some people get a check and have nothing to pay out that week. They can go out and splurge a little, or they have maybe one bill to pay. But it's never that way with me. I have bills every week. And it's the little bills that worry you. Not the big ones because you know you gotta cope with them. It's the little bills that come in every once in a while. If it was just me, I wouldn't have much to worry about, but I have two kids. And they gotta have school clothes, school supplies, bikes, and they want to go places. . . . You can't help but worry about it.

I always try and add up my bills a month in advance. I keep a list, with everything I have to pay that month. That way you know, when the check comes in, you gotta pay this bill and that bill with it. I mark it off every week. I try and have enough to buy groceries after paying off the furniture, the rent, stuff like that. Sometimes I don't have enough money to give the kids an allowance. And sometimes I don't have enough to buy gas. Or I just have $1 or $2 left during the week if I want to buy something. So I sit and try to figure it out, and I worry so much. Just last night I was sitting up figuring, trying to go a month ahead. And I'm gonna have to stretch, scrimp, and scrape because now I'm down to $122 from $170. It makes a big difference. And I caught myself sitting there on the bed and staring. You know how your eyes get when you stare so much and sit so much? You can't see anything. Well, you can see, but you're not looking at anything. I noticed the clock. It was after 12:00 when I started. One time I looked and it was 1:01, and then I looked and it was 1:25, and then 1:45. I said, "Why should I sit here and worry about this when I don't really have to worry about it right now?" You shouldn't let things worry you before the time comes, but I do. How can I help it? Now I have nothing but $122 to cope with. It's gonna be kind of hard. I'm gonna try and cope with it, but I don't know how.

I have this girl friend. She doesn't have to go back because she's got just about everything she wants. Her old man is working at AMC. He works overtime. That's one of the things that kind of get next to me. How can they afford to let them work overtime, even though they have more seniority, when all of us are being laid off and can't work at all? So my friend tells me she don't want to go back. But I do. I look forward to that day. And I hope it's not more than two months of waiting. I think I can sweat it out for at least two more months. I don't really want to, and I don't look forward to it; but I have no other choice. I just hope they come up with something because five months of sitting at home is a long time. You think, "Half a year!" Because it will be half a year on the eighth of next month. And that's one heck of a long time to sit down and wait for a job to call you back. It's enough to kind of drive you nuts. But you try not to let it get next to you. You try and block it. Try and keep the faith.

LEO JOHNSON

In recent years he has been a college student (briefly), a housebuilder, lumberjack, record salesman, farmhand, and riverboat man. Now he is hitchhiking around the country to see old friends. We're talking in a backyard in Richmond, Indiana. His pack lies nearby; later he will shoulder it and head for home in Phoenix. The interview begins at 9:00 A.M., and by the time it is over he is drinking his third beer. He is twenty-nine.

The last job I had was for an explosives company. One of the largest in America. They deal in slurry explosives, which are used in open-pit copper mines and also in coal stripping. I quit in April. Been free since then [*laughs*].

I had a technical job, making the explosives. It's kind of the equivalent of making a cake. You follow a recipe. You have to get it right or else it doesn't work. It won't blow up unless you have everything right. It's fairly complex, but anyone who'd had any chemistry at all would be able to grasp it. You just have to be awake most of the time. If you start dreaming, then you're gonna foul something up, and the stuff won't explode, and if the company loses enough money they could get excited about it.

Did you like the work?

OK. That's a tough question. I like to play a lot more than I like to work. I like to work as long as I'm learning something. I think most people I know are that way. Everybody in the company was that way. They used to like it and now they're bored. Most of the people I worked with had been with the company ten years or so, and they were in a different situation than I am. I'm not married. I have no kids. I can be almost as irresponsible as I choose to be, whereas most of them couldn't. So while I was learning, the job was a lot of fun. I kept it about eight months. That was the longest job I've ever had. I always seem to get bored. You learn 90 percent of what you're going to learn from a job in a short period of time. So why keep doing it? Especially when they pay you chicken feed anyway. Out in the West, wages are not very high. I was making something like $4.50 an hour. I started bitching with them all the time about "Come on, I want more money. I want more money." They said, "We can't possibly give it to you," and then you read their profit statements in the newspaper, and they make $17 million. What do they mean, they can't give it to me?

So you catch on quick that you aren't gonna get it, and it becomes a joke. With me it became: How long should I stick? How much money do I want to save before I go? Meanwhile, I was negotiating with this guy from the company who wanted me to go to Pennsylvania. I wrote a letter at one point, telling him all my demands. First I wanted eight bucks an hour. I thought I'd put it high enough so that they wouldn't meet it [laughs]. Then there were certain questions on my expense account that I didn't want them to ask anymore. There were phone calls. and I wanted a certain number of plane tickets home. To my amazement he met them all. It was kind of flattering, but on the other hand I knew he needed somebody badly. He needed somebody he could trust. And I knew that as soon as I was no longer useful, they'd let me go.

So he met all the demands and said, "OK, here's the job we want you to do." They were having trouble with this mine in Pennsylvania. The equipment was always breaking down, so they weren't able to deliver explosives. The mine was pissed off. And I had to do something about it. Most of the guys who worked at that plant—there were eight of them—had worked for the company for ten years. I'd worked there for eight months. And this guy was gonna have me go in as an equipment maintenance troubleshooter, called in special to solve the problem. Now it's obvious that I know less about the equipment than those guys did. I hadn't been to the mine, but it was fairly clear to me that the reason the equipment was always breaking down is because the workers didn't give a fuck about fixing it.

At this point I was on leave from the company. I was in Los Angeles, and I was supposed to fly to Pittsburgh on a Tuesday. I was going to stop in Denver to do some business, so I called a friend there, and he said, "Listen, Bob Dylan and the Rolling Thunder Review are coming to Denver on Tuesday night and we got you a ticket in the front row if you want it." I had wanted to see Dylan all my life. So I called the guy in Pittsburgh and told him I'd be a day late. I flew to Colorado and saw Dylan. It was a great concert, and since I was back on expense account, I checked into the Holiday Inn. Talk about abysmal, man. There's nothing worse than a goddamn motel. That Holiday Inn seemed so fucking negative, and I thought about being out in Pennsylvania, and I said to myself. "I don't want to go back to that snake-pit company to while away my life." [Laughs.] So I sent them a telegram and said, "I'm sorry, due to new developments I'm not gonna be able to come there." And I didn't go. Instead, I started this tour.

When I left the company, I knew I was gonna have to go back to work pretty soon. It's always been that way when I quit. I've never been able to quit when I had a lot of money. Maybe I had $600, $1,000. How long does that last in today's world? Not very goddamn long. Especially if you tend to like to spend money, which I do. If I have a lot, I get off on going out to a really great restaurant and ordering their best wine and spending $100 on dinner. I can't do that very often, but I try not to let my lack of money stunt my tastes. Either get the best, or starve [laughs].

I figured on a two-week trip, but it's been more like two months. Met a lot of nice people. The American people are great. Really great. Very generous. But there was no work around here. I stayed for a while, ran out of money. Sold a tent. Went to Kentucky. I used to work on the riverboats there, the towboats on the Kentucky River. We would take barges of sand down the Ohio and up into central Kentucky. I checked on the boats and it looked as if I could get back on if I stuck around very long. But I wasn't really in the mood to stick around 'cause that was my second stop and I had at least three more friends I was committed to spending some time with. From there I went on to Baton Rouge. A friend of mine is a blacksmith there. Louisiana really struck me nice. I checked around for jobs on shrimp boats. I've never worked on the ocean, and I'd like to do that. I looked around and got some contacts, and if I went back there I could get on a shrimp boat. Fairly sure thing. Might take two weeks. Then I left Baton Rouge because I had promised to be in New York on the Fourth of July. Now I'm on my way back to Arizona, and then I'll probably look for work seriously.

Do you think a lot about where you're headed?

When I do, I get very depressed [laughs]. So I try not to, I guess. I try to be glad for the things I have right now. And I feel like I deserve a wonderful future, so maybe I'll have one. I just try to be as honest as I can. If I get so I don't like a job, I feel it's my responsibility to quit. Not to stick with it. I think too many people are security-oriented, where they get some rotten-tasting little slice of the pie and they figure that's what they better keep. I think that's real bullshit. If people would just quit more often when they got sick of what they're doing, that would mean you could always find work. There would be no problem [laughs].

I work for two reasons. One, for money. You gotta have money. Well, maybe you don't, you can read Ram Dass or something and reach the point where you don't need money anymore. You can be happy without it. I would like to reach that point. But I need money to do my hobbies, the things that bring me pleasure. I like to buy things for my friends. I like to go out for dinner or cook a nice meal. Nobody's giving that stuff away. I enjoy camping, so I need equipment. I need gas for my car. And I don't like to camp for the weekend; I like to camp for the winter. That

108

means you gotta work and save up a couple thousand bucks. And then I also work because you get to learn new stuff. That's the other reason.

So being out of work obviously doesn't bother you?

OK. It depends. I don't have a hell of a lot of control over how I feel at this particular time. Sometimes being out of work can really be depressing. It depends on whether I feel strong at the time or not. I felt real good on this trip. It hasn't bothered me. Everything's worked out nicely. But I know at other times, being out of work has been very depressing.

What makes the difference?

I don't know. It's very subtle. You'd have to ask Ram Dass, I guess [laughs]. I don't know. It's just that I don't feel worried about being broke right now. I haven't felt worried on this whole trip. When you start to worry about whether you're in trouble or not, then you're in trouble. Because my responsibility is to be as happy as I can. I think that's everybody's responsibility. So I try to stay free enough to do what I want. If I want to quit, I quit. If I feel like I need to go back to work and that money will make me happy, then I'll do that. If I feel pissed off enough about something to demonstrate about it, I'll do that. Life is a fragile thing. I feel like if I make too many plans about what my life is, it makes it dead all of a sudden. You gotta have enough faith to do what's right, right now.

On the other hand, if I could find a company that would treat me right, what I consider to be right, I would stay with them. If they would continue to give me opportunity to grow. If they wouldn't bullshit me about little picayune items. If I could get time off when I felt like I needed it. If they would pay me a reasonable wage. Then I would stay with them. I'd see no reason to leave. But very few companies can offer that. They're trying to make a profit. If they offer those kinds of opportunities to all their people, there's not gonna be any profit. It's gonna take all their resources to do that.

The problem with work is that you're usually working for some company where you have no say over what's going on. You're expected to just be a robot. Do this, do this, do this. You're not supposed to ask why. You can be building some kind of trash and you aren't supposed to care about what you're doing. The kind of work I've enjoyed most is helping a friend to build a house or fix his irrigation ditches. Something where I feel like I'm involved in it as a total person. Where I'm not building something without knowing why.

In the West, it's really pretty, right? Well, ten years ago it was a lot prettier. Now there are houses in a lot of places where there didn't used to be houses. This is really disturbing to almost everybody I know. It certainly is to me. Why are we using up the earth if all we're building is garbage? Making things to throw away, to keep the economy going. It's hard to get excited about working in order to do that. I feel like our economy's mindless. There's no plan behind it. And there are so many people. When you come east from Arizona, there's a traffic jam from Topeka on. Just an ungodly number of people. And they need things and want things. and they're gonna have those things. You may not want coal stripped in Montana. But by God, if they want coal, they're gonna strip that coal. There should be some kind of national planning that says, "These mountains are to be left alone. They're too pretty to dig up. And this particular product is garbage. We won't make any more of it." But it comes down to the same old problem. The guys who own everything will not allow that to happen. They want to pump oil until the last drop is gone, so they can sell every last drop. Then they'll worry about solar energy. They're gonna dig up every goddamn pound of coal in the whole world, even if there's another way to heat that's perfectly clean and rational.

So I think that maybe there has to be a bloody revolution 'cause they're not gonna let go of the things they own. They're not gonna let go of their political power just because it makes sense that they should. It's obvious they won't do that. But I'm afraid of a revolution, and I don't think the common people are organized enough to win one at this point. I think the working people are more afraid of some kind of dictatorship of fanatics than they are of the one we have right now, which is a kind of dictatorship of greed. At least in this one they can move around a little.

One of the beauties of America is that it's still pretty inefficient. You can still find a way to get what you want just because there's a lot of incompetence around. If the boss is an asshole, you can walk off with half the shop and there's nothing they can do about it. You can steal any outfit blind. But it's like guerrilla warfare when it would be much easier to just have a democracy in the first place. Why should you have to fight all the time to get by?

I'll tell you an interesting story. I have a friend who's an excellent mechanic on foreign cars, especially Volkswagens, Porsches, those kinds of German cars. He's a very good mechanic. Very generous. He used to work at a VW dealer as a mechanic, but he was forced to do lousy work. That was the dealership's policy. You know, get the car in, make it so it runs, but don't worry about the son of a bitch. Just get it out on the road and charge the bastard his money. Well, it went against his grain. But he needed money so he worked there anyway. He did the best job he was allowed to do, and in his spare time he would fix cars for all his friends. Wouldn't charge them anything. Finally he got enough pissed off at the VW place that he quit. He went on unemployment.

110

Built a little shop in the garage where he lives. And now, while he's on unemployment he fixes people's cars and does a much better job than the dealer ever did. So tell me what that means. He has to go on unemployment to reach a place where he can be productive. That's one of the paradoxes that you're faced with around here. The most competent people are held back all the time. The most generous people are held back all the time. As far as I can tell, all the people who are alive in any sense are held back most of the time. Unless they can somehow figure out a way to get around all the roadblocks.

DICK FRANCO

He is writing his first novel, a detective story. He lives with his wife, Leslie, an unemployed cellist, in a middle-class neighborhood on the outskirts of Boston. Both are twenty-five. The house is run-down, sparsely furnished. A copy of Madame Bovary *is on the dining table. A huge, hairy dog roams about. Seven months ago he and his wife quit jobs in Vermont, "when we had enough money saved," and transferred their unemployment claims to Massachusetts. "We came here for several reasons. The major one is that it's a good city for music. It's right behind New York and Chicago, and we didn't want to go to either one of those. The car wouldn't make the trip."*

Maybe my Protestant work ethic is getting to me. I always get the feeling that the people at the unemployment office think I'm a bum or something. Not that I should care, but I guess I do a little. It probably comes from my parents, who were real go-getters. They live on a farm, and there's a family on a hill around the corner that's on welfare. They've been on welfare for years. And my mother is a pretty incredible woman in terms of being vindictive and nasty and gossipy. She's constantly critical of these people because they're on welfare. That enters into everything else. The way they look, for example. Not the fact that they're dressed poorly, but the fact that they're fat. Those fat people on welfare. Those people with big noses on welfare. Those people with the big green car on welfare [*laughs*]. That's the kind of upbringing I had.

So I have the feeling that I should be doing anything other than drawing money from the government. Morally I believe a little bit in that. But rationally I realize that if I was to take a job as a janitor somewhere, it won't solve anything. I mean, if everybody who had a B.A. went and took jobs as janitors, there would still be as many unemployed people because the people who would have gotten the jobs as janitors wouldn't get them. I mean, Ronald Reagan is ridiculous. But people like my mother believe that anytime you want to go get a job you can go out and get one. A lot of people believe that. And it's true for me. I don't think there's been anytime in my life that I couldn't get a job within a week or two. Some kind of job. But that doesn't mean anything about the unemployment percentage. If everybody like me found jobs tomorrow, it might lower it by half a percent. But it wouldn't change the economics at all because that half percent is probably people who are in between jobs anyway, that are in flux at any given moment. Rationally I know that, but there's something there that says, "Wow, you should be out scrubbing sidewalks, kid." I'm dealing with it, though. I'd rather be doing what I'm doing now.

I get up late usually. I hate to get up early. I probably sleep till about ten. Then I get up and doddle around, and the guilt starts about 10:30. I feel terribly guilty till about noon or one and after I start feeling really bad, then I start writing so I won't feel guilty anymore. I try to discipline myself to a ten-to-four or nine-to-four schedule, but I can't start working that early. Every once in a while I do, and I feel just fantastic. I just feel great. If I do it two days in a row, I feel like I've been doing it for months, and I just feel remarkable. What I do quite often is stop in the afternoon and then in the evening go back and write a little more. It's a lot of hours some days. Some days it's almost no hours. I wish I worked harder at it. I feel like I've got time now, so I should be working at it harder.

I often think of the writing as an apology for drawing unemployment. I think, "Well, some people get grants." I always look at it as a grant. Except that I didn't win it. I didn't have to prove myself in order to get it, which doesn't really make it fair. But if the government's paying me to write my novel, I really don't mind. Whether the novel is good, bad, or indifferent, or whether I'm good or bad, doesn't even matter too much to me. We don't have the de' Medicis anymore to support artists, and I guess that's pretty much how I still look at myself. It's kind of a rationalization for writing and not getting anything for it. The idea that it takes ten years of writing before you write good novels. In a way I hope it isn't true, but it makes me feel all right when I read over something that's terrible. Still, I don't know that the people of the United States should be paying me to do it [laughs].

But if they weren't paying me, they'd probably be paying somebody else to do nothing. Maybe I'm actually being an altruist. I'm sitting here trying to live on these few measly crumbs that they throw me, and I'm giving somebody else a chance to work as a janitor while I work on my novel. I could look at it that way. I guess that's pretty ludicrous, but I could look at it that way.

Really, the only way you can deal with drawing unemployment while you're working in the arts is to rationalize some framework. And part of my intellectual framework is that I don't feel that bad about being one of the eight or nine million unemployed. One of the reasons I don't feel bad about it is because I'm doing something I think is worthwhile. In fact, I think it's infinitely more worthwhile than building Chevy Vegas. Now I'm going to get outraged and philosophical and talk about how nonsensical it is to go out and work at all. Because what people are doing is making stuff like cars that people *don't* need. I like cars. I'm a car nut. But my car is a 1968, and a lot of people's cars could be 1952s—mine could, too—if they were still drivable, and there's no reason why they shouldn't be. But I know it wouldn't work that way. Then there would suddenly be all these people without work. Not that there wouldn't still be enough food, and lumber to build houses, and everything else. There's no reason for everyone in this country to work eight hours a day. There's no reason for me to do it or for anybody else to do it. But that's the way it's gonna stay. I don't think there's gonna be any massive social upheaval, and people are gonna say, "Come on, we only need to be working five hours a day to make what we need." I wonder how many hours a day it would actually boil down to.

Sometimes I think it's hysterically funny. The whole situation. That there should be any question about any indivudal drawing unemployment when there's nine million people unemployed and there's no jobs for them. The whole fact that Vermont would even care where you're looking for a job, that they would make you write it on a form. Of course, I don't think they really do care. The only people that care are the taxpayers. Especially if a good Republican legislator can get up and make a lot of noise about people quitting their jobs. They never get it through their heads that when somebody quits a job, somebody else gets it.

I went through a socialist period. I don't know if that would work any better. On one level I certainly feel it would have to, despite the fact that someone said the purpose of communism isn't to make the poor richer, it's to make the rich poorer. I think some Czech said that. But I don't really give a damn. In my situation I can't relate to socialism, even a very loose kind of socialism. I can't really imagine what it would be like, a situation where everybody is guaranteed employment. Do we wind up in the same boat we're in now, where everybody has meaningless employment? What are we doing, providing nine million more meaningless jobs? Of course, it's still better than having nine million people without any money. It's pretty meaningless not to have money, too.

I guess I'm just scared because I'm kind of an elitist. I feel like I belong in some sort of special place, and I don't want to be leveled out. I feel like I'm gonna make good money at some point. There was a time when I didn't think that. I was going to be a starving artist. I was gonna write what I wanted to write. Heavy things that didn't have a plot. Then it was all right for me to think that artists should be subsidized. They should get six grand a year or some little pittance to piddle around and write heavy tomes. Now I'm starting to get the idea that maybe I'll be able to make a living, and I don't want anybody controlling my income. I want to make fifty grand and buy a sailboat.

ANNA MONTES

She is a Chilean in her mid-thirties, soft-voiced and gentle but with a quick-flashing temper. She has worked in day care centers since 1972, when she came to the United States. Though she left Chile before the military junta overthrew Salvador Allende, her leftist politics now make it dangerous for her to return. She lives with her son in a small apartment on the Lower East Side of New York City and does volunteer work—"more than full time"—with a group of exiles who are compiling a list of political prisoners in Chile, "especially the nonrecognized ones."

I lost my job last December, when New York City had the bright idea of closing its day care centers. People kept telling me the centers were going to be closed, but I didn't think it was true. It seemed inconceivable. For example, where I worked on the Lower East Side they desperately need a day care center. I don't know if you've seen those areas, but it's as if they'd been bombarded. All the buildings are destroyed. The children play in the ruins and the garbage. Most of the parents are drug addicts or alcoholics. The children have no protection, no one to look after them. The lives are actually in danger. The apartments are tiny, full of rats and cockroaches. . . . So it's sad enough as it is. I thought that given the situation, surely they wouldn't close this day care center. How could they close it? Imagine [*laughs*]!

Well, in November they told us it was going to be closed. People started to organize. There were demonstrations and protests. The police arrested some people, put them in jail, clubbed them. . . . I was in all the demonstrations except the one where they arrested people. I can't remember what I was doing that day. Anyway, the people from the city agency started to negotiate with us. They said maybe they'd let the center stay open until June, and then maybe they could prolong it even a few months after that. But those people are such hypocrites and liars. Every time there was a meeting they talked about how much they cared for the children and how worried they were. You soon found out that their worry was a complete lie. For example, if a lamp in the center broke, they might say, "This room can't be open today because there might be a short circuit and the children will touch it and get electrocuted." All you had to do was unplug the lamp and nothing would happen. But they were always inventing pretexts like that to close the center. They would close it for a day or two, and meanwhile the parents couldn't go to work, or they had to let the children wander around alone. And there was much more risk to the children in that neighborhood than in a room with a faulty fixture. But still, I thought that because of the political pressure the center would stay open. It didn't happen that way. Time passed, and we kept negotiating, and then suddenly, boom, they shut us down.

When I lost the job I wasn't so much depressed as worried. I knew I had unemployment, which would allow me to live for a year, more or less. But I had friends who had already lost their jobs in day care and who hadn't found new work. I had another friend who's a secretary, and she couldn't find work either. And when I heard that the city was planning to close eighty more day care centers, I knew there was no chance at all of getting day care work. I said to myself, "OK, I'll have to find work in something else."

There don't seem to be a lot of possibilities, because I don't have experience in anything but day care. I'm not much attracted by the idea of working in a store. I don't want to be a waitress. I don't have a profession. The other day someone told me that women who work in bars make a lot of money [laughs]. But with my political ideas I can't see myself working in some bar, trying to get men drunk.

I think the best possibility for me is to work as a nursemaid. Because in this country there are so many people with so much money—rich people who want nursemaids for their kids. I called an agency, and so far I've gone out to about twenty interviews. Of those twenty there was only one that I could have gotten that suited me. But just at that time came the elevator operator's strike, which looked as if it would last a long time, so the lady told me I might as well keep looking.

It's an amazing process. First you call the agency. They give you some names, and you call on the phone. Then the questions start. If you pass the telephone exam, you go for an interview at the house. You go in, and you have to sit down for tea or coffee. And then it's like they're taking your confession. I swear, if I were looking for a job as president of the Chase Manhattan Bank, they wouldn't ask me so many questions. First, of course, they want to know what country I'm from. Then what experience I've had. How much they paid me. Why I left. What I did with the kids. If I smoke, if I drink. Whether I go out. What they want you to do, what they don't want you to do. The hours of the job. On and on.

Of course, whenever I go, I try to look as square as possible. I always wear a dress. I put on the best clothes I have—and well ironed, too [laughs]. I want them to think I'm very square. And from what the agency tells me, I've made a good impression on most of them. I don't really know why. I have a feeling that there's a racial thing mixed up in there somewhere. Lots of women who go for these jobs are black women, and some rich people don't want their kids to be in such direct contact with a black. Heaven forbid the child should learn that blacks are people just like them.

Frankly, if I take a job like that, I don't know how long I'm going to last. I don't have the kind of character that will stand for people pushing me around very much. I have no patience with people who bother me about little things. Sometimes I'm immediately aware that I couldn't work for the person. But by that time I'm already there, and I have to go on with the whole show. For example, I went to one interview with a woman who had a two-year-old daughter. Listen to this. She had a doorman who opened the door. She had a cook. She had another woman who took care of her other kids. She was about forty-five years old, and you know how old her husband was? Seventy-five [laughs]. She was offering $200 a week. That's good money. But right away I knew that if it was $500, I wouldn't do it. First of all, I saw that the other nursemaid had to go trailing around after the kids every second. It was incredible. And she was completely dependent on the mother. So I told the woman that if I took the job, I would want to make my own decisions about the little girl—whether I took her out, when I put her to bed. I didn't want to be in the position of telling her no, and then her mother would say yes. Well, I don't know how the woman really reacted to that. She said to me that of course I was right, of course. But if she saw someone being mean to her daughter, she would have to intervene.

I would never work for someone I didn't like. Some people don't understand that. But I couldn't do it. I've never worked directly for a rich person before, and I don't know how they're going to treat me. But if they insist on making me feel very subordinate, I'm not going to like it. Some of them look at you, and you can see them thinking, "This person is my employee." Then they treat you that way. So you look for someone who's more human, who treats you like a person. Not really like a friend, but . . . more kindly. A few of them are like that. They're different. When you're talking with them, you feel like it could be with a friend. So that's what I'm looking for. Someone like that. Since I'm still getting unemployment, I don't have any reason to take a job until I find the right person.

Are you very worried about money?

Well, I don't know. Sometimes I feel that nothing worries me anymore. I always live with the knowledge of what happened in Chile and what's going on there now. So I say to myself, "Jesus, in Chile people really have no way out. There's no solution to their problems." Whereas here I may not have any money for the moment, but I can always find something that will support me. Even if I have to do something I hate, like working in a bar. I know I'll find something, so I don't worry. In fact, I've even started sending money to my family in Chile. They aren't rich, but they were never poor either. Now everybody's destitute there. It's funny: What the Allende government couldn't do in three years—get everyone to the same level—the junta did in six months. Now you're either the son of a bourgeois with huge investments, or you're poor. People in Chile are happy if they think they're going to have enough to eat *today*. They don't even think about tomorrow. I've never had to send my family money before. So the only thing that bothers me about not working is that I'd like to be able to send more.

One thing that's absolutely incomprehensible to me is that some people feel ashamed of losing their jobs. I find that absurd. I just can't understand it. It's the same as if you felt ashamed of wearing glasses because you're nearsighted. It's not your fault. And it's not our fault if there's an economic crisis here—whether it's artificial or not—that affects people who have to work. So I don't feel any shame. I think it's this country that's shameful. I think it's shameful that when I was walking along Thirty-fourth Street last night, I saw at least ten beggars sleeping in the street. Ten! Ten! I swear to you. They were sleeping outside the big stores with their huge neon signs and advertisements in beautiful color. That's what I think is a shame. It's something I'd like to film, so I could have proof of it and show it to people. Because a lot of people in Latin America are fooled. They don't realize how things are. They see American movies about a lovely *gringo* couple, who live in a beautiful house with a garden and the latest model car and two beautiful kids. . . . Everything's perfect. They don't realize that it's a lie. And the ones who haven't been here don't believe you when you tell them. They say, "You're just a communist." It's those things that are shameful. Nor am I ashamed of taking unemployment money. I think every little thing I can get out of these *gringos* is well taken [*laughs*]. I ask myself, "How many millions and millions and millions of dollars have they robbed from

117

Chile?" The little bit I get from unemployment, or that I might get from welfare, is nothing. Over the years they've probably taken twenty times the entire value of Chile. Not to mention Argentina, Bolivia, Ecuador, Peru.... So I don't have any prejudices about being unemployed. That's just one more thing they've put in your mind to make you think the way they want.

BILLY WONG

He has worked in construction for fourteen years, specializing in floor work: tile, carpet, parquet, linoleum. He is a slight man with blurred Oriental features: half Chinese, half Irish. He grew up in San Francisco's Chinatown and now lives with his wife and three children in a white working-class area of Redwood City. In the apartment he shows off the profusion of plants and two large tanks of tropical fish. He would like to find a job in horticulture, "so I can watch things grow."

On the day we talk, 24 percent of Bay Area construction workers are unemployed, and the percentage is even higher in his carpenters' union local.

I haven't worked a full week for six months. Maybe two days, three days. And I haven't worked at all the last seven weeks, not one day. There's no work. I talked to the business agent of the local, and there's nothing.

What happened when you got laid off the last time?

The job was finished. Every job you go to, you stay on till it finishes. Being that we're floor layers and we have to do a certain amount every day, we only last in the building maybe two weeks, a twenty-story building. Two, three weeks, and we wrap it right up. So then you call in to the local and put your name on a list, and they put it on a bulletin board, and you can walk into the union hall and see your name on the list. They rotate the jobs around. If you have two days, they don't count it. You stay on the same spot on the list. Only time it changes is if you have three days; then you go back down to the end. Or if somebody's losing their house, they can't meet their mortgage, then they jump the list. Usually you're not off work long enough to get unemployment. You're off a week, two weeks. But I'm on unemployment this time. Ninety-five dollars.

I get moody, very moody. It feels terrible. You have no ambition to do anything. You're disgusted. The only thing that's keeping me together is that my wife works. She works at a drugstore. So we make ends meet.

Sometimes I say to myself that I should have gone into something else that has more security. Because construction, when it's busy it's secure, but when it's not busy it's not secure. In a year you might work for maybe thirteen, fourteen bosses. It's crazy, y'know, 'cause you get laid off constantly. And you make big money but your expenses are really high. Because you travel from job to job. I worked as far away as Santa Cruz, it cost me $50 a week easy, plus union dues, plus telephone calls to the union hall. So by the week you don't really make that much. I mean, they bullshit you—oh, how good you're making. Years ago I used to work on overtime jobs, but the last five years I haven't seen an over-time job. So I make $14,000 or $15,000. A couple of years ago I went up to about $20,000, but you have to have the breaks, fall into it right. If you don't fall into jobs right, you make crap.

And the insecurity. It makes you feel bad in a way but good in another way, because I can put up with it, where if somebody else is working steady and gets laid off, it's a big drastic thing. I can always jump back because it's not steady. You can always jump in and out. So you get used to being laid off. At the beginning, when I first started in the trade, it bothered me very bad, but now when I'm into it, it doesn't bother me. It's just a crazy business, very cutthroat. All the bad points of a human being come out in construction. Because you're competing constantly. Everyone is competing. Not only the bosses are competing, but each man is competing down the line, right on the job. Looking for security. They got their hope that they'll have a secure job. Nail another guy. This is the way it goes. It's a rat race. You always get somebody doing tricks. That's why I dislike the business very much.

Have you looked for other work?

Yeah, I'm trying to get something in horticulture. I want to put in an application at the Arboretum. I called up a friend who works there, but he's getting laid off. This week or next week. So, wow—I feel pretty crummy going in there with an application and them getting laid off. I went to a couple of other jobs. The pay is crazy. I was asking about the starting pay, and it's like $140. By the time they take taxes out you bring home $95. On unemployment, doing nothing, you collect $95. And most of the jobs are around that price. So like, wow. Just very bad. But even if the money was large, I'd rather work for the Arboretum because I really enjoy it. I don't care if I make under $95. I enjoy it.

Y'know, it's very hard to find something to work at that you like. I think a lot of people really bullshit themselves. I don't know, maybe their expectations on life are very little. It's hard to understand. I got friends that love construction. I mean, how could you love that friggin' trade? You crawl around like a roach on your knees; you get arthritis in the spine, arthritis in the shoulders. I got bursitis in the knee. . . . And I'm supposed to love this job? 'Cause you're working seven hours crawling around on your knees. And you're constantly moving; you can't stop. How could you like it? There's gotta be a better way. I mean, you're not a fucking machine. But you have to do that in order to compete against the next guy.

I had one offer to work under scale off the books. They were going to pay me $300 off the books. But I couldn't because my benefits are running out. With the union you get $15 and change an hour. But you only see $10.45 of it—55 cents is for vacation and the rest cash. And the other $5 is for fringes. The boss pays into the union to cover your medical, pension, and everything else. And you're supposed to have about 450 hours a year. If you don't have it, you can't be covered. You got to keep that going. If you're working off the books, you can't keep nothing going. And even with fringes taken out, we're supposed to bring home $400 and change. At $300 he's making a lot of money off me. But yet he still wants the same numbers, even though he's getting your body cheaper. It's like, wow—he wants your blood, too. But my wife wanted me to take it because it looked pretty good. We always lived good, and now at $95 a week you don't live so good. 'Cause I have a boat, we go away for the weekends, we go hunting, fishing, boating—everything. To go away and do these things costs money. And $300 off the books, that's money. Plus what she makes, we're living pretty good again. But I can't do it. It's like cutting off my nose to spite my face. Because I work out of the hall, I'm a union man, and my benefits are running out.

So I stay home. My wife wants me to go fishing or hunting or do something because I get uptight. Not really angry. I try and calm down. I just feel uptight inside. She sees me, I'm all a bundle of nerves. Because I can't stay in the house during the week. I try to do things, get up and just take a walk or take the car and go for a ride. Just ride around. I feel terrible staying home. Some of my friends lay down in a bed and sleep all day. But I'd feel like life was passing me right by. I'd feel terrible, like it's a wasted day. At least I get out and talk to people, see them, it's not as bad. If you just sleep all day, wow. I park the car. Walk. I go window-shopping [laughs].That's what I've been doing! I just hang around like a friggin' bum. This bugs the shit out of me. I feel really bad. I meet my friends, we're all out of work, and we go for ride, bullshit, we go have coffee at somebody's house. We just chew up everything. The job, the world, everything. We get pissed at everybody. Together. Then, after you leave, you feel worse than when you went in. Because *everything* sucks, everything [*laughs*].

I don't know if the kids worry. I really don't know, because they're still getting theirs, y'know what I mean? They keep asking for things: I need shoes, I need this, I need a gown, my daughter's graduation, and my two little ones made their confirmation. . . . Wow. It's crazy. But they're kids, I guess. When I was a kid, I never worried about what was going on. But I worked, I never had to worry. Always worked part time, since I was twelve. So I never needed for nothing. I always kicked into the house, gave my mother money. So I never had to ask. But you try and make things better for your children. And I don't know if that's so good. You wonder if they appreciate it. They'll tell you to go and take a walk afterwards, when they get married. Another phase of life. It's crazy. You don't know whether you're shoveling shit against the tide or what. You just want to know, when do you count? When you're in the ground?

You don't know where you're gonna go, or when it's gonna end, or what's gonna happen. And you start looking at life like—very bad. You look back on the years and you say to yourself, "What did you accomplish?" Three kids, you raised them. But what did you do for yourself? Not a fucking thing. Just broke your ass and broke your ass to be in the same place where you started when you were a kid. I try not to think too much. I try very hard. 'Cause when you think a lot, you become very critical about everything.

And the president keeps bullshitting: "We've passed the bottom; we're coming up. He's fucked up, I think. He said that a couple of months ago, too. They don't know whether they're coming or going, but they figure they'll say a few good words, maybe they got some gullible people around. I think this whole fucking thing is a plan to fuck up the workingman, so they could have you by the balls and squeeze when they want. 'Cause they're making it real easy for everyone to get welfare and everything else. And what's unemployment now, $104? Too high! You get that kinda money, who wants to work? Start living off the government, right? So you start leaning on them, and then they got you by the balls. That's what it looks like to me. Too many things is too easy, and too many others that make for independence look too hard. Nixon started the ball rolling to wipe out the unions, and it's working. Little by little, it's working. What we're going to end up with is a socialist government, that's the only way I can see. When the government's paying your bills, you can't say too much to them. So many people on welfare, so many on unemployment, they raise this and that, and after a while they have all the workingmen on friggin' welfare and unemployment.

Then they run the show. If the government says, "Shit," you're going to turn that color. Don't it feel that way to you? It scares the shit out of me. I think it's a plan to fuck up the people of the United States. Millions of people living off the government, and that's not counting back east, they're worse than us. That's a lot of people.

It's funny, you get all kinds of theories, you don't know what to believe. But I mean the thing that worries you about it is you won't be an independent human being no more. You always want to be independent.

I don't think it's the union's fault that there's no work. All right, they have a tendency to get greedy from making too much money. But that's what comes from competition. Today everybody wants your blood. Everyplace you go, everyone is competing. Competition has become very great. A lot of times I wonder if everything collapsed, if it would be the same like in the Depression years ago. People were a lot closer then. Today nobody is nice to each other, everybody hates each other. There's no compassion. Nobody could give a fuck. They say, "Fuck you," and "Fuck it." Bad feelings all the time. Nobody couldn't care about a person he meets in the street, nobody can give a shit about what's happening, because they're dying in a shell by themselves. It's very bad. I know it wasn't that way when I was a kid. You could walk down the street and you felt a fucking glow in your whole body. Today you just keep going. And I don't know why it's changed so much. A lot of time I second-guess myself. I say, "Maybe it's me, maybe I'm fucked up." Then I say, "No way." 'Cause when I was younger, if you were in trouble, somebody would help you out; you didn't have to worry about it. Always somebody to pick you up. I wish it was back in them days.

Today it's like, wow. Competition. It stinks; it's what's fucked up this whole world. Y'know, it was good on the ballfield or something like that, but they brought it down to regular everyday living. A lot of people become animals. I'd like to withdraw from everybody, but you can't because you got to live with the wife and kids. So you have to jump on the train with everybody else. What I try to do is jump on the train a little bit and then jump off. I've been on and off so long I feel like a fucking yo-yo. To compete all the time, anything you do. You can't relax. You always gotta be on guard, somebody's trying to do you in. And it's gotten worse the last few years, or maybe—I say to myself—maybe it was always there, and I was too young to see it. But I really don't think it was there. Even when you talk to someone, they're competing with you in the conversation. It's like terrible, you never feel relaxed. Me and my friends, we all feel the same way. Everything has changed.

3

SCHEMES TO GET BY: "You Can't Live on Air, Right?"

The pinch of reduced income—or no income at all—affects nearly all jobless people. Few can support themselves on unemployment checks; others aren't eligible for benefits or have exhausted them and their savings, too. To meet the need, they invent innumerable survival schemes, ranging from the most common—the illegitimate claim for benefits—to mild forms of larceny, to esoteric small enterprises. Here are seven examples, legal and illegal, of how people get by.

PENNY BAXTER

She is an attractive black woman of twenty-seven, living with her twelve-year-old son in a city on the East Coast. She studies part time for her B.A. Eventually she would like to work in a social services program organization or a women's center. "When my unemployment runs out, I'll have to get a job, I guess. But I'm not really excited about getting into a profession and fighting my way up the ladder. I hope I don't have to get into that. The first job I accept after I get my degree would have to be at a bracket where I can live comfortably so I won't be pushed to do more, more, more. I see people get into that, and it's horrendous.

"Right now I read a lot and daydream about the million dollars somebody's gonna hand me someday. . . ."

I quit my job about three months ago. I was a secretary in the customer relations department of a big lumber company. I just got sick of it one day. It happened all at once. I couldn't take it anymore, and I said, "The hell with it." In the first place, I don't see myself as a secretary. I hate office work. It's a skill I picked up in high school before I knew I'd have a chance to go to college, so over the years I've sort of naturally fallen back on it. In the second place, I don't like to get up in the morning, and I had to be there at 8:00. Not at 8:05 or 8:02 either. Preferably 7:55. So that's a hassle. And there were no windows in my office. It took me three days to figure out why I felt so weird in there.

For the first couple of weeks I was bored. I just sat around the house. It was still cold, and I don't like cold weather. I was going to college at night, so that took up some time. That went right on into the warm weather. And then I started having a ball. Now I go to the beach as a regular thing, in my uniform: cutoffs and a halter top. I have a couple of friends who live by a place where there's a swimming pool and tennis courts. They've adopted a bunch of us, and we go by there just about every day. I play Frisbee and volleyball in the park. I'm a night person, so I sleep till about eleven in the morning and then stay up till three or four in the morning, dancing, playing music, playing cards, swimming, getting high, whatever comes along. Some unmentionables [*laughs*].

Are you on unemployment?

Of course. There was a penalty period because I quit my job, but then I started collecting. I earned that money, and they took it from me. This is a way to get it back. They make me play games about getting another job in order to get my checks. The whole thing is twisted. I mean, where's the guilt? My conscience isn't overworked on too many subjects.

I suppose I should also mention that I have another income that makes me worth about $1,000 a month. . . .

What's your other income?

I ain't telling [*laughs*]. You want to know why I'm so happy being unemployed and other people aren't right? Well, I just have an outside source.

Is it illegal?

No, it's not illegal. It's just befriending an old man, that's all. It's a job in itself, the way I look at it. He's old and he's rich and he's lonely. He's closing his life around him, letting his money build him a little cocoon. And he drinks, and now and then he runs down to take the treatment and get detoxed. He just wants somebody to call and come over and talk. And for my friendship, he pays me. What makes it really nice is that he's so old, you don't have to deal with the physical part. I just have to sit and talk with him, like I'm talking to you. I go and see him two or three times a week, and he gives me $100 a visit. Been doing it since April. That's what helped me decide to quit the job in May. I just fell into it, like poof! And I said, "Well, thank God or whoever is responsible for it."

His name is Carl. I met him through a friend of mine named Sal. One day at a club Sal introduced me to Carl. He was sober that night, and I talked to him. Later he told Sal, "She's really a nice person, she seems intelligent," and all that. I said, "What does he want? He can forget it." Because when you see an older white man in a black club, and when he starts talking about a nice-looking girl, you know immediately what he wants. But he didn't want what I thought he wanted. I'm glad I pursued it.

He's got a home right on the ocean. It's brand-new, with three bedrooms and a kitchen like a whole apartment and everything color-coded, wallpaper, carpeting. . . . It's really beautiful. And he's into a routine, and his routine is within his four walls, his restaurant, and his baseball team. He's really into baseball. And he's into this thing of liking a certain kind of treatment, so he only goes where he's known. He goes to one place for breakfast, lunch, and dinner. He does all his business dealings in the same place because that's where he's known. He has his laundry sent out to a certain place where they treat him right. Even his breakfast is a routine. He eats a soft-boiled egg with toast, no butter, every morning at 6:30.

He's the nicest person you'd ever want to meet, but all he does is sit.

Say we're sitting here, and there's the bay window. He looks out at the boat, but he never goes out on the damn boat! It's a beautiful boat, sleeps eight people. And he has his own private dock, his own private beach area, fishing tackle, everything you could want to have a ball. But he just sits there and looks at the boat. His big thing is eating his egg and measuring how much it rains. He has one of these water-depth things that they use to measure rainfall. It's like he says to himself, "I'm gonna ignore that things around me are changing because I have enough money to ignore it."

But in his loneliness he drinks something awful. If he starts drinking today, in two weeks he'll need to get dried out. He'll be stumbling around, completely out of it. It's a yearning in his mind. No matter how happy he says it makes him for me to come and see him, he still wants a drink. When I first met him, he'd just come back from the place he gets detoxed. He pays for all these services so it keeps him from feeling it, but he could be a bum on skid row in any town if he didn't have the money. 'Cause that's all his life is about. But he gives me $200 to drive him down there, and I get the car and all the credit cards that go with it. The only problem is that as soon as he wakes up the next morning, he's ready to come home, and he hasn't completely detoxed. His doctor just tells him, "Well, your liver's fine and circulation's fine. Didn't do too bad this time, Carl." 'Cause he's tired of hollering at him about it, and Carl's paying him well. Carl goes to this hospital because he gets treated the way he wants to be treated.

So I talk to him. He's lonely, damn it. He's just really, really lonely. Probably in his mind it's almost like a girl friend—boyfriend type thing. Minus sex, simply because he ain't able. And I think if he was, he'd have to find himself another girl friend, because he's—he's not old, sixty-three isn't old, but the alcohol has taken its toll. He doesn't have palsy, but it's like the shakes.

I talk about anything he asks me. My life, what I'm doing. See, since his life is so narrow, it doesn't have to be anything big. I can say, "My front-door lock is broken, and I called the landlord, and he's gonna come over and get it fixed," and that's interesting to him. Little tiny things that happen in the course of the day. If my tire is flat, then we figure out how to get it fixed. That's a big event to him. Usually I go in the afternoon, like at two. That's when Archie Bunker comes on. I've been watching Archie Bunker for damn near three months now. But that cheers him up; he likes to laugh at Archie Bunker. Sometimes we might get into heavier discussions of attitudes, mostly racial. He seems to deal with that a lot. Sometimes he'll come across with some really bigoted thoughts, and it just turns me off, and I have to say something. But I don't carry any of that too far, because people get set in their ways. No matter what it is, whatever you believe now you're gonna believe it even more strongly if you hold onto it for fifty years.

It's a job to me. A psych job more than anything else. He's living in a pretend world, especially about his drinking. He might say, "Penny, do you think I can have a drink?" I say, "No, if you don't need a drink you don't want to go through that again. Not so soon. Wait another month." Or maybe he'll call me. He calls just about every day. Since I live alone, there's no boyfriend hassle that he would know about, and whatever I do away from him he just shuts out. So it's a job. I'm going along with his pretense that this is it. He's saying, "Isn't it beautiful to just sit and look at the ocean?" And I'm thinking, "The ocean ain't changed in an hour."

Of course, getting paid makes me feel a little better about it. Because that's what you do at work, if it happens to be a job you don't like. You give them eight hours for two breaks, lunch and a paycheck [laughs].

How do you feel when you're with him?

Bored. In a word, bored. I don't know how long it's going to last or how long I can keep it up. That's why I'm making plans to go to work. Because who knows, he may die one day from all this alcohol. Anyway, he gets on my nerves. Like tomorrow, I know I've gotta go see him. I don't want to. I just don't want to. I want to get up when I want to get up and do what I want to do. I don't like the drive. I don't like any part of it. Plus he started drinking yesterday. He gets drunk fast, not dead drunk for the time being, but progressively drunk. His speech is slurred and his comprehension is off. It's like watching someone get sick and degenerate mentally before your eyes. I don't want to do that, and I don't want to take him down to the hospital. I don't care if it is worth $200. So I don't know how long I can keep it up. But I think I can hold out until I get a job.

MIKE GUNTHER

A year ago he quit his job as professor of history at a prestigious small college. He had worked there for twenty years. "The working conditions became more than I could bear. We had been having internal political difficulties for ages. I also wanted to change jobs. It's not that I didn't like teaching. As a matter of fact, teaching in the last five years was the most pleasurable of all my career. But I had been teaching for thirty years. Can you understand what it's like to be doing the same thing for all that time? It's like giving up a meal you've eaten for years. It's no great sacrifice to give up the chicken and potatoes, even though you still enjoy it."

He is a small man with clear blue eyes and a sharp-boned, angular face. He is careless in dress, careful in speech. We're sitting on the terrace of his house, set among rolling hills and fields.

At the time I quit, the dean of the college was a slick New Yorker, Dan Weinstein. Well, I thought I would be just as slick. I didn't send in a written resignation. I just went in to see him and told him that I couldn't stand it any longer and I was quitting. I said I had a whole bunch of reasons that I couldn't even talk about, but that I wanted and needed to stop. And I told him that if he liked me, he would like to help me out, I wished he would be thinking of ways to get me on unemployment. I said, "I could go berserk or throw bricks through windows or whatever the hell I would have to do to get you to fire me, you know. That's kind of silly, but I'd still like to get the unemployment."

Dan was a little reluctant about the whole thing, but he said he would talk to Carey Gregory, the dean of finance. Quite a while went by. Finally I called Carey and said, "Did Dan talk to you about it?" He said, "Yeah, he talked to me about it, and there's just no way we can do that, Mike." So that was it. I just put it aside. But then I discovered that it wasn't true at all. I was in town one day shopping. This was in November, six months or so after I stopped working. And I thought, "What the hell am I doing? I might as well go over there and see if I'm eligible." So I went to the unemployment office and talked to a guy behind the counter, and he said, "Oh, you don't have to be fired. You can quit. It's just a matter of going through an appeals court and a group decides whether you're eligible or not. You want to?" I said, "Sure." So I applied.

That's when Carey dug in his heels. He was trying to save money all along the line, and he wasn't gonna give it to me at all. So I went to see Dan Weinstein again. I said, "Come on, Dan, I don't know how much this is gonna cost the college, but you said you wanted to help me out. Carey Gregory is making it hard." Well, just about that time they were launching an enormous fund-raising drive, and they were being very successful. They raised $4 million in no time. So I guess Dan felt magnanimous. He said, "Oh, never mind, Mike, I'll tell Carey to put it through. Don't you worry." And he did put it through. I don't know how much it cost him.

And I still don't know about this quitting business. They never told me what the conditions are for getting unemployment if you quit. I got into a hassle down there even after Carey approved it. Somebody called me in and started talking to me about the discrepancies between the reasons I gave for my quitting and the reasons Carey gave. I said, "What did he say?" And she said, "He says they did away with the position." I said, "Oh, he did?" [Laughs.] I had learned enough by that time to keep my mouth shut. Then I dashed back to Carey and said, "Look, we've got to get our stories together here if you want me to get this thing. Tell them I quit for the reasons I gave." And that's what he must have done. In a couple of days I heard it went through.

Did you have any qualms about taking unemployment?

None. None whatever. Absolutely none. And there's a simple reason for that. When I first started to teach, man, this capitalistic system of ours really did fuck me over. I was getting $1,900 a year when I started. When I think of the years of eating organ meat and all the shit I put up with . . . years and years. The least they can do now is give me one year of unemployment [laughs]. No, I haven't the least qualm about it. Does anybody? I don't see how you could talk to the people at the unemployment office very long and have qualms. Who are you feeling qualms about? To whom do you owe this moral debt? To the American people? Certainly not to the administrators of the unemployment program. They're just a bunch of machines. They're hardly people. They don't have any relationship to you. Who do you have a relationship to, Jimmy Carter? Bert Lance? I don't know who the hell I should be feeling immoral about. Should I feel immoral about the people who are paying for it out of their taxes? Fuck that—for years and years and years I have been paying my taxes to people on unemployment. I never complained. Why should they suddenly complain about me? [Laughs.] Anyway, it's just peanuts.

I did feel some funny things in the beginning. The first thing that strikes you is how difficult it is to get the relationship straight between you and the people behind the counter. I'm not quite certain how they see their role. But I've learned that for the most part, the way they see it is that they've got a whole series of regulations. Things that tell them what to do. Things that tell them what to say. For example, somebody must tell them, "Never ask for evidence, and if it's offered to you, don't look at it." Somebody must tell them that because they don't give a damn if you can prove what you're telling them. So you get this feeling that you're dealing with automatons.

And they don't tell you anything. They don't tell you what the rules and regulations are. They never tell you any of that. They just ask you questions. And you soon come to see that if you give the most noncommittal answer possible to fish out what you're supposed to say, eventu-

130

ally they'll tell you. They don't want any trouble with you. I went to Florida last winter, right? I did check into some jobs at community colleges there, but mainly I spent my time fishing. So you go to Florida, and you goof off and have a two-week vacation. Now they know you've had a vacation. They're absolutely convinced of it. They've seen enough cases of people going down there for vacation. In a way I was even an exception because at least I checked on some jobs [laughs]. But they don't care. They want you to get that money. They just feed you the right answers. It's really a crazy experience you go through. You're talking to somebody who knows you are lying and is trying to help you lie—but without breaking any of these regulations that they have. So the people behind the counter don't feel as if what you're doing is anything immoral. They're encouraging you in your immorality, if that's what it is.

I'm also curious about the reaction of poor people toward the bureaucrats. Have they ever seen bureaucracy before, in the factories or wherever the hell else they'd come across it? I wonder, because this is my first experience with American bureaucracy. That's amazing, isn't it? Such innocence. I'm fifty-five years old, and this is the first time I come to see what a bureaucracy is like.

The most awful thing is that you're being dealt with through regulations. Nobody is looking at a personal case as if it could be personal. It's out of the question that one case could be one case and dealt with as a unique case. Absolutely out of the question. For example, you have to be classified in a certain job category so they can help you get a job. They give you a number for your job classification, and it goes down in your little booklet. And the way they classify you is to bring you downstairs to this office where you find all these people waiting. They're being classified. Finally you get an interview, and it consists of them asking you what it is that you've done in the past. You tell them. And whatever you've done is what you get classified for. They don't care what you *want* to do or what kind of jobs you're applying for now. I don't remember exactly how the conversation went, but I said to the man, "What is this for? Why am I being classified?" And he replied that they make efforts in some cases to get people jobs, or they try to match jobs with your qualifications so they can tell whether you should try for the job or not. Well, if that's the purpose, one part of me wanted them to get the classification right. I didn't want them to have me down for the wrong number. I didn't want to be a professor any more, even though I knew they were never going to find me a professor's job anyway. But I didn't protest too much. Because I could see that if you keep up with your personal story, it just fouls up the machinery that they have, and its going to slow you up. You're not going to get your damn money. You think about that. You don't want to be sent to more people to be interviewed more times until they get it straightened out. It's far, far easier to go along and get out of there faster. Particularly since I'm not gonna get a job through them anyway. I can't believe they could find me a job. Maybe if I was a drill press operator or something like that.

So that's your strategy. And theirs is not to tell you anything. Suddenly they say to you,"Well, you'll have to have an interview with Mr. So-and-so. If you sit in that chair, you'll be called. Go sit in the chair." Now the logical thing for me to do is say, "Who is Mr. So-and-so? Why am I being interviewed?" But no. I sit there, get called, go up to the desk. . . .That's how I found out I was being classified. I went up to the guy and he started asking me questions. He didn't tell me why. So finally I had to ask. I said, "What am I doing here?" But all the while what you're thinking is that you're a marginal case since you weren't fired, and maybe they're reconsidering your application. Maybe Carey screwed me up again [laughs].

Another thing that's absolutely screwy is the little booklet they give you. Every week you have to list three places where you applied for work. OK, you do that for a while. But then you realize they make a point of not looking at it. They just flick through it. I think they must look at the dates. But they don't want to see what you've written. I don't think anybody among those people has ever looked at one of those booklets. And nobody ever will. It gives you a weird feeling. Each week you write stuff down that nobody's gonna look at. Is that crazy? So you start making up places that you went for jobs because you know it doesn't matter. And then you start getting a tendency to write really insane things, just to shock them into paying attention to you. "Pay attention!" It's like the Willy Loman story. He wanted somebody to pay attention to him, not to act as if he wasn't there. If I were really hurting, and I didn't have anything to eat, and I had kids and so on, I think I would get very angry at that. Especially if I were looking for a job and the guy was classifying me and not paying any attention to what I was saying. I'd get really angry. It helped me envision 1984. It gave me my first insight into what that kind of state would be like, even though this was on a kind of silly level. I don't want to exaggerate the seriousness of it, but it tells me what it would be like if everybody treated you like that.

I think in Europe people are much more used to being dealt with as numbers or exactly the same as everybody else, not as a particular case. But I don't think that's the American way. There is something in me that wants to insist that I'm a person every time I'm down there. Also, being a professor, I'm used to being treated personally. We all think we're big shots, great celebrities. And one of the things we do if we're being mistreated is demand, God damn it, that you be dealt with as a single person. And you get it. You generally have enough clout to get it. So when you bump up against a bureaucracy, a real one, it's pretty awful.

It's only for about twenty minutes once every two weeks, so I can take it. But if I ever had to live that way, I'd go in there with a shotgun and shoot it off just to wake everybody up. Tell them, "Here I am!" What I wonder is if the other people I see down there feel the same way. Or if they're treated like that all the time. Like if they work in a big factory or something. Are they angry about not being dealt with as individuals? How angry are they? I wonder.

BOB ANDREAKIS

He is twenty-six, a college dropout living in a small city in Wisconsin. The apartment—half of a two-family house—belongs to his girl friend. Printed bedspreads from India hang on the walls; one corner of the room is littered with record albums: Joni Mitchell, The Eagles, Pink Floyd. He lies in a reclining chair as though talking to a psychiatrist. "I think I'm somewhat intelligent. I think I could be successful in some venture, but I refuse to budge this time around until I find something that's at least challenging to me. I'm not gonna compromise and take a job just for the sake of working. . . . I'm thinking about going into my own business. I think about it all the time, but I don't have capital. Everybody wants to do that, you know. I don't know what the statistics are, but 97, 98, maybe 99 percent of the people aren't happy with their jobs."

From last September until this May I worked at a Sears store. I was the automotive manager. I ran the department. And I put forth a good effort at first. But after a while I realized that it was too structured. I was running a department, which was what I wanted, something where I could call the shots. But it was too hierarchical. I realized I couldn't do anything major. You can't be a freethinker there. Everything I decided to do had to have five stamps of approval. So I got tired of it, bored with it. The hours were bad. And if you want to know the truth, I think the real thing that made me quit was tennis. I play in tournaments and made the state championships last summer. When the tournament season came, I wanted to change my hours so I could do that. The company was pretty flexible, but I found myself having to go to my boss a lot. I'd probably still be on the job if it was a forty-hour Monday-through-Friday job. But I didn't want to work weekends, and I didn't want to work so many holidays and other times that all my friends had off. So I said, "I've had it." I just quit and filed for unemployment.

I really blew it, too. Because the goal when you file for unemployment is to get it right away, and I had a plan in my mind which would allow me to get it. I read the law over really closely, and I came up with a plan. But I didn't do it because I'm really flighty. I think things up, and I get a lot of solutions to things in my head, or I'll do something that's creative, but then I'll drop it halfway through and move on. People say that in astrological terms I've got a lot of air in me. I'm an Aquarian. I get grand visions and I start out, I'm creative, and then I seem to drop it and go to something else.

Anyway, my plan was like this. I had to have a connection to do it, and I did. All I had to do—and I'm sure people are doing this, even though I haven't heard of it before. It's staring you right in the face if you've got the connections. I should have called Sears one day and said, "I'm quitting for a better job." Even if I had to work a few extra days, I would have. "I got a better job offer. I'm leaving the company." That would have gone down on my record in personnel. And I've got a friend who's got his own business. He was going to create a dummy job for me at a higher wage. I was going to work two weeks for him, and then he was going to lay me off. We figured it out. He would have had to pay roughly 3 percent into the general unemployment fund. It worked out to about $40 in taxes and unemployment. I was just gonna give it back to him and collect unemployment immediately because I was laid off. And Sears would have paid most of the unemployment. I'd have to pay my buddy $40 and I'd be sitting there with $100 a week all summer long. Which ain't too bad. Plus an extra $1,300 because I wouldn't have been penalized thirteen weeks for quitting.

But I didn't do it. I didn't get around to it for three or four weeks. Then I said, "Jesus Christ, I've been out of work for a while already. I'd better get down there and file." I hadn't talked to my friend and I wasn't even sure he would do it. I still could have worked it after I quit. All I had to do was tell the unemployment people that I got a better job. I was thinking of that plan right up to the point where I went down there and was standing in line. By that time it was too late. So I devised this other bizarre plan. I thought it could have worked. I thought I could pull it off. But it was certainly bizarre.

I was standing in this line, right? And I decided to come up with some story. There were about twelve people ahead of me, so I figured I've got about half an hour to think of one. I'm thinking, and I've got the booklet in my hand, skimming through it, trying to learn the law. I decide that the only way I'm going to get it right away is if I can show that they fired me and the firing was unjust. Now the way I quit was that I called on a Monday and said I wasn't gonna be in. OK, I didn't show up. Tuesday I called personnel again and said I was having personal problems. Didn't show up. I was thinking of quitting, but I didn't have the guts to go in there. Same thing Wednesday. This went on for three or four days, and then I just stopped calling. So I figured they had it on record that I did call in every day. And I never called and said, "I quit." After three or four days of calling, I just stopped showing up. Then about a week and a half later, when I got the guts to go in because I was broke and they had a check for me, I went in, and my job had been filled. It was understood from my side and the employer's side that I had quit and they had replaced me.

So I was standing there on the unemployment line, thinking, "If I could show that I didn't really want to quit or didn't have any intention of quitting, maybe I could get unemployment right away. I did call in sick, and when I came back my job was filled." So I concocted this story. It was bizarre. I made it bizarre on purpose so it wouldn't sound like your everyday cock-and-bull story. I pictured these claims examiners going, "This is too bizarre to be contrived. And if it's real, if it really happened to this guy, then his dismissal was unjust and we should give him benefits right away."

My story was this: I got off work on Sunday. I went to tennis practice. I took some paperwork home with me. This had to be done at Sears. Every other Monday I had to place orders for merchandise, and it took a little while. So after practice I went to a bar. I was sitting there with my friends and I mentioned that I was going to have to stay up late to get some paperwork done. And a friend of a friend offered me a head of speed to stay up. It turned out to be LSD, and I tripped my brains out for like three, four days. When I called in, I was incapable of working, but I did call in. They have records of me calling in.

I wrote all that down. And—oh, I forgot one other thing. I had even called my boss at his house, but he wasn't there. I talked to his wife and said to have him call me. And he didn't return the call. I thought that was even more evidence on my side. I called in but they went out and hired somebody else.

But the story wiped out. I'm telling you, when it looks like you quit, as far as they're concerned you quit. Unless the employer says, "I laid this guy off, and I laid him off for these reasons," then you quit. It's standard. So I filed and lost my determination. Then I filed for redetermination. I didn't hear anything. I went in again and again. They told me, "It hasn't been completed yet." Then one day—this is really bizarre—the girl goes, "You can wait right here, and they'll do your redetermination right now." I had pictured them taking all these redeterminations and going off with a couple of people, discussing them, maybe doing a little research. Horseshit. I said, "OK, I want it done right now." The lady took my papers and read my countercharge, that I called my boss because I was ill and he didn't return the call, and it seemed like they just replaced me. She goes, "Have a seat over there." She just typed it out: "Your redetermination is that your initial determination of a thirteen-week penalty is valid, and you have to serve that time." So I'm doing that at present.

It was funny how they reacted to the story. The people down at the unemployment office treat their job as something not very challenging. It's not stimulating work. It's monotonous, that's the best word to describe it. And I think their dealings with people are monotonous. You meet a large cross section of the populace at the unemployment office. All the way from the legitimate breadwinner with a family who's laid off legitimately to some bum who just doesn't want to work. I'm sure they take a lot of abuse because of the long lines and short tempers. So when you talk to the claims examiner, there's no big deal. They don't make anything big out of it. There's no emotion. There's no sympathy. There's no understanding. There's no relating. I'm sure there's a lot of distrust. I'm sure they know there's a lot of bullshit. And I guess my story didn't come off like I wanted it to. It's pretty hard to be sincere or sound credible with something like that. But I thought because of the outlandishness of it and the bizarre story that maybe I could pull it off.

FRANCISCO CIENFUEGOS

He stands all day outside an unemployment center in Houston, hanging around a curbside stand that sells tacos and spicy barbecued meat. The sidewalk is crowded with people waiting for their names to be called inside. Most of them are Latin; many speak little English. He helps them fill out unemployment forms.

He is tall, broad-shouldered. At sixty-two, he moves slowly but is still trim. He began his working life with ten years in coal mines. When the coal gave out, he learned the machinist's trade and has also worked on the docks, in construction, as a meat cutter and truck driver. He has little hope of ever working again. "I'm getting used to it. I'd like to be working, but now that I'm getting old I figure I'll just collect my social security. Heck, let somebody else have a job."

He shares a tiny house with his wife of many years. The children are grown up and gone. In his garage he has built a miniature machine

shop. "I fool around making fishing tackle—leaders and lures and stuff."
As he reminisces, it is sometimes hard to separate recent events from
those that happened years ago.

The last steady job I had was for this company that made all kinds of accessories for farm equipment. I went there as a machinist and I worked eight years for them. I was head machinist for them, and assistant foreman.

But in November of 1973 the plant was closed down completely. First they started laying people off. There was only six of us left of the whole bunch. We was cleaning up and fixing up everything, and then they sold it all and let us go. So I went to collect unemployment, and I collected the first claim. It was twenty-six weeks, and at that time you could only get three weeks' extension. So they gave me those, and then the lady asked me if I had worked during 1973, and I told her that I had made over $8,000. She said, "Well, you have another claim coming." So I made another claim. Altogether I got ninety-one weeks, and then that ran out. So I've been out of work now for about three years.

I started looking for a job right away, but I've got two things against me: my age and the wetbacks. All these companies around here have too many wetbacks working. All they want to pay is $2.00, $2.25 an hour. Even the big companies hire wetbacks. 'Cause the Anglo or the legal immigrant will demand a higher wage, whereas the wetback, if he gets smart, they'll fire him and he can't say nothing. There's ten or fifteen more behind him, so they fire him and get another one. See, a lot of the wetbacks have fake alien cards. There's a lot of fake cards around. The companies look at the card and say OK even though they know it's fake. Because you can tell by looking at it. It's like a dollar bill, it's got little lines that run up and down the side, and you can tell that the fake cards don't have it. The immigration department's got a special thing they put them under and they can see it right away. But if you call the immigration department and tell them some company is hiring wetbacks, 99 percent of the time they won't show up. I've done that a few times, and they say, "We'll go down and do something about it." But I go back to see if they did something, and they never do. I think it's a big racket. The big companies are paying off somebody. Senators, you know, and all them guys.

Then there's the companies that tell you you're too old. That makes a guy feel like hell, 'cause you're down already, being out of work. Some companies say, "Don't you think you'd do better collecting your old-age pension?" They tell you that right off. Some companies just say, "Sorry, ain't got no job for you."

After a while I just stopped looking so hard. Heck, I knew it was useless for me to keep going the way I was. I was getting my unemployment, and I used to spend around $15 or $16 on gas a week. Just looking for jobs. And that's not counting what the other guys used to give me. There was a couple of other guys, and they used to give me $6 or $7 a week. We'd use that for gas in my car and just keep going all over.

Now I spend most of my time down at the unemployment center. I go down there about 7:15, and I stay till about 2:30, 3:00. I help the guys down there fill out their forms. You know all those forms they got? Well, most of the people around here don't know how to fill them out. So I fill out the forms and tell them what to do when they get inside, what window to go to and all that. Then when they go in there, they already know what to do.

I started doing that way back in 1965. I was working for a company that moved away and left me out of a job. I went to claim my unemployment, and when I was filling out my papers over there, there was an old man outside and he was filling out forms for people. Real slow. He was an old man, real slow. So I was filling my forms out and there was a lady next to me. I filled mine out, and she said, "Will you fill mine out for me?" I said yes, and I filled them out for her. Then she said, "Here." I said, "What?" She says, "Fifty cents." I says no. She says, "Yes, yes, I got charged outside." So she gave me the 50 cents, and then another girl came over and then a guy, and I stayed there and filled out forms and I came out of there with about $8 [laughs]. They said, "Are you gonna be here tomorrow?" I said, "Be here tomorrow?" They said, "A bunch of girls are coming tomorrow. They need somebody to fill out papers." I said, "OK, I'll be here." So the next day I went down at 7:30, and the girls were there. I started filling the papers and I came out with $23 that day. So I started going every day and pretty soon people knew that I filled out papers, so I stayed there. I stayed there about nine months and then I went back to work.

Then when the farm equipment company closed, I was collecting unemployment again, and one day a guy came by and told me, "You used to fill out papers here before, didn't you?" I said yes. He said, "Fill mine out." I started filling his and then said, what the heck, I might as well start doing this. A lot of people that I knew before were coming back there, so I stayed around to help them out. I used to go out and look for jobs, and then I'd come back and fill out forms. But about two years ago everything went down. It was bad, so bad. It was slow at factories, machine shops, construction work, everything. There was hundreds and hundreds of people at the unemployment office. So I just stayed around there. I didn't go out and look for a job. There was no jobs. And now I just stay there most of the day, every day. I'd rather be working, but since I got nothing else to do, I go over there and help them out.

They give me a quarter or 50 cents, whatever they can afford. I go home with $7, $10, $12, $15 sometimes. It depends on how many people come around. Then sometimes you get people with special problems. One guy came in there and he had a whopper form. Jesus Christ, it was about thirteen pages, and they've got ten questions on every side. You've gotta answer all those questions and then fill out the form. Some guys with forms like that are pretty nice. They give you about $2. Other guys kid around, they throw you a quarter [laughs].

Did you see that hypo when you were there? That colored guy with the tie? Well, he's a hypo. Always on pills. He fills out forms for people and then tells them, "You owe me $1." But they can get you for that. That's soliciting. The way I do it, I tell them, "Whatever you want to give me." Whatever they want to give is OK. If they give a quarter, it's all right. I know this one girl who comes in all the time, and whenever I see her I run around the other way. I don't want nothing to do with her. She brought me a bunch of papers one time and gave me a dime. So every time I see her coming I always go the other way [laughs]. She's a nice girl, but. . . . I told her one day, I had about six customers, and I told her, "You see that guy over there?" She says yes. I says, "He fills papers, too. You go over there with him." She went over to that guy, the guy on the other corner. I said, "He's not busy right now." She went over there, and pretty soon the other guy comes over and says, "Hey, you know what?" I says, "What?" "That girl came over with papers, and I filled them out for her, and you know what she gave me?" I says, "Yeah, she gave you a dime." He says, "How did you know?" [Laughs].

AL SALVATORE

He lives in a new apartment building in the San Fernando Valley outside Los Angeles. On the Formica counter that serves as a dining table in his apartment are a set of scales and a large plastic bag of marijuana. Talk is punctuated by customers coming and going, each of whom stays long enough to smoke a sample. He is generous to a fault, even with people he hardly knows or doesn't like. Twice he calls the corner liquor store for delivery of a bottle of cold champagne. He is jovial and wryly funny; a sort of wide-eyed innocence makes him seem younger than his thirty-five years.

Not long after this interview, police raided his apartment. He now faces a long jail term for possession and sale of marijuana and cocaine.

The last job I had was in a film production company, making low-budget public relations films. I dealt with clients, selling them an idea for a film. Sometimes I would write a film. Then I'd produce and direct it. The clients were PR agencies, corporations, trade associations—things like that. And what I was trying to sell were what they call electronic press releases. They're like sponsored news films.

At first I loved the job. I saw it as a step up. I figured I would move into classier productions, with bigger budgets. Get into commercials. And the ultimate, at the end of the line, was my soul film [*laughs*]. *My* picture. So I planned to stay at the job for a couple of years, get some experience, get a reel together, and go to an ad agency to get a job as a producer.

Then business got very slow. There were a lot of cutbacks because of the economy, and the first thing to go is PR. Especially television and radio PR. It costs too much. What the hell does it cost to put out a printed press release? Nothing. But to make a little film might cost five grand, and that's a lot of money for a PR budget. So basically there was no business. I went one month without shooting anything. And I didn't get along with one of the partners. He was this real tight-assed, miserable shmuck that you had to fight every time you wanted to spend $10. He regarded me as an unnecessary expense because there really wasn't work for me. So he wanted me to sell, sell, sell, which I didn't dig. The tension kept building. Plus at that time I was hung up on this chick, and I came in drunk a couple of times, which didn't help. I mean, it was nothing unusual at this place. You'd go out to lunch and get loaded. But it was like the last straw, and they had to cut back, so this one partner said, "So long."

When it happened, I felt terrible. I felt shattered. Even though I hated the job at the end, I felt very insecure, very scared. It was almost like losing my identity 'cause I had been this guy who does such-and-such, but now I'm just ... well, who am I? And I felt the insecurity of not having that paycheck coming in every week. I got unemployment right away, but I knew I couldn't live on that. It would just pay the rent and the phone bill. It wouldn't take care of anything else. I already had a little something going on the side. I was dealing a little dope. Just a little sideline to bring in a few extra bucks. But I couldn't live on that either, so after a couple of weeks of being totally blown away, I put together a résumé, put together a reel of some of the films I had done, and started setting up appointments with people at advertising agencies.

The big problem was getting appointments with these people. If I saw one guy a week, I'd feel like I was doing good. Almost invariably it had to be through somebody I knew. That's the only way to get them to take the time. Then they'd listen and say, "We don't have any jobs right now." It was a bad time to be out of work. The economy wasn't exactly booming. All I kept hearing about was people getting fired. I've also got to admit I wasn't killing myself to get a job. Being rejected by that chick had really messed me up, so I was very miserable. I was doing a lot of partying, a lot of drinking, a lot of getting stoned. And I was dealing, trying to build that up into a full-time job.

How did you go about doing that?

Well, first I put the word out. I tried to contact people that were into more weight. Tried to get some bigger things going. And I got on the phone with a lot of people. You know, I encouraged them, if they knew anybody that was looking, to send them my way. Again, I wasn't killing myself. I wasn't getting up at the crack of dawn and getting on the telephone, nothing like that [laughs]. Let's see. . . . On a typical day, I'd wake up with a hangover [laughs]. A hangover and a hard-on. Have some coffee, maybe go out and get breakfast. This would be about ten o'clock, unless it was a real bad hangover. Then I'd make some phone calls for the dope thing. Make some phone calls for the job thing, trying to set up appointments to see somebody. Bop around all afternoon. That's about it.

How about a typical day now?

Not much different [laughs]. OK, it's ten in the morning, and the phone rings. I'm hung over. I answer it, and some guy says, "Hey, listen, I need a quarter pound right away. I'll be over in a half hour." I say OK. I get up and brush my teeth. I wait for this guy to come over, and I sell him a quarter pound and rap to him a little bit. Maybe try some stuff out. In that space of time a couple of people turn up, and I take care of business. Then I get dressed up and maybe go into LA. A lot of my customers are people who work at ad agencies: copywriters, technical people. I go down there, drop something off, and rap to them. Tell them I need a job, and ask who I should see here. Maybe they'll put a word in. I try and set things up, try and arrange for interviews. I'm there a lot. Trying to keep in touch with things. Then maybe I go see my supplier and pick up some more stuff. Pay him and come back home. Then in the evenings I go out unless I got stuck here doing some dealing. Go out, get drunk, get high, go to a party, whatever.

But lately it's been a problem because I've neglected business. I never was exactly busting my balls because I don't have that kind of motivation. I sort of had it a little bit in the beginning, when I thought I was gonna go out there and get a producer's job. But it became apparent right away that this was gonna take a long time. So I keep busy, but maybe I'm just spinning my wheels. I'm certainly not as industrious as I could be, that's for sure. I would say I was doing $300 a week in dope at one point, when I really had it built up. That's tax-free. Now it's dropped off to maybe $150, $200. It's hard to say because it goes in spurts. Some days you won't sell anything, and then the next day everybody . . . [laughs]. I don't keep any kind of written record.

What I've got is like a retail business here, you know. The only guys that make real killings in the dope business are the importers, guys that are dealing in really big weights. And the higher up you go that way, the more risk is involved. Still, I guess $300 a week steady, off the books, would be a lot of money. Except that I acquired a coke habit in the process [laughs]. See, that's the problem. As soon as I lost my job, my expenses went up like crazy. I got a phone service. I started going to a shrink [laughs]. I acquired a coke habit. It's crazy. But I had to have the phone service so I could look for work and for the dealing thing. My customers couldn't call me at the office anymore. I guess I had to have the shrink since I was in bad shape. And the coke thing . . . I don't know. I started cultivating it. I had done it before, and I had gone on little binges, you know, when I'd say to myself, "What am I doing spending all my money on this shit?" And I'd stay away from it for a time.

I don't know. I see myself now, as long as I can make the rent, take care of everything, and have some spending money, as being free in the sense of being an entrepreneur or a hustler. This is just one hustle. And I don't care if the hustle is legal, illegal, or what, I want to keep my fingers in all the pies. I'd still like to get back into film, but I have a certain fascination with being in the dope business. There's a certain connoisseurship. And there's a future there. Fortunes are gonna be made when they legalize it. There are certain regions, like the Bordeaux and the Burgundy regions of dope growing. I don't know if there's a future in it for me personally. I ain't no businessman. I don't know. Maybe. I'd like to keep in touch with it. If I had an opportunity to make a killing on something, and it was safe enough, I would certainly give it a try. But I don't see myself as working up to taking over this territory [laughs]. I just have a little retail business.

It's strange, my life these days. I don't feel guilty about being on unemployment. There's no stigma attached anymore. And it invites cheating. If they're gonna give you a certain amount of money that ain't enough, what are you gonna do? Unless you happen to have a lot of dough socked away or a benefactor or something, you're gonna figure out some way to make the rest of the bucks. But every day for me I confront—it's like looking in a mirror. Because I was looking for a job as a producer in an ad agency. And now I'm selling dope and trying to sell this friend's music to producers and ad agents. It's a funny kind of thing, because I almost see myself on the other side on the desk. That could be me. I dig the glamour of it, you know. Ad agents always have a lot of foxy chicks walking around. Everything's real swank [laughs]. I like that. But I also know that these guys are under tremendous pressure. There's always the ax behind them. Things get bad, they lose the account; there goes their job. They're working nine to five. If I feel like taking the day off, I take the day off. They can't do that.

Still, if somebody offered me a job as a producer tomorrow, I'd take it. I probably would. What I used to love about it was the film part. I love the medium. But I don't know. Right now all I can think about is making money, supporting my habit [laughs]. My God, I've lost all my ideals and ambition [laughs]!

GIORGIO RICUPERO

He is an electrical engineer, born and educated in Italy. In 1951 he came to the United States. "I had relatives in New York, and they said, 'Come over here to the paradise of America.' At first it was hard. I couldn't get work on certain projects because they required secrecy clearance. But in the 1950s they relaxed the requirements and I got my clearance. Slowly I built myself up. I worked in the East and the South and the Middle West and the West. Finally I went to an aircraft company and stayed there about eleven years. My last position was as advanced systems staff engineer, which was management already."

He is sixty, a small-boned, precise man with wispy white hair, wire-rim glasses, and a lingering Italian accent. He lives on Long Island. He has not worked as an engineer for seven years.

In 1969 came the big blow. The space program was running out, and there was not that much new research going on. The Vietnam War was coming to a close. There weren't enough jobs. The government didn't give enough money in contracts. This was a big blow we had in many of these aircraft companies. At my company in 1969 they let go almost three thousand, and then in 1970 another fifteen hundred left. Almost five thousand were let go in that period. The impact here was very, very big.

After getting laid off, the initial phase is very bad. You're very down. You think you're good for nothing. You feel a lot of resentment for the company. You think they could have done something to keep you, especially since you're in management already and you have a lot of contacts. But that's another thing. As soon as you are laid off, all of your friends—even your best friends—it appears that they want nothing to do with you anymore. There may be a feeling on their part that "If I get near this guy, maybe I am more or less obligated to do something for him." So they withdraw a little bit. Slowly, of course, you get them all back; but it's an initial phase, and it's a little bit difficult.

Then suddenly you recover a little bit and think, "What can I do?" You live on unemployment insurance, but that time goes fast. Then, of course, you have a lot of savings. What I did first, I got my savings and even some money I had put into the company, and I paid off all my debts. I was free of any kind of obligation. And my wife is a girl who takes things in hand pretty rapidly. She went out and found work. First she did some housework, which was fairly well paid at that time—$3 an hour or so. At least we made a living from that. And a few years later she got a job at a hospital as a nurse.

At first you spend a lot of time trying to get employment. You go and write a résumé. I sent away probably about 350 of those things. I gave up in the last years. I don't do it anymore. The answers all sound very nice. The wording is always the same. It says, "You certainly have wonderful experience and so many years in the field. But right now, for this particular field, we have no opening. We feel very sorry we can't offer you a job; but we'll keep your résumé on file, and you probably will hear within the next year." You never hear from them again.

So time goes by. I decided I'd have to do something on my own. I'm good at working with my hands. So my wife had an idea. She said, "Why don't you try to start your own business with the money we have? You're good at woodwork." We had an old spinning wheel which my wife brought from Italy, and she said, "Why don't you try to do something similar?" So I made one. I carved the legs and the wheel and did all the detail work. I made various types as working models, and we offered them to friends. Immediately they all sold out. At that time I offered them relatively low because wood was much cheaper then. I think the first ones were running about $90. There's a lot of work in them. In order to sell them, you have to lower the price of your labor very much. With some things that I make I'm working for about $1 an hour. That's the only way I can sell them, because there's a lot of competition from foreign countries like Hong Kong and Japan.

Next I started making toys. Wooden toys. I started off with a little locomotive and a tender and a flatcar and a caboose. I painted them all different colors. Now I make fifty different types of toys. I make all kinds of little horses, rocking horses, fire engines. I make them out of all kinds of wood. The cheaper ones out of pine, Douglas fir. A little more expensive ones from oak and maple and even cherry wood. Then some of the customers said, "You're always making things for boys. Why don't you make something for girls?'' That's when I started to make doll cradles and doll houses.

It's unlimited what you can do. One of the local school boards asked me to make some wheels for the kindergarten kids. Just little wheels that you turn down on a lathe. They gave me the first order for five hundred, and out of that order came a second one for fifteen hundred and a third for three thousand. For weeks we were sitting in my garage and turning out wheels. We were really wheeling around down there [laughs]. Anyhow, now we've got contacts in the schools, and I have orders from as far away as Albany.

I start working in the morning about 8:30 or 9:00, take a break for lunch and dinner, and sometimes work till 10:00 or 11:00. Not every day, of course. And I make about $1 an hour for my labor on most things. Sometimes I can charge a little more. I have to figure it out, to compare my work against what's available. For craftwork, like for spinning wheels and looms, I can charge a little more. Maybe $2 an hour or so, depending on the customer. I have to see how much money he has. My normal spinning wheels run about $160 to $180, and I can't go much above that because there's one offered in the Sears, Roebuck catalogue for $190. And sometimes their work is very good because it's imported and made out of very good wood, which I can't use because it's much more expensive in this country. Plus my overhead is high. You have to pay electricty and gas and machinery. Right now I do it in the garage. I have it full of equipment and machines. I've invested almost $3,000 in machinery. Saws, drill presses, lathes. So you need money. And basically I work alone. My boy helps a little bit. I need more help, but as soon as you hire somebody, then you get other problems. You have to pay unemployment insurance and disability insurance, and as soon as the state comes in, they want all kinds of taxes. As a matter of fact, right now, even with my little operation there it's really bothersome. Before you even sell anything, the state and the local government already want money. The city wants you to have a business license for $20, and you have to have a resale license, which costs another $20. Before you've even started, it's $20 here and $20 there. But we struggle along.

The first year we sold about $600 in merchandise; the second year, about $1,800, and the third year, about $3,000. So it's been picking up. But at the same time my taxes go up, and the price of materials, so the total amount is larger, but not the net profit. I would say $3,000 only brings me a net profit of maybe $800. That's for a year's work of maybe thirty hours a week. But it gives me satisfaction and some extra money, and there's the possibility of making a real business out of it. One of the limitations now, as I said, is money. For example, I'd like a larger place to work and some place to display what I make. I've gone to some of these little shopping centers, and for a display window about a foot wide they want $75 a month. For a little workroom I'd have to pay between $300 and $400 a month. There's just not enough money in the job to pay for that. So I stay in the garage. Fortunately I have ample work to do now, especially at Christmastime.

What I really want to do is move into making more scientific toys instead of the simple type I make now. One school board said they would like to have some scientific toys because if they buy through commercial companies, they have to pay a lot of money. Some of these little units they use to teach physics might cost the school $300 or $400. So I made some prototypes, and I can make some of these things for half the price. So the school is very happy, and I like to do that work. Another thing I've been doing with my son is developing a noise generator for model locomotives. That involves electronics. We take a transistor and operate it in a reverse polarity position, and it becomes a noise generator. It makes a sound like *shhhhhhhh*. Then we have a tiny device that makes it go *sh sh sh sh*, like a train. It's completely electronic, and you can build it into a locomotive. We also built a little ship with electronic control on the rudder. That's what I do to keep up with my field a little bit.

But I've pretty much given up hope of ever finding a job in electrical engineering. There comes a time when you realize you're losing contact. The progress in science and engineering goes so fast that unless you're constantly keeping up, you're losing sight of it. There's a lot of new things now which I vaguely know about, but particularly the ones in the military, the new systems that are classified, I have no way to even look at what they're doing. So I think the best bet for me is to have my own business. It's more rewarding. As a matter of fact, I think I'm more healthy since I'm not working. It was a difficult adjustment, and basically I feel bitter about it. I think it shouldn't be that way. But I have enough things to do that fill up my time. And as long as you work at something, no matter what it is, it keeps your thinking off those bad thoughts about your old problem.

ANDY DILLON

He is a climber, a would-be tycoon. "At the age of nine I had a job after school. Fifty cents an hour. Big money. I put myself through school. I've always, always had a job. If I didn't, I created something whereby I would make some sort of living or income off it." He is friendly but self-contained; he doesn't try to hide his depression, but neither does he seem vulnerable in any way. He tells his story of financial collapse in a sourly matter-of-fact tone while drinking Miller High Life from seven-ounce bottles.

Over the years I picked up a pretty good electronics and administration background, and I wound up working for the state government. I was with them until about six months ago. Then I resigned. I guess the reason I resigned was the pressure that I was under. It wasn't a normal forty hours a week. It got into fifty, fifty-five, sixty, sixty-five hours a week. I worked on lunch hour, in the evenings, and on holidays. The job was very demanding. And I got absolutely no additional pay or recognition. Sure, my supervisor might say, "You worked Thanksgiving Day, so take tomorrow off." Well, hell, everybody else gets paid for that day, and if they work that day, they get double time. Why shouldn't I get compensated for it? So I hit a point where I wasn't gonna tolerate it any longer, and I resigned to go into private business.

Actually I had been in private business for quite some time. I've always had an investment in something or other. But I guess my luck really turned on Easter Day of this year, when one of my places of business was broken into and burglarized to the tune of $19,000. So at this point I'm down to the nitty-gritty. When you bumped into me the other day, I was going down to the unemployment office. That's what I mean by nitty-gritty. 'Cause I realize $95 a week isn't gonna take care of my bills. Even more discouraging, they told me I couldn't draw it because I had voluntarily resigned my job. And according to state law, they're absolutely right. I can't draw it. So I've hit a point of desperation, you might say. I reapplied to get a job back with the government, and I'm eligible to be reinstated. I'm certain I'll get a job because I have an excellent working record and people with the administrative experience I have are hard to find. But when you apply for a government job, it takes months, so I just have to wait until they call me.

What was the business you had?

Well, I purchased a liquor store [*laughs*]. What happened was that a burglar broke into the store and took $19,000 cash money. See, the store cashed a tremendous amount of payroll checks every week. So I made arrangements with the bank to loan me about $50,000 each week. If you don't cash those checks, you can't do the volume of business that you need. And I had a triple alarm system. But the guy was a pro. He really knew what he was doing. He managed to jump the entry system and disarm the motion detection system. We didn't know he was in the store until the third alarm system went off when he opened the safe. He cracked it with a hammer and chisel, which I didn't know could be done so easily. He sifted through what was in the safe, got the cash, and made his getaway through the rear. Apparently nobody had enough sense to go around back to see if there was a hole in the wall or something.

That's really what put me out of private business. The cash was uninsured. I couldn't cover the bank loan. That put me in bad face with the bank, and I couldn't go there and borrow money on a weekly basis to cash checks with. They were afraid they'd get hooked with another loss, and you can't blame them. So then the business in the store began to fall off because I couldn't cash checks. That meant I couldn't cover the loss, and I was left with nothing to do but sell the store. I've got a buyer now. We're supposed to close the deal on Monday.

Sometimes a small incident like that happens, and you get yourself caught up in something it's difficult to get out of. Because there was a time when my financial statement reflected personal assets of $300,000 to $400,000. Today it's probably down to $15,000. All in a three-month period of time. The problem was that I had a lot of money tied up in real estate, in pieces of property with big mortgages. And sometimes you have to give something away in order to get out from having to pay the debt. To cite you an example, I had a piece of property that was worth $250,000. I paid $200,000 for it. I had a $50,000 equity in it. I couldn't meet the principal and interest payments, and I couldn't sell the property fast enough. So I ended up in a foreclosure, which means that I lost probably about $80,000.

There's only one word to describe how you feel when something like that happens: depression. Complete depression. Because it had taken me years of scraping and saving to acquire what I had acquired. I had built up trust with bankers, and that takes a long time to do. But it only took two or three months to lose it all. So you're very depressed. You're depressed to the point where you don't want to do anything, you don't want to see anybody, you don't want to be around people. You just want to sit and look out the window and say, "This couldn't happen to me." My medical friends tell me if it would've happened to most people, they probably would've taken a gun and gone and blown their brains out. But I don't look at it that way. I'm thirty-three years old. I made a lot of money. I've had a good time. I've lived a good life. And now I've lost practically everything I owned. So why destroy my life when perhaps in a year or two I'll be back on my feet and I can get into some other things and make some more money?

The worst period was during the months when I was trying to save it all from collapsing. There were days when I sat and figured all day with a pencil and paper, trying to reach some sort of solution to bail myself out. In the back of my head I knew that if I didn't reach some sort of solution, I'd be wiped out completely. And finally it just dawned on me that this was it. I might as well face facts: What I owned was slowly slipping away from me. I went through a lot of sleepless nights. I might lie down and doze off and sleep thirty minutes or an hour, perhaps even two, depending on how fatigued I was. And then I'd be up again, in the kitchen. I'd fix coffee or get a beer and drink that, just sitting there. I was trying to figure out some way, some means, some method that I could put it all together on a sensible basis and get myself out of it.

Then, after you've exhausted all your efforts to bail yourself out, the only other thing that you can possibly do is contact your creditors and say, "I've had some bad luck, and here is what I plan to do." They will not be unreasonable. I've never found one yet that will be unreasonable. They'll say, "Well, pay what you can when you can. Keep in touch, and let us know how things are going." This is where a lot of businessmen make their mistake. They just run off and leave those bills or run down and get their attorney and immediately file bankruptcy. When a person files bankruptcy in this state, it takes seven years to overcome it. They ruin their own selves by doing that. I'd rather tell my banker, "Look, I realize my payments are $2,000 a month. I'll pay you $500 a month, or $100 a month, or I'll pay interest only. Let's rework the loans." This gets the FDIC off his back and gives you some relief. And this is what I did.

But the thing that haunts you most of all is the depression. The thought of once having success and letting it slip through your fingers. The first thing you have to do is accept that you failed. That's difficult for a lot of people to do, to say to themselves, "I have goofed. I have failed. I have made a blunder of everything." Now this may not be your fault directly, but indirectly it is. Because it's your problem. You inherited it. But many people want to blame somebody else. I blamed the police department at first, because they failed to go around back and stop the guy from getting out of the building. Then I said, "No, that's not true because I was stupid to start with. I wasn't thinking clearly when I put all that money in a safe, thinking that a triple alarm system was going to prevent that burglary." So I finally accepted the fact that I had goofed. I had failed. It was my fault. I think once you've overcome that, then you can begin to deal with yourself mentally a lot better.

What are you living on?

Ah. Now we get to the point of desperation. Let's talk about desperation.

You can't live on air, right? And you can't live on love. A lot of people tried it and a lot of people failed. They found out that you just can't feed yourself off of love. So you gotta do something to generate some sort of income. But a lot of people just will not use their heads. If they would just stop and think a minute, and say, "Now, what sort of talent do I have that I can use to make some money with? To at least feed and clothe myself and keep a shelter over my head? I may not be able to pay my creditors, but at least I can provide the bare necessities." A lot of people are so caught up in panic that they fail to stop and think. Well, I thought about it and came up with something. And I've found myself recently dealing in stolen goods. It's not something I want to do, but I hit a point where I have to. I can't draw unemployment. I'm not generating enough money in the store at the moment to draw any kind of salary from it. I can't go back to work for the government right away. The jobs that I find in the papers are so low-paying that if I took the job, it wouldn't be worth my time and effort.

So you turn to something to provide an income until you hit a point where you can find a job that will pay you something you can live on. And as a result, I think I've ended up dealing with stolen goods. I can't swear that they're stolen because I don't know where they're coming from; however, I strongly suspect that they are. Strongly suspect [laughs]. I buy these things at very reduced prices, and I'm able to turn them over for probably twice, or a little better sometimes, what I paid for them. I never touch the stuff. I never see it. The guy calls me on the phone and says I've got X amount of this and X amount of that. I say, "How much do you want for it?" He tells me and we dicker about the price. We finally reach a price and I tell him where to deliver it. Then I collect the money and he gets his. That's what I'm living off of, and I'm just barely living. I'm not paying any of my bills. I'm just providing myself with bare necessities, a place to live and food.

A lot of people don't know this, but liquor stores for some reason attract people that deal illegal. I've had everything offered to me in that liquor store that you can think of. Everything from stolen office goods to meat products. You name it, and there'll be somebody at that store to let you know how much he's got and how much he wants for it. I don't know why, but every store experiences this. Well, for a good long time I just said, "No way am I going to be involved in anything like that because I feel it's stolen." They'll produce bills of sale to show you how they paid for it legitimately. So perhaps some of it's not stolen. However, I still believe it is. Because you can't buy a $200 CB radio for $25 in a CB store. You just can't do that. So I put these people off and I put them off, and now I hit a point where I have to have some sort of income. So I said, "Well, maybe it's not. Maybe some of it's not stolen."

I try to be very choosy about what I deal in. I won't deal in anything that I know is obviously illegal, like marijuana. I could sell five tons of marijuana in a week. The offers are out of this world. I can buy the darn stuff for anywhere between $75 and $100 a pound. And I could turn it and probably double or triple my money on it. But I won't do that. I just flat refuse to do it. But radios, stereos, TVs, meat products, grocery products, dry goods. . . . I try to scrutinize the guy that's selling it to me first of all. I want to know who he is and where he's coming from. I like to know a little something about him. And then I like to know where the product's coming from. Well, he won't always tell me that. He'll say it's surplus from a warehouse or fire-damaged stuff. And knowing as many people as I know across the Midwest, I can move that stuff pretty good. So I'll tell him I'll get a truck, or that he should have it at such-and-such a place and somebody will come by and pick it up with a truck. A lot of times I have to pay for shipping on it myself. Then I haul it over to Missouri, Arkansas, Iowa, Nebraska, sometimes Chicago. To people that deal in fire sales and merchandise of this sort. I make a little off of it. I don't make a great deal. What I'm mainly charging for is the point of contact.

It was a hard decision to come to when I decided to do it the first time. I said, "What if I buy this stuff and get it loaded and the cops drive up and say it's stolen?" I may have a bill of sale from the guy I bought it from, but there's no reason why they can't confiscate it and take it to use as evidence. But I said, "Well, I've gotta do something."

How do you check into the backgrounds of these guys that are selling the goods?

The first thing I do is ask him where he lives, and then I tell him I'll be by to see him. I'll go over and take a look at what he's living in, the environment he lives in. I find out where he's working, because that may be where he's getting his goods from. If he's a warehouseman or working for a truck line, he could be stealing the stuff. And I ask: Does he go to church? Where does he go to church? What are his social activities like? What does he like to do? Does he like to fish? Does he like to run with the women? Just by being around the person, you can tell things. I'm sure that in the two hours you've been here you probably figured out things about me that are very true. And maybe I've got a gift that I don't realize I have. A lot of people say, "You're a pretty good judge of character. You can usually figure out people when I can't." This may be true. Maybe I've got that gift. I don't know. But I can usually tell by being around a person. And I never, never judge a book by its cover. I never use first impressions to judge a person by. I like to be around them for a while. Because you may just be around that person on a day when he's not feeling good. Or you may be around on a day when he's feeling exceptionally good. Ninety percent of the rest of the time he's a real damn devil. So I like to be around people for a while, and then I go from there. I try to stay legitimate with whatever I do. I always make the guy produce a bill of sale or sign a bill of sale that says he sold this merchandise to me and he's willing to admit that he sold it to me.

I still think it's illegal. The only way I could prove it is to actually follow the guy to see where he's getting it from. So if it is illegal—and I know that it is—there's no way for me to say *absolutely* I know that it is. To be very frank with you, I have thought seriously about marijuana. And I don't feel guilty about that, because scientists haven't proved that it affects your mind or your body any more than cigarettes. Probably less. And the aftereffects are nowhere near like alcohol. So if our generation must have some sort of depressant, let it be marijuana. And I really have given that some thought. It's illegal. You and I both know that. I could make some really big money. I mean huge money. A great deal of money in a very, very short period of time. But I won't because it's illegal, and if I were to get caught, which I think would be rather doubtful, the consequences would be serious.

With the stuff I'm selling now, it's different. I never see the merchandise, and I never come in contact with it. All I'm doing, really, is saying I know a guy that'll buy it. And tacking a buck or two onto each item for my fee. I've been fairly careful, too. The business would really pick up if I let it. But I don't want to get that much involved. I certainly don't want the law to point their finger at me. And believe it or not, come April of next year, I'll report what I've received [*laughs*].

4

LOOKING FOR WORK:
"Just Give Me a Chance . . ."

For some people, looking for work is the most difficult part of unemployment. It can be bitterly frustrating, particularly if it goes on for many months, and the constant rejections can grind down the most durable self-esteem. In this chapter, people talk about the obstacles they face—high blood pressure, a college degree that's nothing but a hindrance, a family at home, or a fresh discharge from the Navy as a Vietnam veteran—and the more desperate measures they seize upon to get work.

PAT GRODOWSKI

He is a stocky young man, twenty-three, with an anchor tattooed on his forearm and close-cropped hair. He lives with a friend in a new building near the waterfront in San Francisco. The apartment is comfortable, with modern furniture, psychedelic posters on the wall, and a view of the port. "I want to stay here 'cause San Francisco isn't a rowdy town. I was born and raised in Detroit, and that's a rowdy town. This is mellow. The people out here are a lot friendlier."

When I was nineteen I joined the Navy. The way things were at home, it seemed like my best bet. When I joined they was takin' billets for Seabees. So I ended up goin' through three months in Marine boot camp, and then I got attached to a battalion of Seabees. I went over to Vietnam when it was just ending, in '74 and '75. We were there for six months, building a city for refugees. Then I was in the Philippines for a while. And then they sent me to NDRC, the Naval Drug Rehabilitation Center. They caught me getting high, so they sent me back.

I think I never should've been sent back, that's the truth. I was snorting heroin and smoking pot in Nam, but it was part of the whole situation. There was two or three thousand guys in my battalion, and I'd say out of those guys only two hundred were straight. I'm serious, man [laughs]. We had to 'cause we were afraid of getting shot. Afraid of dying, man. 'Cause you knew you were gonna die. Rockets was landing around us, and we could hear fighting. They was actually shelling the airport we was building in that city. So the reason we was addicted to drugs was because the situation over there was just so hectic. People say, "Well, that's not an excuse," but it is if you were over there. You had to keep looking over your shoulders. You didn't know if someone was gonna shoot you or not over there. People was crazy [laughs]. It was depression on your brain, man.

In the Navy's eyes I was addicted, but in mine I wasn't. An addict, he fires up every day, right? We was snortin' maybe every other day. But it was getting bad. I'd say if I would have been there another month, I would have been addicted. Anyway, after a while in the NDRC they let me out. Then they gave me an honorable discharge with all benefits.

When I got out, I thought I'd have a pretty easy time of finding a job because of my background. I had done electrician's work, and I had cooked here and there. I knew most things about waterway transportation because I got that in the Navy. So my first step when I got here was to find a job. Mostly I looked in the want ads for electrician work or waterways work.

Well, I'd say I've had interviews for about thirty or thirty-five jobs. No exaggeration, thirty-five jobs. All skilled labor. Most of 'em I had the qualifications for. But I didn't get a job. And the feeling I get is that it's because I was over in Nam. It just seems that nobody anymore wants to hire anybody in the service, man. Especially when they find out you were overseas. They say, "Where were you overseas?" You say, "Well, the Philippines and Vietnam." Once they hear Vietnam, that's it. Probably because they think, "Hey, he's just come back from Vietnam." And what do they read in the paper about the people who were in Vietnam? Either they're addicted or their brain is messed up from being there. So people don't want to have anything to do with you.

Here's what happens. I take an application and the first thing that's usually on it is military service. OK, you write down U.S. Navy, discharge such-and-such a date. Then it has "Veteran of Vietnam or Other." You have to write "Veteran Vietnam" because if you don't, they look and they're gonna see you lied and they won't hire you because you're lying. But once they see you've been in Nam, they ain't gonna take you because they don't trust you. That's the point I get from it all. They look at you and say, "Uh-huh, you were over there," and I say, "Yeah," and that's it. Mostly it's just a feeling I get because they all say, "OK, we'll get in touch with you in two or three days." But they never get in touch. It can't be because I was in the NDRC 'cause there's no way for them to find that out. The employer can check to see if I was in the armed forces, but the Privacy Act stops him from finding out what I did in the service. So it comes down to them giving somebody a chance, man. If he messes up, you let him go. But if he don't, and if he shows he's gonna work, let him stay. They don't do that. They don't do that. It's pretty bad.

Christ, I think I looked all over the city for work. I've been to the piers, to the suburbs, to downtown. Just can't find a job, man. Oh, you can find them, but if you're gonna work, you want to work at something you're gonna enjoy. There might be jobs cooking, or pumping gas. But I can't see doing that. It's pretty pathetic when you have to do something like that. I like working with my hands, like with wires. I dig working with wires. But nobody's gonna hire an electrician that just came out of the Navy. I tell them, "Give me a chance. Let me show you what I know, OK?" "Can't do that." "Why?" "It's against company policy." "OK." "We'll let you know. We'll call you." "I got a phone, man, I'll call you." "No, we'll get a hold of you." "OK, see you later."

OK. I've got my seaman's papers. I'm qualified to join the merchant marine if I want to. And I can drive a two-ton forklift. So I hear there's a sign down there at the pier that says, "Hiring. Merchant Marine." I went and checked it out, and they're looking for forklift drivers and people to go overseas. I went in there and showed this guy that I'm qualified to drive. It's a government document, I'm qualified. I asked him if they was hiring. The dude says, "OK, here's your application, fill it out." I fill it out. Military service is on the other side of it. Now check this out. I fill it out, turn it over, and fill that out. He skims over the front side, turns it over, and once he hits military service he stops and takes five minutes or so to read it. He turns it over and says, "You qualify to drive a two-ton forklift, work with electrical systems, such-and-such. . . . Where were you when you were in the Navy?" "OK, I was in the Philippines, and I was in Vietnam." He says, "Did you ever get in any trouble with drugs?" So I says, "Well, I've come to apply for a job, not to talk about my past life." He got kind of mad about that. He says, "Well, as the employer I feel I have the right." I says, "Wait a minute, man. As my employer you mean you want me to tell you my past history in the Navy?" He says, "Yeah." I says, "Yeah, well, I told you." He says, "No, I'm not talking about that. You went to Vietnam?" I says, "Yeah, I went to Vietnam. I built a city for them." He says, "Did you get hooked on any drugs?" I says, "What do you mean?" He says, "That's exactly what I mean. Did you get hooked on any drugs?" I said no. I told him I didn't. We carried on a conversation from there about the freights and what I'd be working on. That was in April. They told me if they needed me they'd get ahold of me. They still haven't got ahold of me.

There was plenty of incidents like that. Like a construction company downtown that does the electrical wiring for buildings. They were rewiring the north side of this building. They had it advertised. They still have the ad in the paper, as a matter of fact. For electricians. I went down and applied, and I showed them my discharge and everything. They said OK. And the foreman says, "Since you were overseas, did you have any addiction with drugs?" I had to stop for a minute, you know. I just thought, wow. I said no. He said, "Are you sure?" I said yes. He says, "Well, we're gonna check on all this, and if you're lying we're not gonna hire you." I said I was sure. I don't know if he checked. I'm sure he couldn't have gotten anything because of the Privacy Act. But they actually come out and ask you if you've had anything to do with drugs.

Even at this gas station at the bottom of the hill. I don't want to work in no gas station, but I'm going to if I have to. And this guy asked me if I had any drug involvement. This is a gas station! "Have you had any drug involvement when you were overseas?" No, man. "Are you sure?" I said yes. He even asked me to bring down my discharge to prove to him who I was. He wouldn't believe me. So all I can say is if you're gonna look for a job, don't mention nothing about the service. Grow your hair to where it's got to be grown, and don't say nothing about the service. Because they will hassle you for sure.

157

I think it's getting to the point where some people get off on telling you, "No, you can't have a job." Really, it's getting to be that way. It's pretty bad. As a matter of fact, this guy down at the unemployment office told me that. I came out and asked him, I says, "What do people in this town have against people in the service?" And he says, "Well, the whole thing comes down to this army issue." I says, "What do you mean? They advertise the Army right here in the unemployment office." He told me that when all the news came out about people in the army experimenting with drugs and chemicals, it made a big impression on people. They think that if you go into the military, you're experimenting with drugs. He said that once they find out you've come out of active service overseas and was in the war they're gonna look at you and say, "Uh-uh." And they're gonna enjoy telling you that you can't have a job 'cause they figure you're like one of the people on the street that do use drugs. He actually came out and told me this.

It makes you feel pretty bad, man. Especially when you know you were overseas fighting for them. Then you come back and find they won't hire you. It makes you mad. But you can't do nothing. They just shrug their shoulders and say, "Oh, who are you, man? You're nobody." I'm so sick of it that I don't feel like looking anymore. That's why I went down to unemployment the other day. I decided that if people don't want to hire somebody who wants to work, hell, why even go out and try? Stay home. Collect money from the government.

Was that the first time you went to unemployment?

Yeah.

Why did you wait five months?

'Cause I was looking for a job. I'd rather work than go on unemployment. I thought I could find a job with the skill I had. I'm kind of against drawing unemployment. I figure the government's got better things to spend that money on. If somebody is eligible to go out and work, they should go out and work. Not sit back and draw money. The government can spend that on defenses and stuff instead of people. And I know I'm eligible to work, man. The Navy did teach me that much. I know I can go out and work. But people won't hire me, man, so the only thing I could do was go down to unemployment.

It seems like people are always bitching because so many people go on unemployment. Now I see why so many people do that. Because nobody wants to hire anybody. All I can say is that if you're in the Navy or any service, man, stay in [laughs]. 'Cause if you come out, you're not gonna find a job. I wish I would have stayed in now, to tell you the truth.

I would've put up with all the shit I had to. At least you always have a roof over your head, three hot meals, and a steady income. But I can't get back in because they gave me an R-4 reenlistment quota. It means you can't join again unless Russia bombs us [laughs]. It's pretty bad, man.

ELLEN ROGERS

She is what's known as a retread, a woman beginning a second (or third) career. In the 1960s she and her husband were figures in an experimental theater group in New York. Now, after a period of work as a housewife—and after returning to college for a degree in business administration—she is looking for a job for the first time in fifteen years. She lives in a small New England city with her five-year-old daughter. The house is 150 years old; she boasts that it was built by a runaway slave. The rooms are cluttered and messy. She is thin, pale, blonde, wearing a halter top and baggy blue jeans.

I think what happened between Lewis and me had something to do with my studying. I haven't figured it out yet, and I don't think he has either. Maybe someday we will. But there's this thing, especially for women in my generation and older, where we've always backed our husbands. We're staunch backers of the husband. We work to send them through college, some of us. We raise the kids, we stay home, we're the secretary, we're the nurse, we're the housekeeper, the manager ... everything. Well, I wanted to better myself. It was fine when Lewis and I were in New York because we worked on projects together. But then Lewis got invited out here to teach, and he stopped working with me. He decided he wanted to do his own thing. Suddenly he had all these students to work with. And that got me into doing my own thing. But the more I did on my own, the more I learned, the more uptight our relationship got. I didn't feel his presence there beside, supporting me. He didn't feel it either and admitted that to me. He had problems with that. He's a brilliant man, and I love him and respect his work; but I think he's a victim the same way a lot of older men are victims in our society. So the marriage started to deteriorate, and we made the decision to separate.

Now I'm five credits away from getting my B.A., and I'm getting a little scared. I haven't been in the job market for so long. The whole interview process is very strange to me. But I've been doing it for a few months now, sending out résumés and going to see people. I've applied for jobs as administrative assistant and theater instructor at two different colleges. One university had a whole range of things I applied for: personnel director, theater teacher, faculty adviser. So far I've been to seven interviews. I haven't heard anything, so I'm getting a little bit frightened.

I guess what's scary is my lack of experience in being on the market, on the block, selling myself. It could be, on my part, a lack of . . . but I believe in myself. I know that I can do it. I know that I can teach theater damn well. I know that I have excellent training in business administration, and if given the opportunity, I could probably do a hell of a job at that. But I get really uptight. One thing that sets off the fear is the question "What/who/where was your last employer, and how many years were you employed?" And the thing about being a married woman with a child makes it hard. Because first of all, at my age I'm not going to go out and take a job as a waitress or something like that. It wouldn't even cover my expenses, my house, and my child's education. And I figure I have about twenty-five working years left. In that time I have to prepare for my child's future and my old age, so I have to hold out for a position rather than a job. And companies aren't too crazy about giving married women positions of responsibility. They kind of hold back. Especially if you're being interviewed by a male. They make you feel kind of low, like you're not worth too much. It's just a feeling I get. I wish I could put my finger on it. For instance, I went into one man's office for an interview, and he was immediately pulling out my chair, saying, "Oh, let me help you." Like I'm so helpless that I can't sit down by myself. And holding my arm while I'm sitting down, which probably is just a social courtesy, but it makes me feel uncomfortable.

I suppose a lot of my fear stems from not having the experience of being really aggressive to get what you want. That's a thing males are taught, but I haven't been conditioned for that. I've been conditioned for taking care of the male, taking care of the children, budgeting, and cooking, that kind of thing. To be assertive and aggressive is not something I've been pushed to do.

What about those years when you were working in the theater? Didn't that involve being aggressive?

Not much because I didn't have to go after any of that. It came to me. I don't know if this is the usual procedure or not, but the people I was working with—we were later labeled the "underground"—suddenly got discovered. Newspapers and magazines all around the country started writing about us, and with that kind of PR, things start coming to you. Foundation presidents would come and see our work and say, "Do you want a grant?" [Laughs.] "Would you accept it?" It was definitely nothing like having to go out and apply for a regular position.

I thought that the experience, and all the PR, would help me this time. But people around here don't seem to care about it. Even though we spent years of hard work and struggle trying to open up new areas for artists. For a while, in the early sixties the whole art scene was like living in a Nazi community. If you performed nude in this country, you were considered a freak and you were doing pornography. They called us avant-garde. I remember going to court for one play I had worked on, and the judge didn't even know the meaning of the word. He said, "What kind of an artist are you anyway?" I said, "I'm a member of the avant-garde. I'm trying to change things in society. There are a lot of us who are trying to do that." And he said, "What the hell is avant-garde anyway?" I said, "If you don't know what it is, you shouldn't be sitting up there." [Laughs.] I got thrown out of court. Well, that was a long struggle, and I feel like I'm still struggling now because of my sex, because of my wanting to work and be responsible for myself and my child. That doesn't seem like it should be too terribly avant-garde, but it actually is. I'm sure it's going to get a hell of a lot better for women as time goes on, just as the underground movement made it better for artists in general. But I'm getting tired of being in the avant-garde. I'd like to be in the derrière-garde for a while [laughs]. Just sit back and relax and get some of the cream.

I keep redoing my résumé. It's a constant in my life. With every job I apply for, I have to send out a new one. I have one for academic positions that has my professional accomplishments. I've got two pages of plays I wrote, directed, or performed. There's one for business administration that's about two pages. It just has honors and activities and a few other things. But I always feel pressured by the résumé. Things like "Status, marital." If I put down "Married," they might not hire me because they'll think, "Well, she's thirty-nine. She could have another child. What if she gets pregnant? If we get her in a good position, pay her a good salary, and she gets pregnant, we're going to lose money on her." So all these questions dealing with status really worry me. "Children"—if my child gets sick, maybe I won't come to work. I don't know, maybe I should put "Childless Widow" on the résumé and see if they take pity on me [laughs].

And the problem isn't just being married. It's more basic. It's being a woman in a world where most employers are men. The man who interviewed me at one college was a very fine person. I was able to open with him and discuss administrative procedures and ideas, and he wanted to know how I would do things. That was very good. I had a lot of respect for him. I could see that he wasn't treating me any differently than he would have treated anyone else coming to apply for the job. That was very much appreciated. I should bake him some cookies [laughs].

But I often get the feeling that men are afraid of me. They back off, and that worries me. I don't like isolation. And I don't see any reason in the world why a man should be frightened by a woman who knows something. I always think it would be a very nice relationship to have—challenging, creative, interesting, pleasant. It would never get boring. But I feel that fear coming from them, and that sparks off anxiety in me, and I say, "Oh, what do I do now? I don't want him to be frightened of me, because I'm not going to hurt him. I'm not going to kill him. I'm not an ogre; I'm not a shit. I'm just a person."

At one point I caught myself playing the game that a lot of women play, which is to wear a short skirt, put on some makeup and act dumb. I did that one time. It was such a speedy interview. I hardly said a word. I let the man do most of the talking and asked him to explain everything to me, twice. I asked the meanings of different words. I was living a lie, sitting there lying to this poor dude who thought he was building up his ego. Oh, it was awful! I was ashamed of myself after I had done it and he had offered me the job. I knew that if I took the job . . . OK, the income was pretty damn good, and there would be opportunity for advancement. As an actress I could sustain the role indefinitely. But then I thought, "I know I'll have to go to bed with him. And the boredom of playing dumb is either going to drive me into a mental institution, or I'll slip and let him find out I'm intelligent, and then I'll lose the job."

So I told him I'd like to think about it for a couple of days and I'd call him back. I called him and told him that I couldn't do it, that the responsibility was too much for me. I played the game right through to the end so that I wouldn't fuck him up. And I didn't fuck myself up either. I just learned something: that I'm not capable of role playing anymore. There was a time in my life, especially in high school, when I was very much into role playing. But I can't do that anymore, not at my age.

What made you do it in that interview?

Desperation. I was really uptight. My husband and I are separated, and I have no job. I don't want to get into the thing that so many couples do when they separate, of going to court and saying, "You're to blame, you're to blame." I am myself, and he is Lewis, and we have a child, and I don't want to suck him dry of all his financial resources for the rest of his life. It would seem like a pretty horrifying thing. I have made a decision that I want to be responsible for myself and for the child, and if he would like to be responsible for the child, too, then I think that's wonderful. But I don't want him to feel he *has* to. I don't want him to feel forced into it because I think he has just as much right to do as he wants as I do. The child wants to remain with me and I want the child. I'm willing to accept that responsibility.

So out of desperation I'm thinking, "Oh my God, how am I going to face next year's school tuition? How am I going to pay the doctor bill? The car needs new brakes. Taxes are due in July." So I did the interview out of desperation. I knew there was going to be a financial crush that I had to be ready for. But after that one experience, I know I can't go that route. I just can't.

KRISTEN JACOBS

She is twenty-two, a recent graduate of the University of Michigan. She has a B.A. in art education and some experience in library work. After leaving school, she worked for a year in a state-funded special education program, but its funds were cut. "I was really upset. I was thoroughly disgusted with the government. I tend to get very involved in working situations, very loyal, and I knew we were doing something good. So it's hard when they just pull out the rug from under you." She has been unemployed since then: fourteen months.

She lives with her boyfriend, Jack. "We're getting married in three weeks and going to Jamaica for our honeymoon. And I've resigned myself to the fact that my unemployment runs out right around the time we'll be getting back, so I'll probably have to get myself a part-time job for $2.50 an hour."

The contract with the government ran out in June, and I didn't hear that we hadn't been funded for a new project until sometime in October. So during the summer it was sort of a nice break. I missed the routine of having to get up and go every day, but I liked not having to work in the summer. That was really great. I had mixed feelings because I knew that I shouldn't count on having a job in the fall. But I said to myself, "Yeah, you kept saying that last year, and it was a shoo-in. You practically got

163

the job before they even interviewed you." I've had very little experience in looking for jobs, and that one just fell in my lap. So you hope that the silver plate keeps getting passed around and you don't drop it.

Things changed after October when the job fell through. I felt helpless. I got a lot more moody than I had been. It wasn't until January that I started looking for a job. Until then I had been sitting around being down on myself. I'd say, "Here I am with a college degree. I'm not trained to do squat, and what I am trained to do I have no desire to do. Where does that leave me? It leaves me in the middle of nowhere. So what am I going to do?" Well, I couldn't think of anything do do. The only thing I could look forward to, if I was lucky, was to be a secretary, which to me is even worse than working in a five-and-dime [laughs].

At one point I decided I would go to the university's career planning center. I was really excited. I thought, OK, I've got these skills. I have skills. I know a lot about art. I can draw, design. I have certain skills that . . . I don't have skills such as accounting or being a clerk, or retail or sales. But I have things like being responsible [laughs]. More nonbusiness skills. Nondefinable. I thought, "Well, I'll go in there and maybe they can help me." I made an appointment with this man and explained what I wanted. He said, "Move to Dallas." I said, "What?" He said, "Move to Dallas or Houston. You'll never find a job here. That's the only place you'll ever find a job." I said, "Well, can't you help me? At least give me an idea of something I might look for?" He said, "Well, take the occupational directory. That big book. All I can suggest is look through that and see if you can find something you'd like to do." And I said, "Where do I go from there?" He told me that from there I should make a résumé and start walking around to every social services agency and fill out six hundred applications. For a job that I know doesn't exist, but just in case something might come up that I might be able to do in the next ten years. I practically cried when I heard that. I said, "It just can't be that hard to get a job. It just can't be that hard."

I was really down about that. But I got my résumé together and started looking for jobs in the papers. There wasn't much there. General jobs were all that were around. I didn't want to waitress. There's nothing clerical. Under "Professional" three-quarters of the ads are for nurses. So there wasn't much in the papers. I got ahold of a state bulletin that announces "professional" jobs that they have. But these were all things that I wasn't trained for. I just had a college degree which qualifies me to look for those jobs.

So there's always this feeling of "What am I going to do?" I suppose I'll have to go be a secretary, but I can't type particularly well, and God, I don't want to be a secretary. I could always go get a job at Woolworth's or McDonald's, but Jesus, I don't want a job at Woolworth's or McDonald's. I want to do something. I want to use my intelligence. You know, the whole time I was in high school and college was when they started saying, "Well, gee, women, you've got to get out and do something." "Women are people," they were saying. So you spend six years trying to erase the last fifteen years of your life, saying, "Hey, I am a person. I can do something. I'm really worth something." You finally start really believing that, and then they kick you right in the teeth and say, "You're not, you can't be anything but a secretary. Go to the end of the class."

I started going down to the unemployment office, and I had some very bad experiences there with some of the counselors. They would say, "What do you want?" I say, "Well, I'd like a job that at least pays $3 an hour, full time." "We don't have anything that pays $3 an hour full time. We could get you—well, here's something that pays $2.50 for twenty hours a week." I'd say, "But I can't even pay my rent on that." They'd say, "I'm sorry, but that's all we have." There was one job, just one job, that I could've possibly gotten. It was taking microfilm out of a projector. That was all you did. It paid $3.60 an hour. Thirty hours a week, I think it was. I called, and they said they already had three hundred applications [laughs]. That's about as close as I got to anything.

Those people not only couldn't offer me anything, but they certainly didn't console me at all. They were very cold about the whole situation. Who was I to think that I could earn more than $2.50 an hour part time? I remember this one lady. I went in there and told her I was looking for something that paid at least $3 an hour. I said I needed to earn at least $400 or $500 a month before taxes. She said, "Let me look through the files." So she goes and looks through the files and comes back. There was a job as a night clerk at a hotel or motel where there had been a shooting death a few months before. I just looked at her and said, "Are you kidding? You want a female to go into an unguarded place to work in the middle of the night where there's been a shooting? That's all you have to offer?" She said, "Well, what do you expect?" I said, "I have a college degree. All right, so I don't have much specific training, but I have all these other things. You have to learn on any job." She said, "There just isn't anything. You won't be able to find anything either."

Her attitude was typical. It was like: "Oh, here comes another one. Here comes somebody else looking for a job when there just aren't any." You could sense there was a lot of hopelessness around the office in general. I know that some people down there really care, but after you work there for quite a while it must get to be a real drag. 'Cause you can't offer people anything. Maybe you can to some people, but the vast majority of them you can't help. So there was this attitude of them not being able to help and you being desperate for something. You keep going down there with so much hope. "Maybe they'll have something today. Maybe they'll be nice to me. Maybe I won't have to stand in line so long." And you come out of there saying, "Oh, I'm so stupid for going down there. They can't find me anything."

As it went on I started feeling dumb. I started feeling incapable of handling any type of job. I thought, "Well, maybe I really can't do anything good. Maybe I should just accept the fact that I'll have to go to McDonald's and get a start there." I wondered a lot about just what was going to happen to me. I have this terrible fear of being penniless, walking around in the street, trying to find a job. You know, the whole melodramatic thing of turning into a drunk and falling into the gutter. That's a very real picture to me. I'm afraid something like that is going to happen. It crops up on occasion.

Sometimes I'm so down on myself that I can't get anything done. Partly it's because I don't feel I'm making the supreme effort to get a job. I mean, I'm not following up absolutely everything in the paper that I might have. And I'm having a hard time trying to decide whether I should just stay on unemployment or take any job I can find. If I didn't have the unemployment I certainly would have had a job by now. And when it runs out I have to have a job. That's all there is to it. That's a fact of life. So I ask myself: "Am I ripping off the government or am I not ripping off the government?" I ask myself, "How far do you compromise?" Because $94 a week tax-free is a lot of money compared to what a lot of people make. So do I go out and try to get a job which would take me off unemployment, which would relieve the government? Doing something that may let me bring home $50 or $60 a week? Or do I just stay on unemployment and be happy because the government's fucked anyway and that's their tough luck? They haven't done anything particularly nice to me, why should I go out and do something particularly nice to them? I feel that conflict a lot. And I talk to people. Some people go, "Yeah, yeah, it's hip to rip off the government." Or, "You might as well stay on unemployment, why not?" Or, "When are you gonna get a job?" I think it's just really hard to figure out what to do. Do I go and do my patriotic duty and help my country and my government by not being one of the unemployed welfare bums? They had an excellent thing on "60 Minutes" on unemployment, about these guys who were like golf pros from Ohio who went down to Florida to work and draw unemployment. After watching that show I felt guilty as hell, and I thought, "Well, shit, I'm not doing that. I'm not ripping them off by moving south for the winter and collecting down there." But I felt guilty.

I keep coming up to these blind alleys because I can only see so far. I go to people and say, "OK, what can I do? Can you at least give me a direction? Someplace I can look? Even an area of jobs I might be qualified for?" And everybody says, "Sorry, no, we can't help you." It makes me upset with the government and with the whole economic system. I am very disgusted with big business. It's just that they make all the money. They get it all. And the average everyday common person is getting screwed down the drain. Whether it's your taxes, or not being able to find a job, or them telling you that you're a person and you can do anything you want—not literally, but you have the potential to do a lot—and then they turn around and tell you you don't, and make you feel stupid and bad. I don't know, I guess I tend to put my college degree on a bit higher level than I should, but Jesus, I spent I don't know how much money going to college. Yet I'm supposed to go out and get the same amount of money, doing the same job as somebody that just got through high school. I don't think that's fair at all.

GRACE KEATON

In Chapter 1 she talked about being fired from a publishing house without warning after twelve years. Here she describes her efforts to find new work.

It's funny—I can hardly remember the days after I got fired. But I do remember one thing: I immediately started to look for a job. I started the day after I was fired. I don't know where that energy came from, but it came from somewhere. It's an energy I'm unaware of, and that I don't feel that I muster; it's just there. I immediately started calling people, and wrote a résumé, and went to somebody who was very savvy about résumés, and rewrote it there, and got it printed and mailed out. I wrote a million letters, called everybody in New York, Boston, Washington . . . and so on.

Well, the publishing industry is not in terribly good shape now. And nobody would offer me a low-level job. They all said something like: "It's bad policy. You'll get discontented. You wouldn't be happy with the salary. I can't offer you a job like that; it's too low-level for you." Apparently it's just considered impossible. And all I could think of was the woman in *Chorus Line.* Did you see *Chorus Line?* One of the lead roles in *Chorus Line* is a woman who has had one or two starring roles, and they won't let her back into the chorus. And she says, "I've got to eat! What do you mean, you won't let me back into the chorus? I want a job!"

But there were not that many jobs around. It was a long time before I realized that all these good, warm, friendly interviews were not going to lead to jobs. And people didn't call me back. Or they didn't write. I couldn't believe that people would do that. But then I searched back and tried to remember how often *I* had done that to people asking for jobs. And I'm afraid I did do it to people. They would call, and I just wouldn't call back or wouldn't tell them the results of an interview.

I was dogged about going for interviews. I would interview for anything. I tried outside the publishing industry because I am not wedded to the publishing industry at all. And mainly they laughed. I tried to get into banking [*laughs*]. I went to Headhunters, who service other industries. Nothing came of any of that. Nobody's very interested in a senior person from another industry. Apparently you're not allowed to switch. If you're a specialist in left-handed crochet stitches, you are not given a job in right-handed knitting stitches.

I would see people I had done business with, who were helpful about introductions. But that doesn't get you a job if the people who interview you don't like you or if there are no jobs there. I did get a consulting job that didn't pay badly given the amount of time I spent on it. But after that I turned down a couple of other consulting jobs and stopped trying to develop others. I really don't want to do consulting. I don't want to be free-lance. I want a full-time job with steady income. If I had any common sense and inner calm, I would have tried writing, which is something I'm very interested in. I might have been able to hack something out of it. At least I would have been trying. And I had the time. The time I spent worrying, I could have spent writing. But I didn't. That's because of the kind of history I've had, the kind of person I am. I really do regret that.

Sunday was the most depressing day of the week because the want ads came out. Reading the classifieds and replying to them was the most depressing thing I did. I can't tell you why, but I knew it was hopeless from the beginning. And I knew I had to do it. It's as though you have to put in your time. You have to do a certain number of things, and that's one of the things you have to do. And I hated it. But I did it. I went through the classified section and the business section. I answered ads and wrote letters. I went on interviews. I went to see employment agencies. I did far-fetched things. I would go up to my sister's for a weekend and meet a man from ITT or Union Carbide at a party and get my brother-in-law to press a résumé on him. I called people in California, where the publishing industry is in even worse shape than it is here.

The funny thing is that through all of this, everybody thought I

168

looked—and apparently I was—genuinely very competent. I would come through in any crunch. If I had to go on an interview, I was fine suddenly. I never felt that way, so there was a big discrepancy. But I did all these things, and they looked fine from the outside. Of course, a lot of people knew how I felt. I didn't make any secret of it. Very often I would call people up and tell them how awful I felt [laughs]. But I kept busy. Sunday I read the classifieds, and Sunday and Monday I sent out résumés. My résumé is a masterpiece. Occasionally I would write letters to go with it. I would reply to letters. I would see literary agents. I would have lunch with people. Everyone was very good about feeding me. I gained five pounds, which I really didn't need. And after I would have lunch with them, they'd go back to work, which was where I wanted to be going, and I'd go home. That was devastating, just devastating. As I said, if I'd had any sense, I would have come home and written. But I couldn't even read, much less write.

I'll tell you what I did: I spent a lot of time crying. Oh, my God, did I spend a lot of time crying. There is really nothing more boring, and it gives you sinus headaches.

Did you adjust to it over the months?

No. I still haven't adjusted to it, even now that I've found a job. I did not adjust to it when I was consulting and making some money. Everyone would say, "You can free-lance until you get a job." But I didn't want to free-lance. I think it has something to do with how old I am. I grew up at a time when the ravages of the Depression were still being felt, in the thirties and early forties. If you were alive in that period—even if you were an infant—and your family had been heavily affected by it, something magic and neurotic attached itself to work. So that it became in many senses the central definition of your life. Which is . . . I hear myself saying this, but I know that that way lies madness. I mean, there's just no fun, no party that way. It's crazy.

WILLIE HAWKINS

A duplex apartment in a Birmingham, Alabama, housing project. He has just moved in and cannot yet afford furniture for the lower half; on our way upstairs we pass through two empty rooms with bare white walls. He is a big man, on the plump side, with a gift for speech like that of a fire-and-brimstone preacher. He doesn't simply talk—he declaims, in a powerfully resonant voice and the heavy cadenced drawl of the rural South.

My name is Willie Hawkins. I was born in a little place on the other side of Birmingham, about sixty miles away, in a place called Oakman, Alabama, which is located in Walker County. I was born February 13, which they say is an unlucky day, but I think it's pretty lucky because I'm here since 1953, which makes me twenty-four years old.

I got out of high school in 1971, and that's when I started working. But due to the Vietnam War, the draft was mandatory at the time. I had to worry about the service. I had a lottery number, and my number came up. So I went and joined the Air Force. I went into the Air Force in 1971. I was a field specialist, which I knew was gonna benefit me when I got out of the service. 'Cause what I had in mind was to make my four years and get out and use the skill as an aircraft refueler that I had learned. I knew that being in the service would help me get a job. But what I found out when I got out was that it wasn't so. I was discharged in 1975, and that's when my unemployment problems really began.

When I got out I already had one job in mind, which was at the post office. See, before I got out, I went into this program where they learn you and school you about jobs. So what I did, I took a test to qualify me for the post office, to make sure I had a little something going for me when I got out. But I found out they wasn't hiring. There I was, stuck without a job. So I went for my next best skill, which was dealing with airplanes. I had a friend who worked at an airline, and he put in a good word to his supervisor for me. I was interviewed by a lady. She looked the application over carefully and fixed my paperwork up. I went and took a physical. But when I got back to the office, the results of the physical weren't in and the lady wasn't there. They told me they'd contact me through the mail. I did hear from her about a week later, but the letter showed there were no openings. Now they had already told me there were a lot of openings. This really discouraged me. I wanted to know what was going on.

The only reason I can see is that they didn't want black people with a little knowledge. This is my own opinion. But there's a lot of this going on. And that's the only way it could have been because everybody I know that works out there, they don't have any knowledge. There's some dudes out there I went to school with. And they're not high school graduates. They don't have no kind of experience. They don't have no military experience. They aren't qualified to do skilled work. They're just there to keep people from issuing a lawsuit. OK, if you go and say, "I want to issue a lawsuit against the airlines because they're prejudiced," you can't really prove it. Because they got blacks working there. But the ones they got working there don't have any knowledge. This is in order to keep black people from advancing in the business. But if they was to look at me, they'd say, "Well, looky here. This man here, he got potential. We don't want him. We want to keep him down." You see what I'm saying? This is what they're doing out there, which I think should be investigated.

Now, at that time none of the other airlines in town was hiring. So I started looking for any kind of job. It was seven months before I found anything. And the more time it took to find a job, the more aggressive I got. I even went to the point where I shaved and got a haircut. Because sometimes you have to impress people in order to get a job. So I figured, "Well, maybe I'm looking too much like a hoot." I wasn't dirty or nothing. I was clean. I had to wear brogans and messed-up clothes, but I made sure they was clean. But yet and still, they were looking at my physical appearance. So I shaved off my beard. That's how desperate I was.

One day me and my brother drove out to this industrial area. We parked the car and walked to every factory. I think it took us something like three hours to run up on a place that would even talk to us. Everyplace we went, they wasn't hiring. They wasn't even accepting applications. Well, we came to this warehouse. The receptionist told us they wasn't hiring. But I had got so aggressive that I told her, "I'm not trying to run your business, but would you make sure? Will you call back there in the plant and ask to speak to the general foreman and ask if he'll accept an application?" She said, "Well, I'll do it, but they're not accepting applications." So she called back there, and he answered the phone and told her that he would accept one. She was all in shock and she told me, "Yeah," and she apologized.

My brother was in need of a job, but he knew I was in need worse than he was 'cause I had a family. So when the foreman came out, I talked to him. I really had to sell myself to him. I had to show him that I was desperate for a job. He run a game on me, telling me, "Mr. Hawkins, we work hard out here." I told him, "I was brought up hard. I was brought up on a farm in Oakman, Alabama." I said, "I know what hard work is." I said, "I don't come here looking for no pillow job." I said, "If I was looking for a pillow job, I'd have stayed home." He was kind of trying to discourage me from getting the job, but since I was so aggressive, he had to give it to me. He would say, "Mr. Hawkins, we come to work at six o'clock." But everything he would say I had an answer for. I said, "In the Air Force I used to go to work at four o'clock." Which I did. He ran it on down, saying, "We work hard. We work twelve hours a day." I said,

"In the Air Force I have worked eighteen hours. So don't try to tell me about no time." I said, "I know about the time." I said, "You give it to me. I can take it." I said, "Physical-wise, I know I can take it because I'm a pretty good man." So I sold myself. I went to work that next morning at six o'clock.

I worked there one full year. Then the place went out of business. So this not only put me out in the street; it put about fifty people in the street. We were out there facing the challenge again. And man, it was terrible. I went and reapplied for unemployment, but my old lady couldn't foot the bills. The landlord threatened to put us out. So we called my old lady's mother in Virginia and told her to send out a truck to come get us because we were going to be out in the streets. We put the furniture in storage, and my wife and two kids moved back in with her mother. I stayed with my brother in Birmingham. And I was out of work that time for seven months.

For a while I would get up early, just like I was going to work. The old saying goes, "The early bird gets the worm." I believed that could help me. But it got so bad that I really gave up. I even tried to get back into the Air Force. But to show how bad my luck was, they wouldn't let me back in. I called this recruiter, and he told me that due to the new rules and regulations, you have to go back in under your old Air Force Specialty Code. And my AFSC was crowded. They didn't need anybody. I had to wait for a slot to open. At the time when I was discharged, you could come back in under a different AFSC. But they had changed that. So I had to suffer it out.

Now this is when things started going through my mind. It started to be a problem. Because I started thinking about things that were against the law, see. I thought about pushing a little dope, which is quick money. But I thought about the law and what would you get if you got caught. I'm not saying I would have got caught, but nine times out of ten the law of averages catches up with you. So I didn't go that route. But I used to walk around, and I'd see people with money. And things would go through my mind about ripping them off. Things had got bad. I needed money. I was about to lose my family because my wife was in Virginia and I was here in Alabama. I knew I couldn't get no job in Virginia, but it didn't seem no better here. And I was watching the dudes who was doing things. They was influencing me to do it. Because I could see how they was doin'. Oh, man, they was getting over! Yeah! And here you is sitting back here with nothing. You're trying to live right, but your financial problem won't let you do it. You don't have no money. You don't have no place of your own to stay, and the only food you get is something that your people give you. And to me it was worser than that because I had a family and I'm trying to save my family. I have to worry about whether I'm ever gonna have my family back together again.

You even get so far down that you start thinking about God. I'm a Baptist even if I don't go to church that much. I'm not gonna lie. The last time I was in church was at my father's funeral. But I started feeling like God was punishing me for some reason. He would let me get so close to a job, and then He would take it away. I do believe He was punishing me because I didn't do right by my family. This was after the warehouse had closed down, and I started hanging out in the street. I was just messing around. Out smoking reefer and drinking with the guys. You know, I was just out of the service, and I wanted to get back in the streets with my friends. But after I got out there, I found out it's a different thing. Everything was serious now. I wasn't no kid no more. And now I'm looking for all the friends I had four or five years back. Looking to do some of the same things. But I have responsibilities. While I'm out there having a good time, my family is suffering.

So I believe God was punishing me for that. And it began to be a mind thing. I was thinking things that I didn't want to believe, but I was believing them anyway. In other words, it was something like the devil fighting against God. The devil's trying to overpower you to go out and kill to survive. You know this ain't what you're supposed to do, and it ain't what you want to do. But you feel God is punishing you for something, and the devil is saying, "Oh, go ahead. It's the only way you're going to make it." I didn't want to take that route because one thing about stealing and robbing, you have to be prepared for the situation that you're either going to kill or be killed. That's what you'd be asking for when you start doing things that are against the law. You either kill or you're gonna do some time. And when you rob in Alabama, you're gonna do a lot of time. So all this here was going through my mind. At one point, that's *all* that was on my mind. But I didn't let my mind lead me to do nothing that was wrong. I turned to the Lord. I let Him work it out. I said, "If He wants me to have something, I'm gonna get it." And finally, one day, He provided me with a job.

I got this job through a friend I played basketball with. He worked out at a factory, and he told me to put in an application out there because they were going to be hiring during the summer. I went out there and they told me they would call me when they got an opening. I was so depressed that I wasn't looking for them to call me. But they did. That surprised me. And then I thought about the money they were paying: $2.95 an hour. I said to myself, "That ain't no money, but yet and still, I have to start somewhere, so I might as well start right here." I said, "I ain't doing nothing out here now." I said, "At least they're gonna give me $2.95 to work." I knew it wasn't nothing for a family of four. But I went on out there and got the job. I was packing crates.

I made friends with this dude out there whose name was Drew Washington. He was telling me about jobs at the auto plant. They wanted to hire some blacks out there. I started thinking about it, and I said, "I'm gonna give this a try." So what I did, one day I swung by and put an application in. They were paying $6.20 an hour. I said, "I know I'll never get a job like this." I figured I'd hang on at the factory and make $2.95. Well, about a month later the auto plant called my friend because he had put in an application, too. The next morning I woke up and something was on my mind to tell my cousin the phone number out at the factory. I just had a strong feeling that I was gonna get that auto job. So I gave my cousin the phone number and said that if anybody called me about a job, to call me right away. That was on Tuesday. On Wednesday morning, about 9:30, I got a call. They wanted me to come in for an interview.

I got off from work right then and caught the bus to town. At that moment everything was going through my mind. I said, "If you fail this physical, you ain't gonna get this job." See, I have high blood pressure. I already lost one good job 'cause my blood was too high. And that morning I could feel my blood was up. What made it worse was that I had ate some pork meat the night before, so my blood was really up. And I had run out of medication and didn't have money to buy no more. I didn't have no business eating pork, but I had to eat what my cousin ate at home or I didn't eat nothing at all. So this job pops up. I had to really put on my thinking cap. The appointment was at two o'clock. It was a little after ten. I had to think about some way to get my blood pressure down because this was the job that was gonna get things back like they used to be. So I went down to the free hospital here. And I gave them a pint of blood. Because I figured this way: High blood pressure ain't nothing but pressure on your blood. You have to take medication in order to treat it, but it ain't nothing but pressure in your body. So I feel like this here, if you lose blood, your pressure can't do nothing but go down. So I went and gave them a pint of blood.

Then I caught the bus home. It was getting to be around 12:30. And I'm thinking, "I want to impress these people." I had growed another beard. So I had to shave. I didn't have nothing to shave with. So what I did, I borrowed a razor blade from a friend next door, and I shaved with nothing but a naked razor blade. But I was still thinking about my blood pressure. I was thinking, "I don't think my blood pressure is down enough 'cause I can still feel it in my head." So I called my brother and told him, "Charlie, bring me some Epsom salts." I had heard people say that Epsom salts is good for high blood. And I figured I ain't got nothing to lose. I want this job, so I'm gonna try everything. I said, "I can't take no medication now and get my blood down fast enough. I have to have it right now, in order for me to get this job." So my brother hurried over with some Epsom salts and I took a dose. By now it was about two, so I went on out and got interviewed for the job.

I was interviewed by the warehouse manager. And man, I was so aggressive that I just made him laugh. It was like that other job. I had an answer for everything. He said, "We hire a lot of people that can't do the work." I said, "Well, looky here. Just give me a chance, and I'm gonna prove it to you." He was telling me they go to work at five every morning. I said, "Looky here, I had to go to work at four in the morning in the Air Force." He said, "We love for people to be on time. We pay good, and we expect that you will work good." I said, "Let me show you." He said, "They give you thirty days to learn the job, but we expect you to do it in ten." I said, "There ain't nothing out here I can't do. All you have to do is show me one time." I said, "You don't even have to show me twice. Just show me one time, and I'll do it. Just take your time and go through it and show me, and I guarantee you I'll meet your qualifications out here in five days." I said, "Give me four days, and on the fifth day I'll do just as well as anybody out here." Well, he laughed. He said, "OK, Willie, I'm gonna fix your paperwork up. Can you take a physical now?" I was a little skeptical about the physical. I wanted to give it another day and make sure my blood was down. But I said, "Yeah, I'm ready." I just had a feeling.

Now, they got a limit. Your blood pressure is supposed to be within that limit. If it's over the limit, they disqualify you. The limit was 150 over 90. And that's exactly what my blood pressure was. Can you dig it? You might think I'm kidding, but that's right. My blood pressure was exactly 150 over 90. The lady told me, "If your blood pressure had been one point higher, you would have been disqualified."

So now my troubles are over for employment. 'Cause that's where I'm working, and that's where I figure I'm gonna retire. Right now we're on strike, but we should be going back in a couple of weeks. And when I get my year in out there, I think my unemployment days will be over. I think it's a brighter day now. When I think back on them bad days, I figure everything's got to be smooth sailing for me now 'cause I've been through the rough part, and I survived it. I remember when things had gotten so far down that I don't think it could've gotten lower.

Really, the whole thing changed my mind completely. It made me conservative. Made me put back for a rainy day. It made me appreciate people giving you a job, because these days if you mess up on a job you might not be able to get another. You got to be real conservative. You have got to be prepared, because everything you do is very serious. Life is much shorter now than it was a long time ago. You got to get up and try, man, and I think people are learning this here. They know how the unemployment rates are. They're much higher than ten or twenty years ago. You didn't worry about unemployment in them days. You could quit a job every day and still find work. You could quit a job this morning and go out and find one this evening. But you could quit a job today, and it'd take you two years to find one.

The interview seemed to be over. I was about to turn off the tape recorder. He said he had one more thing to add. As he spoke his voice dropped almost to a whisper.

Since you say you're gonna change the names and everything, I'm gonna tell you another experience that happened to us during the time I was unemployed and had no money. My wife got pregnant. She had to have an abortion because we didn't have no money. I think that really hurt me. But there wasn't no other way. That was the last choice we had. That's something I left out, but after you and me talked, I just wanted to show you. You thought it was bad, but I told you something worser than that. I figured, "Ain't no use to let the baby come and have to starve." She really felt upset about it, you know. She cried. My wife would call me up on the phone and cry. But I didn't see no other way around. It's a hurting feeling. It gets you down when you start thinking about it. You think of what the baby could have been. But then again, I didn't want it to starve either. I know if that had happened, I would've really did something illegal. I couldn't stand for it to go starve. So that's the story.

5

MINORITY YOUTH: "Natchez Is Natchez All Over the World"

In every American city, large or small, a high percentage of young people from minority groups cannot find work—or work only sporadically—for years after leaving school. The current rate of unemployment among minority teenagers approaches an astronomical 40 percent. The reasons for this employment blight are obvious, including lack of vocational skills, lack of advanced education, the flight of industry from central cities, and racial prejudice. The remedies are not so obvious, and some proposals, such as reducing the minimum wage or outlawing the widespread demand for a high school diploma as a certificate of employability, are highly controversial. Government job programs like the Comprehensive Employment and Training Act (CETA) are useful but far too small. As a 1977 report by the Vocational Foundation, Inc., of New York notes: "For minority youth, these are the years of a great depression, far worse in its impact on them than any depression that the country as a whole has ever encountered."

Perhaps the most remarkable thing about the young people in this chapter, then, is that they still cherish high hopes for the future.

JIMMY GREEN

A wooden shack in the black section of Natchez, Mississippi. Two tiny rooms: a kitchen/living room and a space barely big enough for a bed and crib. The roof leaks; windowpanes are cracked. In the front "yard" of red dirt are a car up on blocks, a pickup truck, and auto parts scattered about. He lives with his wife, Letty, and two kids: a son, three, and a daughter, one. "Sometimes we get angry and maybe holler or something. It's just the idea of us stayin' here. She's tired of us livin' here. I'm tired of it, too, but there's nothin' we can do at the moment. So maybe the reason we holler is because of the way we're livin'."

He is a Vietnam veteran with an undesirable discharge, the result of a "little riot." He has a high school diploma but is unskilled. "I took this correspondence course from a commercial trade school. It was studying to be an electrician. Due to money problems I wasn't able to finish. I've still got everything they sent me, but I owe them $400 and some. They can't get the money if I can't pay it, unless they can get it out of my hide."

Letty listens silently, as though letting the man of the family speak for them both. During the day she studies secretarial skills at a business school, leaving him to watch the children.

For a year after I got out of the service I mostly sat and didn't do nothin'. I was at home, see. Didn't have to work. It was like rest and recuperation. Take a year and relax. Then I met Letty, and after that we got married. By then I had a job. I left that one to seek for a better one. I had a bunch of jobs over two years. It wasn't that I would leave them just to be leavin'. I always left with intentions to seek a better one, but it didn't work out that way. I did a little of everything. I worked a week or two, sometimes only a day or two on some of 'em. Some I blew because we didn't get along, or the pay wasn't right, or I wasn't really satisfied. Some little thing that I didn't like or my boss didn't like. I've probably been at the unemployment office more than anybody in Natchez. Always lookin' for another job.

I can't say that I'm the easiest person to get along with. I can understand most anybody. They can talk to me, and I'll understand. So I'm not really hard to get along with. . . . I mean I'm not crazy. But whatever you're gonna do to me, I'm gonna do to you. I don't care who you are. And I'm always thinkin' big, thinkin' ahead. I want a whole lot for my family, and so far I'm just not gettin' it. So I ask myself, "Why work eight hours a day for a $2 job when I could be workin' eight hours a day

179

for a $3.50 job or even a $4 job?" Even if I'm workin' for, say, $4 an hour, I say, "If I can get a job at $4, I might get one at $6." That's the way I feel. Just continue and continue thinkin' big. I guess you might say there may not never be no end to what I think. I might get a job for $100 an hour, and maybe I'd be thinkin' about $1,000 [laughs]. That's just the way I am, man. It's not that I'm greedy. I just want the best for my family since I got one. If I was by myself I wouldn't care. I'd be sittin' at home right now and it wouldn't worry me. But since I have a family, that's the problem. And I figure I never could be earnin' enough to do what I want, even if I was makin' $100,000 a year. Only time I'd be makin' enough is if I was like all the rich people, sittin' at home and orderin' people around. And I always say, if I don't have it made by forty-five, I'm just gonna quit anyway.

What do you mean, "quit"?

Just sit home. Grow old, I guess. It don't make no sense for a man or a woman to work all their lives. Like my mom and dad. They're old and crippled, and they're still workin'. I don't want to be fifty and sixty years old and still tryin' to go out there and make a dollar. If I'm gonna be poor, I might as well be proud poor. That's better than being sorry poor. At least I can be proud. They'll say, "Well, he died poor, but he died proud." That's the way it's gonna be. I mean, who wants an old person like that at work anyway? When you get past that age and you go out there tryin' to get some job, that's a strike against you. 'Cause even if they hire you, they probably goin' to pay you less than a young man is gonna make. Nobody wants you when you get old, and I don't want to go out there and embarrass myself lookin' for no job at that age.

What was the last job you had?

Well, the longest one I had, and the last one, was at this gas station. I stayed there for about six months. Makin' about $150 a week. That was about the best one I had, too. Then me and the man got into an argument and he let me go. I went to file for unemployment and they wouldn't give it to me because they said I was fired due to the loss of customers. The man said he was losin' customers because of me.

Was that true?

No. All I did was speak my mind. I don't care who you are or what you are or what you're doin', I feel that I should speak my mind as well as you can speak yours. Even if that means you won't be comin' to my service station for something. I mean, if someone has somethin' wrong with their car and they ask me what would be the best place to get it fixed, why should I tell them to fix it here when I know I can't do it or he can't do it? You can maybe get it repaired better somewhere else. Well, this maybe tends to lose the man customers, so I guess to him that's wrong. I should try to bring people in instead of send 'em away. But I figure, why pull the person's leg when you know you can't do nothin' for 'em?

Like a couple of people asked me if I tuned cars. I told 'em, yeah, I could tune cars, but I couldn't tune 'em there. I could tune 'em up at my house or maybe at their place. Well, the man thought I shouldn't be talkin' like that on the job, tryin' to get customers for myself. People figure that you work for them, so your mind and soul and body should just be thinkin' of them and that work. You can't take a moment to think about yourself or somethin' else. As long as you're on their time, you got to do what they say and think as they say. That's just not me. If a person asks me for advice, I'm gonna tend to give it to him. Girl, boy, black, white, green, makes no difference. I guess they wasn't ready for that.

Then I made a careless mistake. I had to put a fuel filter on a car. I put it on there, but I should've cranked it up to see if it worked. I didn't crank it up. I went home and another guy cranked it up. I guess he was under the impression that I had checked it, and he took it out of the bay, and it blew up. It caught on fire and all the wires in the motor burnt. I naturally had to pay for it. And I could understand the man bein' angry. I told him, "Well, it's my negligence and I'm sorry. I'll pay for the damage." Then he sent me somewhere to get a trailer and a hand truck. I got the trailer but I forgot the hand truck. That's when I blew it. He started callin' me names, you know, "stupid" and stuff like that. And everybody can take only so much. It got to the point where I couldn't take any more, so me and him got into it and I told him what he could do with his job. He paid me off and I left.

I was plannin' on quittin' anyway. I knew it was gonna come to that, but I thought maybe I could last another month or so. See, he was screwin' me on my paycheck. I was workin' from sunup to sundown, six days a week. I was goin' in from seven in the morning to six in the evening. It was a sixty-hour week. And he was payin' me $2.50 an hour, all straight time. I never got no overtime. So I knew he was screwin' me, and he knew he was screwin' me. And there was another thing. He tried not to show it, but I knew he was prejudiced. I was poor black and that still drew a big line between us. In other words, it makes no difference that he left the key with me and let me run the cash register. That was as far as I was gonna go. He never thought about maybe a raise or maybe even so far as my bein' a partner after so many years. You know how things like that go. I knew I wasn't goin' nowhere.

So after he fired me, I went to the unemployment office. They took my claim. Well, I always say you can tell when somebody is leadin' up to somethin', and this was one of them times. I went there week after week. From the first to the third week I didn't worry about it too much because it always takes that long. They told me to keep goin' every week, so I kept goin'. Usually about the third week they'll tell you how much you're drawin'. But they didn't tell me and I didn't ask. They said they were havin' trouble hearin' from Jackson. By the sixth week I was gonna make it my business to find out what was goin' on. But by the time I wanted to make it my business, they already had it waitin' for me. They had a paper sayin' I was disqualified due to some article, Section Twelve. Misconduct. They had verified statements from the gas station that due to my conduct or behavior, the station was losin' customers. So I was disqualified from August through October. On October 11 I can file again, but that won't assure me that I'll get it. If they figure I still shouldn't have any, I'm disqualified again.

I couldn't believe it when this happened. I had never heard of nobody getting turned down for unemployment. This was the first. When I got the disqualification paper, I said, "Hey, this can't be me." I mean, why disqualify me? I thought this never happened to nobody. It really came as a big shock 'cause it meant that until I found a job, I wouldn't have no money comin' in at all. I couldn't believe my eyes. I looked at the paper three and four times: "Disqualified." How did they know? I figure it was just my word against his, so what made me really mad was the idea that they're gonna sit up there in Jackson and rule on what I should have and what I shouldn't have. How do they know what was goin' on down here? In general they took his word that I lost his customers. I guess the board figured he had a more better statement than I did. He had a better reason to say I shouldn't get it than I had a reason to say I should.

Of course, they said I had a right to appeal. But what's the use of appealin' something? You're gonna get the same answer. It's a funny thing about the right of appeal. It's only a nice way of sayin' they're not gonna discriminate against you, because they say, "You have a right to say this is unfair. So we give you a piece of paper, and if you feel it's unfair, you write down that it's unfair." Then all they do is say no again, and they'll tell you they gave you a chance. So what's the use of sendin' 'em an appeal if the same answer is gonna come? That's only wastin' their time and my time as well. So I didn't worry about it.

But I still feel it's altogether wrong. They favor the employer over the employee, which I feel should be the reverse. Because I got a family and he's single. He's the owner of the place and I'm unemployed. And it's not gonna hurt the state to give me that $43 or $45 or whatever it is once a week, to try and support my family. I guess it's sort of punishment, so that the next job I get I'll cool my temper or something. I know I ain't no high-tempered person. But if I was to appeal my case and say, "I'm not this, I'm not that," it ain't no good. I wouldn't have got nobody to come here first hand and talk to me. All I woulda had was papers. They would've sent me papers and I would have to send 'em back papers. All paperwork. And when you're correspondin' on paper, you don't get no feelin' you're talkin' to a person. You got to see 'em and look at 'em and their reactions, and they look at you and get a feeling of how that person is.

This all happened about two months ago. Man, it came as a blow. 'Cause you wonder what you're gonna do next, with no money comin' in. How are you gonna get money? It's been a rough two months survivin' without any money, period. I managed to get along by fixin' this, cuttin' that, washin' this. . . . Somethin' to get me a few dollars every now and then to keep goin'. But every day it's gettin' thinner and thinner. If I don't come up with some money soon, it's gonna thin out completely [laughs].

Have you been looking for a new job?

Yeah, but not too hard. I got to the unemployment office and they give me cards for different places, but either they want experienced people or there's a hundred people applyin' for the job. Like a couple of weeks ago they sent me to a plantation. I've never been no farmhand. I've never been on a farm. So if I give the man a line, like "Yeah, I know everything about farming," he's just gonna end up firin' me 'cause I don't know. It's only makin' a fool of myself. This afternoon I applied for an oilfield job, which I have a little experience in, but the man said to call him back. Most of the time you might as well not even bother to put in an application 'cause they're not gonna look at it. If you're lucky, they might store it. That's if you're lucky. They had a new place open up around here, a grocery store. Letty and me was gonna go put in an application, but during the first day of takin' applications there was seven hundred people there in the store. What's one or two more gonna do? You can imagine how many people in Natchez and the surrounding area that's out of a job. They swarm into Natchez from all the little towns 'cause Natchez is about the biggest place around here.

I used to go around to all the plants, Armstrong and Wilco and International Paper and what have you. But IP was the only one where I passed the test, and they wouldn't let me in because of my discharge. I passed all their tests; but they started talkin' about military discharge, and that's where it stopped. That's the killer in most of these factory jobs. That's the reason why I don't say nothin' about bein' in the service when I go for a job now. If they ask I tell 'em, "No, what's the service?" 'Cause I know if I mention it, they're gonna bring up what kind of discharge I have. That's ruined me so much in the past that I don't mention it no more.

Mostly I just sit home. I reckon if it's gonna come, it's gonna come. I live day by day. I think about not havin' work, but I don't get into a panic. I know I'm bad off. My wife knows we're bad off. And the Man up there knows we're bad off. So if He wants to change it, He'll say, "Well, I'm gonna give this man here some money, or I'll give him a job. Get him together." I just keep on hopin' to find somewhere I can get work. Most of the jobs I've had I didn't really look for. The unemployment office came through many times, and I'm lookin' for them to come through again. And I look in the paper for ads.

You might say our financial situation is very dim [laughs]. We might have a nickel between us, and I'm gonna keep that for tomorrow. So I got nothin' to spare tonight, man [laughs]. A lot of people ask me how we live with no money comin' in. Well, we ain't got too many bills pilin' on. We might have a $12 gas and light bill. Then we got the phone bill, and the rent, which is $25 a month. Which ain't bad, but it ain't good either. So the majority of times our bills come to about $50 a month, and I can usually raise that money. Sometimes we get a week or so behind. But nothing has been taken away from us 'cause there ain't nothin' to take. Everything here—well, it's ragged, but it's ours. The car's ours; the furniture's ours. We just have to worry about light and phone and rent bills.

But we've been cuttin' back. Oh, yes. You'd be surprised how much you can cut back when you ain't got nothin' to cut back with [laughs]. It's like that commercial on TV where the man says, "You have three meals a day. Why don't you cut back and give one to CARE?" Well, we cut back, too, and it ain't to CARE neither. We have to economize. Actually it's more than economizin'. We're on rock bottom. At first we had some money saved up and some food stocked up, but you get down to a point that it's a day-by-day thing. You gotta find some money to get somethin' to eat for the day or think about ways to get money to buy somethin' for tomorrow. We don't go to movies no more. We don't play the TV all the time. We used to put on the air conditioner when it's hot, but now we put on the fan instead. We just put one light on in the house, so we can barely see. I know it's not gonna help much, but in the long run it's gonna help some. And if we don't have enough food for the next day, we cut down on the meal and save some. What you call stretchin' a meal.

I don't know how, but somehow we manage it. I do little various things that I can do. Handiwork stuff. Fix this or that for my mother, Letty's mother, other people. I get a couple of dollars out of it. Sometimes we have to borrow a little money. But somehow we get by.

You seem in amazingly good spirits.

Well, why be down about it? I can't do nothin' about the way I'm livin'. I'm hopin' to get a job, and that's it. Both Letty and me know what the situation is. And what's bein' mad gonna get you? That don't get you nowhere, bein' mad. I mean, just 'cause you're angry at bein' unemployed, that ain't gonna make nobody jump up and give you a job. You get better treatment if you're pleasant and smilin' than if you go in with a frown on your face and say, "I want a job." I always go in with a smile on my face and hopin' to get a job. If people meet you with a smile, why can't you meet them with a smile, even though you're hurtin' inside? Might as well smile. Might turn out to be your lucky day. Like I say, I know what the situation is. Letty knows what it is. I know the fault's on me 'cause anytime I lose a job or quit a job, I know it's my fault. And my family suffers for the mistake I made. But there's no point cryin' about it. Maybe it depresses us sometimes, and we get angry and holler 'cause of the way we're livin'. But you calm down and come back to normal. The kids are still eatin'. They don't go indecent or unclean. They still eat. We haven't gotten to the point where if I eat, they don't eat, or if they eat, I don't. So I just go on with a smile.

Have you thought about leaving Natchez?

I've thought about that many times, but where would I go? Natchez is Natchez all over the world. The other places are only bigger than Natchez. If I knew a specific place that was hirin' for a specific thing, I might go. But just to pull up roots and say, "I'm goin' to Minnesota," and try to get a job there, it's farfetched. Or people in my family might say, "Come on up here, you can find a job here." I ain't gonna go there when all I have is their say-so. How do they know I can get a job? That's as farfetched as pickin' a city out of nowhere. You may be livin' with them, but they're gonna get tired of that. If you don't find a job in a month's time, they're gonna be ready for you to pack up and come on back.

If I saw on TV or written in the paper that they have a specific job in a specific place that I may be qualified for, I would go and apply for it. But like these days everyone says they're hiring in Houston, Texas. Well, whereabouts exactly are they hirin'? This is just hearsay. I don't want to go to Houston, Texas, just because somebody said they're hirin'. I want to know for sure.

Do you ever think about getting together with everyone else who's unemployed in Natchez and marching on Washington or City Hall?

No. Never think about that [laughs]. Because it's so very hard. I mean, it takes money to march on Washington. And then the people in the White House, or wherever you're gonna march to, they sit up there in their cool offices and don't even hear you. And if they do, who's to say they're gonna come out and meet your demands? There've been so many marches on so many things, like civil rights, where people got together and went different places. Only about one in five was heard. I know there's a hope that you'll get heard better than as individuals, but it takes a long time. Look at all the time the civil rights movement took. And I guess poor people are even worse off than minorities 'cause they're unemployed and probably don't have no money to take a walk or a plane to Washington. They're probably under stress, bein' unemployed, and maybe they're too busy lookin' for a job to protest about one they lost.

So I'm not one to protest or buck the system. I did in the service, but I had good reasons. I mean, I have good reasons now. I realize that. If it really came down to a few of us gettin' together and goin' over to the mayor's office to protest about bein' unemployed, I would be willing to sign a petition or maybe go along with it. But as far as me goin' out there in front of the unemployment office to start gettin' together a group, callin' people together and sayin', "We're unemployed . . ." well, I'm not gonna be the first to make the move. I guess the rest of 'em feel the same way; they're not gonna be the first to make the move neither. Therefore, there's no move to make, and the system goes as it is.

KEN DUTTON

He lives with his girl friend in a black neighborhood of one- and two-family houses, declining but not hopelessly blighted, in Seattle. A late-model Ford and a Honda 750 motorcycle are in his driveway. He wears shades, an Afro, sideburns, and a Fu Manchu mustache. He is high-strung, brash, funny. During the interview his phone rings half a dozen times. When a friend driving a delivery van stops in front of the house and honks, he goes to the door.

KEN (shouting): *Hey, stupid!*
FRIEND: *Hey, man, my name's not stupid, it's George.*
KEN: *I call 'em like I see 'em!*

I was born in Portland, Oregon, on January 23, 1956. Grew up in Seattle. I went to college at San Francisco State University, where I did a year and a half before getting drafted into the United States Army.

When I got out, I started doing sheet metal work. Joined the Laborer's

International Union. But there's so many men out of work that the jobs only come once in a while. Last year I worked nineteen days for a steel company. Then I worked twenty-three days for a ship repair place. And that's it. Nothing for the last three months.

So I've been waiting for my name to get to the top of the list at the union, and at the same time I'm looking for something steady. This will give you an idea of what it's like. A few weeks ago I got a hint that Alcoa was starting to take applications. So I went to Alcoa in Vancouver at about 5:30 in the morning for an interview at 8:00. When I got there, there were already twenty people, and it just so happens they take twenty applications a day. The twenty people were already there, so I left. Came back the following Monday because they do it once a week. OK, I went there that time at 3:30 in the morning. There's twenty people there. OK, the next week I went back again, and it was at 2:10 in the morning. Twenty people there. So the next Monday I pulled a gimmick. I went in and talked to the night watchman to find out just about when people start coming. So me and a friend of mine, we rode out there at ten o'clock Sunday night. Camped out [laughs]. And we stayed from ten o'clock till eight o'clock to get interviewed. The fun thing about it was on that Monday, instead of taking twenty, they took thirty. And the thirtieth person didn't get there till about eight o'clock in the morning.

But we got interviewed. You fill out your application; then you get interviewed. And then if you passed the interview, which only seven of us thirty did, you get scheduled for a physical. And I mean a Class A physical. Everything from the doctor sliding on his little rubber gloves. . . . And I passed the physical. So I was told to call back the next day and find out what was going on. I called, and the guy told me we would end up on the waiting list. Meantime, while all this is going on, my name got called down at the union hall and I got scratched because I wasn't there to go out on a job.

OK. Since then, I been to the electric company, pestered Alcoa a number of times, been to Boeing, White Freightliners. I've been to a lot of places I can't think of offhand. And I've been to the Federal Building, making inquiries about what kinds of jobs there are. Openings for veterans qualified to shoot tanks. I'm a gunner and a driver on a tank. Nobody wants to hire me [laughs]. Nobody runs up and down the street with tanks no more, so. . . . If there's another riot in the United States, I might get a gig. If they need tanks. Probably wouldn't go, though.

So my basic day is running around. I ride my motorcycle, do favors for my friends. I could sit up and read, but after a while that would get monotonous. I don't like playing chess with myself. I could go shoot pool, which I really enjoy, but that could get tiresome. I'm learning to play tennis, but it gets tiresome by yourself. I can go see a few of my partners, the ones that don't work, but that would get tiresome 'cause all they're gonna do is sit up and get high and talk about the old days, think of something dishonest to do, and look to see how many police cars are passing their house. That would get tiresome. So what do you do all day long? I dabble in all those things. I may do one for a week or two, and I'll quit that. Take up something else just to break the boredom.

A lot of times I sit up and watch the Late Late Show. It goes off at three o'clock in the morning. My old lady and the kids are in bed. And I sit up and look through how much money I got to pay out this month. And wonder, well, which source am I gonna pluck it from? And I just say, "Look at me. I'm doing nothing. I got nothing to show for it." I got television, stereo, car, motorcycle, and stuff. I got a little more than other people have. But when it's time for me to die, I want to have something to show for my life. I mean, I don't want to have an outrageous bank account; I just want to have something to show for it. I have intentions of buying a boat one day. And I don't mean a boat; I mean a full-size cruiser. 'Cause when I do things, I like to do them right. I don't want everything the rich have got. I just want to have something so when I feel like I don't want to ride my motorcycle today, I want to go ride on the Sound, I can go do it. I don't think I'd be happy with so much money that I couldn't spend it all. I believe in spending money. That way I know somebody else has got a job to build whatever I want. And as long as they spend money, somebody else has to work, and it just goes around. But whenever somebody up on top decides they're not gonna invest money, the thing stops. And that means boredom. Thinking about knocking off a whole bunch of rich people just for the hell of it. See how far the money falls down, and to who [laughs].

A man has to be able to have something to show. Because when you get ready to sit back, take it easy, you don't wanna. . . . I don't intend to work the rest of my life. I don't want to have to work thirty-five years to be able to draw those benefits or all that other jive. I want to have mine where I don't have to have a lawyer jump on the Teamsters or whoever to say, "Where's my check?" And I don't really appreciate having to accept unemployment. I mean, right now, today, I can get out and break laws and make a bundle of money right now. 'Cause I watched other people and seen their errors, and I learn from my own errors, so I don't make the same mistake twice. I could get now to where I don't have to work. And I can drive a big Cadillac, live in a penthouse apartment, all that. Have women working for me. And have the police always trying to kick in my door. See, that's fast, easy money, and it can't last long. And I don't want it. And see, you got to make an awful lot to be able to get in and get out of it. If you get into big business, if you get in there and get good at it, they ain't gonna let you out that easy 'cause they know they got somebody good. The only way you ever gonna get out is in a box.

But I think about it. When I got on a plane flying back from Vietnam, my mind said, "OK, when I get out of the Army, either I'm gonna do it all or I'm gonna hang it up." When I say do it all, that means organized crime, because it's easy to get into. I mean, up in the big-business organized crime. You may not be up on the high ladder, but you'll be making a nice income. Knocking over places, touching people up for somebody. But to me, to be able to do all this, a fellow's gotta have about $10,000 to $20,000 in his bank. That way you can buy your own lawyer, buy your own doctor to look after you. Then you gotta have two or three good nuts. They're stone crazy. When you say, "Kill," they kill [laughs]. They don't ask any questions. But they got to be just smart enough to have sense. You don't walk up in broad daylight and blow somebody away. You got to use tact. You use silencers. You bump 'em off at your convenience. I got that all figured out, good enough to where I know I won't get caught.

At least it's an alternative. They always preach about whatever trade you learn in the service, you can use in civilian life. Well, nobody's hiring any gunners today. I distinguished on an M60 A-1 tank, which is a medium-size tank. I'm a qualified sharpshooter with the M-16, submachine gun, .45 automatic. You know anybody that needs one of those [laughs]? I can break a lot of military codes 'cause I worked with the company commander. Nobody's trying to get me to spy on anybody, so that's out. It wouldn't do me any good anyway. I ain't patriotic, but I ain't gonna be no fool.

But if the rich people can do it, why can't us little criminals do it? And if I get caught, well, what the hell, all they can do is put me in jail, and I was born in jail. I couldn't ever do things I wanted to do, so I'm in jail. Same thing a person in jail goes through. He can't do everything he wants to do. He can live. He wants to live. But he's locked up. I'm locked up, too. I ain't gonna go through all this to get ahead since nobody gets ahead except the people that are already born ahead.

So if the president and all the power structure don't think of something pretty soon, and everybody's unemployed, that seven point whatever it is of the population that ain't working is going to get tired. They're gonna start making jobs by tearing up shit [laughs]. They're gonna have to build that shit back. Somebody's gonna have to build back. See, if all those geniuses up there don't like to get dirt under their fingernails, they're gonna have to pay somebody to put all that shit back. So . . . phooey.

KAREN LEWIS

We're on the front porch of an aging wooden house in a southern Mississippi village. She is twenty-two, a small black woman with two

*children, no husband, and few prospects other than training in business
skills that she receives at a trade school in the county seat, twenty-five
miles away. Her schooling is paid for by the Comprehensive Employment Training Act (CETA).*

*Her voice at first is neutral, guarded. It changes as she talks about the
village—still ruled by age-old racial codes—in a bitterly matter-of-fact
tone. It's the tone of someone trapped but not yet resigned.*

When I got out of high school, I started work at Talvert Industrial. I
quit that because it was too far away from home, and I got a job at Alltree
Fashion. It was sewing and making shirts. You have to make so many a
day, and I couldn't keep up. I worked there for eight months. You're
only supposed to stay there for a three-month trial period, and then if
you can't meet their qualifications, they're supposed to let you go. But
they were gonna let me stay because the work I was doing was good.
The head boss said I could stay. But they got a lady at this job, and if she
say she don't like you and she don't want you to work, you don't work.
We had got into an argument one weekend, and the next week I got laid
off. They said it was because I couldn't keep up, but I knew it was
because this lady wanted me to go. So I went.

Besides Alltree and Froeling Electronics, there's hardly anyplace to
work around here. They got this gravel pit, and they got this rock place
where they make little rocks that go in goldfish bowls. I tried there and
they told me they wasn't hirin' right then but they would be later on.
They told me to come back in a week, and I went back in a week and
they had hired this white girl. If you don't know the white people here,
you don't get no job. So I was out of work about six months. Drawin'
$35-a-week unemployment. Then it started to run down, and I decided
the onliest way I could get a job was to take a trade. I decided to go to the
trade school.

What do most blacks here do when they get out of high school?

If they have children, they go on welfare; if they don't, they have to go
out of town to get a job. Most men work on the railroad or offshore. They
got a few at Froeling 'cause Froeling knows they're gonna do whatever
they tell 'em to do. And the hard job is at the sawmill. That's mostly
black 'cause white people don't want no hard job.

Why didn't you go on welfare?

Well, when my unemployment ran out, I went to get welfare. It took
from March to July to get my first check. And then they told me to go

back and check my unemployment. I didn't know I could re-sign and get an extension. The man told me I could re-sign, so I just got that one check from welfare and went back on unemployment. 'Cause the unemployment was more money. On welfare they give you $86 a month if you're alone and $112 if you have a child. Well, $35 a week is more than $112 a month. And even after the unemployment started to run out again and I was getting $17 a week, I decided to let welfare alone. I didn't want to go through it. You got to tell who your boyfriend is, and they come to your house and check on you. Nobody wants to go through that 'lessen you're extremely lazy. Lazy people will do it. But I just didn't want to, and Momma told me, "Don't worry about it."

So I finally figured school would be my best out. See, this is a small town. And everything here is run by white people. The onliest way to get a job is to know 'em. Like the lady who got me fired, she works at the boss's house and then works at the factory for the same salary. She goes to the house and starts work at seven. The boss has to be at work a little bit before seven. So she goes and gets his little girl off to school. She stays there, cleans up, cooks. And when she gets through there, she comes to work at Alltree Fashion till about eight at night. That's if she doesn't have to go back to the boss's house and cook. She works both jobs for the same salary. So you know they're gonna keep her.

The white people have to know your family. If somebody hadda known my mother and father real good, I coulda got a job. But by them not knowing them, it was hard. Somebody else black could come along, and if the personnel lady knew her family real well, she coulda got a job right then. The personnel lady is the most important. 'Cause mostly the boss is gonna say to her, "Well, do you know her? Do you think she'll do?" And if she says, "Yeah," you're hired.

How do you get to know the white people?

If your family don't work for 'em or somethin', you get to know the white people by starin' up in their face grinnin' . . . [*laughs mockingly*]. Sayin', "Yas, suh," and things like that. And if they tell you to lick the ground, you do it. That's how you get to 'em. 'Cause this is something like still a slavery town. It was so much under slavery at one time that most people are scared to let themselves go and say, "It's not slavery no more. I'm gonna do what I'm gonna do." There's some places you're not free to go in. Like in the drugstore, they got this little counter where you go and buy ice cream. If you're black, you can't sit there. And at the café, black people don't go in the front. They know better. There's a table in the kitchen, and you sit in the kitchen.

They got this man here, his name is W. B. Davis. He's white. He owns the loan company. If he knows you well or if you owe him, you go and tell him you need a job 'cause you can't pay your bills next month. He'll get on the phone and call, and you're gonna get a job. No doubt about it. You're gonna get a job somewhere. If they ain't got no openings at Froeling, he's gonna call around till he finds you a job. And if they don't want you there really, when he says you're through payin' him they might let you get one more check, and then they let you go. That's why most people say if you owe him, stay in debt if you want to keep your job. It don't have to be that much, but stay in debt.

Like this one lady, she came to town and she said she wanted a job. She looked to me like the type that didn't want one. But she had to get one 'cause welfare wouldn't give her nothin'. So people told her, "All you gotta do is go and tell W. B. a lie and borrow some money. When you miss the first payment and he comes to you and asks you why, you tell him you ain't got no job. Tell him where you want to work and you'll get a job." She did it. She got a job. All you got to do is borrow some money and miss the note.

Why didn't you borrow some money and get a job?

I did borrow some once. I borrowed $6 and I had to pay him $7.25. He's high interest. But it don't make no sense to get no job that way. You either be owin' him the rest of your life, or you're gonna get laid off. I wouldn't want to work awhile and then be laid off and be broke again.

I knew it was gonna be hard to find a job, but I didn't know it was gonna be as hard as it is. 'Cause I've heard most people say to get your high school education and you can get a job. Well, you don't have to have no high school. You can have a eighth-grade education, and if the white man knows you, you got a job; you can have a college degree, and if he don't want you to work, you ain't gonna work. Not unless you go out of town. A white lady can be dumb and not know how to write her name, and I can fill out the application and spell everything right; but by her color being a little lighter than mine she gets the job. And I can go on back home and start all over again.

My friend Sally, she went to college and got her master's degree and went out there to put in an application at the welfare office. They told her straight out they don't hire black people. They didn't hardly say, "We don't have no openings." They told her, "We don't hire black people." Now, if I hadda been there and they would've made me mad enough, I would've went further. I would've took 'em to court and took it as far as I could. Then, when I found out that I could get the job, and they know I could get the job, I would've just left it alone.

Right now I'm studying to be a clerk-typist. I got seven months to go. We take record keeping, filing, English, math, typing, office procedure, accounting, and personality development. Personality development tells how you should act around people. How to groom yourself, stuff like that. I like it 'cause whether or not you get a job when you get out, you've still been and learned something. Even if you can't get a job in what you majored in. Most government jobs, like the post office, you have to have the civil service test. And you have to leave Mississippi in most cases. 'Cause in Mississippi you won't get a black person in the post office or a black person in the bank. No way. You don't get no job in the post office, not black. Oh, you might get a job carryin' mail to the houses, but if you want a job in the office, you don't get that. Working behind the window, you don't get that. Black people not qualified for it, so they say.

I want to be a clerk-typist, but if I can't be a clerk-typist and I pass the civil service test, I want to be a state trooper. Which I doubt they'll let me be. At least I'm gonna try. I'll have to go farther than Mississippi. Up north or west, somewhere like that. Not in the South. These people in Mississippi are not right, I'm tellin' you. Not on the job thing, not on gettin' money. No kinda way. Everybody here know that no black faces ain't gonna get behind no desks.

THEODORE CARDENAS

We meet at the Youth Employment Society (YES), a private, non-profit agency that offers high school level classes and job placement help to New York City dropouts, most of them ghetto kids in trouble with the law. In the reception area, teenagers lounge in metal chairs and pore over textbooks. Down the hall, counselors in suits talk to clients in jeans and Pro-Keds. Photographs, abstract art, and posters with pointers on jobhunting decorate the walls. We talk in an empty classroom.

He is nineteen, of Dominican ancestry. He is hefty, bullnecked, with short, curly black hair; he wears slacks, a double-knit shirt, and a cross on a chain around his neck. His soft voice comes as something of a surprise.

I was born in New York, and I lived in New York all my life. I was raised up in Manhattan, on East Broadway, the Lower East Side. Then we moved to Fourth Street. And here's where I began to get myself into lots of trouble. I was only ten. And I grew up seeing so many things—drugs, stealing, everything. The works. Even before I moved to Fourth Street I used to get into a lot of fights. I always loved to box, and my father would sometimes see that I was scared of fighting. He would say, "You better fight, and if you don't fight I will whip your ass when you get upstairs." And then again he would say, "And if you lose the fight, I will still whip your ass." So I grew up and I always wanted to win the fight. But about a year after we moved, my father booked the premises, you might say [laughs]. Now my mother has been separated from him for about seven years. So she was taking care of us. There were five of us altogether—three boys and two girls. She was on welfare. She still is.

When I moved to Fourth Street, I was doing good in school for at least a year. I was doing good. But then I see that the younger generation—and I was that age, too—would just smoke cigarettes behind their mother and cut classes, and as I seen these things, I was doin' 'em, too. I would say, "Well, follow that person 'cause what they're doin' is right." So I went up through the tenth grade, but after that I think I just went about a month and then quit. I found that school wasn't no good for me. In class I would act like a regular little kid, start jumpin' here and there, playin' with the people. Plus I always had the street in my mind. I always thought the street was better than school. I wouldn't know why. I found myself cursing teachers out, throwing erasers, hitting teachers in the necks with paper clips, stuff like that. I was a menace [laughs]. So after I came out of school, I wouldn't go home and study. I would go downstairs and call one of my friends and go cop an ounce or half an ounce and just smoke and drink, whatever.

We just constantly kept on doing this every day. And pretty soon everybody was gettin' into this. More and more drugs kept on comin' in, and there wasn't no embarrassment about it. People doin' it right in the street. And the buildings were kinda getting abandoned. We'd throw garbage inside of buildings, try to burn them down—arson and stuff like that. 'Cause sometimes we would go into a building and get hurt. We didn't want to get hurt no more. We'd see glue sniffers goin' in there, drug addicts. People would get raped in that building. So we'd decide to burn it so that they won't use the building. We'd try to knock it down completely. We didn't want to see it no more. We just wanted to have it plain, like a desert. These days I sometimes wind up comin' down there just to see how it looks, and there's only two buildings standing up. Out of at least fifteen or sixteen that were there.

When I was about thirteen I started stealing, mugging. I would go into apartments, just open up the window or break the doors down. Me and a group. I was also stealing in churches. Some people say not to steal in churches 'cause it's bad, but we would go in churches and just wreck everything and steal what was there. And on my same block there was a grocery store right on the corner. Everybody seemed to be hitting this store all the time. They would hit it through the side of the walls, the ceiling. . . . Me and my friends managed to break under it from the basement through the floor. Sometimes we would try to get into a check-cashing place or something that's worth something. We would just keep on constantly hitting churches, grocery stores, apartments, beating kids off their bikes. I was also in a gang, called the Young Dynos.

I had a pistol. I remember one time, right across the street from where I lived, me and my friends put on masks, and we went with the pistol and knocked on a door. We put the gun to the man's face, told him to take off his clothes and just lay on the floor, and we racked up on the place. Just tore the whole place apart, and took our time 'cause we wasn't really scared. And another time they grabbed me trying to burn the school down. With cocktail bombs. Y'know, you take a bottle and fill it with gasoline and put a rag in the top. We wanted to get rid of the school. Burn up one of the classrooms that was one of my major classes I didn't like. There was nobody in there; the school was closed. But I didn't say this in court. I said to them I wasn't there, and a friend of mine was telling the same story so we managed to beat that case. When I was young I was going to court constantly. Since I wasn't over sixteen, I knew they couldn't do nothin' to me, so I would keep on doing these things.

I was getting busted like every week, you could say. But I was never hooked on drugs. I always managed never to get hooked. I would take dope once or twice a month. Coke, I would take maybe once every few weeks. 'Cause I would see what it had done to my friends. I would hold the belt around their arms, help them take it, but I never put it in my arm. Never. Never. I just snorted. I can't tell you why. And the cops would pick me up and look for scars. I always had scars, but from burglaries, burns, beatings . . . but never no track marks 'cause I never used drugs through my veins. Never skinned. Just snorted once in a blue moon. My thing was always grass.

I never had any jobs, not where I was actually hired. Sometimes I would go in a restaurant and ask the man if I could wash plates for him. Or in supermarkets, I'd pack things. I got those jobs because maybe sometimes my friends wouldn't be around. Or I might feel like trying to win money honestly. A few dollars, just chump change, to buy some glue or a joint or something. Not really to win $15 or $20 'cause I would say to myself, "That's too much hard work." Because I'm the kind of guy—when I was younger—that if I'm gonna be wasting my time in the supermarket trying to win $20, I'd just go around the corner and mug somebody for maybe more.

Every now and then I would go out and look for a job because my mother wanted me to do it. And I figured that maybe if I did have a job, it would keep me from stealing too much 'cause I was doing that every day. Like I would get up in the morning, and right there [*raps his hand on the table*] my friends would be waiting for me, just to look around all day for a house, an apartment, a factory. I always had my mind on stealing and mugging. So when I went out to look for a job, I found I wasn't too persistent. I'd go for a half an hour, an hour, and then I'd say, "Psheew. Forget it. These people don't wann ... I don't give a fuck anymore." Sometimes I'd just go for the walk. I'd go to Delancey Street, Fourteenth Street maybe. I'd ask one store and come back. "Yeah, Mama, I went out, but. ... " She'd say, "Well, that's good, at least you tried."

But little by little, when I got older, I seen that I was constantly doing these things, and I wanted to do better for myself. I would look at my mother, and sometimes I felt real bad, seeing her, 'cause she suffered a lot. I seen how much I made her suffer. And my mind started changing all of a sudden after I went to jail on Rikers Island. I had got into YES before that. I talked to my probation officer from when I was a youthful offender, and she got me into here. My mother was on my case, and my father was on my case even though he wasn't living in the house. So I came to YES and they got me a job over here on Sixth Avenue. I was doing very fine over there. People were willing to help me. I was enjoying it 'cause people were recognizing—not seeing me just like a Puerto Rican who ain't worth nothing. But I seen that I wasn't making very good money, and I would always think of my so-called friends. So I kept on stealing and stuff.

Then one night, when I was eighteen, I was busted for stealing a taxicab. I was with a group of four people, and I was high on Placidyls, the first time I ever took it. I took three Placidyls, and since my mother was always nervous, she had Valiums, and I opened the bottle and took some of them. And I was smoking. So I went with the fellows, and we were all ripped. We were walking through midtown. My friend managed to see a taxi with the keys in it. The owner of the taxi was talking to another man on the corner about three feet away. So I told my friend, "Go around the taxi to the passenger side, and I'll take the driver's seat." We wanted the money in the taxi. I turned the key, and the man heard the engine turn over and he tried to grab the door. I was panicked, and I wasn't looking at the shift, but I just managed to hit the gas and get the taxi in drive. When I turned the corner the man was still holding the door. The street was a two-way street and I went up it the wrong way. And a cop stopped me and he said, "You got registration for this taxi?" And I go, "Yes, sir," and I stepped on the gas again. I ran seven or eight blocks. They chased me. I turned the corner and crashed into three other cars. My friend's face hit the windshield, but he managed to get out of the car and hide under another one. So I got busted. And when I went to court I tried to impress them by showing them I had a job and I was going to school at YES. But the judge said, "You gotta learn your lesson." So he sentenced me to a year. I didn't take it too hard 'cause I always thought that if you do the crime, you gotta be ready to do the time.

That conviction was my first—except when I was a youthful offender—and I think it'll be my last. 'Cause I don't want to go back behind bars. It's a whole different world in there. Always gotta be fighting, all the time. I think I never fought so much out here as I fought in there. I think I had about sixteen or seventeen fights, and that was in five and a half months. Y'know, fights over commissary—things you eat. Your sneakers. Clothes you wear. State stuff. It's crazy. If you don't know nobody in jail, you might as well hang it up. I'm lucky I had some fellows I know from out here. They would say, "Keep away, don't be botherin' him."

In jail there's a thing they call PC, protective custody. You can ask to be put in a cell with another group that don't like to fight. I didn't play that 'cause I figured I could do my time in a regular dorm. And they look down at you if you play PC, especially if you have a friend in there; he'll say, "Ah, you played PC." And like I said, if you can't do the time, don't do the crime. Well, I did the crime, so I showed them I could do the hard time. But if people woulda kept on fighting with me, I think I woulda played PC. 'Cause I just wanted to get out. My mind was runnin'. For two months I had a lot of problems. My mind was tickin' all the time: how my family feels, what I wanna do with myself, am I gonna spend my life in jail? I see young fellows go from Spofford* to Rikers, from Rikers to upstate. They spend all their young life in jail. And that scared me. Even though Rikers is just an institution, it's not like a jail where you're behind bars. It's fences and everything. Where you're really talking about jail is upstate someplace, Attica, Dannemora. Where you see nothin' but bars and rifles pointed at your face. Rikers is just everyday punk-ass motherfuckers like out here in the street.

So I did seven months in Rikers and four in a rehabilitation program. And it changed my mind around. When I came out I wanted to do the good things. I came back to YES and they found me a job in a clothes factory. But I quit that place 'cause I felt it wasn't enough money, and I was comin' from the Bronx—I moved my mother and family up to the Bronx 'cause Fourth Street was too much—to Brooklyn, then to Manhattan to go to school at YES, and then from Manhattan back to the Bronx. I couldn't do it. Now I'm trying to get a job in Manhattan near YES. But it's been five months now, and it's kinda hard to find a job. Some places won't accept me 'cause I got a record. Other places want references, and I ain't got a good reference from the factory 'cause I quit.

---

*The youth detention facility of New York City.

Some of my friends who got jobs, they tell me to go to such-and-such a place. They give me the address, and I go check it out. Sometimes they turn me down; they say, "No, we don't got no openings." So I keep on going from building to building. I ask the super to give me the address of where the landlord is, and I go to the landlord and ask if he could put me into a super's job, where I could clean and mop down the building. But they say no 'cause you have to be able to work the boiler, too. I go into clothes places, where they sell clothes, and they say, "No, you can see we have too many people already." I've been all along Thirty-fourth Street, Twenty-third Street, Fourteenth Street. It makes me feel real down, bad, that they don't want me. But I always have that persistence, like if I'm knocked down, I'll keep on getting up and doing it again. I always manage to keep it up.

My intention now is to finish in YES and get my GED,* and then I plan to go to college. What I'm gonna do is get myself into computers, electronics, something that pays for the future. I always have it in my mind to start stealing and mugging, but I always try to see the positive side and say, "No, it doesn't pay. It's not worth it. You don't want to see yourself behind bars." Hangin' out? I don't believe in it no more. So even though it goes into my mind, it goes outa my mind, too. Like my brother, he's still stealing. And once I said to him, "Bro, I'm gonna go steal with you." He said, "No, man, you ain't gonna go steal 'cause I don't want to see you in jail." And I said, "No, I'm only kidding you." Really, it goes through my mind, 'cause I see my brother do these things, and he gets away with them, some of them. And I say, "Boy, if he can get away with it, then maybe I could." But then I say, "No, I can't do it. I'm not interested in trying my luck." And I sit down and talk to him and I say, "I wanna see you better yourself. I don't want to see you in a position where I have to go visit you in jail." And he understands. I think his mind is getting together, too. He got busted twice for breaking and entering, so he sees it's starting to catch up to him.

I'm gonna show my mother I can do it. That's my goal. To make my mother happy. And to make myself happy, too.

TOM BURDETTE

Another YES client. He is eighteen, a gangly, shy black youth in a striped T-shirt and jeans. His right hand is wrapped with gauze tape—a basketball injury. He looks contentedly around the classroom as we

---

*General Equivalency Diploma

198

talk. "School is different here. If you miss a day, they don't send a letter home. It's more like a grown-up atmosphere. And they don't know me here. My rep didn't follow me. They just took me for Tom, instead of "Oh, that dumb nigger, that bad guy."

I was born in New Jersey. Lived there till I was two. My father, he went crazy on us, so we had to move to Brooklyn. When I was ten we moved to Harlem, and it seems like that's when everything went downhill. It started out like I couldn't behave in school. One week I'd be in school and one week I'd be expelled. Then I'd come back and cool out for a week, and then I'd be out again. By the time I hit the seventh grade none of the teachers wanted me in the classroom. It got to the point where I'd come in school, and I'd be plannin' I wasn't gonna stay. And the first time the teacher said somethin' like "Sit up," I'd say, "What!" And I'd go. That would be my excuse. I'd be gone the rest of the day. I don't know, I never could handle school. I couldn't take the confinement. The problem went as far back as kindergarten. As long as I can remember, I couldn't juggle it. I had to go 'cause my mother still had the reins on me then, but I wasn't doin' nothin'. I can't think of one day I went to school that I wasn't in trouble.

Then I got to junior high and that's when the reefer broke out, and the gangs and all that. That's when everything was just the streets, the wine, the herb, and all of that. The more I hung out, the more I learned. The first thing I learned was to jump up on the trains for free. The next thing was how to snatch a pocketbook. How to yoke . . . that's like you follow a person, and instead of goin' in their pocket and takin' the money, you just grab 'em by the neck like this [mimics a headlock]; then you take their money. You learn that, and you learn the hustle with the cars and the watches. That's when two of you walk up to a car, and the person on one side, he ask 'em the time. They tell you the time, the other person snatch the watch off their hand. That's all I learned in like four years. It wasn't happenin' that quick, but it went from one to the other. The older I got, the more they would let me into. 'Cause it was like the big dudes was schoolin' the little dudes on how to do it. So when the big dudes got too old to do it theirself, they'd get to be our boss, and we'd be givin' what we made to them.

When I was fourteen I got kicked out of my house. I was sittin' there smokin' reefer and I got high and I left a joint in the ashtray, and my mother had always told me that if she ever caught me with it, I was out, y'know. So that was like the beginning of the end. She busted that, and when she was packin' my stuff, she found an ounce in a shoebox, and that was really it. She threw me out. So I was livin' in the back of my aunt's house in a car. I was sleepin' there, and in the daytime I'd be out in the streets.

By that time I was dealin' dope and reefer. I used to see it all the time. The brothers that was teachin' me to steal said, "Here, sell a little reefer, too." And I saw dope before I even saw reefer. I'd be goin' to school and used to see the guys, and I'd say, "Wow, what's wrong with them?" They'd be sittin' here like this [*mimics addict nodding sleepily*]. And they'd say, "Those are dope addicts." And when I came back at night, I'd happen to see 'em passing the money and the dope. So I saw that before I saw reefer. But I never did it myself. I smoked all the herb and all the coke, but I wasn't shootin' no dope. Nah, I'm scared of needles. I couldn't put no needle in my arm. Nah. Unh-Unh. Especially when I was dealin' because then you be shootin' up the profits. You can't do that. That's why if you're a reefer dealer, you can't smoke and deal 'cause you got it right there and you smokin' up what you supposed to be dealin'. I learned that the hard way. If you dealin' for somebody, usually how they run it down is you can smoke three or four joints as long as you get off ten or twenty. And it's hard to sit there if business ain't too good and you ain't high. So you say, "What the hell." And the next thing you know, bang, it's gone. I think I still got the lump on the back of my head from the time I learned that. The nigger beat my ass. He beat it bad, too. He was a big, black nigger. Big ugly turkey [*laughs*]. I think it was about a good hour's ass kickin' that night. I never got beat that bad.

So for about a year and a half I was dealin' both reefer and dope. I would go to the methadone center around the corner and cop, and then I'd go out to Brooklyn, to my old neighborhood. Dealin' mostly to brothers a little older than me. But after a while I figured I gotta deal just reefer 'cause the dope was drawin' too much heat. Too many wrong people. And I was just a skinny dude. It seemed like I'd be gettin' took off more than I'd be dealin' if I kept on. 'Cause soon as the word get out that you don't walk with a piece or nothin', when you go to sell somethin', the niggers as soon as they see it, they gonna jump you and take what you got. And then I mighta been dead. So I jumped out of it before it could happen, before I got a real rep. I can't really explain why I stopped right then. It's just a feelin' sometimes that says you better stop before something really goes wrong. Anyway, I wasn't gettin' all the money to myself, and I couldn't give any to my mother, which is why I got into it in the first place, because she wouldn't take none. I moved into it because I felt funny taking money from her. It was a feeling like I was pimping, in other words. Her workin' seven days a week, and I'm takin' and never givin'. I just felt funny that way. But when I was dealin', she wouldn't take anything from me. And I was only makin' about $100 a week. I would bring in $400 or $500, but I had to give it mostly to the dude I was dealin' for. And I had to buy all my own stuff, my clothes and all that.

But I never then thought about gettin' a job. Not no job. I felt like, who would want me? I just felt worthless. I used to come in the house and my aunt would say, "You still out there?" "Yeah." "Why don't you get a job?" Then everybody in the family would start in. "Get a job!" They'd sit around me—I'm sittin' like this, Uncle Leon and everybody else standin' around me like this, and I'm sittin' here like I'm on trial or somethin'. I'm sweatin' and everything. . . . [laughs]. So I'd say I was gonna do it to please them. But as soon as I go out of the house, it'd be "Joints and bags! Joints and bags!" Work? That was a curse. That was like a bad word.

I just felt like, who would want me? I realize now I never even went out and looked. It was just that things was really down. Nothin' to look forward to. Every day was the same. And I just said, "Oh, what the hell, I might as well go out there and be on the street as go out and get my feelings hurt tryin' to find work." And I always heard if you ain't got that piece of paper, you can't get it. And I knew I didn't have that. So it just seemed like everything was sayin' no, so I just didn't even try.

When I was fifteen I went and pleaded to my moms to let me back in the house. So she let me in, but that got messed up again. The house got robbed. And being as how I hung out with all these people, she thought I had set it up so I wouldn't be there, and I had told my friends when she wouldn't be there. She thought I robbed her. That was it. I was gone again. Back to the car in my aunt's driveway.

I was dealin' reefer for a long time. It wasn't a lot of money, but it was money. I did it in Brooklyn in the same neighborhood, around the school. Joints, bags. I brought back the trey bag 'cause nobody was dealin' treys. And I was tryin' to figure out how could I get a name, y'know? So I'd just give 'em five joints for $3. It was really the old five-for-three, only it was in a bag instead of in joints. I don't know what it is—people wanna take bags instead of joints. They'd rather have a bag. They're gettin' the same thing. So I figured that out, and that's what I did.

And I used to—I'll never forget this [laughs]. I had bought an ounce of gold. And somehow we smoked just about all of it. And I said, "Damn, what I'm gonna do? I don't have no money." So I shot upstairs and looked in my uncle's room and I pulled out the oregano. And I poured oregano in there and mixed it up with that. Then I went out there and told them it was the stuff, and I got all my money back. And they got high. That's what cracked me up. They got high. I'm sittin' there and they're sayin', "Yeah, this is the joint," and I'm sayin', "Yeah, I know," and I'm tryin' to keep from laughin'. So I started to do that, just jerk 'em off for all their money. But later I said, "No, I better just not smoke it all up." I don't know, it mighta got 'em high. I had a little bit of stuff in there, just a little bit. You put a little at the beginning, a little at the middle, and a little at the end. So when they light it, it smells like herb, and then they smoke the tea till they get in the middle, and when they get to the end they smell a little more weed. That way I keep 'em goin'.

I'd go out to the school, and I'd be playin' ball or somethin'. People would come in the park, they'd say, "Who got the joints?" I'd stop the game, go in my pocket, give 'em what they want, keep playin'. And by them sayin' who's sellin' this or that, on a typical day I'd just sit there in one spot. When business got slow, I'd yell, "Joints and bags," just in case anybody new came in. But mostly you'd just sit there and somebody walk up to you and say, "Anybody got that herb?" And you say, "Yeah, I got, what you want?" And that was it. The reefer didn't last long 'cause I didn't have enough money to buy right weight. So I'd make maybe $30 a day. Some days I'd make $30; some days, $20. When it rained, I didn't make nothin'. When it was cloudy, I didn't make much.

I never done no mugging or breaking and entering, stuff like that. I never had the heart for that, I don't know why. I used to have a partner named Larry, and he used to say that all the time: "Let's go break in a house." I'd be high enough to want to do it but sober enough to know I better not. So we'd get to the house and I'd look at it, and I'd look at him, and I'd just say, "Oh, wow." I'd have some kind of excuse and I'd just break away. I just couldn't do it. I could sell dope, but I really had a heart. 'Cause I knew how it felt to be robbed, so I wouldn't rob somebody else. You come home, turn on your lights, and everything's gone. I couldn't juggle with that. I had less conscience dealin' dope than robbin' somebody's house.

When I went back in the car the second time, it was about a year. About the time of my eighteenth birthday I figured it was about time to check in and see if I could get back home. 'Cause by then I was sayin', "Wow, I'm really sick of this. I'm tired of doin' this." So I went there and I rapped to my moms, and at first she really didn't want to let me in. She had the door on a chain lock. But I told her I ain't got nowhere else to go. The car was gettin' smaller by the day. She said if anything, *anything*, break crazy, I was never comin' back. So I moved back in. 'Cause there just nothin' happenin' with the streets. Nothin' out there. Just standin' on the corner, drink beer, smoke herb, sell reefer. At first it's fun 'cause it's something new. But after about a year of seein' the same faces coming back, the same streets, the same boulevards, the same people, the same stores, the same numbers runners. . . .

So one day I said, "Yeah, I think I know what to do." I pulled out my ounce of reefer and poured it on the bus floor. I just said, "I'm *through*." Just poured it on the bus floor. God strike me dead right here. I was sittin' on the back of the bus. I was sittin' and thinkin'. And I said,

"Damn," and I had it in my pocket, and I pulled it out and threw it on the floor. Opened it up and poured it all out. Took out the Bambu, the joints, and everything. And I said, "I done threw away my money, somethin' gotta go right."

It was just—I guess I grew up. I just seen it wasn't right; it wasn't gettin' me nowhere. I guess 'cause I seen a lot of people that had been doin' what I was doin', I seen them gettin' jobs and stuff. "Wow, how do they do it? Has that nigger got a job?" We used to sit there and talk about him: He's stupid; he ain't gettin' no money. But in the back of your mind you're sayin', "Damn, I wish I had that job." 'Cause when you see people gettin' things, and they can be proud, I guess. . . . He'd come back, and instead of like stoppin' and smokin' a joint, he stop and talk about his job. A lot of us, we used to act like we was interested and then go off and talk about him. But I guess when we all broke up and went by ourselves, we really wish we was him. We'd say, "Yeah, the nigger think he a Rockefeller now just 'cause he got a job." Then we'd give the same old excuse, you know: "I wouldn't get no job if they gave it to me." All the time wishin' somebody *would* say, "You want a job?" It got so he wasn't one of the boys no more 'cause he wasn't doin' wrong. But I guess everybody was wishin' they had a job, but everybody felt like, who would want you? What could you do? Ain't got nothin' to offer. Never finished school. Never seen the inside of a high school. Wasn't nothin' else to do but talk about him and wish you had what he had.

But that night, that's really when it changed. That night. I was tired, it was hot, and I just said, "I'm really sick and tired of everything." And I just looked up in the sky, and I said, "Wow, I hope there is somebody up there." I looked at my reefer and all that, and I kicked it and all that. . . . By that time I was wishin' I hadn't done it. But a weird thing happened. I was talking to my grandmother, and she was talkin' about the Bible. And I said, "Oh, hell, not this again." She's kinda old, and they always get into that Bible stuff. And I said, "Yeah, Grandma, I'll read the Bible." And she said, "Read the Lord's Prayer," and I read that, and I didn't understand a thing they had in there. But I read it, and I was lookin' at it, and I put it down and forgot about it. And a few weeks later I got into YES and things started breaking right.

I knew about YES a year before I came here. I was standin' on 165th Street trying to get my stuff off, and my aunt caught me. My aunt Elaine, this was a different one. I turned around and said, "Oh shit!" [*Laughs.*] "Hi, Aunt Elaine!" I don't know how long she was standin' there, but she must have been there long enough to see what I was doin'. She said, "Oh, you're sellin' joints now, huh?" I said yeah. She took me to her house and showed me all this stuff about CETA and all this. I kept it and just put it away. I didn't jump into YES for a whole year. But after I moved back in with my mother I started thinkin' about it, and I called up. But I had to come through an agency, so it took about two months. I was sittin' in the house goin' like this [*stares at ceiling*]. But I never started dealin' again. Not to this day. That was the end. So I really didn't feel that bad because I knew I wasn't doin' nothin' bad. And my mother, she never said stuff like, "You're worthless," or nothin' like that. She just said, "One day, when it's ready to happen, it'll happen."

For the last few months I just been schoolin', mainly. And when I really feel like I'm gonna jump back in the streets, I go talk to my grandmother, and she soothes me for a little while. When you first come in here, it's fun, but then it turns into a regular school. It ain't always fun. Some days you get discouraged, and you be thinkin', "I don't wanna come no more." Whenever I felt that way, I just went and talked to my grandmother. I'd say, "Grandma, I ain't got *no* money." And she'd say, "Yeah, Tommie, but there's some people that aren't even alive." Stuff like that. Make you think. It seem like she always got sense, make me look at the other side.

So it seem like the sun is shinin'. Feels good. Feels real good. Now I'm goin' down and talkin' to all the fellows out there. My main partner, I talked him into gettin' a job. I talked his brother into gettin' a job. I be walkin' in New York and don't be walkin' just to see what you could steal, but walkin' 'cause I got somewhere to go and somethin' to do. That's nice. I dig that.

MICKY ELDRIDGE

He lives with his wife and two sons in an old town in the Deep South that was once an important trading port. Then the river changed course and left the grand old homes of the town facing onto a picturesque but useless—except to the old men who fish there in the evenings, using long cane poles—backwater. Today the town functions mainly as the civic seat of a rural parish; it attracts tourists rather than industry. Unemployment is high.

A jovial man of twenty-three, he seems more puzzled than enraged by the economic conditions and racism that condemn so many blacks in town to long days of drinking and dominoes on the corner of Market and Pine streets.

෧ৡৄ

The last time I had a regular job was back in '76, around August of last year. Today makes a year and about fifteen days. I was a machine operator in Atlanta, Georgia. Me and my family had moved out there because there wasn't no jobs here when I got out of the Army. But then my mother-in-law took sick, and we had to make a choice of the whole family movin' back here or just my wife movin' back. I decided that I had been away from home so long that things must have changed. So we moved back, and when I got here I started lookin' for a job. I wanted a job that was worth somethin', that gave you somethin' for your strain and hustle. But the jobs that was open was mostly seasonal jobs, like pickin' cotton or hauling cotton to the oil mill. Workin' three months out of the year, and after that you don't have nothin' to do. It wasn't the type of job I wanted. And I found out that things around here hadn't changed. They had got worse.

How were they worse?

Oh, man, you had guys with master's degrees and teachin' degrees on the corner smokin' dope and drinkin' wine. Trying to ask themselves, "Why did I go through all that if I'm gonna end up like this?" You had guys with no education at all makin' more than guys that went to college for six years. When I saw that, I knew it was gonna be rough. Because not only here but everywhere in the South, you got to hustle to make it. If a guy is payin' you $3 an hour, he's payin' you good money down here. So you got to bust your butt to get the job and do the job. I found a few construction jobs, like if they needed a few guys for a week or two to lay concrete. But it got to the point where everything was wrapped up. The government stopped building. People stopped building. The one thing I had to rely on was gone. I found myself hangin' around the streets, just asking myself, "Why? Why should I be here? What's goin' on in this town? Why couldn't it be like other places? Who's keepin' the work out of this town?"

I asked a man one time. He was runnin' for mayor, so I asked him, "If you become mayor, would you get jobs in this town?" He says, "I'm gonna tell you honestly. What keepin' work out of this town is three rich men. Some people want to put factories in this town. But as long as those three men got everybody workin' for them on their farms and plantations for $1.75 an hour, they gonna keep other things out. They don't want factories in here because they're afraid it's gonna cut their end of things." They don't want no competition. Don't want no other rich men to move in. Some of the guys I know work for these men, and if they get into trouble or anything—I'll give you an example. There's this man named Steve Charlton, he owns half the town. And if any of his guys kills somebody or shoots somebody, he just gets the keys himself and goes and unlocks the door to let 'em out. On one occasion he wanted to get one of his guys out of jail. The man told him, "Well, Mr. Charlton, we can't let 'im out." So he said, "You let 'im out, or y'all move off my land." It was as simple as that. They had to let 'im out. So those rich men won't let nothin' in. They want everything for themselves.

Day after day you go to the unemployment office, and there's nothing. They did open up a paper mill here in town, but during the time they was takin' applications I was away. And when I came back they had changed their policy. They had to interview so many people that they had turned it over to the unemployment office. The unemployment office would interview you and then send you out to the job. The people that owned the mill didn't have to be bothered at all. So if the guy at the unemployment office didn't know you, you still didn't get no job. He picked the people that he knew or that he thought might deserve that kind of money. Like if he knew Steve Charlton, and he knew Steve Charlton was used to big money, he'd try to help his son, so his son could continue to make big money. But if you was just a little ordinary person, he would try to fix you up with a little ordinary job. A job that might be payin' $2 or $3 an hour, and you're lucky if you get one for $3.

A lot of it has to do with being black or white. Because like I said, the only good job around here is the paper mill. That's the only job you can find that's payin' $4 and $5 an hour. Well, sometimes I hear guys sayin', "They doin' any hirin' up at the paper mill?" They say, "Yeah, they hired three white guys just the other day." I go over there and ask do they have any openings, and they say, "Nothin' goin' on right now." I just say, "All right." I don't want to start no trouble in there. But even if they did have an opening, it would be for something like sweepin' up floors. This town is so behind, they think the Negro can only do common work. They're not up-to-date. They don't want to realize, or they don't want to give you a chance. I look around and see things like that, and it makes me disgusted.

The young blacks start to get a bad feelin' when they realize these things are goin' on around 'em. They have seen their fathers go through it, and they didn't like it. They see their fathers and grandfathers calling young whites around the age of nineteen, "Yes, sir, no, sir," and the whites calling them, "Yes, boy, do this or that." No respect. And they can be workin' on a job for twenty years and have all that experience, but they never reach a stage where they're managers. They always remain what they were when they first hired on. So a lot of young blacks, even if there's openings in them jobs, kind of fade away from it because they don't want to go on with that. They're afraid they might do somethin' they don't want to do. I have heard a lot of 'em say, "If I was workin' there and he told me, 'Boy, do this,' I'd probably pick something up and knock his head around. 'Cause he didn't hire no boy. When he hired, he hired a man."

And right up here on the square there's a liquor store. I can't understand it because this store is in the heart of a black area, and there's not a black person workin' in the store. I went there and asked them for a job, and they told me they don't need anybody. And a couple of weeks later I go by and they got three or four new guys. People tell me, "They ain't gonna hire no blacks 'cause everybody else went up there and asked." So I wonder. I say to myself, "The guy can't be that prejudiced 'cause he's in the heart of a black town. There's nobody white around for about a mile or so. And he's makin' a killing." But I went there for a job, and it's just "No way." It makes you bitter, very bitter. You get hate inside. Something you thought you'd never have. You don't realize you're doing it, but you're hating all the time.

So that's why you get all these guys on the corner. Unemployment. I asked one of these guys that went to get a college degree, "What made you do it?" He said, "Because I thought that after I got out there would be something. But I found out that I couldn't even get a job." He told me he would take a job doin' anything, and I believe him. You know, unemployment shows you a lot of things. More guys get into drinking. The ones that wasn't winos begin to be winos. The ones that was smok-in' a little dope begin smokin' a lot of dope. It begins to be an everyday thing. Guys start messin' with other guys' wives. I noticed when guys get on unemployment, hassles begin to be in the family. You begin to have a lot of breakups and stuff. The guy is home all the time. There's more arguments than if he went to work at 7:00 and came home at 3:30. He's home all day. She says, "You ain't lookin' for work." It's a hassle on him because he can't find no work. It's a hassle on her because she wants her man to get somethin' for her. She wants support that he can't provide. So he's out on the corner, and he's wondering, "Where can I get some money?" He can't go home because she's gonna fuss, so he gets messed up, gets stoned on dope, gets to drinkin' his wine, and just lays up on the corner somewhere all afternoon. Then he goes home, and he's so messed up I reckon he just falls out.

Do you hang out on the corner, too?

Well, yeah, in a way. I never did have no mind to smoke no dope or anything like that, to go that way. But I get with 'em and I talk to 'em. Whatever they do is all right with me. That's what they want to do, so they're gonna do it. There must be three hundred blacks in my area alone that's unemployed, can't find nothin' to do. Disgusted. Stealing. Some of 'em are really hung up on dope, and they'll do anything to get money. So I hang out and talk to 'em about jobs, 'cause some of 'em are so hung up that if a job came around they wouldn't take it. If somebody comes around lookin' for someone to work maybe one day, they tell me, "Such-and-such a person came around, and I don't feel like workin'."

They get high and they don't look for work, or when they're drunk they don't want to work.

I have a kind of routine. I get up and leave here, say, at six in the morning. Everybody goes up on the corner there of Market and Pine streets. People know they can pass by there if they need somebody to do something. They pass by and ask, "Do you want to work for a day?" So I stay there there sometimes all day. Just sitting around talkin'. That's mainly what we do, just sit around and talk about how many politicians got busted [laughs]. We ask a lot of questions. A lot of blacks have things like that on their minds. They have a lot of things against the white man. They'll say, "Well, how come every time a white man steals somethin' there's somethin' wrong with his mind? Or if he kills a lot of people, there's somethin' wrong with his mind? But if a black man does somethin', they're gonna hang him." The law is for the white man, not the black man. Only the hard part of it is for the black man. You know, every prison in this state is jam-packed. Before unemployment you never did hear about that. Maybe one or two guys would get sent up. But now the guys are stealin', and every jail is jam-packed.

Boy, I'm tellin' you, Carter better get off his butt and push some jobs into these towns. Push it so the guy with the money don't have no voice unless he's gonna get somethin' goin' here. Carter should push some federal factories in here, so these guys with the money cannot say no. 'Cause as long as these little enterprises are gonna come into town and ask, "Can I put up a factory?" they're gonna tell 'em no. They're gonna keep it out. Carter better get off his butt or this country's gonna get worse and worse. 'Cause the United States is a nice place to live, but the system is too loose. You meet Mexicans, Chinamen, any guy that comes from a foreign country can get a job just like that. They send 'em to school with no problem at all. But here you have to fight to go to school, fight to try and get some money, and these guys are comin' from Japan and Israel and invadin' the country and gettin' jobs. I've never seen a Japanese layin' on the corner. 'Cause the government is helpin' 'em. The only people that's on the corner down here is blacks.

On the corner you tend to get into a debate. You get into politics, hard into politics. Because the average person on the corner, he's got a lot of smarts. You don't find too many morons on the corner [laughs]. Mostly smart people are alcoholics or dope fiends. 'Cause they feel the pressure on 'em, and they have to do somethin' to ease their minds. Lots of 'em don't like the system that's goin' on, but they can't express themselves the way they want to. So they get high and let themselves go. They might buy two or three half gallons of wine and just sit on the corner and chat. Just let everything out of 'em.

Of course, it's not only bad around here. Some guys get pushed back from California. They was on their own out there, and they couldn't find jobs, so it pushed 'em back home because they couldn't hardly make it and they figured probably in a little town they could at least eat. Around here you might not have some money, but if somebody's got a piece of bread, they're gonna give it to you. And on the corner the guys will give you a drink before they'll give you something to eat. There's a lot of guys out there who were away and came back. They don't want to go back there either because it was pretty bad. At least here you can sneak out in the woods and steal a watermelon or a potato or something. In the city you can't. I know a lot of guys that steal potatoes, watermelons, cabbage.

Have you?

Oh, yeah. You know, it's a hard thing to run with a watermelon [*laughs*]. It's a hard job. You just *cannot* run with a watermelon. You ever try to run with two watermelons? Goddamn, it's a hard job [*laughs*]. Try it one day. Them watermelons jiggle, and you're tryin' to adjust 'em. . . . It's hard [*laughs*].

I haven't had to steal much food. My grandfather always raises a garden, and I do a lot of fishing. Blacks around here eat a lot of fish, so when I don't have anything to do, I go fishing. I've sold fish, too. Sold a great deal of fish. Mostly buffaloes and a few bass. Had regular customers. All these schoolteachers want fish. And the farmer's market, I've even sold at the market. I got caught once. Well, I didn't get caught, but somebody turned me in to the game warden. Told him I was catchin' game fish. He showed up one day and told me he had to come out and check on it. It was a good thing I didn't have any game fish that time. All of 'em was legal fish. He told me that if I had just one bass it could've cost me $150. Didn't make any difference how long it was, it would've cost me $150. From then on I had to be more careful.

I used to fish down by the river. That's where I went to catch the bass anyway. Boy, if the game warden only could've seen 'em [*laughs*]. I did that about seven months, and I'd pick up anywhere from $4 to $6 a day. You string out your net, and about fifty yards away you string out another one. You might let 'em sit there all night. And when the fish runs into the net, he gets tangled. The next morning you go back and take him out.

But I had to go out of business. A lot of guys was stealin' my nets. They wanted to try and make that little extra change, too. Times are hard, man. Shoot. These guys wanted some money in their pocket, and they would watch you. They might be out settin' traps or somethin', and they would watch when you put your nets in the lake. Shoot, when you leave, they go right back in there and take it. Might set it again right around the corner from where you had it. So I would make something like $5 or $6 a day, and the nets was costin' me $30. I was tryin' to save to buy another net. If I could get one, then I could make a little more money. I was tryin' to establish myself to where I might have six or seven nets. Shoot, I couldn't win. 'Cause the more I'd buy, the more they'd steal, and I found myself workin' for nothin'.

Now I pick up Coke bottles. You can get five cents apiece for coke bottles. A guy made me see that when I was in Texas. He said, "Would you take a nickel and throw it out of your pocket?" I said no. He said, "That bottle you just kicked there is a nickel." I began to realize what he meant about that. If I kick one bottle and kick another one, that's a dime. And it goes on up. As easy as I can kick it, I can pick it up. So that's what I do. If you find ten bottles, that's 50 cents. A pack of cigarettes. So if I run across a bottle and I need some money, I pick it up. I don't go around town lookin', but you get guys to do that. They make sort of like a wheelbarrow and go down by the highway, pickin' up bottles.

Then we have a lot of races. Races for a fifth of wine. Races for $1. All kinds of other games. Drinking contests. Domino games. I don't take part in the drinkin' games, but I play dominoes. You can't imagine how time passes when you're playin' dominoes. I think it's an education. Teaches you to be quick.

Anything that comes up, I'll try to make a little money. Like my father used to mess around with plumbing, and he taught me when I was a boy. If somebody needs a pipe put in or a leak fixed, maybe I'll do it and charge 'em $2 or $3, where a plumber would charge 'em $20 an hour. Or I work haulin' hay. They pay a penny a bale. Five hundred bales, that's $5. It's hard work. One of them bales weighs 100, 150 pounds, and you're throwin' 500 bales and then have to get in that barn and stack it, too. Wow, that's a hard job of work for $5, I'll tell you.

And I've picked cotton. That hasn't started yet this year. It'll start around the middle of next month. It used to pay $2 a hundredweight, and some days you might not even pick one hundred pounds. That was when I was younger. If you never picked before in your whole life, you might not make but $1 a day, or 75 cents. You got to be a fast and strong picker to make $4. You ever seen a cotton row? A cotton row is about a mile long. You have to drag that sack through there, pickin' cotton. The sun's beatin' down, and the poison they put on the cotton makes your nose itch and sneeze. Then, once you get the sack down the row, you have to pull it down to the other end to weigh it. It's hard work. You have to pick a lot of cotton to get one hundred pounds.

But when the season comes, if I don't have work, I'm gonna be out there pickin' cotton. The pay's gone up a little bit now. Lots of the guys will be out there 'cause it's the only thing people get to do around here. I swear to God, even at $4 a day, I'll be doin' it. It gives you somethin' for your mind to do.

EDDIE VARGAS

*He lives in the Chicano ghetto of Los Angeles. He grew up in the
streets, a gang member from an early age. "Then I met Dorothy, my wife.
She was different. Other girls I just picked up to throw away, picked up
to throw away. But I seen something different in her. She started talking
to me, changing my ways. Even though I came from a Christian family, I
was still bad. So it's not inherited. I listened to her and started changing. I went from an F to a B average student."*

*He is twenty-four and has a child of school age. A visitor to his living
room soon notices a huge aquarium against one wall and a dog-eared
Bible, the only item on the coffee table. He is a recent convert to fundamentalist religion, describing his past with the phrase, "When I was
in the world. . . ."*

When I graduated from high school, I got a scholarship to go to
college. They knew I came from a Mexican background, so they wanted
to help me. I went to a technical college for two years. I was taking a full
load and working nights. It was a real ambitious time for me. I was
thinking, "Wow, I'm going to college." I graduated after two years with
something like seventy units and my qualification in machine shop
work. After I graduated, I got married, and then I went to another school
for more training, to finish my apprenticeship program. When I did that,
I thought I really had it made. I figured, "Wow, I graduated, I had a good
average, I've got my apprenticeship credentials." I thought I had a lot
behind me. Then I went out there in the streets and started looking for a
job. That's where I started getting hurt.

The first place I got work was at Fudd Engineering Associates. They
told me, "We can only start you out at $3 an hour." Well, one of my
teachers in school used to tell me, "Never settle for anything small.
Always aim high." That's what he got into my head: Always aim high.
So I told them I wanted more than $3. I was aiming high. But he said,
"I'll start you off at $3 and see how you are." I finally said OK. I started
doing machine shop work, and there was one job I didn't thread right.
He told me, "I gotta lay you off."

Then I went to another company. They wanted to pay me $3 an hour,
too, and I said no. I was still aiming high. So I lost out on that job, and

the same thing happened at another place. I lost out on two jobs. I was asking for $3.50 an hour and they wouldn't pay it.

Then later on it started getting rough, and I had to settle for whatever I could get. I'd be looking for a job, and they'd be telling me they need ten years' experience or five years' experience. I told them, "Look, I don't have the experience. I have the knowledge and the know-how on up-to-date machines. I got my tools. I know what to do." They'd say, "I'm sorry." So after looking all over the place I got kind of disgusted. Everybody wanted ten years' experience, and I was twenty years old [laughs]. Finally I came to a company called Winston Corp. They wanted ten or fifteen years' experience. I was so disgusted and run down by this point that I said, "Give me any job." So I started working on the assembly line. I did that for three years. I put aside my knowledge and my skill because I had to work. I had a little girl, and I had to feed her.

After three years they closed down and went back east, so I got laid off again. Then I started working for another company driving a forklift. After a while they put me on cutting metals, and then I started running the machines. The lathes and mills. It was machine shop work, the first I'd had since I got out of school. I was pretty happy with it. For a while there was a lot of work. But then the work went down, and they laid me off for two weeks. They called me back because there was work again. I worked a week. They laid me off again. And now I've been off for eight months. I'm looking for a job, but not in machine shop. I figure I'll go back into shipping and receiving. Working with the trucks. Plain labor work, in other words. Because I have some experience in shipping and receiving. And I've been looking at the unemployment office for whatever odds-and-ends type jobs they have. One was for a chauffeur, chauffeuring coffins. A hearse driver. That was $3.50 to $3.75 an hour, but I didn't get it. The problem is always experience. I have a friend, he's Mexican, too, who went for a job sweeping floors. And you know what they told him? He had to have two years' experience. Two years' experience in sweeping floors for $2.30 an hour! He said, "You guys are crazy. Two years' experience? I sweep floors in my house every day! There's nothing to it!" [Laughs.] So that's the situation I'm in right now.

It gets to me. There are times when I cry about it. I knew it was gonna be hard, but I wasn't expecting it to be this hard. But this is where the Lord comes in. See, I came to the Lord just before I got laid off. If I was still in the world now, I think I would be going crazy. Hollering, nervous, upsetting my family. Hating everything like I did when I was in high school. But there's a Scripture that says, "I am in the world, but I am not of the world." People can't understand that. It's what's keeping me sane right now. Because to me the Lord is the truth. He's the one I'm living for. I believe in God, and He is true in my life. I had a personal experience with Him, and I know that the word of God says that if you have heavy burdens or heavy labors, put your cares upon Him. So I have been trusting the Lord to supply me with a job. The Scripture says, "Seek ye first the Kingdom of God, and all his righteousness shall be added onto you." As long as I put Christ first in the picture, I know He is going to supply my needs. And He does in different ways. Two days ago somebody gave us some food. My mother-in-law gave us $50. People help out here and there, but I know it's the Lord doing it.

So I feel that if I get a job, I get a job. If I don't, I don't. I just keep on looking. Simple as that. I'm not gonna quit and say, "Forget it. I'm no good. I'm not worthy. I'm not a good father. I can't support my family. My kid don't want me, and my wife don't want me." I don't have that attitude because I know my wife has confidence in me and the Lord is going to keep us. It still bothers me about the job, but I have Christ in my heart. I've got something to base my life on. I live not for material stuff or the desires of the flesh, but for Christ. I owe Him my life, because I know He did a miracle for me. I'm a completely different person than what I used to be before. Completely different. If you would've met me before, I probably would be cussing and telling you to get out of here. I'm a new creature in Christ.

In fact, I wasn't looking very hard for a job until about two months ago because I was working for the church. We have a program called Street Line. We work with gang members and drug addicts. I go into the ghettos and tell those guys that they don't have to live that way, fighting with each other, in fear every time they turn around, getting hooked on heroin. I tell them that Jesus is the answer and He is the way. See, there are a lot of organizations trying to get these guys—social services and group therapy and such—but they don't have the answer. Christ has the answer. So when I first lost my job, I was working full time for Street Line. Then I had to slow down because my unemployment is running out, so I have to get a job. I can't be at the church so much.

I enjoyed that work. It wasn't a job like unloading freight. It was a job that dealt with human beings. It was a responsibility job. I like to work with people. I can feel their burdens. I get a satisfaction when I talk to them, and witness to them, and see a different glow in their faces. I rejoice when I see a person convert themselves out of that rotten life they're living. And it's not easy. It's not an easy thing to go into the ghettos and talk to these guys. Some of them . . . están locos, they're crazy. But there are a lot of them that put up a mask. And we know they put up a mask. Inside, they're crying, crying for help. So you go and explain to them that you came from a rough life, and you know what they're going through. You explain to them with love. And they open up.

It helped me another way, too. I started out feeling bad because I don't have a job. But some guys out there don't get anything to eat. There are people out there who are crippled. They're suffering more than I have ever suffered. I saw people on skid row. Man, I thought my life was rough. They've got a rougher life, living out there in the cold. Or a heroin addict going around in the middle of the night, making connections, stealing, and getting killed. So I say to myself, "You know what? You ought to be happy with what you have. You have a family together; you have a home; you're surviving. You're not rich. You're poor, but you're not on the ground." I praise God that I can think and talk and move around. I can go out for a job, and either I get it or I don't get it. I still make my effort.

But the time's gonna come soon when my unemployment runs out and I'll have to take any job for any money. See, a man has a lot of pride, but the Lord has been taking my pride away. When there's no money left and I'm not getting any money, I'm gonna accept a job for $2 or $2.50 an hour. I got no choice. It's either life or death, and I'd rather take life. I'm not like Jack Benny, you know: "Your money or your life!" "Take my life!" [Laughs.] When the time comes, I'll automatically have to take that job. And then by some miracle, maybe I'll advance in it. Right now I won't accept $2.50 an hour. Three dollars, yes, but not $2.50. Even though it's only 50 cents' difference, it adds up.

I'm very discouraged at this point. I mean, I'm not gonna get any worse. I live day by day. I'm not gonna worry about what happens tomorrow. But there are times when I feel, "Man, I can't go on living like this." I'm only human. There are times of doubt, when I get hate into me. I feel like they're not giving me a chance. I start turning against the society. And there's times when I feel like I'm not worth anything. Sometimes I think it's all my fault. I should have opened my mouth at such-and-such a time. I should have taken such-and-such a job when I had the chance. I shouldn't have listened to that teacher when he told me to aim high. Because I don't care for that idea no more, that "aim high" thing. I feel that if you can get a job that's reasonable, take it. Don't be greedy. Don't be selfish and want more and more and more because all you're gonna do is lose everything. Take what they offer you, and start from there. You'll start moving up. But "aim high," it's no good no more. I just hope that teacher's not still teaching his students those things.

Sometimes I cry when I think about all that. How come I didn't take advantage when it was there? There were times when I had it in my hand and turned it down. Now if they offer me a job for $3 an hour, I'm gonna take it. Regardless of what the job is. I'm not gonna make that mistake again. I know I can't make it on $2.50. That's not a mistake, me turning that down. But if I turn down a job for $3 again, that's a mistake. So when I pray at night, I pray I don't make a mistake like that again. Take it! Three dollars an hour, take it!

MAHMOUD DAUD

He is Lebanese, a member of the Arab community clustered on the southern edges of Detroit. It is midafternoon when I come to the door of his house, on a leafy street, but he has just gotten out of bed. He is dark-skinned, handsome, shirtless, with wild black hair. As we talk, different members of the family come into the room to be introduced. His mother serves thick, sweet coffee; she has tiny tattoos on the back of each hand. Afterward they insist I stay for dinner and feed me quantities of zucchini stuffed with ground meat and pine nuts.

He talks in heavily accented English, with a kind of passionate despair. Seven thousand miles away a catastrophic civil war is raging in his country. Half a mile away is the mammoth River Rouge Plant of the Ford Motor Company—a Mecca to which he cannot gain entry.

I was born in Lebanon. I came here around six and a half years ago. When I was fifteen. Now I'm twenty-one. Trying to find a job. In six years I had one job. I worked at Frank's Pizza for one year. When I first came here, I was new. I didn't know how to drive. So I started learning how to drive. I drove the car and the truck for Frank's. I used to get lost. Then after one month, two months, I knew the streets. I went around delivering. But then they gave me another job. See they don't want me no more, right? They want to get rid of me. How they gonna do it? They don't want to tell me, "You're fired. We don't want you." They say, "We're gonna give you a job inside the place." So I went on the inside job. Worked a week. My check came around, and it said $80. On the truck I was making $150. After they take taxes, $107. So I know they don't want me anymore. I don't know why. They just don't want. So I says, "No, I'm not gonna work no more. I quit." Since that day I'm looking for a job.

We got fifteen people in this house. Eight of them, they're still under age. And my father is the only one working. He's working at Chrysler. Me, I'm just trying to find a job to give him money. I go to all my friends and other people, and I ask them. Every time I ask they say they don't need people at their factory. Or they say this other factory is needing people. So I go there, and they say, "No, this factory is laying off people. What's your name?" "Mahmoud." And that's it. When they know my name's Mahmoud, they say, "We can't help you, no."

215

Because you're an Arab?

I don't know. Maybe. Also lack of experience. And I don't talk good English. I talk English but I don't talk it good. And I don't have experience in this kind of work, in a factory or inside to be a manager.

You see this drum? I play it. This is the only thing I learned here. I came here and there was nothing to do. I used to play tambourine in the old country. Then I came here. I said, "Well, I got a drum, so I'll make some money out of it." I started it. Now I make some money. I play at weddings, anniversaries, birthdays, conventions, anything. Sometimes they pay you $75 a night. At nightclubs, $30. That's why I didn't go to work yet. This is better than working in a gas station or a store. In a gas station I'm gonna make $75 a week. That's why if I work in a factory, I don't care about this drumming job no more. If I find a better job, like $3 an hour, then I'll leave the drums. But this is more money than a gas station. I didn't find a job yet that pays me more than this.

How do you get through the day?

Well, I don't have a job, right? So what I'm gonna do? I go look for a job, yes. But all the time I sleep, wake up, watch TV, sleep, wake up, watch TV, sleep, wake up, watch TV. Every day I sleep twelve, fifteen hours. I can't just go outside because I don't have the money. Sometimes I even scream at my mother 'cause I feel sick inside. When anybody talks to me, I swear at them. I don't want nobody to talk to me. Sometimes I sit by myself for twenty-four hours a day. I get up, watch TV for twenty-four hours a day, believe me. Around two months ago I stayed in the house one whole week. I didn't go outside. One week watching TV. Because of the job. The job, that's the only thing to bother me. Give me a job and believe me, you'll see me different.

I get so nervous sometimes, I lose my mind. I don't know what to do. I go outside looking for people to fight. I don't mean I look to fight them. But I go outside and I'm so nervous that if somebody talks to me, I fight them. And I don't want to do bad things. Like go steal or kill or something like this. I don't like it. I could do it. It's easy. But I know I'm probably gonna lose everything by doing that. But if I'm gonna need it, I'm gonna do it. You know what I mean. I hope not, but if I need it I'm gonna do it. I don't care what's gonna happen. Sometimes it comes in my mind: "What the hell, I'm not working. I don't have any money, and I can't work, and I can't make no money. So which is the easiest way?"

That's why a lot of people take drugs. So they can forget. I tried it once or twice. I took some hash. It was the first time in my life I took hash. I came over to the house and everything started going dark. My father and mother, they say, "What's wrong?" They got scared. I didn't tell them. I says, "Everybody stay out of my sight 'cause I don't know what I'm gonna do. Just call the ambulance and let me go to the hospital." I called my brother, and he came and said, "What's wrong? Did you take any drugs?" I says, "Yeah, I took some drugs." He says, "That was wrong." I went to the hospital, took a shot, slept and slept. Since that day I never touch it. I lost my mind the last time, right? Maybe the second time or the next time, when you want something and you wanna get it so bad and you don't know how, you're gonna take some drugs and go get it. Whatever you want, and whichever way you wanna get it. See, I don't want to be a bad guy. I still want to be straight. But if it's gonna be my life, or my brother or my mother or a friend's life, somebody's gonna be sorry. I think it's me.

See, whatever you want to do, money will let you do it. If you want to be a king, money will make you a king. A lot of people say money is nothing. Well, if you're living good, money is nothing. But it's because you have money that you're living good. Like me, I don't need a lot of money. With $5,000 I could do something. For a lot of people here, Americans, $5,000 is nothing to them. With $5,000 they get a car. But I'm different. I got plans for $5,000, because I know what the dollar means. I got plans for them when they come. Like to open something. My mother is a professional launderer. So with $5,000 I could open a laundry. A small laundry, any place. Just a small corner. My mother could do it. When you start with something small, you get something big.

But I can't even get something small. And I feel so sorry for my father. I can't give him money. My father, he wants his family to be a big family. He wants to give from himself till he dies. That's what he is. He's been carrying me for six years. I worked one year and I gave to him. Now I play drums and I give him a little bit. But how much can I give him? Sometimes I don't get work. Then I'm gonna go to him and tell him I don't have money today. I need $2 to get someplace. I'll tell you the truth, this is the only thing that's making me feel bad even more than jobs. When I ask him to give me a couple of dollars. He gives it to me. Just like a child.

Sometimes I get so hopeless I can't look for work no more. 'Cause you don't have to. Just look in the papers, you'll know what's going on. Believe me, this country has gone down 50 percent. Like I saw in a paper that there's 200,000 millionaires in this country. And the paper said, we don't want 200,000 millionaires. Instead, we could have 200 million people with a little bit of money. That's what it said in the paper. We need some money for the people. They're dying of hunger. Now in Lebanon, my country, they're dying of hunger. It's a revolution there. But revolution between the Christians and Moslems, between leftist and rightist, between Americans and Russians. Nobody knows what's going on. A lot of people, they don't have money. They're gonna die 'cause there is nobody to help them. So what they're gonna do? They're gonna get a machine gun, go someplace, kill somebody, get his food. And it's gonna be in this country, too. Dying of hunger. That's what I think. Because I can see it now. It's gone down 50 percent. A lot of people are getting hungry. Over at the unemployment office I saw thousands of people. Remember the unemployment office where you were standing? There were people standing to the other side of the street. Standing up everywhere. And what they gonna get? Ninety dollars a week? What's that gonna do, $90 a week?

My brother, you know, he works in a meat shipping plant. You know how cold it is where he works? Forty-five degrees. And he's standing on his legs for eight hours. How long is his break? Fifteen minutes. He works like a slave. And he can't bring his family from Lebanon. You know, sometimes my brother sits talking to God. He asks Him, "Why are you doing this to me? I'm gonna do this and that to you." He got so nervous, he don't even trust his God no more. Sometimes he says, "God, I don't believe in you." I don't believe there is a God. If there is a God, what is He doing right now? Why doesn't He see? Why doesn't He look at what's going on? A lot of people dying of hunger. Why don't He help even one guy?" You know, we have a joke. One guy says, "Jesus or Mohammed's coming back." You say, "He's coming back where? To the South End?* Where is He coming from? What's He gonna look for? I think if He comes here, He's not gonna find a job. He's gonna go back up there." Believe me. Day after day you lose your trust in God. Not just in God, in yourself, too.

Once I stayed over by an auto plant for two months. Waiting for a job. Can you believe it? Do you know how long is two months? When it's freezing below zero? That's why maybe I hate everybody. They hire like a hundred blacks, twenty-five whites, one Arab. Believe me. So I stayed there in line. I'm thinking maybe they didn't get enough Arabs. I fill out the application and give it to the guy. He takes it and says, "Come back some other time." He don't tell you, "We're sorry," or something. Just "Come back some other time. Get out of here." Second day, third day, fourth day. I stayed there two months. Then I got so nervous, I want to kill that guy. One day a Palestinian guy gets in there. He's tall, smart, strong. He stayed in line just like me. He gave the guy the application. The guy didn't look at it. He took it from him and said, "What's your name?" "Ali." "Oh, Ali. Come back some other time." So that guy Ali, he got nervous. He held him by the neck right there and took his tooth out with his fist. He says, "I don't want your job. I just want your . . .

---

*The Arab neighborhood on the outskirts of Detroit.

when I give you this paper . . . I don't want you to hire me. When you take this paper, just look at it and say you're sorry. Or don't say you're sorry. Just look at it and say, 'We don't have a job for you.' Don't tell me to come back tomorrow. It's below zero and the ice is on the sidewalks."

You know what I used to do? I used to take my blankets from the house and put them over me to go wait in line. 'Cause it's too cold, man. It's below zero. You wear five or six jackets, two pairs of pants, something under the pants. Do you know what it is when it's below zero, to stand outside six hours? Sometimes I would go there at 2:00 A.M. till 8:30 or 9:00. I used to sleep outside. Sometimes you take newspaper or something and put it on the ground and sleep on it. 'Cause if you come at six you find at least forty people standing in line, and they only take five guys. So I used to say, "Well, I'll go first. Maybe they'll take me because I'm first." I used to go around at two and find some people sleeping before me. It's two, man. And I knew they were hiring. I filled out applications for about fifteen people, and they got in for interviews. I filled out applications for three blacks who didn't know how to even read and write, except their names or something. They got inside; I didn't. I don't know why. There's nothing between me and the guy who's sitting there. I never met him in my life. It's unbelievable. Ask anybody on the South End. They'll tell you. It's true what I'm saying.

My father was lucky. He came to this country. He's got fifteen people to support. I don't know what happened. He went into Chrysler just like that, and he's working there now. But I'm twenty-one years old, right? Who do you think is gonna work better than me? An old man? I could work twenty-four hours a day, but they don't even think of it, those people. It's like you're trying to fight a war. And that's not just my opinion. You could go to the South End and just watch those people there. It's almost all Arabs. A lot of them don't have experience, but a lot of them do have experience. And they're smart. Believe me, there's a lot of smart people there, but they haven't found a job. If they have got a job, they work like slaves. Not like workers, like slaves. 'Cause they don't know how to speak the language. They get the bad jobs. Work and work and work and work, and they're gonna die, man. But I'm gonna do it, too. If it comes to me, I'm gonna do the same thing. I'm gonna be a slave. That's all there is. But I'm gonna be a slave because maybe if I'm a slave, then my brother, the small one who's five years old, when he gets to be eighteen, he won't be a slave. You know what I mean? That's all my father's doing. My father is working as a slave for Chrysler. He supports us so we won't be slaves.

6

OLDER PROFESSIONALS: "Sic Transit Gloria Mundi"

The middle-aged white men (and one woman) in this chapter live with the fear that they may never work again. Laid off from highly skilled, well-paid executive or professional jobs, they face two insidious kinds of discrimination—against the older worker and against the "overqualified." Some of them have involuntarily retired.

JIM DIXON

He is a gangly man with the beginnings of a paunch. His long, bony face is ruddy with sunburn; his gray hair, cut short, is just beginning to thin. He spends much of the day sitting on the patio of his modest apartment in the heart of "Silicon Valley." He gives a feeling of nervous energy not easily contained. There is an ironic aspect to his unemployment, which he appreciates: He spent his working life as a personnel manager or recruiter.

I joined Instruments Unlimited in 1961. At that time I didn't know what a semiconductor was. I didn't know how to spell it. It was the first time I ever worked in the electronics industry. Prior to that I had been with a construction company for five years. Anyhow, it worked out fairly well. I was with them for nine years. Then they went through a series of massive layoffs, I think in 1969 and 1970. These were huge layoffs. I don't know how many thousand they let go. My guess would be that it probably numbered around six thousand to eight thousand. Those figures are very hard to verify because nobody will tell you the truth about 'em *[laughs]*. Well, my number finally came up. One week before Thanksgiving, they called me in and said, "Thank you, good-bye." And that was it.

At that time there were obviously no jobs around. Christ, every organization and company in the area was laying off. So I did nothing. I didn't even attempt to look for a job for six months. Then I got a call from a headhunter named Larry Sanford. He was a good systems engineer, and he had heard about me, so he asked me if I wanted to go work with him. I did, and we got along very well. But in the summer of '74, I think it was, all of a sudden the bottom dropped out of the business altogether. We were finding engineers for companies, you know, charging a fee. But we were pretty narrowly based. Larry worked mainly with the systems houses 'cause he was in systems, and I mainly worked the components houses. So when the semiconductor firms started laying off, that was the end. I've been out of work a little more than a year now.

It's funny. I knew the day I was laid off from IU . . . I could have damn near wagered money that this is how it would end. Just the way it is. Because I had been in the electronics industry for almost ten years, and I know how they think. There's no security in that industry. You make your own security. I look at it as being my fault because I didn't have the intelligence or good sense to realize that anyone who has not put himself in a position by the time he's fifty to not ever have to depend on industry for a job, I think he's asking for trouble. Especially in "Silicon Valley." I didn't realize it before, but I sure as hell realize it now. And it's the advice I would give anyone. If you have to depend on that industry past the age of forty or forty-five, you're in bad shape.

Even if I had the chance, and I know I won't because of the age factor, I would very much dread going back to that industry. To me it's an industry without a soul. Really. They just don't care about people. They'll manipulate 'em and use 'em, but the minute they don't need you, you're gone. What's always amusing to me is that they emphasize loyalty to the company. Shit, that's a one-way street in "Silicon Valley." Of course, other industries aren't as exciting to work in. Public utilities, oil. . . . There's something about electronics that keeps you going. At the IU research division, when I was fifty I must have been the oldest guy there. You have to be nimble on your feet 'cause you're dealing with a bunch of real bright young engineers and scientists.

But that's the problem. I remember Harry Stevens, who was one of the founders of IU. When I came there, I don't think he was yet thirty-five years old. And over the ten years that I was with him, there were many occasions when we'd have someone come in and Harry would say, "Gee, he's an old guy." You know, the guy was forty! They want the bright young tigers. They want all racehorses. And if you ask around "Silicon Valley," you'll probably find that IU is the most notorious of them all for getting rid of the older employees. As I said, I was the only older guy in my division. And this is interesting: IU has a retirement program, and after you have ten years of service you have vested rights in it, OK? I was laid off after nine years and ten months. Now, I don't say they laid me off just because of the nine years, ten months. In all honesty, for the last year or so I was pretty fed up with the place. But it seems to have been a pattern. There were so many coincidences like that.

I still don't know why they did it. I honestly don't know. No one gave me a reason. I said to my boss, "Christ, you just reviewed me two months ago and said everything was fine." He said, "I still feel that way. I still feel the same about you, Jim, and about your work. But it's out of my hands." What he meant by that I don't know. And you sure as hell could never get a reason out of IU, any more than you could out of any company. They don't operate that way. It may be that the personnel function is sort of a frontline spot. I think they preferred to have younger people. It's not a company policy, but they do it. Trying to prove it, that's another thing.

Over the past couple of years I've had damn few interviews. Maybe a dozen, no more. But I think the industry has made it painfully clear over the months that I'm considered unemployable because of my age. And there's no way I can buck it. Now, I haven't applied for too many jobs either. I didn't blanket the entire area with résumés. Because first of all, until you get to a point where you need the money, you're a little selective about the companies. And second, you quickly realize what's going on. You have a background in the industry, so you know how they feel about older people. Then you apply for jobs that you know would be cakewalks for you, and you get turned down. It isn't hard to figure out why. What the hell other reason is there? They always wind up hiring some youngster or some female. There are an awful lot of females in personnel jobs down here now. So what other reason is there? No one can tell me that it's because my performance wasn't all right. Shit, if it hadn't been, they wouldn't have kept me for that long.

So I've had maybe a dozen interviews. Some of them were genuine, I think, but later on I still got the Dear John letter. Others were courtesy interviews. I was down at one place a couple of weeks ago. I spent an entire day with them, interviewing. They were looking for senior technical recruiter in the San Francisco office. That's a job I know well. But everyone I met in that group were young tigers. And it became pretty evident after the first hour that I was being given the old courtesy interview. I could tell by the people's lack of interest in talking to me. They didn't ask me the right questions. You can tell, for Chirst's sake. If someone sits down and doesn't talk a bit about the job, or how you would handle a situation, or how you'd go about looking for engineers, but instead talks about the weather and how the company has grown, and all this crap—I know how they've grown; they don't have to tell me that.

It's the hardest thing in the world to prove, discrimination. A few weeks ago I was talking to a friend of mine down south, and he asked me how things were. I said, "Roger, you should know. At my age, things are lousy. I can't get a job." And he said, "Why don't you file a claim against any of the companies you feel have discriminated?" I said I didn't think it would be worthwhile. He said, "Wait a minute, Jim, I have a friend in Washington. He's in the government. I'm gonna call him right away, and you can expect to hear from him within the next hour." Well, I never thought I'd hear from the guy. But I'll be darned, about twenty minutes later the phone rang, and this man identified himself. He said, "Roger tells me you're having a problem. You feel you're being discriminated against because of your age." I said, "Yeah. I am." He said, "Do you have any handicaps?" I said, "No, I don't have any handicaps other than being fifty-five years of age." [Laughs.] And I said I was toying with the idea of going to the EEOC and filing a claim. He said, "Jim, I don't like to discourage you, but if you're not black or female, forget it. They won't do a damn thing for you. The only way to handle that is go out and hire yourself a good lawyer." I said, "I can't afford a good lawyer." He said, "Well, unfortunately that's the situation most people who are laid off are in."

It does you a tremendous amount of harm psychologically. Not necessarily because you feel that other people don't want you. You get over that feeling. At least I do. I've come to the conclusion that it's just pointless to try to get a job in the electronics industry. I have other concerns now, financial concerns, that are more important than whether or not people like me [laughs]. I have to get a job out of self-preservation, for Christ's sake. You can imagine what this does to a pretty active guy, sitting around the house like this all day. It affects me tremendously. Between worrying about finances and crawling the wall because I have nothing to do, it has a great effect on me. I just try to get through the day, that's what it boils down to. And it's *difficult* to get through the day. Even if you had a lot of food for thought, there comes a point where you've digested all that food [laughs].

The worst part of it all is the embarrassment. Great big grown man, and he can't even support his own wife. It's hard for me to stomach, seeing my wife get up every morning. I drive her to work, say good-bye, and then come back to what? Nothing. Either sitting here or going fishing. But what can I do? I live with it. Suffer with it. I think any man would feel the same. Everyone knows you're not working. Everyone knows your wife is working. People put two and two together. You're not supporting her, so it's obvious she's supporting you.

A friend of mine is a doctor, and I went to see him about a year and a half ago. Not for anything serious, just a case of nerves. And he said, "Well, Jim, you supported Ginny for many years, what's wrong with her supporting you for a while?" He said, "I'm sure if you asked her, she'd be the first to tell you she doesn't mind it." Well, that may or may not be true. But I don't feel that way about it. I think a man should be in a position to support his wife. Period. It's that simple. Absolutely. And the fact that I can't makes me feel pretty friggin' useless. Whether or not it's my fault, that doesn't change my thinking any. The fact remains that she's supporting me. I couldn't care less whether it's my fault or not.

She's been great about it. But I'm sure she thinks about it, because she'd like to quit work and relax. Both of us think about it. I don't talk to her about how I feel because I can't alleviate the embarrassment by talking about it. It's not something I discuss with anyone. But it's something that's always here in my mind. And whenever I tell her that I have a prospect or an interview lined up, why, my God, she gets on cloud thirteen. So delighted and excited. It's gotten to the point now that when I went to the last interview, I didn't even tell her. I didn't want to disappoint her. I had a pretty good idea it was a courtesy interview, so I didn't even tell her. It would just upset her more because she can't understand why Jim Dixon is not hired by these companies. She just can't understand it.

That's one of the reasons why I've tried for *every* job in the past few months. I mean menial jobs, like pumping gas in a gas station. Shit, yes. First of all, just to relieve the boredom. Christ. Plus the fact that I need the money. When this began we had some savings, and we had some stock; but it's just about gone. Ginny doesn't make enough to support us. Do you know what rents are in this area? You know what the cost of food is? You just don't get by on an income of $600 a month. You just don't. By the time you pay your rent, electricity, gas, telephone, some dry-cleaning bills, you know, there's not much left. And even if it were enough, that still wouldn't help the situation. It would ease the situation a certain bit, but it certainly wouldn't change my thinking about my wife supporting me.

Then I just happened to see a sign, "Help Needed," at the station where I buy my gas. I said, "How about me?" And the young man who was managing the station at the time said, "Are you kidding?" I said, "No. It's only a few blocks from my house." And he said, "Well, as far as I'm concerned, great." It wasn't much of a job. It was $3 an hour, but you could work all the hours you wanted. So I looked at it this way: Even though it's only $3 an hour, it's close to where I live. It's outdoors. They furnish the uniform, and if I can put in seventy hours a week I can earn enough to survive. Still, it made me feel a little strange [laughs]. This young man didn't have the final authority to hire me. The station is owned by some gentleman from Fresno who has about a dozen stations. So the young man said, "I don't see why not." And then he said, "Would you take our little test?" It was just a mathematics test, very simple. A guy buys five gallons of gas at this price and gives you a $20 bill, what's his change? OK, I took the test. I think I got them all. Then he said, "Would you fill out an application?" I brought an application home, typed it out, and took it back. And that's when it started to look a little ridiculous. You know, here's this job pumping gas. Not that there's anything wrong with pumping gas, believe me. But a guy comes in and he has a fairly heavy background in supervision and management, with a fairly good salary history, applying for a $3-an-hour job. It didn't hurt my feelings any, but I wondered what the owner's reaction would be. And apparently it wasn't too good, because I wasn't offered a job.

Just this last week I tried for a job overseas. I have a friend who has spent most of his life on foreign construction. He seemed to feel that he can help me get placed overseas. If things weren't tough, I certainly wouldn't consider it, because it's single status. And when you're fifty-five, it's a hard thing to leave your wife because you don't have that many years left together anyhow. But these foreign construction jobs are single status. They're good jobs; they pay extremely well. We'll see. My friend's optimistic, but I've talked to optimistic people before. I've been optimistic and nothing materialized. At the moment, though, that seems

227

to be about the only possibility. I talked it over with Ginny about going alone. What's the alternative? What's the choice? There is no choice. I could survive it. I think every sixth month they allow you to meet your wife in Europe for a certain length of time. And time passes quickly on a construction job because you're usually working a minimum of six days a week. There's nothing else to do. You're out in the boonies. So that remains to be seen.

You asked a while back if it affects my family life. Well, it does. And it's not Ginny's actions; it's mine. I'm always on edge, and I have a tendency to fly off the handle. Things that should not annoy me do. But I think it's really myself I'm angry with. I'm so goddamn frustrated because there's nothing I can do. At least I haven't found anything. So all this builds up. You know who's working out there. You know that when there's a job opening, it's pointless to even send in a résumé. If you do send one in, you do it with the almost certain knowledge that you'll get the old letter. Then you check around and find out who's accepted the job, and in one hundred cases out of one hundred it's somebody twenty years my junior. Things like that can be goddamn frustrating. You can't just crawl under a stone. No, I think the facts of life are that this may be a fantastic country for young people, but it can hurt like hell when you approach middle age.

DOROTHY FEIBERMAN

She belongs to the 40-Plus Club, a self-help organization of unemployed executives. We're in the cramped office of the club's public relations committee; in other rooms, men in suits (and a few women) practice interview techniques, make phone calls, or revise their résumés. There is an air of dedication and an almost familial warmth.

She is a forceful woman with silver gray hair. "When they asked me if I'd be interviewed, I said, 'I sure will!' If somebody's going to publicize this situation, they deserve all the help they can get. Everybody's getting older. Everybody's going to face this sooner or later. So maybe a guy of thirty-eight will think twice about leaving his job if he reads your book. . . ."

In 1971 the company I was working for decided to move its offices from D.C. out to Virginia. The bosses lived out there, so they made it

convenient for themselves. But I live in Maryland. I was very independent and had been very successful. And never in my life had I had any
trouble getting a job. I started working for that company at the age of
thirty-four, which is the ideal age to get a good managerial job. You're
not too young—not just a kid out of school—and you're not too old.
I didn't know it at the time, but that's the prime age. After that, forget it.
I had been with the company for ten years, and when they moved I
figured I didn't want to go to Virginia. I had a very beautiful house in
Maryland, and I didn't want to move. So I quit. Had I known what lay
ahead of me, I would have moved to Timbuktu with that company, I'll
tell you.

For the first six months I didn't really want to work. I was enjoying
the newfound freedom, because I had worked since I was seventeen
years old. But finally I started to look for a job and got no response. I was
absolutely flabbergasted. I had sent out a résumé with all my marvelous
experience, knowing how marvelous I was, and no answers. I couldn't
believe it.

Well, your first reaction to that is: "Maybe there isn't the right job out
there right now." I'm married, so the situation wasn't that desperate. My
husband has a very good job with a management consulting firm in the
city. He always wanted to start his own business, something he could
build up, and then move to Vermont when he retired. I never liked it
there that much, but having nothing else to do and no jobs panned out,
we started this direct-mail business. We sold handmade wood and
metal objects. Very nice stuff. He designed them and I ran the business. I
took out ads, sent out catalogues, handled correspondence . . . and I
hated it. I got progressively more depressed. I had worked in cities all
my life, and I like to work with people. I do my best work running a
department. And there I was sitting in the house, doing this work alone.
A day could go by without speaking to anybody. I couldn't stand it.

So I started looking for a job again. Meanwhile I'm getting older and
older, right? I'll be fifty this month. When I started looking I was forty-
nine, and I said, "This is it. I've got to get something this time around, or
I'm finished." Well, I still was getting no response to the résumés. And
one day my husband said, "Did you ever hear of this 40-Plus Club?" I
said I vaguely knew about it. And they happened to have an ad in the
paper that day. I seemed to fit the qualifications, and my husband said,
"Why don't you go in there? You're exactly who it's designed for.
Maybe they can help you." He realized I had had enough of the business, and I agreed to keep doing it at night and on weekends. He knew I
couldn't stay in the house, so he said, "OK, go to the club and see what
happens."

Well, the minute I walked in here I knew I would like it. You feel a
tremendous empathy the moment you walk in. First of all, there are
people your age. They've had jobs on your level. And they're all unem-

ployed, so obviously there's something you have in common. The man who interviewed me knew what my problems were before I told him. I signed up right away, but it takes awhile before they approve you. That in itself makes you feel good. They're very fussy. They insist that you give references, so you have to be at least a halfway decent manager to get in. The whole thing is to make you feel comfortable and build up your ego a little bit, which everybody needs. Most people who come in here do it as a last resort, after they've tried themselves and failed.

By the time I came I was depressed, very depressed. I'd sit at home and cry. I'd eat a lot. I didn't know what to do with myself. I'd go out for walks, but it was all very meaningless. Well, it depends on the kind of person you are. There are many women who are used to staying home, and they love it. They don't have to get up and make trains every morning. They have all day long to do what they want. But I was a liberated woman a generation before my time. I always wanted a career. I never wanted children. I have to feel I'm doing something that the world thinks is worthwhile and pays me for it. I like to be involved in things. So I think maybe not finding a job hit me harder than a lot of other people. I don't have children or anything to keep me home. I had a dog, but I didn't see how I could get along with a dog as the meaning of my life.

I started out by using all the personal contacts I had and by answering ads. I did go the employment agency route, but let me tell you, I don't know how those people make a living except by placing secretaries and young people that are easy to place. Some of them even tell you—maybe you strike a chord, and they feel they can talk frankly—they tell you, "Hey, look, over forty is hard." It's against the law to talk about that, and I suppose in a way it's good that it's against the law. But on the other hand, you don't know where you stand. It was almost better when it was legal because only a very few feel they can trust you. The others don't say anything. They just have you fill out a lot of papers, and they talk to you, and you never hear from them again. And you know what it is. I'm registered with eight or nine agencies, but they've never once gotten me an interview.

It's a rotten situation. It makes me feel like I've worked all my life for nothing. I'm at an age now where I know a great deal. I'm capable of handling problems that it would take a younger person years to learn to handle. And I don't think I'm that old. I can work another fifteen years, but I feel that they don't want me anymore. It's such a terrible form of discrimination. Very bad for your ego. It makes you feel worthless. You put in all those years, and they don't want you anymore. You ask yourself, "What's it all about? What am I going to do with myself?"

I now understand what black people have felt for so long. For example, you answer a blind ad in the paper. Sometimes you do get a response. Then you walk in there and you can see the muscles tighten in the person's face. They're trying not to react, but they're maybe expecting someone twenty-eight or thirty. It's horrible. You can't imagine. As soon as you walk in, there's that reaction. Then, of course, they try to be very pleasant. And you never confront them on it because you think maybe they'll hire you anyway. And they would deny it if you said anything. They have to interview you because age discrimination is against the law. They have to say they talked to everybody, young people and older people, and they picked the most qualified person. Who's accidentally going to be thirty.

There's another problem with big companies. They don't want anybody over forty because they have to pay more benefits to older people. But a lot of us would waive the pension plan. I don't need it. My husband has a pension plan, and I could have my own plan today, with the Keogh and IRA systems. I'd be willing to waive it, but they never ask you. The personnel office just says, "At this age, stop." In fact, personnel officers are the worst people you can talk to. If you get past personnel, you're halfway home. In general, someone who would hire me would be someone my age. You normally don't get to be a vice-president of a company until you're fifty. To that person I don't look old. But the personnel office usually has an army of interviewers, and these are kids in their twenties. I look like their mother. There's a tremendous resistance right there. And you mostly have to go through them, so you don't get very far.

You get pretty disgusted at things like that. But that's why the club is so helpful. I've been here about six months. Some people don't get jobs for two years, and others are out of here in a month. However long you're here, it's helpful. It had a marvelous effect on me. It gave me more courage and confidence immediately. I made friends here, which is nice. And it keeps me busy. Part of the membership requirement is that you devote two and a half days a week to club work. There are no paid employees, so somebody has to do it all. What we do is come in three days one week and two days the next. That way you don't have that five-day week ahead of you that you don't know what to do with. For two or three days I have to go into town, and the other days I can cook up something.

Another good part of it is that it's a disciplined situation. When you come here, it looks like an office, not like a social club, even though it is social to some extent. There's work to be done, and you're in a disciplined atmosphere, which is very good. All the members belong to at least one committee, and they usually put you on one that your background suits you for. Since I was in advertising, I'm on the public relations committee. Then there's the membership committee, the treasurer's office, the secretary's office, the marketing committee—they try to get companies to list jobs here. We give courses on interview skills that are tremendous. And we have a team of people who help the new members to write résumés. That's an important feature of the club because at our age it's bad to have a chronological résumé that talks about all the years you've worked at various places. It goes back too far. So they teach you to write an achievement-type résumé that says what you've done. Instead of just saying, "I worked at such-and-such a place where I did layouts and wrote copy," it says, "Because of the ads I designed or the copy I wrote, sales were increased from this to that."

For me it also makes a difference to be with other people. I'm a social being, a herd-type person. But I don't like to be with people on a social level. I like to be with people who are interested in business, so the conversation is on that level. That's very important to me. And another thing: When you can't get a job, you think you're the only person that can't get one. You begin to feel, "There must be something wrong with me. Maybe I don't have it anymore." But when you come here, you realize that's not true. As a matter of fact, you think to yourself, "What am I doing here? There are men here that were vice-presidents and presidents of companies. They had much more important jobs than I ever did." And you see that if it can happen to them, of course it can happen to you, too. We had a man here who just got a job for $60,000. He was looking for $80,000. He compromised [laughs].

If I get one interview a month, I'm doing well. Sometimes you get a couple together, but I don't have many interviews. People here keep telling me if I was a black woman I'd have a job like that. Companies want these token people. A token black, a token woman. But it's still easier for men to get jobs, don't kid yourself. The companies don't really want a woman when they can get a man. With all the talk, it's still harder for a woman. And the field I'm in is terrible because advertising is young-minded. They think you should have young ideas, young approaches. They take people right out of school so they don't have to pay them very much. I'd be very happy to change my field because I can do a lot of things. If you've been a manager in one situation, it doesn't take long to learn a new one. But it's very hard to change fields. There are people in the club who have twelve résumés. I'm not exaggerating. Unless your résumé uses the exact words that appear in the ad, then people say, "He's never had the right experience." I myself have three résumés. One says "administrator," one says "manager," and one says, "executive assistant." There's so much competition that they can get exactly what they want. So if your résumé doesn't say it, they don't listen.

One funny thing is that people can't understand why I'm so desperate to work. My friends say, "So what? You don't have to work. It's about time you stopped and enjoyed life a little bit." My mother can't understand it at all. "Well, you've worked for twenty-eight years. It's enough. Everybody has to stop." Well, yes, everybody has to stop. If I was sixty, I think I could stop. But it's too soon for me. I can't stop yet. So many people who retire fall apart and die. I go through this business about whether I should dye my hair. That's a big thing I think about. If I dyed my hair, maybe I'd look younger. I asked some of the people here what they think. They tell you the truth; they're very frank. They all said no. I said, "But I'd look younger." They said I wouldn't because it would only harden my face, and the employer's going to find out how old I am anyway. I'm starting to think they're right. Maybe I'm really making a statement by leaving it this way. What difference does it make what color hair I have? But then it occurs to me, maybe I should get my face lifted. If I could get my face lifted, then I'd dye my hair because then the whole thing would look right. My husband says, "Stop it, why are you carrying on like that! If they don't like you the way you are, tough." He's very encouraging in that sense. His attitude is: "It's their loss if somebody doesn't grab you up."

But it even creates problems in my feelings towards him. I'm the kind of person who likes to be in control of my own life. There are many people who don't care about that. Many women love to have their husbands protect them and support them. But I like to have my own money. I like to be a separate person from my husband. I don't like to exist because of him. As I say, I was in women's lib a long time ago. I was afraid to say these things thirty years back because people thought you were crazy. But I've always felt that way. I like to be married, but I don't like to depend on my husband. Our relationship exists because we like each other, not because I need him to feed me. I like to be able to buy clothes if I feel like it without asking anybody. But now I don't feel I'm in control of my life. I'm dependent on him. I don't like that feeling.

Maybe the worst part of it all is that it makes you fearful of a lot of things. Fearful of time, that's the first one. You used to welcome it, but now you're afraid of how you're going to fill it up. You're fearful of general economic conditions. Maybe they're going to get worse, and you'll never get a job. You get so insecure and nervous about it that you advise anyone who has any kind of job to hold on to it, which may not be the best advice. How is the person going to advance? But I find myself saying to people, "My God, don't leave or get fired when you're over forty." I tell my husband that. He has a good job, but sometimes he'll see an ad in the paper and say, "Gee, maybe I should go after that." I say, "Don't do it." I'm afraid for him to give up that security. Whereas before I never felt that way. I had a lot of confidence. I never lived by fear.

You start going over your life: I did this wrong; I did that wrong. I knew that advertising wasn't secure, but when you're young, you don't listen to people. Now I think they were right. The security was very important. Why didn't I listen?

GIORGIO RICUPERO

Besides producing hand-crafted wooden toys (see Chapter 3) he is active in The Experience Advantage (TEA), a group of unemployed professionals based on Long Island. Unlike the 40-Plus Clubs, TEA does not try to find jobs for its members; it functions more as a pressure group, aiming to win support for programs to help the unemployed—especially those in glutted fields such as aerospace—to begin new careers, either through retraining or by means of seed money for small businesses.

We talk in the TEA office on the second floor of a church.

I was fifty-three in 1969, when they laid me off, and that was already a little too old. As a matter of fact, now I understand that in some places you're already starting to be too old at thirty-five. The main reason for that is the cost of fringe benefits: health insurance, life insurance, and pensions. On pensions, the employee usually pays half, and the other half is paid by the company. But a manager who's got a department with a hundred people in it, he looks at the average age. Let's say it's forty-two. Life insurance is based on that, and so is health in a certain way, and pension. If somebody is at the company only five years, the pension fund payments aren't that high. But another guy who has fifteen years puts in much more, and so the company has to put in more. The manager looks at the average age, and if he can figure out a way to lower it from forty-two to thirty-nine, he may save quite a lot of money. The only way is to get rid of the old ones. You can't blame the manager for it. It's just company policy. I've seen it happen so often.

Some families never get over it. They may have been living this good life. They have lots of money. They have a big house. Suddenly they can't meet the payments anymore. They have to get out of the house and get a small one. The kids want things. They have always had everything before. Now it's all gone. The wife has to work. You often see these families break up. We have had a tremendous number of divorces in this area as a result of the layoffs. But my wife and I are not that type. We went through very bad years during the war, you know. My wife was bombed out three times, so she knew what it meant to be at the lowest point, when you have no furniture and nothing to eat. I don't know if you have an idea of what it is to be hungry when everything's rationed.

You get maybe three loaves of bread for the whole month, one ounce of lard, and four ounces of meat. No vegetables, no fruit. It was a very bad time. So even when I was laid off, I didn't suffer that much. But there were a lot of people here who really suffered.

In fact, TEA was set up to fight this specific situation. It was started at the end of 1972. We found that we didn't have any success in getting attention from the government or the companies, so we tried to be a lot more political. We have been several times to Albany, and we talk to our local legislators and congressmen. We know them all very well, and they know us, too. We found out that if you don't get anywhere, the only way to get people to listen is to get a little violent. I don't mean physically violent, though we got to the point a few years ago when we were ready to start throwing Molotov cocktails around [laughs]. I mean in speeches, in letters. So now they're a little more responsive. But you can write an awful lot of letters, and still nothing happens.

These legislators come around and talk. We've gone sometimes to places where they have open sessions. For example, a congressman comes to a school, and we go and we talk about our problem. And he says, "Oh, sure. I'm aware of that. That's a very serious problem that you're showing me here. I'll try to help you. Give me something in writing." And we say, "Here, we have this in writing. Here are the facts of it." But do we ever hear from them? Sure, you may eventually hear from some secretary there in Washington. She sends you a letter and she sends you all these forms. You fill them out, send them back. Months go by until you finally hear again, and probably the things you were asking weren't even answered, because they just send you standard letters.

What we wanted a couple of years ago was money from either the state or federal government to help us start our own businesses. We had found out that employers wouldn't take us anymore, so we thought we'd use our experience to start a business. But you can't raise money. For instance, at the Small Business Administration—I have been there—the first thing the man says is: "How long are you unemployed?" You say, "A couple of years." "And what are you, are you Caucasian?" "Yes, I'm Caucasian." (This again is a bad point, a negative point, that you're Caucasian.) "Do you belong to any kind of organized group? A union?" "No, I don't belong to a union. I'm just a simple engineer. I would like to have some money loaned by you people so that I can start a business. I would like $2,000 or $1,000." Immediately the man says to you, "No, we can't give it because our policies and guidelines don't allow it. There's nothing set aside for you. It's only for blacks and Hispanic-Americans. They can get money, but not you." He actually said that openly to me.

Or you go to a bank, and what happens then? You go in there and you want them to guarantee a loan so the SBA will give you money. They say, "What collateral do you have?" You say, "I don't have any collateral because my money is all gone. I'm unemployed. I don't have anything left." "Oh, you don't have anything." "I just have a few assets. I still have a house." "Then you have to put the house up for collateral." But I didn't want to do that, because what would it leave us with if we lost it?

So as I said, we tried to be a little bit more political. Our key man here was very outspoken. He was a good speaker and he wrote numerous letters. All these file cabinets are full of his letters. But now he's gone. He's employed. So we're not so active. It's getting a little bit slower now. We also found that to be a political activist doesn't really get you anywhere unless you belong to a minority group. As a matter of fact, sometimes people even feel that if you're too outspoken and you do something about it, then you're a rabble-rouser and bad for society. I remember one time when one of the local congressmen came to an open session with county government. We came in there and went into the newsroom. There were all these newspapers there, and they had a booth. We wanted to impress upon them that they should put a little more emphasis on writing about the unemployment problem in the area. So we went in their booth and they immediately threw us out. There was a little—well, not a fistfight, but some pushing. They threw us out of the room. Now it's interesting what came out of that. The next morning the papers appeared, and they all talked about the bad unemployed people, who came and rabble-roused and made a lot of trouble. They didn't even discuss the reason why we went there. The only thing they mentioned is that somebody was fighting with them. That was it. We were rabble-rousers. We were activists.

Another example of that was when we went to Albany. We were invited by an assemblyman who felt the unemployment problem might be something he could use in his political strategy. This was during the last campaign, four years ago. So we went up there, and he had invited television stations and all the newspapers. Everybody spoke a little bit, telling little stories of what we had gone through and what the age discrimination problems were. The television and radio and newspaper people were all listening, but the more we talked, the quieter it got. There was no response from the people there. Apparently they didn't want to hear about it because it's a hard problem. The newspapers would rather talk about easier things. So nothing came out of that. The assemblyman dropped the issue because he felt there was no reason to follow through on it.

So in recent months we've been a little more quiet. Our best activist is gone, and we felt it was no use because you don't get anywhere unless you have money. The only thing you can do if you feel discriminated against is bring a first-class suit against the government or the state or the company, but we don't have the money to do that. So we lose out.

ABRAHAM ROSNER

We talk in the backyard of his house in a New York suburb. A sprink-
ler revolves slowly, spitting long jets of water; the wrought-iron table
near our lawn chairs is covered with magazines: Newsweek, The New
Yorker, The Atlantic. *One side of the yard is strewn with branches from*
a tree he trimmed yesterday. He is fifty-five. He has troubled eyes and
deep lines around his mouth. His voice is toneless, brightening only
when he talks about his good years as a stockbroker.

In 1964 I got laid off from an insurance company. Well, I had been
interested in the stock market for some time. I'd been doing some dabbl-
ing and had some investments. One day I was talking to my broker, who
had become assistant manager of his office. I was unemployed, and I
was sort of jokingly saying that I'd make a million dollars if I had his
job. I said, "You've got the greatest job in the world." He said, "Why
don't you come in and apply?" Then I got a call from him two days later
that somebody had just left and there was an opening. He said, "Just
come around and throw your hat in the ring." I did, and I got the job.

At that time I was already pretty knowledgeable about stocks. In fact,
when I got in I soon discovered that I knew more than most of the
people in the place. And I had had one big winner, which makes a
difference. In other words, I knew it could be done. I had had a stock
that went up twenty times beyond what I paid for it. Which has an effect
on people's lives. . . . But that's a subject for another story. Anyway, it so
happened that a new manager came there a couple of months after me
who wanted his own trainees. So I wound up out. Eventually I got
another job with another brokerage firm. I stayed there four years. Then
I went with somebody else for a year, and they merged, and I wound up
out of there. Probably there were other reasons, too. I might have of-
fended some people. I guess I was doing pretty well, and I didn't care.
After that I worked for another insurance firm for a while. I wasn't very
successful at that. Then I managed to get into another stock brokerage
firm. But I had a hard time and they got a little impatient. They wanted
more business. I wound up out of there, and I've been mostly unemployed since 1974.

I'm not sure just what went wrong at the last firm. Coming back there
from insurance, I just didn't have many customers, and I wasn't the type
who was going to go ringing doorbells or spinning the phone all the

237

time. I don't know, I felt that it was rubbing me the wrong way. In the brokerage house they essentially wanted salesmen. The manager of one house told me, "I'd rather have a successful Fuller Brush man than a Harvard M.B.A. I need somebody who can sell. I don't need your knowledge. The brokerage house will give you all the ideas you want. All you do is convince people to buy and sell stocks. That's where we make our money." The ethics of the brokerage industry are far from what they try to make them out to be.

I don't know, I just can't get on a phone and do that kind of selling. I guess I've always looked down on people who did that. I built up the business before without doing that by having a very good batting average. I came up with a lot more winners than losers. I got a lot of business by word of mouth. But when I came back to the business again, one of two things had happened. There had been some bad years in between, and the customers had pretty much lost their money, whatever broker they were dealing with. And those who were fortunate enough to be dealing with a broker who didn't lose their money, they were inclined to be loyal to that broker. So it was a bad scene. And the manager finally said, "Look, you're simply not doing the business, and I don't know how you're gonna get business unless you want to spend a lot of time on the phone. You're not inclined to do that. So I would suggest you resign."

I was a little bit discouraged by it all. I decided I would never go back to a brokerage house because I just couldn't be a salesman like that. I also knew it was ridiculous even to try and get another brokerage job. After that failure, it just wouldn't work. Nobody was gonna buy me.

Actually I did check around at brokerage houses because unemployment compensation requires you to look for jobs. And I checked into some other things. I tried to get into some banks, in the areas of portfolio management or securities research. But there were a lot of experienced people looking for that work, and if the banks were inclined to hire somebody new, they would get somebody fresh out of college. They're reluctant to hire somebody my age because the fringe benefit costs are much higher, like pension plans and medical costs.

I didn't take it as too much of a personal failure when I left the brokerage house because I'd been successful in my own speculation in stocks. I've made a lot more from buying and selling stocks than I ever made from salaries and commissions. Which has had its effect as far as my family is concerned. In other words, my son grows up and he sees that I didn't make my money from hard work or labor. I made it from shrewdness. What does that do to a young fellow who's growing up? He thinks that the way to make out is to be shrewd. Or maybe even just to be lucky, coming in and out of the stock market at the right time. It's like being a winner in a poker game. Is it because you're smart or you're lucky? I think a little of each. But recently I haven't been a big winner.

There aren't too many people who know more about the game than I do, but for the past few years I haven't been that good at it. I'd say for the last five years I haven't done anything brilliant in the stock market. It's just more difficult for me, and I think it's my mental attitude. I think half the battle is being in the right frame of mind.

See, this unemployment is bad for people. I could adjust to it in some ways. But even though I'm sure I have more assets than most people, I feel insecure. I don't know how far inflation is gonna go. I might easily make the wrong moves in the stock market. Another tumble would really hurt me if I'm in it. I don't have any pension. There's a feeling of insecurity about the future. So let's say my broker suggests a course of action and gives me the reasons for taking it. If he catches me on a day when I'm in one frame of mind, I will act on it. And if he catches me on a day when maybe I'm in a negative frame of mind, I'll find reasons for not doing it. Even though I'm the same person. I don't think I have as balanced an outlook as I used to have when I was doing better. The insecurity preys on me. It affects my judgment. It affects my moods. So much of this is psychological.

There was a period of time when everything I did seemed to work out beautifully. Jesus, every move turned out brilliant. I know I did better than the other brokers in the office because one of them told me. He said, "You've done far better than anybody else. If I'd just been doing the same as you were doing, instead of listening to the manager and the house, I would have been infinitely better off." And that was true. I had a feel for doing the right thing. It's an intangible. I remember reading a story of a gambler who was successful. He did pretty well. But he broke a promise to a friend, and psychologically that hurt him because until then his word had always been good. He was supposed to take a trip and he didn't make the trip, or something like that. He left his friend hanging. And he was a loser after that.

While things were going well, I really enjoyed it. Business was picking up. Everything was breaking right. I got much more satisfaction out of choosing a stock that did well than out of making a big sale, like some of the others did. They were excited if they sold, say $20,000 worth of mutual funds and got a $1,000 commission. I always came up with unique ideas, too, that other brokers would never think about. But on a couple of these deals I got in hassles with the house. On one unusual deal—most brokers have never even heard of it—the house made an error which cost them quite a few thousand bucks. They wanted it to come out of my account, and I had a big hassle that wound up with my leaving that house. Actually I got everything adjusted to my satisfaction, but in the meantime, I'd made all the arrangements to leave. Which turned out to be a poor move, because at the next place things didn't go right anymore.

I guess you could say I should have been more loyal to that house because they gave me a really good break when I came up there, and I did pretty well. They carried me when I was doing poorly. But it got to be an impossible argument, and I guess I was looking for greener pastures. I thought it'd be better somewhere else. That was a mistake, looking back on it. And I was hurt by the bear markets over the last few years. However, I could have sold short as easily as bought stocks if I'd been smart enough to do that. Maybe it's possible that I could've made myself a fortune and wound up with a lot of self-esteem that I was one of the few people who was smart enough to recognize what was happening and make the right moves.

These days I spend a lot more time studying than actively trading stocks. I do a reasonable amount of trading, and I devote a lot of time and attention to it. But I don't think I can beat the game from where I'm sitting this time. I don't think my chances of doing things right are much better than random. The commissions are higher, so it's harder to trade actively and be successful. And my sources of information are not as good as when I worked for that particular brokerage house. I try to check with other brokers, but I find there are few decent brokers around who can come up with good information. I would love to find a broker who is the same broker I was in my good days. But it isn't to be.

But I still work at it. I read the *Wall Street Journal* every day. I get it from a neighbor who finishes it before he runs to work. He leaves it in front of the door, and I pick it up, so it saves me the job of buying it. Otherwise, I'd probably go over to the library and read it there. My wife yells that I spend too much time reading it, which I probably do. But I'm not pressed for time. Generally I get out of the house in the afternoon and go to the library. I enjoy reading all kinds of magazines, mostly nonfiction. And it ties in with the stock market if I read something like *Business Week* or *Fortune*. Occasionally I might get some ideas that might help me.

I often think of a customer of mine who was the president of a small company. His father had also been in the stock market. He quit somewhere in the 1930s, and for the rest of his life he never went to work again. He'd go to the poolroom every afternoon. Or he'd bet on horses. That's the way he spent his time. And sometimes I wonder where the hell my time goes at the end of the day. What did I do? And I don't enjoy the leisure. If I'm at home too much I get into hassles with my wife. I'm not inclined to do anything. We cut down those branches yesterday and they're still lying around. The shower needs fixing. The house needs work. But you get lazy.

It also affects your ethical outlook. I used to have contempt for people who cheat on their income tax. Now I'm becoming aware of how unfair the tax laws are, and I realize that people just do whatever is to their advantage. I'm no longer eligible for unemployment compensation, but if I found some gimmick that made me eligible, I'd use it. And I don't look down on somebody who does some work and is getting unemployment. I might if he was working full time, but if someone makes $50 a week and doesn't tell them, I think that's fine. So your ethical outlook changes. You feel inflation is hurting you, and you figure that certain people have things stacked to their advantage. Like government employees, who automatically get increases. And people in powerful unions and in certain occupations like lawyers and doctors. Everything goes their way. They strike; they get increases; they raise their fees. Sometimes I wish I was in one of these powerful unions. Or working for the government. Though I'm sure some people would envy my position if they knew it. My capital situation is quite strong. I could go a number of years without working. But eventually I would run out. Well, it depends how smart I am with the stock market. Maybe I'll never run out. But you kind of run scared all the time. Which is not a good way to be.

I'm just hoping my son does well. He's a little disoriented, too, I think. He doesn't have the patience to finish college. He's sort of running around doing a bit of painting, but I don't know if the painting is any good. I don't see any future ahead in it. But I think being unemployed has messed me up as far as his attitude towards me. My attitude towards my father was one of great respect. He was a successful businessman who was looked up to by other people. But I think my son's attitude towards me is that I'm really doing nothing. I get the feeling indirectly. He hasn't made it that obvious. But I think he's pretty disappointed. I guess he figures one should be successful in this world. By the time he's my age he expects to be famous. And he once made a remark, he said, "I'm gonna end this pattern of failure in the family." Something like that. I don't know, I interpreted it to mean he was talking about me.

So family life has been kind of rough. It's easy to get into squabbles. My marriage has been affected, probably by my being home so much. Well, you never know, but I'm sure my family life would have been much better if I was in some kind of job with a steady income. Right now it goes in cycles. We have fights. Don't talk to each other for a while. We were close to breaking up at one time, but somehow we held together. Sometimes I don't know what brings on a fight. It's just like it's on some kind of cycle. Some trivial thing brings it on. Moods. I get into moods and I explode about something or other. Like my wife will ask me to clear the dishes and I resent doing it. Which I shouldn't because she's done the cooking. But I feel, "Well, I've reached the stage where I'm a dish clearer; that's all I'm good for." And then maybe she says, "Hey, you didn't do a good job. You left this, you left that." Usually I'll grumble and finish. The other day I exploded. There was company here, so it wasn't too good.

241

We haven't been hit too hard financially, though if I had a job and was making $1,000 a month or so, I'd be a lot more free with my spending than I am now. I'd be pretty well on top of things because I have a pretty good capital situation. I try to save where I can, but in many ways it gets a little hopeless. For example, let's say this was a down week in the stock market. My stocks may go down several thousand dollars. And that's a real loss, like it came out of your pocket. So I may save a couple of dollars eating at home, but I can lose a couple of thousand in a week. So what does it all mean in the end? From that perspective, all the saving doesn't mean that much.

I think a lot about what I should have done. I should have stayed with that one house where everything was breaking right. Maybe with the changing market I would have fallen into trouble anyhow, but I always managed to come up with unique deals there. Maybe I would have sold short and come up rich. I'm a little sorry I didn't get into real estate a little heavier. I almost got into it a couple of times, but the deals fell through both times. I suppose if I was more persistent, maybe I could've gotten into it. I kind of let things fall where they may. I have this feeling of insecurity. Fear, sometimes. There have been times, not too much recently, when I felt a little bit suicidial. I don't think I was ready to do it, but I was thinking, "What the hell." One of my friends asked, "What happens if your money runs out? And I said, "How does the song go? 'Suicide is painless, it brings on. . . .' " Some song from TV. That shocked him [laughs].

It's the loss of self-esteem, I guess. I sort of gave up the fight after a while. I've been unemployed at various times before, and it was a bit of a struggle to get something; but I always had reasonable confidence I'd get it. This time, after a while I decided that nothing is going to happen. This is pretty hopeless. And even though you rationalize and say, "Well it's not my fault. It's the fault of the economy. It's beyond my control," you still feel it. If I had done something brilliant with the stock market or commodity market in the last few years, my self-esteem would be much higher. If I'd become a millionaire or successful, maybe I'd have said, "Gee, I'm really brilliant." Or, "I'm smart," or something. But I kind of feel like the years are wasting away and I'm not accomplishing a damn thing. I don't think my life has been a fruitful or a happy one.

SCOTT BURCHETT

He is a television director, "one of the pioneers, actually." He lives with his wife, Mary, a teacher, in a wealthy neighborhood on Manhat-

tan's East Side. His living room is crowded with antique furniture, a piano, art objects. A Manx cat prowls about; he thumps it affectionately, calling it Cat.

He is sixty. Since being fired as a director of a network show, he has not had steady television work. "That was . . . gosh, five years ago now."

It was a political move to get rid of all of us. The show wasn't working. The network kept fussing and fussing with it. They spent $2.5 million decorating sets and making showrooms with eighteen different kinds of color telephones, the whole works. But the show wasn't making the ratings. So the program department decided they had to suspend some bodies to justify the amount of money they had put into it. They had to fire somebody. Now, even *Variety* pointed out that firing the director doesn't help the ratings. It's perfect nonsense. The producer is the first one to go, right? So I was pretty sore about that. I was sore about a lot of things actually. It was pretty abrupt. I didn't know all this infighting was going on. So I had dinner with the producer on a Thursday night, and he said, "I hate to tell you this, but tomorrow is your last show." He explained to me that they had to have so many bodies. I was being cast overboard like Jonah.

It didn't hit me hard at the moment. I guess doing shows five times a week for five years, you get sort of bored with it, no matter what kind of money you are making. Your first reaction is relief that you don't have to go to work again, to the same old grind. A pretty hard one at that. Production meeting at noon, and you wouldn't get off the air until eight o'clock at night or later. It was a long day. And it's a grind because you really don't have much creative control. It gets to be pretty much of a bore.

So I suppose my first reaction was—I don't know how to describe it. I sort of looked forward to it. Then after a while the unfairness of it hits you, and you say, "Why me? Why not the writers, the producer?" Looking back, I think I was crushed when I was first let go. We were fired in November and my contract went until April, so all that money was still coming in. But I felt pretty rotten about it. My pride was knocked down. I kept thinking, "Maybe it's a big mistake, and we're all going to be hired back again." It never materialized. I think we all just sat around waiting for it, twiddling our thumbs, hoping they would change their minds.

From November to April I played it by ear. If people wanted me, they could call me. I didn't make one effort to get another show. It wasn't until the money stopped coming in that I began calling people myself, which is rather stupid because I should have hit them right away while they remembered me. After that many months people don't recollect that you're out of work, so they don't think of you. Maybe that's part of a guilt complex I have, that I didn't really try that hard.

Of course, the only real resource I have for finding a job is the telephone. There's no way for a guy in my business to go around and see people. Who do you talk to? You can't go traipsing around. People don't necessarily want to see you. So you sit around the house, hoping someone will telephone. Well, that was OK for a while. I was full of things I wanted to do. I'm a bookbinder, so I can happily work at home. And then I'd dream up schemes with pals of mine about what we're going to do. But they never materialize. It wasn't until about this year that it really hit me that I'm not getting any younger, and I'm not working, and all the schemes we've dreamed up aren't materializing. People with wild ideas would come and say, "Listen to this," or, "Try this and that." I'd be enthusiastic and say "Let's do it." But I'm no salesman, so I have to leave it to them to sell the idea. Then months would go by, and I'd suddenly realize they weren't capable of selling it. That would be a little depressing. Then someone would come up with another idea. Like I was very much interested in cable television for about a year. We were going to do cheap programs for cable stations. And people were wildly enthusiastic about the idea. But to make a long story short, people in cable TV just haven't got any money. They're all mom-and-pop operations, these stations; they haven't got ten bucks to put their own shows together. That was disillusioning. It took some time to find it out, and in the meantime, something else came up, so it wasn't too much of a blow. What happens is a sort of gradual diminishing of enthusiasm.

Usually something interesting comes up every week or so, something that might work out but never does. Like someone says, "I think we got a commercial for you to do," or "Stick around, we're going to have a lot of work for you." This is what you usually get. Everybody says, "Why don't you go to the West Coast?" Well, they're in just as bad shape; 80 percent of the entire Director's Guild is out of work. At least 85 percent of Equity is out of work all the time. So I don't blame myself. The only thing I wonder about is what am I not doing right now? Should I go to the Coast and play it by ear? I should be calling somebody. I should be reminding somebody who I am.

A couple of years ago a friend of mine who's manager of the Ivy Club said, "We need a good guy, a knowledgeable guy about food to act as a maître d' down there at the club. How about joining us?" Well, I fought it for a while and finally it got to the point where we needed the dough so bad that I went down there and signed up. And I hated it. It was too bad because it ruined our friendship. The guy was a good manager, but I didn't like the way he worked, the way he treated help. I was part of the dirt under the carpet as far as he was concerned, once I started working there. And you had to know everybody's name, what their favorite table was, what their favorite drinks were, that sort of thing. And he had all those sets of rules. It was just too much for me. I'm used to giving orders rather than taking them, I suppose. I finally gave up. I was there for six or seven months, and then I suddenly abandoned ship. I made enough money so I could get back on unemployment. But on that job for the first time I realized how angry and upset I was. I felt terribly lonesome working there. There was nobody to talk to. I was completely isolated. My friend was too busy up in the office taking care of paperwork, and you aren't supposed to talk to the guests at the club. Absolutely no one to talk to for hours. It just couldn't have been more lonesome. I realized how isolated I was from everything I knew. Finally, out of pure lonesomeness one day I said I couldn't stand it. We had some falling-out, but it wasn't important; I can't even remember what it was. It was just too much. I couldn't take it.

Then last year I latched onto something called American Executive Careers, which works out of Washington, D.C. It's actually an international operation. I had to fly down to Washington and be interviewed by them, a whole collection of guys and gals. And afterwards they had a meeting and decided maybe I'd be good at public relations or teaching communications. Because they said, "We don't know anything about television direction. That'd be something you'd have to cover yourself." I don't know if I concurred with their decision, but I went along because there was nothing else. I had to try everything. So for $1,500, which I laid out, they went to work on it and made up a résumé and a letter, and they must have sent out—I don't know how many. Look at this folder. There must be five hundred in here now. They mailed out covering letters and résumés to all these people. In fact, that went on till about two months ago. We kept on sending out letters. Here are all the returns, all negative. Hundreds of them. I only had one nibble out of these five hundred companies. I don't remember which one it was. Look at this— they just send a printed notice. It makes you pretty nervous. They don't even bother to answer you personally. All saying the same thing: They just haven't got any work.

I used to have an agent who I called regularly, who never called me. And I gave up calling him because nothing ever happened. I'll never forget—I called him last year, I think it was, and his office said, "Oh, didn't you know? Mr. Thomas is dead." So I've never had another agent. I just gave up. It's perfectly ridiculous; nobody ever called me to tell me my agent was dead.

So I sit at home. Lately I'm beginning to not get up with the bell in the morning. You suddenly find that you *cannot* wake up. It's just impossible because if you do wake up, there's nothing for you to do anyhow. That's the main psychological thing I have: I've lost all my energy. Everything turns into a chore. I have to make myself get up and do *something*. So I fill the time going shopping or doing the cooking and the housework. Then in the afternoon I head for a bar where TV people go. I'm in there every day. Everybody knows by now that they'll see me there from about four o'clock for an hour and a half. At least I have people from the business to talk to there. And often they're in the same boat, out of work. Actors, directors, actresses, production people. All the people that I might be employed by go there at one time or another. I used to make it at lunchtime 'cause they all come for lunch, but now I gave that up, because . . . the hell with it, I can't afford it.

In fact, I'm just about at the end of the line now. I don't have enough money to keep up any kind of appearances. The bar bill alone runs around $125, $130 a month, just bar bills. That's not even eating there. Every drink is $1.85, no matter what you drink. I drink sherry; it's still $1.85. So that gets to be a pretty heavy expenditure, but I don't know what else to do. I'd go crazy if I didn't have something like that to go to. Other than that you just sit here and go out of your mind. You can go absolutely bananas if you've got to sit here all day every day.

It's just getting pretty disillusioning, the whole thing. And besides, I'm sixty. That scares me. And I'm scared to death about the amount of money that's coming in and going out. There's nothing put away. We're practically at the end of our resources now. I know it, and my wife knows it; but we don't talk about it. We just keep hoping that tomorrow something great will happen.

MARTIN PENN

He is a dapper man in a blue blazer and white slacks. He shares a small apartment with his wife and twenty-one-year-old daughter in Cambridge, Massachusetts. The rooms are immaculate, everything in place. The decorative motif is Oriental—scrolls, statuary, vases in glass cases—a taste he picked up during three years in Japan in the 1930s.

"I've given up all ego trips and manic career ambitions. . . . There are just too many people around Boston. They're cranking out the Ph.D.'s and master's in fields that are overcrowded, and these are young people with more on the ball than some of us older guys. . . ."

My professional career really began in 1962, when I got my first job at a think tank. When I was younger I worked in various jobs, but I finally decided that I needed more education if I was going to have any sort of interesting career. So I went back to school and got my Ph.D. in anthropology in 1962. At that time the think tanks were headhunting for Ph.D.'s. They almost didn't care what your degree was in. I succumbed to their overtures and went to work for a research institute. They sent me to various places around the world, on government contracts. I was a research adviser. I traveled for seven years and finally came back to the home office in 1969.

Those were my peak years in terms of salary, interesting work, and so on. When I came back to Boston, the government was starting to terminate a lot of the contracts that were our bread and butter. It's a very treacherous employment market, contract research. There were many black Fridays, and eventually my turn came. They were cutting off whole departments and divisions. People who had been there twenty years got the ax. And it wasn't just happening there. Most of the think tanks were hit the same way. It was a case of *sic transit gloria mundi* for many of us who thought, "God, I've got the world by the tail. I'll always be in demand."

After I got fired, I said, "OK, my training was to be a teacher anyhow, so I'll go out and get into the academic game." Well, I was kind of naïve. I was fifty years old—this was in 1970—and there were a lot of eager young guys with good teaching credentials and Ph.D.'s hitting the bricks looking for jobs. I got a couple of part-time teaching positions, and in 1972 I was offered a job teaching in Latin America. But when I got down there, I found that the conditions weren't exactly the way they had been described to me. So after a year there I left and came back to Massachusetts. That was in 1973. Except for a little bit of consulting work, I haven't worked since.

For a while I wasted a lot of time applying for these long-shot high-paying jobs. I would guess that in 1973 I applied for about twenty-five jobs all told, and the next year about fifty. I watched the want ads, and my alumni guidance office sends out periodical sheets with job listings. I wanted to stay in the area if possible, although I applied for a couple of jobs out west. If I saw an ad where I fit the majority of the requirements, even if I didn't meet one or two, I would apply. By that I mean I'd send a résumé and maybe a cover letter. Then I'd go through the filtering process, and more often than not I'd get a Dear John letter saying, "Sorry, we've chosen a candidate who has marvelous credentials. . . ." On reflection, I'd almost rather have that kind of thing than to get in a long drawn-out process where I begin getting high hopes, only to have them dashed at the last minute. Each time that happens it's another nail in a guy's coffin.

On a lot of these jobs I'd correspond back and forth to beat hell, but I'd never actually get an interview. Perhaps that's justifiable because it seems there's always someone more specialized in exactly what they want. For example, there was one job for a teacher of sociology in Mexico. God, I had a long correspondence with them, but they finally picked somebody else. I've studied sociology and even taught some courses, but I'm not a sociologist. That's the thing—I have to take a sort of shotgun approach. I have some versatility, and I thought, "Well, hell I can apply in all sorts of areas—community work, teaching anthropology, applied social science-type research, whatever." But I'm not sure that's any advantage. Maybe it would be better to be a specialist instead of a so-called generalist. Actually the alumni office has a label for people like me: Miscellaneous Professions. So I'm Mr. Miscellaneous [laughs].

I just recently applied for a good job that seemed just right for me. Well, there were about two hundred applicants for the job. I was one of the so-called final candidates, but I wound up their third choice. I suppose I should take some solace in being third out of two hundred. At least I got an interview. But I don't know if it helped that much. I think when I get an interview I have pretty good rapport with the person except that I have a tendency to put myself down too much. Maybe I'm too apologetic. At any rate, it wasn't until the last ten or fifteen minutes that I began getting the code words that meant "You're close, but you're not the one."

I've pretty much given up looking for jobs like that one. It's just a waste of time. A while back I said to myself, "OK, you can't change the world. This is the way it is. You've got to forget about the past and all this great potential you think you still have." I probably have peaked; but I still have some residual smarts, and I could do a decent job for a good salary. But it isn't gonna happen. So I said, "Look, I need to get some bread to supplement the family income, so I'll lower my sights. I'll take just about any damn job I can get. I have to be realistic." But it's the old story: A Ph.D. goes for a job that a high school graduate could do. They look at your background, and they think, "Jesus, if this guy ever gets a better deal, he'll fly the coop." And the trouble is, I probably would. But Jesus, I don't know whose fault that is [laughs]. Everybody tries to get the best deal they can.

I've often thought, "OK, I'll deny that I have a Ph.D." But something about that goes against my grain. It isn't just ego; it's the principle. There's something wrong with this country when a person has to be ashamed because they got an education. I'm sure a lot of people are downgrading themselves in order to get a bread-and-butter job, but I'm not sure if it's a weakness or a strength.

There are some ironies in my situation. First of all, I like to think I'm a liberal politically. I'm for affirmative action. God knows minorities have been pushed around since the country was founded, and they deserve a break. But I find myself in direct competition with them. And if I go to the university personnel office, for example, the desks in the front tier are all manned by black girls. It's really formidable. If I were to go in cold, I'd never get past the first desk, I know it. "Here's an application; fill it out; we'll call you if we find anything that might be suitable." I've been turned away too many times in that situation. And there are jobs that I know I have not only the education for but the experience, too. I applied for a job as a veterans' counselor at a college around here. I'm a veteran, and I've done a lot of counseling in the academic world. Well, their prime candidate was a young girl about twenty-four years old. She's never been in the service. Maybe she's had some counseling experience, but what does she know about veterans? Nevertheless, she was their choice for the job. So there are some ironies.

Still, I approve of affirmative action, although I think it's often carried out in extreme ways. And I'm delighted that our government has some humanitarian concern for older people, senior citizens, whatever you call them—I think it's defined by the Labor Department as over sixty-five. Maybe they don't get much, but they get something. But I think there's a gray area in the labor market made up of people in their late forties and fifties, up to sixty-four. They seem to be getting swept under the carpet in these grand considerations of what we're gonna do for all segments of the population.

Well, I got that off my chest [laughs].

Like I say, I was pretty naïve when I started looking for jobs. But about a year after I came back from Latin America, I began to realize I was spinning my wheels. Then I went into a period of depression. I guess I had—well, I hadn't given up, but I was pretty damn dormant for a while. I'd ask myself, "What the hell am I doing?" I felt hurt because I had to go looking for these Mickey Mouse jobs that a person with a grade-school background could do. It's a good thing that I'm an eternal optimist rather than a pessimist. Otherwise, I'd probably have cut my throat. I would sit at home and think up schemes. I was unhappy with myself, my life, directions I had taken. There was a certain amount of self-pity. It seemed like I had always zigged when I should zag. I thought about what a waste of time it was to get a Ph.D. in a field that's obsolete. I thought about the humiliations I've had going around cap in hand for these stupid-ass jobs. It's bad enough to be turned down for a job you're fully qualified for. But when you apply for a job that you figure is just an interim thing until you can get something decent, and you're turned down for that, too. . . . You feel, "Jesus, I'm not worth a damn."

For a while I took some refuge in attempting to write a book. I wanted to write some reminiscences of Japan in the days building up to World War II. And it had to have historical verisimilitude, so I spent a lot of time at the library getting source material. That way I could at least go over to the library every day and forget about my problem. But to actually put your research into some sort of literary form isn't easy. It's hard just to drive myself to sit down and do it. So a few months ago I dropped it. I had to come to grips with reality. I guess the book was really a way of reverting to my graduate school days [laughs]. Luckily my wife is a very tolerant, generous-hearted person who understands me. She's had to put up with a hell of a lot.

My wife and I just had our twenty-ninth wedding anniversary. It looks like we're gonna stay together the rest of our lives. But these years inevitably have been a strain on us. When a couple are struggling along, it affects everything, from their sex life to the companionship they have. A lot of times I've just wanted to be alone. I didn't want to participate in the family's concerns. I didn't get surly, but I had a lot of self-commiserating to do. And I'm sure my wife felt trapped. She was saying to herself, "Jesus, I'm fifty-seven years old. I've worked all my adult life, and where are we? He's unemployed, and there's no job in sight." And I saw the injustice of it. She helped me get through college on the GI Bill, and she's supported me every time I've taken off work to go back and get some education over the years. Luckily my wife is the kind of person who would chew her fingernails if she had to sit at home and be a hausfrau. She stays in tune with life by working. That's what has sustained us. But it isn't fair that she has to carry the burden.

There have been two or three episodes when I felt, "Hell, I'm not contributing to the family; it'd be better off if I left." And she has agreed. She even raised the issue herself a couple of times because she's unhappy, insecure, anxious about the future and so on. But each time we both thought about it and talked it over again and said, "Oh, hell, let's try to hack it." I guess I've been the one that's been most reluctant. I don't know, I have some kind of mystical feeling about our marriage. Maybe it's an endurance contest [laughs]. Twenty-nine years, that's a long time. I'd like for us to stay together. So even though I thought I was serious when I talked about leaving, maybe it was just desperation. When I do have some prospects, my wife gets so happy and delighted, and we start what we call "talking rabbits." If you've read Steinbeck's book Of Mice and Men, you remember the moron is always saying, "Tell me about the rabbits, George." The chicken ranch and so on. Well, whenever we're feeling good because something promising has come up and we're sitting around on Friday with a couple of drinks, we start talking rabbits. We're kind of petrified romantics, I guess.

When I pulled out of my depression a few months ago, it was mainly my wife that did it. She's more practical than I am, and she helped me see that this book I was doing was just an escape. The fact is that we've come down to the nitty-gritty, and I have to do something. We've spent all our assets. We've never reached the poverty level, but we're just barely staying solvent. When you get to be this age, you ought to have something saved, but we're not saving a nickel. We sold our house a while back, but this apartment costs $375 a month. That's quite a whack, with me unemployed. But it's a psychological necessity because she'd be miserable if we lived in some tacky two-room plaster place. She enjoys gardening, and this place comes with a little courtyard where she can have her plants. We've collected some nice things over the years, and that gives her pleasure. In fact, some of them are rather valuable. That's a Sung bowl over there. It's been evaluated at $2,500. We've got some Ming vases. We could peddle those, and we could lower our life-style if we had to. We probably spend more than we should, considering the realities, but it's important for our morale.

I may have a real live job coming up tomorrow. I've got an interview for the job of binder's assistant in the library. My only worry is that when the gal called me up about it, I impulsively showed some reluctance. I made some stupid remark like; "Well, nothing's permanent." But I shouldn't sneer because it's a full-time job with regular pay and good fringe benefits. And I honestly would like to learn something about binding books. The job wouldn't be anywhere near what I used to have in terms of salary or prestige. But I've got to take what I can get. If I can weather it out, maybe there will be a change.

7

FIGHTING BACK: "A Little Retaliation Was in Order"

Three women, three battles. These unlikely agitators are among the few unemployed I spoke to who had the opportunity, the political understanding, and the spirit to fight back.

SUSAN INGHAM

She refuses to be interviewed at home, so we talk over breakfast in a crowded drugstore café. She is a short, intense woman of forty; her moral anger has something of the Puritan in it. Her smile is wry, not happy. She has been unemployed six months, after working almost seven years for a large insurance company in a northern city.

It all began when one of the assistant vice-presidents called my whole department in for a big meeting and told us we could decide how things were going to be run. The company had decided to reorganize the department, upgrade the jobs, and so forth. And they said if we wanted a manager, we could have one. If we didn't want one, we didn't have to have one. If we wanted things such-and-such a way. . . . You know. It was a dumb situation. I had worked way above my grade level for years and years. They were always promising me that things would change someday, and still I sat in that meeting like an idiot, believing what they said.

Well, we soon learned that it was not going to be just the way we wanted unless we happened to go along with the method they'd already chosen. That made me furious. Then we learned that they planned to put one woman over us who three of us heartily disliked. So we went in and protested about it. I think I could have survived that, but unfortunately the person we protested to was a very close friend of one of the women who was protesting. After that the friendship went kaput, and I was blamed for it. Judith felt Elice would never have the guts to stand up to her without me urging her on. Which was nonsense. It was her decision. But I should have been intelligent enough to realize what was going to happen.

Six months later they fired me. They worked it very cleverly because we got the upgrading of the jobs, so technically at least I was doing a new job despite the fact that I had been doing the same work for three or four years. And of course the reasons they gave for firing me had nothing to do with the personal conflict. It seems I underwent this mysterious personality change, and all of a sudden I couldn't get along with my co-workers. And since the job had been upgraded, they could say that I hadn't met the qualifications for the job because of my terrible personality.

It may have had something to do with my protesting, but I don't think that in itself would have done it. I've always been a screamer. If I don't like something, I go in and announce it. That was nothing new with me.

255

I think the pertinent factor was that Judith and Elice were no longer friends. It was just a personal thing. And the way they do it, of course, is to offer you an opportunity to find a job elsewhere in the company. I couldn't have gotten one without taking a demotion, and there was no way I wanted to do that. I would much rather have gone elsewhere. So I thought I'd just wait and go when it's time. But I was angry. I felt a little retaliation was in order. I don't go around looking for a fight, but if somebody wants to pick one, they'd better be ready to go a few rounds.

The first thing I did was run over and talk to this woman in personnel. At this point I was incredibly naïve about what kinds of things go on in the average company. I simply could not believe they would fire me over what was essentially a personal problem. So I talked to this woman, and I think she felt sorry for me. She looked through my past record and saw that I'd received appraisals of outstanding all along. Now it's strange that you can be outstanding one day and absolutely unfit the next. So she asked me what had happened, and I told her that I went in and protested. She just looked at me and said, "How could you be so stupid as to do something like that?" And I realized that she had had to deal with this in the past, that it was something that had happened before and would happen again.

Then I thought, "Well, why not go to the FEPC* and see if they can do something?" So I filed a complaint, and this guy assured me that he could go into the company and examine my record and talk to everybody and find out what happened. But it turned out he couldn't do that. He just wrote them a letter and informed them I had lodged a complaint, and they wrote back that he had no jurisdiction whatever in the matter. That was it right there. I realized I had absolutely no recourse.

It was about that time that the union called me. They had been trying to organize the company for several years, and I was in the original group that had met with them. In fact, they had an election in 1971 which they lost rather badly; but charges were filed with the National Labor Relations Board, and the company was found guilty of twelve counts of illegal practices. So they were headed for a new election, and they called and asked if I wanted to work with them. I was ready. I said, "OK, baby, let's go."

That was in November, about a month after the company had given me notice. I worked there until January, and then I went on unemployment and started working full time with the union. From January to April I lived and breathed that organizing drive. It's like political campaigning. You get to the point where you're hooked. You're caught up in it. Every other job I've had started at nine and ended at five, and then

*Fair Employment Practices Committee.

you forgot about it. But with organizing you get so emotionally involved that you feel like it's in your blood. I conducted meetings, wrote leaflets, everything. The most important thing was just to get in there and talk to people and explain to them what a union can do and convince them that a union is what they need. I was helped by being so angry about what the company had done to me, but as I learned more and more about just what goes on in business, I was more and more appalled at what companies do to people. It quickly reached a point where it wasn't so much a personal vendetta. I became convinced that unions are absolutely the only form of protection that the working person can have, and I think I was successful at getting that across.

Until I started working with the union, I hadn't given much thought to the position I had at that company for seven years. I had always known that I was being kept at a grade level far beneath the actual work I was doing. But through my own naïveté I didn't relate my situation to an extensive company policy. I can't claim that I didn't hear things from time to time. Things would happen to people, and I just chose to ignore them. I suppose if I had recognized them I would have fought back right then, and I would have lost my job much sooner. Until it affected me personally, I didn't do anything. Then I began to talk to people, and I found there were a lot of people in my situation. People were getting fired for refusing to do work above their grade level. The company just systematically exploits everyone to the degree that they think they can get away with it. It was mind-blowing.

Of course, you have to take the things people say with a grain of salt. Not everyone is a good worker. Some of them really did screw up on the job. But I met an incredible number of workers who had been badly abused by the company. I remember one woman who had been there at least five years. She was at Grade Nine, consistently rated as outstanding. At one point the company established "D & D" guidelines: discipline and deportment, or some stupid thing. They very carefully itemized what would happen to you under certain circumstances. One was that if you took more than two days off per year without pay, after you used up your sick days and so forth, you would be fired. The woman asked her supervisor if "per year" meant from January to December or from the date hired. The supervisor promised she would find out and let her know. She never did. Well, this woman had taken two days off without pay, and she had to take another one because her child was sick. They fired her. An outstanding employee. She did file charges and got her job back, but what they did was demote her. She still got the same pay, but from Grade Nine they dropped her so that she was doing Grade Two work. It was an incredible waste, and she was extremely unhappy. At least I could give them a good fight, and I think I did. But there were so many people who for various reasons simply couldn't do anything. They were absolutely dependent on these jobs, and they had to take whatever the company cared to dish out, just to keep themselves going.

My feelings at first were directed at the people who had been involved in firing me. Now I just feel angry at the company, not the individuals anymore. I suppose it's reinforced by the fact that not one person in the place had done anything to stop it. They all said, "Well, this may not be justified, but what can we say to a manager?" I think that infuriated me more than anything else. I tend to take strong moral stands on issues, and I not only intensely dislike people who I think are completely immoral, but I have even more dislike for people who tolerate that sort of thing. And the fact is that the company does tolerate it. It's standard practice.

The election finally happened in April, and we won. The outcome was tied up with ninety-nine challenged votes, and we went through hearings on those. The last I heard was that thirty-five votes were thrown out. They were supervisors who had voted. And of the remaining sixty-four the union just has to get one "Yes" to be in. Which we'll get. Then the company will appeal, so it'll be a while before they start negotiations. But eventually they'll have a union, and they'll have good reason to remember me, because that contract is going to cost them several million a year [laughs].

As for me, I still don't have a job, but I feel I gained much more from the experience than I lost. Had I not been fired, I would not have worked for the union. And I think that work definitely made me more self-confident. I seriously doubted whether I'd be able to do it well. I learned that I can do something I never even thought of myself doing. It also gave me a much greater feeling of compassion for people who work. I know much better what they have to put up with. That also relates to the whole area of feminism. Eighty to 85 percent of the workers at the company were women, and I found that one of the greatest problems in talking to them was simply to make them aware of how they were being exploited by the company. It's sort of drummed into women that they must be passive and not make nasty scenes, so they put up with everything. When I started organizing, it quickly became evident that most women have no conception of jumping in and changing things for their own benefit. They would constantly come up with nonsense like "Oh, well, if I don't like it, I'll just leave." That kind of attitude made me furious because it's exactly what they do. Women are notorious for it. They think they can go to any company and work in some stupid, cruddy job for a year and then go somewhere else and somehow translate that nonexperience into an executive position. It just isn't so. They leave at one level and they start again at that level. Often they go through a whole working life without accomplishing anything. Economically they're at the bottom of the scale. So I think this whole experience has given me more insight, not only into what's wrong with society but into what's wrong with women.

In fact, I used to be an example of that. I used to think in terms of "Well, I'm doing OK." I was making an above-average income for a woman and I was getting along all right. But now I think that OK is simply not enough. I should get what I'm worth, and I happen to think I'm worth quite a lot. Whether I'll ever get it is another question. I'm really in a predicament right now about finding a job. I wouldn't mind working as a union organizer, even though it would mean turning my back on all the training I've had in the past. But I don't think many unions are hiring right now. And if I want to continue in insurance, I think I'm going to get a very poor recommendation from my old company. I imagine by this time they're accusing me of everything from arson on down [laughs]. But I'm really quite happy with the way the whole thing turned out.

MABEL LOCKWOOD

She has worked for more than thirty years as a waitress, telephone operator, bartender, social worker, librarian, schoolteacher, and professor. Her appearance is grandmotherly; her manner, commanding. "I like leadership. At the age of fourteen I discovered that the boy who had been the high school's drum major would be leaving. This was back in 1933, and I went to the band director and suggested to him that he try a girl drum major. They had never heard of that before. Well, he was willing to take a chance. I can remember at football games, when the band would pull up in front of the stands, I could hear people say, 'My God, it's a girl!'"

She's divorced and has one grown daughter. She shares her house in a southeastern town with several cats. The sitting room is littered with slides, a slide projector, a screen; she's preparing a talk on the suffragist movement. It has been two years since she lost her last job. "I do a lot of political work. I'm a very strong Democrat. I've written speeches and done PR. People are always asking me to do freebie stuff because I've got the time. They come to visit all the time, or they call. But I also do a lot of just sitting around. And that's appalling, just to sit and do nothing."

I had been teaching high school for about five years when I heard that Anders State University was going to open. I ambled over one day and put my name in the pot, and they called me a year later and asked me to come and teach. That was in 1965. It was a brand-new university, and there was a lot of room for experimenting. I had my master's in library science, but what I wanted to do was more interdisciplinary, involving the various areas of communications. So I taught library courses and at the same time looked for new approaches. For example, the first film courses that were taught at Anders State were the ones I set up. Eventually they grew into the big film department we have now.

The other thing I really pushed—which I think is what got me into trouble—was the women's movement. I started getting interested in it around 1970. I was very excited about what was happening to women because more or less consciously all these years I had been noticing things. Like the fact that my brothers could do all sorts of things I wasn't allowed to do. And the fact that in my various jobs my ideas would get filtered through young men who would get lovely promotions, while I wouldn't. But I didn't think about it too clearly until the late 1960s, when Betty Friedan was speaking and the National Organization of Women was getting organized. I began to look at what was happening with women at Anders State: the fact that we had no women deans, no women in the executive offices, no women in the vice-presidency. Most of the people coming in to take my courses were women, and they were good. Yet I knew that when they went out in the field, the few men who were taking the courses would eventually be their administrators. So I started thinking, "There's something wrong here."

The first thing I did was organize an ad hoc group of women at the university. At that time there wasn't much you could go on in the world of academia. But the bibliographies were starting to come out, and women's studies courses were getting started around the country. So we got together and organized a course. It was the first women's studies course given at a state university in this state. We call it "Women in Motion." One hundred forty students registered for it the first time. It's a big survey course, with lectures on women's sexuality, biology, history—everything.

Well, at about that time—this was in 1971—I started getting calls constantly. I was one of the women who had gotten the course together, and I had been on a couple of local TV shows, and my phone nearly rang off the hook. Please come here, please come there. I had speaking engagements everywhere. It got to be one of those things where I'd be at a conference all weekend, back at the university on Monday, and during the week I'd be speaking at some Rotary Club about the ERA. I was hooked up with the National Women's Political Caucus, and I knew what we were fighting for nationally in terms of legislation. I helped set up coalitions so that we could pass the ERA. It was hectic. I was putting in eighty-hour weeks.

Meanwhile, I had set up the media and communications division at Anders State. I hired the people and designed the courses. But then, all at once, they decided the division was too big for me to handle. A man must be hired to handle something like that. In fact, they hired two men to do the work that I had done. I resented that very much. And all of a sudden it dawned on me that I was up for tenure and promotion. It was your usual publish-or-perish situation, and I hadn't had time to write anything. I had marvelous credentials in terms of my work at the university. I had produced a lot of videotapes and slide shows in my field that I used in my courses. So I asked that those be accepted in lieu of publishing. Also, I hadn't missed any of my classes. My students weren't complaining, that's for sure. I had put a whole new division together, a new concept, a new idea in education. And it was working, because people were always writing for my syllabi or my bibliographies.

Well, I got my notice the day after Thanksgiving. The mailman left a card in my mailbox that I had a registered letter. So I drove down to the post office and signed for it. I couldn't imagine what it was. Then I saw my division chairman's name on the envelope. And I said, "Oh, my God, what's this? Have I received a pink slip?" I couldn't believe it because I was sure I'd get tenure. I knew I wouldn't get a promotion because I didn't have my Ph.D. But there were a lot of people teaching there without Ph.D.'s, including my chairman. I opened up the envelope and read the letter, and I just couldn't believe it. I just sat in my car and looked at it. Sort of stunned. After eight years of hard work, I had been turned down for tenure for the simple reason that I had not published and I didn't have my Ph.D.

I immediately decided to file for due process at the university and ask for a second hearing. I hired a lawyer to represent me. The university organized a due process committee, and I think the hearing lasted two days. The committee decided that I had not been judged fairly and that I should go before another promotion and tenure committee. So the university set up that committee. Now, remember that the person who is being judged doesn't get to appear before the committee. You're always represented by your chairman. It's a Catch-22 situation. If the chairman doesn't want you, you know damn well you're not going to get it, no matter how many times you go through it. So I was turned down again.

Then my lawyer suggested that I file suit aginst them. I said, "But I have no money, and I won't be working. I have no place to go except to get on the unemployment line." She said, "That's all right. I'll take the case on contingency because I think it's important. I think we can use the First Amendment of the Constitution." We're charging they infringed on my right of free speech because apparently they were upset that I was a member of the National Women's Political Caucus. I was an activist. I was working for day care centers, abortion rights, all the feminist things. If I had just done the women's studies program and my own teaching, I might still be there. But I was out in the community, talking and doing things. I've since discovered this syndrome in talking to other women at conferences. The women teachers who move out into the community and become activists get fired. But the ones who just conduct women's studies on campus and don't do much beyond that keep their jobs.

Also, when we started digging, we found out that my salary was entirely different from the men all the way through. And of course, I was always needling them. I used to be very upset when I would see committee lists come through and no women would be named to a committee. Particularly the important ones. I would call the chairman of a special committee and ask why there were nothing but male names on there. I would say, "Why aren't there any women? You know we have 150 women who qualify to be named to that committee." Or I would ask to see the president, and I would go over there and say, "Why don't we have any women in the executive suite?" "Oh, but they don't have the experience." So then I would say, "How can they get the experience if you're not going to put them on committees?" And I was concerned not only with the women at academic levels, but also with the clerical areas and with the women who come in to scrub floors and get paid less than men doing the same job. I kept bringing these things out, and they were regarded as little unhappy things you just don't bring out and continue to work happily at the university.

So we filed suit. That was two years ago. I don't know how many jobs I've applied for since then. Locally it's very difficult because it was in all the papers when I filed suit. I knew that my name would be mud as far as getting a job around here. I'm that women's libber who's suing Anders State. Now that it's two years later, I keep thinking and hoping they've forgotten me, and I file applications; but I don't get very far.

I keep revising my résumé, thinking I'll try another approach. And I've branched out for all kinds of jobs. I have thought about bartending. I make a wonderful bartender. Yet there is something that says, "My God, do I have to go back into that?" I even went to an ice-cream place which was advertising for managers. I know a little about restaurant work. They said yes, I could start as a waitress, and possibly within five years I'd make it to management. I thought, "Gee, I was a waitress back when I was nineteen years old, working my way through college. I don't want to be a waitress at the age of fifty-seven." And I still have enough money that I don't have to do that. But if it comes to a choice of starving to death or not, you jolly well bet I'll get myself to bartending school.

I go through periods of depression because I'm getting older. I'm fifty-seven now, and soon I'll be fifty-eight. I'm not going to get a job around here, but I want to stay until this case is over. I could go out to California or someplace where I'm not known, but I'm not sure there's much point because they want younger people anyway. And I don't blame them. I wouldn't hire myself at this point [laughs]. For the simple reason that a school system has a set amount of money. At this point I come in at the top of the pay scale, maybe $15,000. The superintendent probably couldn't care less about a learning center or a library. He has to have it because there's a state law. So what he'll do is hire somebody with a minor in library science from college, who comes in cheap, about $7,000 or $8,000.

One thing about this is that I'm having to learn patience because of the court. I'll probably be sixty before the case ever comes up. It was supposed to come up this March in the local district court, but my lawyer says that the judge is fourteen months behind in criminal cases alone. So we don't know when it's going to be brought up. It means at least another fourteen months, and I'm going into my third year. This is what happens to civil suits. The university keeps hoping I'll go away. They know I can't live in this area and get a job, so they're hoping that if it goes on and on, they'll never be brought up on the docket.

What we're charging is violation of the First Amendment, freedom of speech and association. Title VII of the Civil Rights Code and Title IX of the Civil Rights Code. Also nonequal pay for equal work. Right now we're suing for cold cash, $2.5 million. What I really hope will come out of it is that I'll get reinstated with a back salary. But at this rate I'll be in a wheelchair. They can retire me the same year I get reinstated. And it all seems so foolish because there are other people who have filed charges against Anders State on the same grounds in the meantime. And there are going to be more as each year passes. To me it would make so much more sense for them to give women equal pay for equal work. Give them equal opportunity for advancement. See that they get placed on committees, chairmanships, deans, and so forth. They have the women there who qualify. Why in the Sam Hill don't they do it?

JULIE JACOBSEN

She is thirty-five, divorced, with two children: a son, nine, and a daughter, seven. She lives on a quiet side street in a small town. The house is sparsely furnished and comfortably untidy, with toys lying here and there. A kitten soon joins us on the threadbare couch. While we talk her roommate, Pat, a younger woman, brings us strawberry ice cream.

She is an attractive woman, shy but frank, with brown hair and eyes and the beginnings of lines on her face. "This is a hard story to tell, because I've told it so many times for other reasons. . . ."

I graduated from college in the summer of '76 with my degree in counseling, and right away I got a job with the Elm Grove Township School District, Lincoln High School. I worked there for a grand total of three months before I made the mistake of telling my secretary that I'm bisexual. Within two or three days things were going on. She told our immediate supervisor, and he called in the principal. All this was going on without my knowledge, but I knew something was happening. Every time I came into my office all the other doors were closed, and the secretary wasn't at her desk, and I could tell she was upset. I thought maybe I was being paranoid until the assistant principal, who was a friend to me, told me that the principal did know and that something would happen. If he hadn't told me that, things would be a lot different for me now because it gave me a little bit of a head start in terms of calling an attorney. The next day there was a note on my desk from the principal that I was to join him and the superintendent at a meeting after school to determine my continuing status. That confirmed my doubts.

I've thought a lot about why I told my secretary. It was a combination of things. There was a student who was gay, who I was counseling, and he had a crush on me. He was always coming in and hanging around waiting to see me. I had talked to the secretary about this student, and she seemed to deal with that OK. I also think I just needed to tell people. I had started to come out, and I felt I could tell her. It turns out I was wrong, but it was something I needed to do.

So they asked me to this meeting. I was pretty scared. It was pretty awesome. I mean, they were trying to be very matter-of-fact, saying, "Come on down to the board office, and we'll have this meeting," you know. But when I got there, it was the principal, the superintendent, and a school board attorney. I was there with my attorney and my NEA representative. I brought them to make sure there were witnesses, and that turned out to be fortunate because what was said at that meeting has become an important point in my trial.

The board attorney did 95 percent of the talking. He said, "We called this meeting to ask for Mrs. Jacobsen's resignation." My attorney said, "On what grounds?" The other guy said, "It's come to our attention that she's been telling teachers at the high school that she is either bisexual or lesbian." He said "teachers"; there's no implication of student involvement. And he quoted a couple of statute numbers that they were acting under. My attorney made note of those and said, "That's all? You're not saying she's not doing her job or anything like that?" They talked back and forth, and then my attorney said that maybe I'd like a few days to think about it. At that point I said, "I won't resign." The board attorney had obviously been prepared for that because as soon I said it, he said, "Then you're suspended immediately with pay." That was pretty much the end of the meeting. They told me I couldn't report to work the next morning.

That's when the waiting started. Waiting has been the big theme of this whole story. What was supposed to happen next was that within ten days I should have received written charges and notice of a hearing. It never came. I would call my attorney and say, "What's up?" and he'd say, "Well, let's wait till the next board meeting." They had one in December and didn't notify me of anything, so we waited for the January one. All this time I was sitting at home. During this thing there have been two periods that were real difficult for me, and that one was probably the second hardest. I really loved the job. I had just gotten into counseling. I had regular sessions established with a lot of students and some teachers. And suddenly I could not enter the building. I think that was the worst because I wondered what was going on in their minds. They had built up confidence in me, and then I was gone.

Finally my attorney filed suit, and two weeks later we were supposed to have a hearing. We were ready with character witnesses and everything, but the hearing didn't happen. Their attorneys and mine met in the judge's chambers and agreed to put me back to work. The judge issued a reinstatement order and said the rest of the suit would be dealt with later.

The following Monday I reported to the principal. We had kind of suspected that they wouldn't put me back in my job, but rather would give me some kind of transfer. And that's what they did. The principal told me to go to my office and clear everything out and report to a certain person in a building across the street they call the annex. I went over there, and they had given me a dark little room that was off a rest room. The door actually said "rest room" on it. They carried in a beat-up old desk and a file cabinet, gave me a pail of water, and told me to clean it up. That's what I did for the first half hour [laughs]. And I just sat there for the next three days. They hadn't come up with an assignment for me yet, but they had my rules. I was to sign in and out of the main building, and they assigned me a lunch period from 10:45 to 11:15, when there were only about fifty students in the cafeteria. Otherwise I was not to enter the main building. And if for any reason I wanted to leave the annex, I had to call the principal for permission, and I had to sign in and out so he always knew where I was.

That started for me the hardest period of the whole time. It would have been hard going back to counseling because of people's attitudes about me and the harassment and so on. But if I'd been able to meet with my kids, that wouldn't have been important. Instead, I was given the assignment to create a proposal for career education for the whole district. It was funny. I mean, it wasn't funny at the time. It wasn't funny because first of all, they took from me a job I loved. The first job I ever totally loved. And they thought up something I liked least of all. I couldn't tolerate the idea of sitting at a desk and coming up with some proposal for career education. But according to my certification as a school counselor, they could assign that kind of thing to me. Technically I should have been able to do it. The whole point, of course, was to keep me out of contact with students.

It was obvious that I was going to be watched all the time. Nobody ever admitted to doing it, but I saw the secretaries write down who called me. They were instructed not to refer any calls unless a person would say who it was. And there was constant harassment. Like they wanted me to write the proposal, and they didn't tell me that by such-and-such a time I should have so much of it done. They just said that when my contract was over, I had to have a proposal. That was the only deadline. Yet I had to have weekly progress reports with the principal, and each time he would act as if there were certain things I should have done that I didn't. Once I had an eleven-page report, single-spaced, with one typing error in it. He called attention to the typing error. Needling me, you know. I got memos all the time. Real nasty ones. The principal made sure he put everything in writing, and I made sure I kept track of everything that happened.

I went through four months of surviving like that, just waiting it out. It was awful. I used to love to go to work, and now I wanted to stay home. But I had to go and be super, super, supercareful about the details. I had to be there, because if I wasn't they'd accuse me of high absenteeism. I had to do everything just right because they'd accuse me of not following policies. I wasn't just an employee anymore. I was being watched, and I had to be perfect. And I had to do the work, too. Even though I knew nothing about it and hated the assignment, I had to come up with a respectable product. And I did it. That was real hard. But I couldn't quit the job without losing the whole case. And it became very important to win the case. Because it was simple homophobia. They did not want me working there because of my sexual preference, and I simply wasn't going to let that go by.

Finally they sent me a letter of nonrenewal with a number of contrived things in it, none of which said anything about sexual orientation, of course. Then it was just a matter of my concluding my term of contract and finishing the proposal. That last day of school was a glorious day for me. And then we filed another suit on the nonrenewal, claiming that it was in fact related to the sexual thing. So we had two suits in progress, one about the suspension and one about the nonrenewal. We asked for $1.5 million in damages on the second suit because of being unemployable. It seemed kind of grand to me then, but it seems a very small amount to me now.

I must have tried to get teaching or counseling jobs at 150 different places in the area. My attorneys told me to apply at every school within a radius of one hundred miles, so I went to the NEA office and got the book of schools. It was a full-time job just writing for applications and sending them out. I used to get fifteen or twenty pieces of mail a day at home, and I got so bleary-eyed from filling out applications that I started to have friends over. I'd say, "I'm having an application party, folks. If you want supper, I'll cook for you." [Laughs.] Four or five friends would come over. We'd get out the stack of applications. I'd pass out pens. I had a big poster made with all my personal information and dates of appointments, and we'd polish off ten or twenty in a night.

Most of the schools would send me back something like; "We're sorry, we have no vacancy." There was no way of telling whether they knew about my case and weren't interested, or whether in fact they had no openings. But there were maybe five or six schools where they asked me to come for interviews. The interviews felt good, and then nothing more happened. They'd tell me they were going to make a decision at the next meeting of the board, and I'd get a routine letter that said, "Thank you for applying for the position, but I'm sorry to say that it's been filled." Those are the kind that my attorneys follow up on, the ones that actually interviewed me but didn't hire me. Because it may help build my case for damages. Of course, a lot of people get turned down, and probably for the same positions I applied for. But part of the process is that the schools check my latest employer, and when they do that, they find two things on the record: the suspension and the nonrenewal. Probably the word bisexual doesn't even come out. In teaching circles they usually don't ask why you were not renewed. They just don't want to touch a person who's got that on their record. So my attorneys are claiming that Elm Grove damaged my reputation by the suspension and the nonrenewal.

It's also been in the news a lot around here. Every time any action has been taken it's been in the papers, on TV, and on the radio. I've sat here and listened to my name being mentioned on the news. "Bisexual counselor," that's always in the headline. And a lot of the stories have been on the front page of the second section, where a lot of people see it. So you have no way of knowing whether the employers are aware of the case—which they very well could be—or if they just call to check on references from your former employer and hear about the nonrenewal.

There were a couple of curious situations right near here. At one I went for an interview and received nothing more than a form letter saying there was no job. It had been a very personal interview, and they acted like it hadn't even happened. At the other one they interviewed me, a couple of weeks went by, and they sent me a letter responding to my original letter and saying, "We have no vacancy in your field." And they had interviewed me for a vacancy.

But the real biggie was at a crisis center and psychological counseling program in town. I've worked there as a counselor and I know a lot of the people, so I applied there for a counseling job. First I had a meeting with three or four people, one of whom had been a teacher of mine in college. They eliminated me from the procedure and I challenged the decision. So they gave me a meeting with the whole selection committee, which is about ten people. And it came out that this ex-teacher of mine, who was wielding a lot of influence in the hiring process, had some terrible thing against me. He hadn't said what was bothering him in the earlier meeting, but he acted like there was some awful thing he knew about me, and that he didn't think I should be hired. So in the big meeting he said he was going to reveal this great personal issue. He said, "Do you remember that cocktail party at the end of semester last summer?" He had given this party and invited everyone in his class. His girl friend was there, too. I said, "Yeah, I remember." And what it added up to was that he accused me of trying to pick up his date. He said, "It's not the competition alone that bothers me. But when you applied for that job at Elm Grove, I wrote you a good recommendation. You deserved it because you're a good counselor. And then you turn around and do that to me." That's what he said. Competition! It was so foreign to me. I said, "Who, me?" It took me aback because it's something I didn't do and couldn't do. I couldn't even imagine how he could be so threatened by me that he would say I tried to pick up his date. And nobody challenged him on it. Nobody said, "Hey, you sound like you're being homophobic"; or, "Would it be the same if she were a man?" Nobody said that. In fact, other people mentioned my gayness as one deterrent to my getting the job. And another guy talked about the suit I had against Elm Grove and said, "That makes me think you have an explosive personality, and if we do something here that you don't like, you'll sue us." So I didn't get the job.

It's easy for me to start taking all the rejections personally, especially if I'm feeling low. I get real naïve, and I think, "By golly, I'm going to put more energy into it and really go out and attack the job market." And then when I still don't find anything, I put the fault on me. It's almost as though I forget the influence this suit has had around here.

And I forget how frightened people are of homosexual people. I forget until I get all excited about getting a job, and then it doesn't come. At that point I can get into a depression very easily. I say to myself, "Oh, yeah, it's got nothing to do with me," but I still feel worthless and useless and tired of trying.

The waiting is the hardest to deal with because all kinds of feelings of impotence, worthlessness, frustration, and anger come up. I can't do what I'm trained to do and what I want to be doing. No matter how much energy I put into getting a job, it doesn't end up getting me a job like it did before all this came up. It gives me such a feeling of power-lessness. And anger, not just for the people at Elm Grove, but anger at the judge 'cause he's just sitting there. He has the power to schedule a trial date. He has the power to rule in my favor. But the feeling I have is that the channel I'm forced to use to right the wrong is biased against me just as much as the people who did it in the first place.

Through all this time I've had no trial date for either suit. Then about six weeks ago a reporter called my attorneys and asked if she could do an interview with me on how I've been getting along in the interim. Not dealing with the facts of the case, but the slowness of it coming to trial. They said she could. The day after it was published, the judge called my attorneys and started to talk about the case. He had just put it away and was not acting on it, until the reporter brought it to everybody's attention again. That was the point she stressed, that I was still waiting.

That was about a month ago. Then about ten days ago a friend called me up and said, "I heard you lost your case. I saw it on TV last night." A friend even came over the next day to buy me a drink to console me, and I didn't even know what had happened [laughs]. The judge had ruled on the first case. He said that it should not be tried, and he found for the school board. He ruled that since my contract was only for one year, I didn't have any property interest in it. But this was the suspension case, and my attorneys are hoping that it will be overturned on the grounds that suspension in the middle of the year deprives me of property interest while the contract is still in effect. The judge even said something like that, that even though I was paid while not working, I was stripped of other benefits.

My financial situation right now is pretty dismal. I had to sell my house to get the equity out of it because there were about four months when I had no income at all. They wouldn't start my unemployment payments last summer because of the teaching contract, even though I wasn't working. So I had to live off the equity in my house. I had to sell my car because I couldn't make the payments. Now it's gotten to another stage because I can't even afford to rent this house. And I bought an old car out of my income tax return, but I can't afford to keep it up. Right now I'm living on borrowed money. I got a loan from the NEA for the next three months. There's no interest; but still, I'm borrowing almost $1,500 just to live on, and I have to start repaying it before I even know where it's going to be repaid from.

There's only one good thing that's come out of it all, and that has to do with my attitude towards being gay. I think at some point during all this, maybe during those two and a half months that I stayed home while I was suspended, something happened internally. I think I just made a commitment to openness about the whole thing. I decided, by golly, that never again would I pretend that I was something I wasn't in order to get a job. And then be forced to live with the pressures and the fears and not being able to talk to anybody about things that come up. I realized that the suits were in the works, and it was going to take a long time, and there would probably be a lot of publicity. It's kind of strange because at the same time I say that I'm committed to it, I know it jeopardizes my chances of work and comfort and all that. I'm committed even though it isn't going to be easy. It hasn't been easy. I am a good counselor, and I am a good teacher, and I should be able to work, and I am gay. . . . I don't know what to do with all the "ands."

8

THE ALTON STRUGGLE: "They Need a Union Bad"

The Alton Products Corporation* is one of the largest multinationals based in the United States. Its American work force numbers sixty-eight thousand, 80 percent of whom are nonunion. Recently Alton built a large plant in Lincoln Valley, an agricultural area in the southeast. After a union drive the Allied Food Workers (AFW) narrowly won the right to represent the twelve hundred Lincoln Valley employees. But Alton refused to make any major concessions during negotiations for a contract. As a result, the union went on strike in October of 1976.

The strike lasted eight months. Then Alton moved to break it by opening the plant gates, inviting the workers back, and threatening to fire those who remained on strike. For five days there was fighting at the gates as strikers tried to discourage the scabs from going in. Many strikers were arrested. Finally, the union, hamstrung by injunctions and with its ranks breaking, capitulated and signed a contract that recognized the AFW but offered few other benefits.

One of the terms of the agreement was that thirty-eight union members accused by the company of violence during the strike would be fired pending arbitration. Among them were several strike leaders. When I talked to members of the Alton 38, as they soon became known in the valley, they had been out of work for twenty months—eight months on strike and a year of arbitration procedures. They hoped to win back their jobs in a few months but could not be sure.

The interviews took place at the offices of Local 1236 of the AFW, in a one-story building next to a bowling alley. We talked in a

---

*This name is fictitious, as are all others in this chapter.

back room, while out front a dozen men and women sat drinking Cokes from the machine and swapping stories. Union members came and went, often with children in tow. Bumper stickers reading "Boycott Gallo and lettuce!" and "Buy an American car!" were stuck on the walls.

CONRAD KELLY

He is the president of Local 1236—a big man, loud, bearish, foul-mouthed, passionately devoted to the union. He belongs to several civic organizations in the area—"It's part of my job"—and has taken courses in labor history, public speaking, and the like. During a long, rambling interview he brings up endless examples of Alton's ill-treatment of workers, asking indignantly, "Is this compassion? Is this what they call a people-oriented company?" Yet he has grudging admiration for the company in which he has spent his whole working life. "It's one of the largest processors of food in the world. In the Lincoln Valley plant they put out five million pounds of food a week. They make anything you can eat. There's nothing that you can tell me you eat that Alton doesn't make. You're eating a doughnut now; Alton makes doughnuts. You go to a restaurant and have lobster tails; Alton makes lobster tails. You're having a shrimp cocktail in the Waldorf-Astoria; it's probably an Alton shrimp cocktail. Alton shrimp is freeze-dried, and you soak it in water with lemon juice, and it restores the shrimp back to the way it was originally. I've tasted them, and they're damn good. Alton makes their own glass to put the products in, their own caps to put on top of the jars, their own labels that go on the jars, the plastic cups that the margarine comes in. They make their own machinery, their own tanks, their own vessels. They have their own railcars. They're a fantastic monster throughout the world."

I'm one of the old-timers around here as far as working for Alton goes. Before I came down here I worked in the Alton plant in Delaware, for twenty-three years. In fact, it was a funny thing—I was on the last negotiating committee in Delaware. We knew they were shutting down the plant and moving here. We got severance pay written into contract. We got transfer rights. We were trying our best to try and get cost of moving. But the company was very much against anybody moving from Delaware to Lincoln Valley. For one thing, Delaware was a union plant, and they wanted to keep this plant nonunion. The Delaware workers were also about 40 percent black, whereas Lincoln Valley's population is only 8 percent black, so the company was worried about getting a bad reputation in the community if a lot of blacks came. So they tried to discourage people from transferring. So out of eight hundred workers only about ninety came down here. I came because I had pretty good seniority and because I would have lost my pension if I didn't. At that time there was no law to give me vested rights in my pension. Once you reached your sixty-fifth birthday, Alton would pay you each month $6 for every year you had worked in the company, *if* you had fifteen years of service and had reached your fiftieth birthday. Well, I had twenty-three years, but I was only forty-five. So I would have lost it all.

After we got down here we found out that Alton had been having meetings with the other people in the plant. They would say, "We're having a group from Delaware come down here. They're going to be starting in a week. These people are very rowdy, very boisterous. They're not a good grade of people. But we had a union contract and we have to let them come whether we like it or not. We're sorry they're coming, and we hope we can get rid of them at some point." So the people here looked at us as if we were animals coming out of a cage when we first got here. And there was a tremendous amount of harassment. I had worked twenty-three years in Delaware, twelve as a supervisor, and never had anything in my work record. I had a perfect record. I was here maybe a week, and I got something in my record. And on about five other occasions things went onto my record card.

So without a union I felt pretty nervous, like a fish out of water. Here I brought my family out of the suburbs into the country, and I bought an old farmhouse and some land in the middle of nowhere, and we're trying to meet all new people, and Alton has me all the way up to a final warning. A final warning means that the next step is out the door. They were doing this to all the people that came down from Delaware. Really putting the pressure on. They definitely discriminated against us. So I felt like, gee, I didn't know what to do except get a union in there.

Luckily a lot of other people were feeling the same way. And when any new company comes into an area, all the unions flock around it, trying to meet people and handing out cards. Two big unions tried to organize the plant, but they botched it. Now the biggest union in the area is the AFW local at a plant about thirty miles away. They have good pay, good benefits. So we said, "Hey, why not ask the AFW to come in?" We got a petition and took it to them, and it impressed the organizing staff. They got permission from Chicago to organize us, and within two weeks over 75 percent of the people in the plant signed membership cards.

After you get the cards signed, then you petition to have a representation election, and the majority wins. Well, the company put on one of the most vicious campaigns you ever saw in your life. Once a week we were forced to watch these movies in the company cafeteria about how unions create bloodbaths and carry knives and guns and how they turn blacks against whites and men against women. The company had big neon signs with flashing green and white lights that said, "Vote no union." Your supervisors would call you in individually. They mailed letters to your house. The president of the company came to speak to us, the first time in his life he did anything like that. So there must have been something bad going on in that plant, because first of all, when it opened, Alton took fourteen thousand applications to hire twelve hundred people, and they only took people who were against unions. So they must have been harassed or mistreated in some form just to get 75 percent to sign cards. And then after that campaign the union still won the election. We only won by twenty-one votes, but we did win.

By that time I was pretty involved in the organizing drive. I got a lot of cards signed and I went around asking people to vote for the union. And after the election I decided to run for president of the local. Since I had a lot of union experience and most people in the plant didn't have any at all, I thought I'd be right for the job. I campaigned like crazy. I really worked to get elected. In fact, there were seven people running, and in the union constitution it says you have to win by a majority vote. It's hard to win a majority with seven people running, but I was able to win it on the first ballot.

Then there was a lot of struggle. The company didn't want to recognize the union, and the negotiations were really a circus. We started to negotiate a contract immediately after being certified. Between June and October we couldn't accomplish a damn thing. The company had this take-it-or-leave-it offer. They didn't want to give us a thing. They even wanted to take many things away that we already had. They wanted to prove to the people that they made a wrong choice. So we had the strike that started in October and lasted till June. The negotiations continued on and off during the strike. The head of the Federal Mediation and Conciliation Service himself was involved in the negotiations, and he said that in all his experience in labor he had never met such an obstinate company to deal with. It wasn't money we were talking about, just the basic rights of the average union worker. We couldn't get half of the basic rights that a contract normally has. Like to get a member of the union on the plant safety committee. We said, "We'd like to be part of your safety program. We want to make the plant safe." Because this plant had one of the worst safety records in the country. Before the contract came into effect, we had people lose eight fingers in one week on slicing machines. One man lost three fingers on one hand. And that turned my stomach so bad. . . . But they wouldn't allow it. They fought us tooth and nail. Finally, we got one union member on the safety committee, where normally it's a joint effort.

Meanwhile I went through hell, and my family went through hell. All through the strike I put in all kinds of crazy hours. I was down here for maybe fifteen or eighteen hours every day. We had to have the strike kitchen going for the picketers. We had to make sure the gates were covered twenty-four hours a day. We had to keep the people's morale high. We had to show that the leadership was in the middle of the strike and that we weren't staying home while they were out picketing. We'd

275

go to the pickets and explain why we're on strike, why we have to remain on strike, why these issues are important to us. Explain the negotiations to them, what the company's position is, and our position. And we'd hold meetings regularly to get votes of confidence. We had meetings to death [laughs]. I really neglected my house and my family a hell of a lot.

We also got into a tremendous financial pinch. During the strike I was getting $50 a week, and for a while I had a part-time job that brought in another $50 or $60. After I got fired I started getting $107-a-week unemployment. My wife had a job for a while, but she got laid off. So we had to cut back tremendously.

I did create a business that gives us an income, though. I don't tell anybody about it. Every Sunday that I'm free I go to a flea market and sell things. My cousin saves me things that she finds on the street in the city. My mother-in-law saves me things from her area. It's unbelievable what people throw out in the street. Ann has given me fireplace and-irons of solid brass, fireplace screens, artificial logs—and that's just talking about fireplace stuff. I just got a leather medical bag that some doctor threw out. A brand-new travel kit made of pure pigskin. Clothes racks, dressers, chairs, end tables. My relatives pick up the stuff for me and put it in the cellar, and I go get it in my van. I have outbuildings on my property that are just stacked with flea market items. And every Sunday I can go down there. I'm there at eight o'clock in the morning, and I stay till five o'clock at night. I never make less than $150 for the day, selling junk. I never run into anybody I know there, and I don't tell. . . . You know, the president of the union, selling garbage. . . . Maybe there's a little bit of image or pride that I have. But that's how I've been surviving.

The worst part of all has been the strain on my family. I don't like to admit it, but one of the reasons I'm not running for president again is that I need to try and get a good relationship back at home. I need a break. I guess I'll always be active. I'm still enthusiastic. If I was a single man I'd continue as president, and I'd never run out of energy. But the job requires too much of your time. It's been a tremendous burden on the family and a mental strain on me and my wife. I would say more on my wife because she can't see why I'm involved in it as much as I am. You know, of the people that were fired we've had about six divorces. Fortunately I don't have one going, but my wife and I have had our first real serious conflicts as a result of all this. It's been nerve-racking on both sides. I come home tense and uptight, and she got to the point where she said, "Don't tell me anything about it. The less I know, the better off I am." And the phone calls! Even now I get at least twenty calls a day. People want my services and I still feel obligated to them. I'm polite and hear them out, no matter who they are or what time of day it is. For maybe four or five months I never had supper at the table. It was

276

always by the phone in the kitchen. And my wife would say, "You're down there all damn day, how come they gotta call you at home?" You'd be amazed the number of times we were in the sack, and I was right there in the saddle, when the phone rang late at night. And that never helps any marriage [*laughs*].

It was only about two months ago that things got seriously bad. It all stemmed from her saying that I treat the kids and her second-rate, that I pay more attention to the people in the union. Well, maybe I was and I didn't realize it. I'd come in, and maybe my kids had thrown their coats on the floor. I'd yell, "Get the hell in here and pick up your coats! I tell you every day not to throw your coats on the floor!" And my wife would say, "Boy, you were just on the phone with a union member and you were kissing their ass. And here you come jumping on the kids." I'm pretty stubborn, and I'd just be cold to her. It got to the point where I felt she didn't give me enough understanding, and if I would've had the money, I would've moved out. I would've left her. But being unemployed, with only $107 a week coming in, I'd have nothing to get a room and feed myself with because they'd need that money to run the farm. Maybe it was best that I was in that situation [*laughs*].

Another problem was the threats. My wife and kids received about eight threatening phone calls. They'd say, "A fire bomb is gonna come through your window and burn down the house while you're asleep," or, "We're gonna shoot your husband's head off." After these incidents my wife became high-strung and extremely nervous. She wanted to leave the state and never come back. I had to talk myself deaf, dumb, and blind to keep her here. I would've gone with her if she insisted, but I explained that these things were common, and they didn't have any substance. We changed our phone number and made it unlisted. I had many threatening calls right here in the office. People saying they were gonna blow my head off. They were just to scare you and shake you up a little bit. And sometimes I was a little shook. I looked behind me when I was driving, and I was careful about going to a lot of public places. I still don't even like to go shopping or to the movies.

All that got worse after I got arrested. In order to be a good leader I had to violate the injunction to try and convince my people that they shouldn't [*laughs*]. I was caught in the middle, and I would get arrested as a result. I think I was arrested five times for violating the injunction. The other kids would say to my kids in school, "Well, I see your father's locked up again. There he is in jail." I also was arrested for hitting a truck driver, which I didn't do. There was this truck that came through the picket line. It happened on a couple of occasions. Usually the picket captain would call me up, and I'd run down to say to the driver, "We have a strike going on here. We'd appreciate it if you'd honor our picket line." Well, this guy said, "Fuck you, I hate unions. I want to make money. I'm going in." And he went in. I knew when he was coming out.

So I was on my way back to the plant in my car with four other fellows. We passed the truck about a quarter mile from the plant. Some words were spoken and he stopped, and one of the guys got into a fight with him. I wasn't in it. But the driver went to the police, and he claimed I was involved. So I was blamed.

That's what got me fired. And right now I'm feeling pretty scared. I'm worried about the arbitration. I feel I'm gonna win it, but what if I don't? My family would be without hospitalization. I've got three kids. I have no vested rights in the pension. And you have to at least consider the worst. For one thing, the lawyers have told me there's only a few people the company is completely out to get, and I'm one. If they're out to get me, they might have a trick up their sleeve. The lawyer still says, "Conrad, don't worry about it. You've got it; it's in the bag. They've got nothing on you. This arbitrator is fair. The situation has happened before, and nobody would set that kind of precedent in labor again. Don't worry about it." But you can't help thinking, "What if the odds are fifty to one that I'll win and that one chance happens?" Maybe the arbitrator will say, "Well, I can please both sides by bringing thirty-seven people back and giving the company the big one." I'm blackballed in this community. I'm in the middle of nowhere. I don't know where or how I'd get a job. I guess I'd never starve because I'm the type of guy that will wash dishes at night and get some kind of work during the day. I've thought about buying my own little business. But it has to worry you. You'd be a fool to say that you've been working twenty-six years, and now you're fired, and it doesn't concern you whether you get back in or not.

I spend many a sleepless night, I'll tell you. I get all tensed up and nerved up. My health definitely isn't as good. I think I'm a strong person, a healthy person, but I can see where it could give me an ulcer. And as president you have to set an example and show that you're cool. People get you so pissed off that you want to kick the shit out of them, but you don't. Also, with the scabs there's certain ones I'll never forget the rest of my life. If I run into a superscab and get into an argument, I just want to smack the shit out of them, but as president of the local it wouldn't be in good taste. But I'm a revengeful person. I'll get even with them. When I'm not the president and I run into them, I will kick the shit out of them. And I'm looking forward to it. I haven't fought a good fight in about ten years, but I used to be able to handle myself pretty good.

Then you have to take care of the thirty-eight. This union hall is a social club, and I made it that way because these people aren't gonna sit home and look at the four walls, wondering what's happening. We spoiled them a little bit, but they deserve to be spoiled. They're special cases. So they come down here and rehash the same story over and over again. They play cards, they argue, they fight, they get drunk, they do what the hell they want, but you can't stop them from doing it. These people were hurt bad, and some of them are babies. They need somebody to lead them by the hand, and if that leadership drops from them, they're completely lost souls. I've gotten to the point where I jump on them. Two in particular. They come in here and I say, "You guys are the clouds of doom. You come in here and look at the worst of everything." I say, "What if I came in here as president and said, 'We're gonna lose the arbitration. Not one of us is gonna get a job back. Not only that, we're all blackballed, and we'll never work another day in our lives. And gee, even our houses are gonna be taken away from us, and when our cars break down, they're gonna rot where they stand. And probably we'll be struck by lightning and our wives will be killed'?" I sit and listen to that fucking shit every single day of my life. But I jump on them and tell them, "I don't want to listen to it; I've heard it a hundred times already." I say, "We're gonna win that arbitration. We're gonna bury those cocksuckers in the ground. They're gonna respect us 'cause we're gonna win every single arbitration. Not only that, we're gonna go back there, and we're gonna hire a bus and wave flags as we go back in that building." You gotta keep their spirits up and have them look forward to something. You've lost everything if you don't do that. If I turned around and said, "We're gonna get beaten into the ground, the company has fucked us, and they're gonna fuck us for the rest of our lives," I wouldn't be a leader.

But all the time that I'm cheering them up, there's something in the back of my mind saying, "You lying fuck. . . . " [Laughs.]

ROSIE ENGELS

She is forty-two and has lived all her life in the state. "Until I went to Alton I never really had a full-time job. I was married after high school and had five children right away. I worked at a steel warehouse for a year until I got pregnant with my first daughter, and that took care of that. But as my children grew up and got to be teenagers, we needed more money. So when Alton opened, I got a job. . . . "

I started on third-shift sanitation, which was very hard. As a matter of fact, I was one of the first women that ever did this job, along with a friend of mine. There had been a woman before us but she disqualified herself, and everybody laughed at her. So we wanted to prove a point, that we could do this work. There were people from Alton headquarters in Dallas standing around, watching us do it, because it was very heavy work. One night we had to take a head off a machine. It weighed about 150 pounds. A friend of ours in there said, "Somebody's going to get hurt." Of course, there was a supervisor standing around, and he said, "Let them go." And I said to Barbara, "I'm gonna do it if my arm breaks off." And she said, "So will I." Well, it was just the first time that was really hard because it sort of grew on you. After that you could do it.

Pretty soon they made me a group leader on my shift, which meant that I really didn't have to do anything anymore. I just saw that the work was done and helped whoever got behind. At that time I felt I could work with or without a union. But I would've voted union for one simple reason: I felt that a man with a family needs job security. If they fired me I could pick up another job as a waitress or something. My husband was working, and my income wasn't the main one. So I wasn't really thinking of myself; I was thinking of the guys with families whose wives weren't working. Even after they offered me a supervisor's job I felt I would go union. I knew that if I took that job I wouldn't have any job security. Anytime I did something wrong they could just say, "Well, out you go." I felt that if we got a union, I'd be more safe. So I turned down that job.

Then they had the election and the union won. But Alton wouldn't sit down and negotiate a contract. They wouldn't talk. So we said, "If we don't get this contract by midnight on such-and-such a date, we're going on strike." And that's what we did because the company wouldn't recognize that the people wanted a union. We had a strike for eight months. I thought it was a nice, clean strike. We more or less had a ball picketing. In fact, that's how my troubles started. I went picketing every Monday night. My husband didn't like that too much because I got to enjoy picketing. And some nights we wouldn't even picket. They wanted six pickets on every gate, so if there were more, we'd just take off and go from one hotel to another, drinking. Ever since this strike began, I've drunk more whiskey and beer than I did in all my life. I never did drink before that.

For a while I only drank on Monday night. Then I started to get really bored. Around January I took a part-time job on Fridays and Saturdays as a waitress in a place that served liquor. So I started to drink on Fridays and Saturdays. My husband didn't want me to take that job. But I was really bored, and I was so involved in the union that I thought it would be good to get away from my family. Because my husband kept saying, "This goddamn strike. This goddamn strike."

I think what really upset him was that it made me so much more independent. Even working didn't do that to me. I think it does to a lot of women, but it didn't to me. I still had my children and my home and my work, which kept me so busy that I didn't have time to think of anything else. I'd work eight or maybe ten hours a day, go home, sleep, cook, clean, and wash. But during the strike I had all this free time. I'd do my cleaning in the morning, and that was it. And I was getting $50-a-week strike pay for picketing. That was like spending money. So it was more or less like that old saying "The idle mind. . . ." You know? I'd sit and think, "Eh, why not?" And I'd go out. I started bowling. I'd go play golf on a driving range. I'd go down to the union hall. And I took this part-time job. My husband didn't want me to go, but I insisted. It got to the point where even if he had said, "We can't be married like this," I wouldn't have given up that job. That's how determined I was.

But when everything really changed was after I got arrested. On the first day they opened the plant gates I wasn't even gonna go down and picket. I had no idea what it was gonna be like. I had no idea that anybody would try to cross the line. But I had a girl friend, and she said, "I'm going down there." She was about five feet tall and ninety-eight pounds, so I said, "If a skinny little thing like you can go, so can I." It was mass picketing that first day, and it meant breaking the injunction; but I figured, if everybody else did it, why not me? So we went down and I didn't do much but kiss and squeeze everybody I saw. That night we had a union meeting, and they told us that people were gonna try and cross the line the next day. Well, that made me so determined and so mad because I could see those scabs going in there and taking my job. I never knew what the word *scab* meant before or that people could be so low as to cross the picket line. I felt that anybody who crosses that line is lower than a snake, and you step on people like that. So the next day we went down there, and yes, I did kick some cars with scabs in 'em. But there were state police all around me. If they wanted, they could've said, "That's it." Then the third day I didn't even go to the mass picketing by the plant. I stayed out on the highway, and when it was over I was walking up to the Sunset Diner with everybody else. I guess I yelled at some cars and stuff. All of a sudden this big state policeman grabbed me. I said, "Leave me alone. I didn't do anything!" He literally dragged me into his car, and he said, "Shut up!" He was going to hit me with his billy club if I didn't shut up. He had no uniform, just a helmet and plain street clothing. He would've hit me because they did hit women on that picket line. They didn't care what you were.

So they picked us up and took us into court. The state trooper said I threw a rock through a windshield, which I know I did not do. I know who did it, but it wasn't me. After they had us in court all day, these two big guys come in, one on either side of me, and said, "Come with us." And I thought, "My God, they're gonna put me in jail." They took me to the barracks, fingerprinted me, and took a mug shot. I felt so bad when they fingerprinted me that I just wanted to die. Then they let me go. I didn't get home until eight o'clock that night, and there were my husband and mother-in-law and everybody just looking at me.

That was horrible. I guess it's because of the way I was brought up, but a fingerprint and a mug shot made me think, "OK, now you're a criminal." That's what Alton made me feel like. I couldn't eat. I couldn't sleep. When I slept, I'd dream of sitting in jail. I think I cried for three days. It's hard to explain. I'd fight with my children, tell them that they had to do the cleaning because I didn't want to. When I was home, I wanted to stay in bed, just crawl away and hide. First of all, I knew I was accused of doing something I didn't do. That hurt. And to get fingerprinted and photographed for something you didn't do. . . . Well, I can't explain the feeling. It's just a horrible feeling. I felt it hurt my family and it hurt my husband. And they put my name in the paper. My son pretended it was funny. He was telling everybody about his mother in the paper. But I didn't think it was funny. I wouldn't have minded having my name in the paper for something else, but not for throwing a rock which I didn't throw.

A few days later we had the union meeting to vote on the contract. They read off the thirty-eight names, and my name was on the list. I knew it would be because I was one of the ones arrested. And I guess I was a little mad at the AFW, because I felt that they let us down, going back without these thirty-eight people. I could see their point, that if they didn't go back, a lot more people would have scabbed. About two hundred scabs had already gone in. These people wanted a union, but they were afraid of their jobs and afraid that Alton would just hire new people. So I could see their point, but when they voted, I still voted no. I still felt that if everybody would stand up and fight for what they want—not necessarily fight, but just be determined, and stay on strike, and let those two hundred people go—then we would have won. I felt that everybody was giving up on me, which made me think, "The hell with you." Of course they told us we'd go into arbitration and we'd probably get our jobs back, but the company has kept that going for almost a year now. And even though I can probably do without the job, whereas a man couldn't, I still have that feeling, like a part of me has been taken away. Something is missing, a part of me.

So after that I just didn't care about anything. I felt that people can lie and get away with it, and they can put you down, so I figured if this is what our world consists of, then hell, I don't want it. I didn't care about my husband. I didn't care about my kids. I did what I wanted to. My husband would say, "Don't do this," and I felt, "Why not?" Because if you don't, life's too short. They just put you down anyway. So I did what I wanted to. That's when I really started to get this feeling of independence. It got to the point where I was going out four or five nights a week. I'd go bowling on Thursday, work on Friday and Saturday, and I was even starting to lie and say I had to work on Tuesday so that I could go out with my friends. I felt like I was single again. Like I had no children, no husband. If I came home and told a lie, it didn't bother me. As a matter of fact, a lot of times I would sit there and think, "Maybe there's something wrong with me." But I would see other people doing the same thing, and I'd say, "Hey, all these other people aren't wacky. Half the world isn't nuts."

Whenever I'd go shopping, I'd say, "I'll just drop over to the union hall for a minute or two." The minute would go to an hour or two, so when I got home my husband would say, "Why'd you go there?" I felt, "It's none of your business." I got like an "I don't give a shit" attitude. I don't know if women's lib came in there and helped a little bit or if I just felt that I'd lived a life that was really like a hermit. But I just wanted to go and go and go. My husband started saying, "Ever since this goddamn strike something happened to you." And I'd go, "Well, what can I say?" And I'd walk away like a cocky kid and think, "Big deal." He kept saying, "This goddamn strike." So one day I said to a close girl friend of mine, "All Tim says these days is 'This goddamn strike.' " She said, "George is doing the same thing." I said, "What did we do?" She said, "I don't know." But she changed, too. I think people were more shocked at her than they were at me because she had that real innocent look, like a Quaker. So I could see that it wasn't just happening to me; it happened to my best friends.

It got to be like a routine on weekends. I'd stay out till two or three. In fact, I'm still going out, and I don't think that will ever change. Ninety percent of your married women are doing this now, and I'm not going to stop. My husband has more or less accepted it. The strike gave me the chance, and I took it. But I think I went overboard. A couple of months after I got fired it got to the point where my family never knew where I was. They'd call the union hall; they'd call different people. If anything had happened, they couldn't have found me. And it wasn't so much that I wanted to be going out; it was just that I needed to be around people who understood about the arrest and everything. And I felt that only the union people understood. A lot of times I used to feel like I wanted to go up in the mountains and dig a cave and hide. If I wouldn't have been afraid, many a time I would've taken the car and went to the mountains for a few days to get away from it all.

Finally I started to ask myself, "Do I really want to stay with my family?" If it hadn't been that I cared about hurting my children, I probably would have wound up in divorce court. But something happened to me, and I thought, "God, Rosie, what are you doing? You have a home, five kids, a husband—what more could you want?" And my husband finally sat down and told me the things I was doing to them. I put two and two together and said, "Yeah, what am I doing?" In plain words, I stopped long enough to think, thank God.

Even now, when I come back from arbitration I get into such a mood. . . . And I get all shook up and nervous every time I have to be involved with a scab. I don't want to have anything to do with those people. Like Fran Richards lives in my neighborhood. I used to know her pretty well. Her nephew is married to my niece. But I don't want to talk to her now. If I see her, I want her to pretend like she doesn't know me because that's what I'll do to her. This is the way I feel about a scab. Even if I got back into Alton, I don't want them to bother with me in the plant. I would never do anything to hurt them, I wouldn't make nasty remarks, but I want them to just leave me alone.

I'll tell you what those scabs are like. About a month ago I was bowling with my girl friend Ellen. I said, "There's a scab." I said, "Now don't say anything to her." Because we were told not to say anything to them. But nobody can do anything to me for staring. So I stared at her. When she went this way, I looked that way. I stared. When she left, Ellen and I walked out, and we stared. She got into her car, and Ellen and I just stared. We knew she was very uncomfortable, but we didn't say anything to her. The only words that came out of my mouth were: "There's a scab." Well, we got down to the arbitration hearings, and the company called her to the witness stand. The company lawyer said, "Were you threatened last week?" And she said, "Yes, I was." He said, "By who?" She said, "Rosie Engels." He said, "Well, would you tell all these people the exact words of what she said?" And she said, "Yes. She called me a scab, and then she said she would stab me in the back with a knife." Well, my arms and legs and everything just went limp when I heard that. Then they told her to go touch me to identify me. Well, you talk about violence. . . . By this time, they had provoked me to the point where if she had touched me, I would have hit her. Because I knew she was lying, and to me, a person can slap me in the face or call me any name, but for her to sit there in that room full of people and lie like that. . . . So I said to someone sitting next to me, "If she touches me, I don't care if they put me in jail or what they do to me, I'm gonna hit her." But she didn't come within five feet; I think she read my lips.

So these are the things that really tear you apart. But I went home and thought about it for a day, and I realized it wasn't worth the time and effort to be so upset. I felt she was as low as anybody could be, and I felt if Alton keeps her on, someday, sometime, somebody will punish her. And I felt that the company wants to get to me, and there's no way I'm gonna let them do that. Even if I don't get my job back and my unemployment runs out, if I ever go back in there and somebody asks me how I'm doing, I'll say, "Terrific," even if I haven't got a penny. I wouldn't let that company know they put me down. One reason I want that job back is to prove a point. I want to go back in there and prove I'm a bigger person than they are or ever will be. That's really what I'm fighting for.

Sometimes I get down in the dumps and I want to quit fighting. I say, "Is this the way it has to be? Is it all worth it?" But then I think, "If you want to survive in this world, you have to fight for what you want and not give up." That's one thing I learned during the strike. I also learned that if people don't stick together, there's no way you're gonna get anyplace.

LINDA FERRARA

She is thirty-four, slight, with dark Mediterranean hair and eyes. She lives with her husband, who works in a cement plant, and three children—the oldest fourteen, the youngest nine—on a farm. "This year we've got fourteen acres in corn, three in alfalfa, and we're raising beef. We're starting to switch over to heifers for milk replacers 'cause there's more of a profit in that." Her children belong to 4-H clubs, swimming teams, hoedown groups; she herself practices sewing and macramé. "I hate sleeping. My husband often argues about this because he takes naps. He enjoys sleeping. It's one of his pleasures. But I only sleep if I have to. I always feel I might miss something good going on."

Since her marriage she has worked "in between kids" as a waitress, sewing machine operator, and salesgirl. "As soon as the third child went to kindergarten, I started looking for full-time employment. Something I could advance myself in and basically earn a retirement." She started at Alton in 1974.

When I first went to Alton I was against the union. In fact, I was one of the people who spoke out against it. In my department I was the only one who outwardly said a union wasn't necessary. I had been in a union before and it didn't do anything for us. That's one of the reasons I was hired in the first place. I heard that Alton would hire you almost on the spot if you didn't exactly like unions. So I mentioned my previous experience with the other union, and of course, once I said that, I was hired.

I went right on speaking against the union until it was voted in. I voted against it in the election. But once it was voted in, a lot of us who were procompany or on the edge felt that, well, the union's in and that's it. Now we have to work together. So I started becoming a little more involved and listening a little more. But the thing that really did it was the company's attitude. Right after the vote they started getting tough. It was like they decided, "OK, you people want this union in; we're gonna show you what it's like. We're going by the book." They started laying people off, switching them around, making us work mandatory Saturdays. You had to raise your hand to go to the bathroom. It just became ridiculous.

Another thing that happened was that I got injured on the job. I crawled underneath a depalletizer and cut my elbow. I had put down plastic coverings, but there happened to be a piece of glass on the floor. I leaned in there, and it cut my elbow. I went upstairs and they put a butterfly on it. Then they told me to continue my job. I asked them to see a doctor. Their answer was that their doctors don't want to be woken up in the middle of the night. Later on the supervisor came over to ask how it was going. They had my whole arm bandaged up pretty darn good, but it was throbbing, and I had to work with a stiff arm, which makes it a little difficult to do my job. So I said to my supervisor that I was going to insist upon seeing a doctor. I asked if I could be run down to the emergency room to see if there was still glass in there, because it was so painful. They said no, they were sorry but I'd have to wait till nine o'clock. Which, like a dummy, I did. At nine I was taken to the doctor. He had to cut the thing open again, and there was bleeding inside. It had cut some sort of vein, so that was why it was throbbing so much. It was bleeding internally and swelling up. I asked him, "Is it true you don't want to see me in the middle of the night?" He said, "Yeah, this can wait. No problem, we just have to cut it open again." Which to me was a problem. I don't like anybody knifing away at me if it's not necessary.

So I felt Alton was showing no concern whatsoever. They couldn't care less. And my feelings about a union changed to just the reverse. Before, I honestly felt that someone concerned about a union couldn't stand up for himself. He needed someone to lean on. But after not being able to handle some situations myself, I felt, "Yes, I do need a shop steward. I do need some advice. I do need someone to protect me from unsafe conditions and bad practices."

When the strike came, I felt both good and bad. I don't think you ever make up the money and time you lose in a strike. I don't think a strike helps anyone. But when you're against a hard comapny like Alton, you have to resort to what's available. So I was for the strike, but I felt bad to be striking. On the other hand, it was terrific not having to work. It felt great to be clean again and let my nails grow and set my hair a little more often. It was hard financially because the strike pay didn't come close to what I was making. But I was very glad to be at home. I'm not a person who wants to be out at work. I'm only working because it's necessary. You can't hardly make it anymore with three kids and one income. I guess if we were just living in a small home, we could possibly manage. But being as we have the farm and we're just starting out, we have to put money into clearing land and buying equipment and animals. So I'm really working to try and get the farm started.

During the strike I started working a lot more on the farm. We spent a few months trying to clear fifty feet of field where the woods were growing in. I started going to farm meetings and talking to other farmers. I started going to the auction at Brownston. I was trying to find out what we could do to make it better. I always felt that if you're breaking your back, you're doing it wrong. But I never had the time before to see what I needed to do. It was always push, push, push. I couldn't ever take stock and see if I was doing things right. I knew that we couldn't ever live just off the farm. In this state you need something like two hundred acres to make a living, and we only have twenty-eight. But if I could make the farm turn a profit, I wouldn't have to work third shift at Alton cleaning up dirty, filthy machines.

At the same time I missed being at work. I used to come down to the union hall every Tuesday, just to hear what was going on. I like the farm and I enjoy outdoor work, but with the kids in school I'd be alone all day long. And I was bored. It wasn't that I didn't have enough to do, but I missed seeing people and having something to yell for, something to fight for. Something that a group of people have together as a goal, that you're talking about and excited about. Some sort of a cause where you could make things better as part of a group.

That's why it was so exciting when the company opened the gates. Oh, it was fantastic [laughs]. I had never been involved in a mob emotion, a mob feeling, and it was definitely that. I would think of it the night before, when I went to sleep, and wonder what was gonna happen. And I would actually think of things to do that would not be exactly harmful, but that possibly would stop the scabs. For example, I came up with the brilliant idea of pumping black paint into an eggshell. I thought this would be great. You could toss it at a car, and the black paint goes on the windshield so they have to stop. They can't go in the plant. It really wouldn't be destructive; you're not harming a person. I tried to think of different things like that. Then I'd get up early in the morning, and sometimes I'd bring my children, whichever ones wanted to go with me. And I'd go down to the gates. It was exciting. It was very exciting, getting out there with the group and seeing who was there, and wondering what we could do. We didn't want our fellow workers walking through our lines, but it was past the point of trying to convince anyone. It was just a matter of strength. How many of us are there? Who will lead? Who will start it? Who will stand fast when the cars are trying to drive through? How far will you go?

First you'd be milling about, just walking around. Everybody would be discussing on walkie-talkies where our people are and where their people are. What they're doing, what we're doing. Do we have people down at that gate? Are we covering this and that? Then the waiting. Waiting for it to come. And they'd say, "They're coming!" All of a sudden your adrenaline pours in. The people are getting excited. They've been waiting for this and they think they're ready. Both sides think they're ready. And no one's really ready [laughs]. It all ends up getting resolved one way or the other, and everyone ends up regretting they didn't do a certain thing at a particular moment. When the scabs got out of their car, we should have turned it over and blocked the whole road—anything that would have accomplished what we wanted. And the mob control police were there. They were afraid of what we might do. That made us feel stronger. So it was certainly different from your normal everyday routine [laughs].

Then when the list of thirty-eight names was given out, mine was on it. They charged me with throwing a rock and damaging a car. I guess some supervisors must have recognized me in the group. There were other people right alongside of me that are now working in the plant. Some of them took pains to dress so they wouldn't be easily recognized. They had little hats on or something like that. I guess I got to be one of the thirty-eight by being aggressive [laughs]. But no more so than a lot of people. We were just picked out at random.

I didn't feel too bad about getting fired. First of all, I felt I would get my job back. It was up to the courts whether Alton could fire me or not. And I didn't think it was unjust because I was a bit of an agitator. Anyway, once I was on unemployment, I was making 80 percent of my salary, so I found it's more satisfying to be on the farm. I'm able to do more. I have the little extra to be able to try an automatic waterer or something. Before, even if I wanted to try something new or remodel something in the barn, I didn't have the extra capital to lay out.

But that brought on a big confrontation with my husband. It came after I got fired. During the summer there wasn't much problem because I was running the children around and it kept me quite busy. But it started bothering my husband when September came and the children were in school. I was home, and I had free time. And he was jealous of my free time. He'd say, "Where did you go today?" I'd say, "I was up at the union hall." "What were you doing up there again?" He was perfectly happy that I wasn't working. He enjoyed it. From his viewpoint it made things much better. But they weren't better for me because I found he was expecting me to change back to the way I was five years ago. For example, he expected me to get his coffee in the evening. Well, I had become accustomed to getting him coffee one evening, and he'd get it for me the next. He thought that since I was home all the time, that was my job. But I didn't want to go back to it. I would tell him that I wear my ring on my finger, not through the nose. I'm a person. I don't want to be there just for his whim. Just because I love him and I married him, that doesn't mean I'm there at his beck and call.

It also bothered him when I got unemployment. He has never collected a day's unemployment, and here I had only been working a year and a half, and I was collecting. But for me the unemployment was important. It allowed me to act as though I was still working. It gave me the feeling that I was still worth something because I had money coming in. It made me feel more confident. It allowed me to stand up and make decisions that possibly I wouldn't have made. I should also say that when I was working, I was always so tired that I just let a lot of things slide. I didn't have the physical stamina to make a fight out of it with my husband, to stand up and say,"No, I want to have a say in this." I just didn't want to have a hassle. I was too tired. Whereas now I not only have the income, but I have the energy to stand up for myself.

After a while it became a direct conflict. It zeroed down. It was his feelings against mine. And of course, you always pick an incident to prove your point. I wanted to go to a macramé class. He thought it was a waste of time and money, but I felt I wanted to try it. Usually on things like that I would try and work something out or use my female ways to get around him, to get him to allow different things. But it came to the point where I had to take a stand. He forbid me to go to macramé. Absolutely forbid me to go. And I didn't listen. I continued going. I deliberately disobeyed him. It was just a simple incident, but I guess he had been holding it in for a long time because he beat me up. Really smacked me around. I guess there had to be a proving ground. And I guess I won, because I ended up pressing charges against him, and I don't think he'll ever try to really assert his rule over me again.

It was a great confrontation. And it happened very slowly. But after the fight I said, "This is the end. This is it. If you ever hit me again, we're finished. You must accept this." He said that he was sorry it ever happened, and he didn't believe it would ever happen again. I interrupted and said, "No, it *will not* happen again." Every once in a while I have to throw that in there. It will not ever, ever happen again. I have to stand my ground, because otherwise he might think that if by chance he should lose his temper and it happened again, I would forgive him. I have to show him it will not be accepted.

He's learning to live with it, but it's hard for him. For so long I never did things without asking him. Now I don't feel I need permission. I just tell him. Like the other day I decided to strip the paint off the door. I decided to do it a particular way and stain it a certain color. He came home and said, "You didn't ask me if you could do that." I said, "I didn't ask you if I could go to the bathroom today either, but I did it."

It's hard for me, too, because now he's pulling switches on me. All of a sudden he said, "Well, you want equal rights? You can go shovel the corn." These are barrels of corn. I believe the heaviest ones weigh 125 pounds, and I had to get them up onto the pickup. Or, "You can pull the tree stumps." He used to drive the tractors. I had to learn to drive three tractors and the loader. In other words, if I'm going to persist in being my own person, then I'm going to do a lot of the heavy work. I don't mind the actual work, but I don't like the way he says I must do it. For example, the children and I just finished fencing off seven acres of pasture. Warren came home at three o'clock and went to sleep. It came to another confrontation, which didn't amount to much because I guess it was a bluff. I told him that either he starts to do work around the place or pack his bags. He laughed, and said,"I'm not going anywhere." He knows that I'll have patience and I'll wait. But he also knows I won't wait forever. He knows it must change.

I think the change came directly from my working. It started the whole thing. Working on the job gave my time value. It gave my body value. It gave me value, where at home I didn't feel valuable. I think being paid good money every week—$5 an hour, that's darn good money for a woman—made me feel worthwhile. It gave me self-confidence. I have quite a few friends that don't work and are completely happy to leave everything to the men. They don't want to get involved. They're content to have everything stay the way it was. So I guess if it wasn't for my drive to be satisified, to find a place for myself other than being a housewife and mother, I wouldn't have gone out for a job in the first place.

And now the unemployment has given me the chance to act as if I'm important even though I'm not working. It's given me the chance to have a say in what we do with our money. The unemployment checks used to go into our joint checking account, and when I suggested different things for the farm, Warren wouldn't hear of it. So after he smacked me around, I immediately opened my own savings account, and every single one of my checks went in. Then he had to ask me what I wanted to do with it because all the extra money was in my name. He definitely does not like that. In fact, he doesn't even like my getting unemployment at all. He feels a man is the sole supporter of his family, and therefore he deserves unemployment if it's absolutely necessary to put bread on their table. But since I'm not the sole supporter, he feels it's like a loophole in the law, and I'm getting something extra.

I guess my husband's very slow to change. He likes the way it was. It's part of our age-group. When we were first married his attitude was normal, but there's been a lot of changes. Most marriages have been having their problems lately with this women's lib. Unless the guy is very, very open-minded and very strong in his self-confidence, it can cause a lot of problems in the home. When a woman goes out to work, the man gets asked to share, not in the housework, but in the responsibility for trucking his kids around here and there. It used to be that any work I did was part time, and I did it providing there was time left over from my family. It must not interfere with my duties as a mother and housewife. So the big change in our family has been that the woman has a right to work. If I want to work, the family has to try and help a little. It's a big change. And it's hard to get used to, especially from a man's point of view.

DIRK ROBINSON

He is a quiet, slow-moving man, built like a linebacker, wearing a work shirt and jeans. Thirty years old and newly divorced, he is living with his parents until he gets his Alton job back or finds a new one. "You get pretty discouraged from people turning you down. That, and from losing everything you worked for: your house, your wife, your kids . . . especially your kids. . . . "

꧁꧂

I worked at Alton Products from the moment the plant opened. I was there from the very beginning. Before that I was a mechanic. I had my own business and everything, but somebody stole my tools and completely wiped me out. I couldn't afford to reopen, so I had to pack it in and look for employment. The Alton plant was opening, and I got a job right away. I worked there for about two years before the strike. And I was happy there. I enjoyed the work, and at first I wasn't in favor of the union.

I started out in the distribution section. Shipping and receiving. Mainly it was loading and unloading trucks. I got along with my supervisor, and I was doing fairly well. He was the best supervisor I ever had. He made you feel like you wanted to work because he left you alone to operate the way you wanted. But he didn't get along with the higher-ups, so he bailed out. Quit. After that we got people that were on our backs constantly. That was the big change for me right there. You know, Alton was always talking about all the money we were making each week—and I was happy about it, I admit. We made good money there. Everybody looked forward to getting paid every week. I was happy with the paycheck. But I was looking to be treated like a person instead of an animal. After a while it got to be like they would say, "Pick up that palette and bring it over here." You'd do it. Then they'd say, "OK, now you brought it over here, take it back." It made you feel like an animal. You know, that's what they said to us over in the arbitration hearings. "You people are just like animals." They called us that. "You people are really animals for being out on strike like that." Well, what do they expect? We worked in a zoo. That's what it felt like with the supervisors we had, a zoo. You treat someone like a person, they're a person. But you start treating 'em like animals, they become animals.

I remember a lot of little things that changed my mind about the union. I saw guys getting hurt because the supervisors were pushing them so hard. Some of them were hurt pretty bad. Legs, arms. It got to the point where I had too much of shipping and receiving, so I bid out of there and went over to the production division as a line operator. By then I was pretty strong for the union. I got a lot of union cards signed, even though a lot of people were scared because Alton told us that if we voted for the union, they were gonna close the plant and move out. I was approached several times by supervisors when I was unloading trucks. They'd call me inside and say, "How do you feel about the union?" I wouldn't tell 'em. They'd say, "I want you to change your mind." They wouldn't threaten you, but they'd say, "I'd like you to change your mind and vote for the company this coming election because we've been good to you." They'd try to convince you. Previously they were lousy to you, and then all of a sudden you're supposed to change your mind and come right back to the company. It just doesn't go in my book.

It got so that every time people in my department wanted union information they would come to me because I was really involved. I was going to every one of the meetings to find out what the union was going to do for us. Lots of people wanted to know, but they were afraid to find out for themselves because they thought they might get terminated if they were seen going to meetings. At that time there was no thought in my mind that I might be terminated because of the union. I just felt that I had a family and that without the union I had no protection whatsoever. They could terminate me for any reason at any time. So I voted for the union, and we won the election. Then, when the company refused to negotiate, I voted for the strike. I wasn't eager to strike. I don't think anyone ever is. Maybe there are some guys that don't care, but I do. I care. I didn't want a strike. But I thought we weren't getting what we wanted. I thought we were being taken. And when you don't get what you want, that's the only way you can fight.

When we went on strike, it was the first time I was ever out of work in my life. I've never been laid off before by anyone. And it hurt. It hurt a lot, because we had quite a few bills to pay. I was only getting $50-a-week strike pay. My wife was working for a hairdresser in Woodbury, but it wasn't that much money. So there were a lot of changes at home. There was no going out. Nothing extra in the house. We had to pinch everything to try and make ends meet. We were cut way down. After a while I started getting side jobs, which brought in a little money. Even when I was at Alton, I had to do that sometimes because with three kids you gotta have money coming in. I went out to find other jobs, but due to the fact that we were on strike at Alton, no one would hire.

The only thing that really helped me out is that I applied for food stamps. We got food stamps, and that was a big help right there. If it wouldn't have been for the food stamps, I don't know what. . . . I'll say one thing, it made me understand the people that are out there that don't have no money and they've gotta get something. They can't get a job. So what do they do? They go out; they steal; they rob. I wasn't that far down. I can't do that. But you get that feeling. You get that feeling inside. Because when you have three kids and they're not eating, and maybe you're not eating either, and you see other people buying things but you can't buy them, it gets you down. I never really got to that point because my parents were helping us out quite a bit, and we got the food stamps.

I felt leery about the food stamps, though. I was really ashamed when I had to go in the store and use 'em. I had never done anything like that before. All my life I had been working and making good money, and for the first time I'm out there using food stamps. It just didn't seem right. And after you get them for a certain amount of time, it tends to make you lazy. You don't look for work because you know you're getting some-thing for nothing. So why go work? It's the same with unemployment. When them checks keep coming in, you have the tendency not to look for too much work. I know I needed the food stamps, but if I could have had the opportunity to work for 'em, I would've felt better. When you're in the store paying for your food and there's people in back of you, you can see them looking at you when you're giving food stamps. There you are, it seems like you're in good shape and everything, and maybe they're saying, "Man, this guy's getting something for nothing." It's like a gift. I feel guilty about it. I feel guilty because I'm able to work. There's a lot of people in the country that aren't able to work, and I think they should be entitled to the money. Whereas when you're able to work, you want to work.

Well, after going through that for eight months, I heard they were going to open the gates at Alton. I didn't like that at all, because as soon as I heard it I knew there was gonna be trouble. I knew there was gonna be violence. I didn't go out there on the picket line intending to hurt anyone. I thought if we went out there in any great number, it would discourage them from trying to go in. But they got their court order that we weren't allowed to stop anyone and that we had to have five people on the picket line and that's all. It just encouraged 'em more and more. They had trooper protection to go in. It was like we were handcuffed. We couldn't stop 'em, and I just seen my job going away. Unless I turned out to be something I didn't want to be, a scab. That's what them people were, they were just scabs.

I was out on the picket line every day I could possibly be there. Some days I had mechanical work that I could do, and the money came first. I had to get some money. Maybe that's the way the scabs felt. They needed the money that bad. And I could see some of the people's point because I guess a lot of them were hurting as much as I was, and they didn't have the same feeling I did, so they had to go in. But the majority of the people that scabbed, their wives were working and they were making a good dollar. It was hurting me more than them, but I wasn't about to turn around and say, "I'm gonna be a strikebreaker." If you're out to get something and you're fighting to get it, I can't see defeating your own purpose. I never even considered going in. I made up my mind that I was gonna stay out right from the beginning because I believed in what I was doing there. I never even gave it a thought. You have certain standards that you live up to. I mean, I felt bad with food stamps in the grocery store, how would I feel about walking around the people I work with every day, knowing that they know I'm a scab, and that I tried to take their jobs away from them? I could never do that. I wouldn't feel it was me. And I gotta be me. It's the only way to go [laughs].

So Alton got me for violating the injunction. In other words, I was out there on one of the days I wasn't supposed to be. I was picked up by a trooper for being on the highway. I was there with several hundred people, but I happened to be in the group this trooper picked out, and I was the one they got. I guess they had to make examples out of certain people. If they had just cleared us out of there, more of us would have been back the next day. So they picked certain people up and put them in cars and made the rest back off. I was never charged with anything. They never read us our rights. They just put us in a car for a while, drove us down to the courthouse, the judge talked to us, and that was it. I was released.

But when the contract was signed, my name turned up on the list of thirty-eight people to be terminated. Now I believe the union was blackmailed into signing that contract. Alton had come up with that piece of shit, and they handed it to us and said, "Take it or leave it." I guess at first there were more than thirty-eight names in there, but they dropped it to thirty-eight. And I actually voted for the people to go back to work, even though I knew it meant I was out. I felt if they didn't accept that contract, it would be a long time till we got another one. There would have been a lot more scabs going in, so it was either take the contract or get no contract at all. It was either the whole plant would be out or just us thirty-eight. So I voted for it, thinking that the arbitrations would be over in a few months. But there seems to be a slight delay [laughs].

I was hurt when I was terminated. Really hurt. It was the first time in my life. I was surprised when I found out my name was on the list. And now, down at the arbitration, they have it that I was throwing a rock, which is totally false. There were no eyewitnesses to it, but they testified that I was in a group where people were seen throwing rocks. It's like being an accessory. But I don't see any possible way I'm gonna lose. If I do, I'm really gonna be disappointed. So the only thing I'm concerned about now is what happened in the past. I mean, when they put in the newspapers that my name is cleared, then I'll feel a lot better. Up until that time everybody I know thinks I'm a criminal. My neighbors don't bother with me anymore. They won't talk to me.

In fact, I've just been divorced because of this whole situation. No money coming in, and my wife just didn't understand. She felt I never should have got involved in any of these things. My wife is the kind of person who always wanted something. I remember being in business and coming home with $275 a week, and that wasn't enough. Well, you can only please people to a certain degree. Maybe when I hit the $1,000 mark, she'll come around [laughs]. So it seemed like we always had little problems, but this developed into a bigger one. I guess it had to come to an end sooner or later. It's like having a bad apple. If you've got one little bad part and you let it go, it just gets bigger. That's the way this marriage was. She couldn't understand why I was on strike and why I did what I did. She'd say things like: "If you'd never gone out that day, you'd be working. If you had gone in with the rest of the people, you'd be working and making all the money." I tried to talk to her and tell her how I felt, but it was hard to make her understand. Maybe I'm hard to understand, I don't know. I couldn't get to her at all.

One day we had a picnic for the thirty-eight. We sold tickets, and all the donations went to the thirty-eight. She went along up there and she mingled in with all the other wives, and everything seemed to be really great because she understood how other people were feeling. When we went home that night, she apologized to me and said she was sorry for the way she acted. She said she understood now, and she was totally for me. But after the arbitration was delayed longer and longer and I still couldn't get a job, she went back to feeling bitter toward me.

We didn't talk about it too much. I tried to stay away from it. We knew it was there, but the more you talk about it, the worse it gets. We tried to do things together, but it got to the point where we didn't have money to do them. We used to go out to clubs and dance, or take the kids to parks, or go to basketball games. Plus the fact that the people who scabbed got all the benefits, medical and eyeglasses and dental, stuff like this. We had a lot of dental work we had to have done, and we had to pay for it. So it kept coming back to, "The next-door neighbor's getting a new car, and we can't get one because you're terminated." That's the kind of stuff that got to me. It got so involved that she actually wouldn't stay in the same bed with me until I got another job. Which is tough. "You get another job and I'll start sleeping with you." I finally got a part-time job, and when I got it, I thought, "At least tonight's the night." But it didn't work out that way.

I guess the worst part of this whole thing was when she asked me to leave due to the fact that I didn't have a job. That's probably the only time I was really depressed. All the other times I kept active. But when your wife tells you she don't want you no more, and you've been married twelve years, and you think you're happy, and all of a sudden it just has to end, you really feel bad about that. I still do, but it's gotta be that way. Sooner or later I'll probably find somebody else and start all over again. But that's what really got me depressed. She said it was getting on her nerves so bad that maybe I should leave for a little while. She said, "Maybe if you're away for a while, things will straighten out." I thought, OK. So I went to my parents' place. I was gone for about two weeks, and I gave her a call to see if things were better. She said, "They're starting to get a little better in my mind. Just give it a little more time." But after the thirty-day mark she changed the locks on the doors and went to the court and told them I wasn't supporting the kids. Which I was. I had the canceled checks. She just wanted me out. So that's what happened to my marriage.

Right now I'm getting some unemployment and working this part-time job, sweeping floors at night. I'm still looking for work, but it's pretty discouraging. It seems like nobody wants you if you're from Alton. Sometimes it seems like you're never gonna be able to work again. Like I went to this one company, and when I first went for the application, the guy said they were really hiring a lot of people. I says, "Good, what kind of personnel are you actually looking for?" He says, "We're looking for shipping and receiving personnel." So I'm saying to myself, "Oh, this is great. That's what I did at Alton." So I fill out the application, and a week later I get a letter in the mail saying I don't meet the qualifications of what they're looking for. And that was the same work I was doing. I felt really bad about that. I felt I should've had that job. So I think we're blackballed really. I think Alton is telling these other companies in the valley not to hire the thirty-eight. The only ones who have found jobs have been out of state. I must have tried at least a dozen places around here. Right now I'm gonna apply at the shopping center they're building in Woodbury. I heard an ad on the radio when I was driving over here. Hopefully I'll find something. If I don't, I guess I'll just have to leave the state.

This unemployment is gonna run out sooner or later, and then I'll have to find a full-time job fast. Maybe the arbitration will be over by that time and I'll be back at Alton. If not, then I've gotta go somewhere. Even though I'm divorced, I've still gotta pay that child support and that mortgage, so I've gotta have a job. I've thought about leaving the state many times, and I would if I knew I could find a job that would pay half decent. The only reason I stay around here is that the arbitration is going on, and I think I've got a good chance of winning. And I'd like to go back to Alton. Even though I feel very, very bitter towards them, I liked the job I had there. And if I go back, I'll be going back a winner. I'll feel like I won the battle; I stuck it out. If the people there can see that I stuck it out, with the divorce and all, and came back in there a winner, maybe it'll change a couple of people's minds. Because I think they need that union in there. They need a union bad.